igall

listo

University

ARNOLD

er Headline Group

d States of America by
Inc., New York

First published in Great Britain in 2002 by
Arnold, a member of the Hodder Headline Group,
338 Euston Road, London NW1 3BH

http://www.arnoldpublishers.com

Distributed in the United States of America by
Oxford University Press Inc.,
198 Madison Avenue, New York, NY10016

The advice and information in this book are believed to be true and
accurate at the date of going to press, but neither the author[s] nor the publisher
can accept any legal responsibility or liability for any errors or omissions.

British Library Cataloguing in Publication Data
A catalogue record for this book is available from the British Library

Library of Congress Cataloging-in-Publication Data
A catalog record for this book is available from the Library of Congress

ISBN 0 340 76332 9 (hb)
ISBN 0 340 76333 7 (pb)

1 2 3 4 5 6 7 8 9 10

Production Editor: Rada Radojicic
Production Controller: Martin Kerans
Cover Design: Terry Griffiths

Typeset in 10 on 12 pt Minion by Charon Tec Pvt. Ltd, Chennai, India
Printed and bound in Great Britain by MPG Books Limited, Bodmin, Cornwall

What do you think about this book? Or any other Arnold title?
Please send your comments to feedback.arnold@hodder.co.uk

Contents

Preface

The purpose of this book is to provide a comprehensive cross-referenced dictionary for those studying international relations and modern and contemporary international history. Whether as a student, or as a general reader interested in world affairs, you will be faced with a great variety of concepts, organizations, movements, treaties, historical and geographical references, doctrines, diplomatic, legal, environmental and other terms.

Readers are confronted with both new and established terms, a number of them widely contested and variously interpreted, 'globalism', 'isolationism', 'nationalism', 'neo-realism', 'pluralism', 'domestic analogy', 'rogue states' and so on. At the same time, interpretative concepts combine with event, movements and historical context – theory with actuality – in a field of study that abounds in allusions. The American novelist William Faulkner once wrote: 'The past is never dead; it is not even past.' In foreign policy and defence, 'Munich' has haunted policy-makers, the 'Vietnam syndrome' is invoked and the 'Maginot mentality' criticized. The supposed 'lessons' of the past influence the present, in a world that is in a state of perpetual movement, flux, change and much instability, and in which theories of order and control are constantly challenged.

You need to understand continuity and change, global and regional interdependence and conflict and rivalry. At the same time, comprehension of international relations and world affairs requires, in particular measure, interdisciplinary understanding. Linkage is of the essence – establishing connections. This, among other things, may be between international and domestic politics, between economic developments and global environmental concerns, between technological developments and strategy, between international law and humanitarianism, between population increase and war, and between arms control agreements and human rights. The range of 1,500 entries in the following pages, then, is intended to meet the needs of ready reference in a world order and a disordered world of much complexity and many interactions and to provide the concepts, terms and factual information to make this task of association easier.

Another major consideration has been the pace of change. The events following the fall of the Berlin Wall in 1989 and the historical sequel to what was announced as the 'New World Order' have altered perspectives, and significantly so. For a generation the cold war, to a major extent, dominated and formed the framework for debate over international relations, in terms of theory and strategy and practice, not least, of course, with the advent of nuclear weapons. One has only to think of the sheer number of terms that the cold war added to our vocabulary. Since 1989 there have been new questionings, reappraisals and agendas. Boundaries have been redrawn and old assumptions discarded. New fears and dangers have succeeded older threats, or perceptions of threat.

The aim here has been to provide the reader with a book specific in purpose, and accessible. For reasons of space, biographical entries have been excluded. Though a number of entries obviously refer also to earlier periods – for instance, 'balance of power', 'Grotian', 'Westphalian System' and so on – the essential historical framework is the period since the French Revolution of 1789.

The entries are presented alphabetically. Small capital letters indicate a separate entry.

Acknowledgements

I would like to express gratitude to Christopher Wheeler for his encouragement and excellent advice with this project, and also Lesley Riddle and Hannah McEwen. I am, additionally, much indebted to Joan Hassock for her preparation of the typescript and to Hilary Walford for her expertise as copy editor.

David Weigall, 1 July 2002, Cambridge

List of Maps

A

ABC states Argentina, Brazil and Chile.

ABC weapons These are also known as 'weapons of mass destruction' and 'special weapons' and stand for atomic, biological and chemical weapons, or weapon warheads. These include toxins and nerve gases. They are synonymous with CBR weapons, chemical, biological and radiological agents.

Abgrenzung From the German word for 'border'. This was specifically applied to the line separating East and West Germany during the COLD WAR. It also meant ideological delimitation and was used in particular to describe the policy adopted by the East German leader Erich Honecker (1912–94), which was intended to counteract the potential impact of *OSTPOLITIK*. He was apprehensive that increased contact between the two Germanys could destabilize the East German system. He therefore argued that there were clear historical and social-cultural differences between the two states that could not be bridged, with the communist German Democratic Republic (GDR) developing a progressive working-class culture after 1945, while West Germany was under a capitalist exploiter class.

ABM See ANTI-BALLISTIC MISSILE (SYSTEM).

Abwehr The foreign and counter-intelligence department of the German military High Command. During the Nazi period it was under Admiral Canaris (1887–1945), who negotiated for it to run in parallel with the Nazi intelligence organizations, as a military rather than a party agency. A number of its personnel were involved in resistance to Hitler (1889–1945) and it was absorbed into the SS in 1944 and formally dissolved.

ACC See ALLIED CONTROL COUNCIL.

Accidental war An unintended armed conflict touched off by incidents caused by human error or by mechanical or electronic failure. In the nuclear age this term relates to the possibility that everything up to an all-out nuclear exchange between the powers could be triggered by a misinterpretation of intentions or by the accidental launching of a WEAPON OF MASS DESTRUCTION. To reduce the threat of accidental war the USA and USSR established the HOT-LINE teletype communications link between Moscow and Washington in 1963, after the CUBAN MISSILE CRISIS (1962), so that discussions could be initiated immediately during a crisis.

Accommodation As used in DIPLOMACY and international CRISIS MANAGEMENT, this term means a willingness of disputant parties to be flexible, reduce friction and make concessions, though with the clear implication that basic interests and objectives are not being surrendered by the parties.

Acid rain High levels of acidity in rainfall, destroying forests and polluting rivers and lakes, became a cause of public and governmental concern in the 1970s. Evidence of this was particularly noted in Scandinavia and CENTRAL EUROPE and was blamed on sulphur and nitrogen oxide emissions from power stations, not least from the United

Kingdom. Accumulating evidence of environmental damage led to a DIRECTIVE from the EUROPEAN COMMUNITY (EC) in 1988 to reduce such emissions. It has been one of the key causes for environmental campaigners and politicians in the Green parties.

ACLANT Allied Command Atlantic.

ACP See AFRICAN, CARIBBEAN AND PACIFIC.

Acquired immune deficiency syndrome (AIDS) The worldwide medical problem, with the destruction of natural immunities following the spread of the HIV virus, was identified in Southern Africa in the 1970s. It was not until the mid-1980s that the widespread prevalence of the condition, not least in the USA, aroused major international concern. AIDS has been particularly highly prevalent in African states.

Acquis communautaire This phrase is used by the EUROPEAN UNION (EU) to describe all the secondary legislation passed by the EUROPEAN COMMISSION and the COUNCIL OF MINISTERS under the provisions of the FOUNDING TREATIES and their subsequent amendments. It covers all the DIRECTIVES, DECISIONS and REGULATIONS adopted by the EU. Any country that lodges an application to join must be willing to accept the acquis commmunautaire as it exists at the time when it accedes. This has accumulated since the Founding Treaties came into effect in 1958.

Acquis politique The collective phrase describing all the decisions and resolutions of the member states of the EUROPEAN UNION (EU) in the field of foreign affairs. The coordinating, intergovernmental mechanism for the member STATES was originally EUROPEAN POLITICAL COOPERATION (EPC) and, since the TREATY ON EUROPEAN UNION (TEU), which came into force in November 1993, has been the COMMON FOREIGN AND SECURITY POLICY (CFSP).

Act of war Any act that is incompatible with a state of PEACE. The idea of an act of WAR comes under the laws relating to the resort to conflict, the so-called *JUS AD BELLUM*. States entering into an ALLIANCE frequently take upon each other the responsibilities to help fight each other's wars. The situation under which an alliance becomes operative is described as the *CASUS FOEDERIS*. The twentieth century saw important changes in the laws relating to war. Treaty law, as set out for instance in the UNITED NATIONS CHARTER, makes a clear distinction between legal and illegal recourse to FORCE. At the same time, use of less direct forms of AGGRESSION, such as in GUERRILLA WARFARE and TERRORISM, have often made it more difficult to apply the laws of war. Foreign INTERVENTION in CIVIL WARS, for instance, has become widespread, and many of the most recurrent and seemingly insoluble conflicts, such as that between the Arabs and Israel, began as communal strife.

Action Committee for a United States of Europe (ACUSE) A significant pressure group established in 1955 by Jean Monnet (1888–1979), the leading advocate of West European INTEGRATION, following the failure, after prolonged debate, of the EUROPEAN DEFENCE COMMUNITY (EDC) in August 1954. Monnet created ACUSE as a selective group of political and trade union leaders who would work for closer European unity and it contributed to the ideas and negotiations that led to the formation of the EUROPEAN ECONOMIC COMMUNITY (EEC). After the ROME TREATY had come into effect in 1958, this organization continued to argue for more intensive integration and the inclusion of further countries. It was led by Monnet until 1975, but subsequently, from the 1960s, became less prominent.

Action–reaction This term is often used in writing about international relations to account for the development of conflicts, whether armed or not, for the way disputants behave in international crises, and for the phenomenon of ARMS RACES. Each party or ACTOR responds to the behaviour of the opposite party with a pre-planned move. The sequence of actions as the crisis develops, though, may become more, or exclusively, directed by the pattern of action–reaction, rather than by long-term objectives or intentions. For instance, MOBILIZATION of forces by one side may have unintended consequences and things may spin out of control. In arms races between powers an action–reaction pattern occurs in the following way: one power may introduce new armaments or a new weapons system that will lead the opposing power to develop the same or a different and more effective system, introducing an almost automatic arms race momentum. Note, however, that sometimes a new deployment may have been undertaken by a power to force the opponent into reacting in the confidence that the cost and strain of additional resources will make the rival weaker.

Actor In discussion of international relations the word 'actor' can refer to any entity that plays an identifiable role. The term is deliberately inclusive, since the word 'STATE' is too limited, and does not remotely reflect the range of influences at play in the global order. Actor can mean states, individuals or organizations, governmental or non-governmental. Some scholars of international relations have argued that the global system as presently constituted is a 'mixed actor model', not least because the relative significance of the state and national SOVEREIGNTY have been reduced.

ACUSE See ACTION COMMITTEE FOR A UNITED STATES OF EUROPE.

Additionality This is the rule that EUROPEAN UNION (EU) funds for regional development must be allocated in addition to, not as a replacement for, the national funds of the member STATES. The EUROPEAN COMMISSION carefully monitors member states' compliance with additionality rules in the disbursement of structural funds, to ensure that governments do not pocket these grants without making an equal contribution to the project under consideration themselves.

Adjudication A legal means for settling disputes by submitting them to the determination by an established court. It is distinguished from ARBITRATION in that the former involves an institutional process carried on by a permanent court whereas the latter is an *ad hoc* procedure. The first international court of general competence was the PERMANENT COURT OF INTERNATIONAL JUSTICE (PCIJ), which functioned as part of the LEAGUE OF NATIONS from 1920 to 1946. It was succeeded by the present INTERNATIONAL COURT OF JUSTICE (ICJ), one of the principal organs of the UNITED NATIONS (UN). Adjudication has been most effective in settling disputes of less-than-vital importance, since, in submitting a case to an international court, the STATES concerned must agree in advance to be bound by a decision that might be detrimental to their vital interests.

Administered territory See MANDATES.

Afghanistan Crisis (1979) In December 1979 the USSR invaded Afghanistan, the first occasion since 1946 of Soviet ground troops being used in any number outside the COMMUNIST BLOC. They remained at WAR with the Afghan guerrillas until 1988, when they were withdrawn, unable to assure victory. The crisis accentuated US anxieties over its strategic position in the Middle East, led to the announcement of the CARTER DOCTRINE, the temporary eclipse of DÉTENTE and some SANCTIONS. President Reagan (b. 1911) followed a policy of very active covert INTERVENTION, supplying large sums of money and armaments to Pakistan and to the MUJAHIDEEN to assist their resistance to the USSR. The consequent further destabilization of Afghanistan with five million REFUGEES in Pakistan and Iran left a legacy that helped to encourage the events of 2001–2, following the terrorist destruction of the World Trade Centre in New York on 11 September 2001.

African, Caribbean and Pacific (ACP) This term refers to the forty-six developing countries of the above regions that signed the 1975 LOMÉ CONVENTION with the EUROPEAN ECONOMIC COMMUNITY (EEC). Most of the countries were former colonies of Britain, France and Belgium. With the accession of Portugal and Spain to the Community, the number of countries increased to seventy. The ACP countries are allowed duty-free access to the EUROPEAN UNION (EU) for most of their products on a non-reciprocal basis. They are also allowed to apply for grants from the European Development Fund (EDF) and low-interest loans from the EUROPEAN INVESTMENT BANK (EIB).

Agency for International Development, US (AID, US) The US government agency that manages foreign aid directed to diplomatic aims, trade and investment, humanitarian assistance and SUSTAINABLE DEVELOPMENT. It amounts to about 0.2 per cent of US gross domestic product in recent years, though 80 per cent of it is not TIED AID – that is, carrying an obligation to buy from the providing country.

Agenda 21 The 800-page programme for the environment that was adopted at the UNITED NATIONS CONFERENCE ON ENVIRONMENT AND DEVELOPMENT (UNCED) (the Earth Summit) of 1992. Many of the points demanding action are very specific. The question of industrial pollution and its effect on the earth's atmosphere has proved the most controversial.

Aggiornamento (Italian for 'renewal') A term closely associated with the pontificate of John XXIII (1881–1963), who became Pope in 1958. It denoted, among other things, a new liberalization within the Roman Catholic Church with an emphasis on natural rights and reconciliation with other religions. In *PACEM IN TERRIS* Pope John encouraged the end of COLONIALISM and pleaded for the abandonment of the ARMS RACE.

Aggravated peacekeeping A term coined by the US Department of Defense to describe peacekeeping operations in situations where neutral troops may be required to use force to carry out their mandate.

Aggression In international relations, an attack by one country or ALLIANCE against another. The literature of INTERNATIONAL LAW has on numerous occasions attempted to define 'aggression' and to distinguish between it and legitimate acts of individual or COLLECTIVE SELF-DEFENCE. It is complicated by subjectivity, so that what one POWER may regard as AGGRESSION another will consider a legitimate WAR of liberation; and by the fact that it does not just involve external conflict but may include internal subversion, aid to insurgents, economic sabotage and so on. It is also the case that the power that fires the first shot, and is technically, therefore, the aggressor, may, nevertheless, have been previously unendurably provoked. Discussion and definition of aggression have been central to attempts to institute COLLECTIVE SECURITY, as with the LEAGUE OF NATIONS COVENANT. The League called for member STATES collectively to take action against any state that was declared an aggressor. This included the use of economic, financial and military SANCTIONS, if needs be. Similarly ARTICLE 51 of the UNITED NATIONS CHARTER provides for sanctions and allows the UNITED NATIONS SECURITY COUNCIL to take action including the use of force.

Agonizing reappraisal This phrase was coined as a warning to Western Europe by the US SECRETARY OF STATE John Foster Dulles (1888–1959). It related to the protracted debate over the rearmament of Germany in the COLD WAR and the plan to incorporate German troops in a EUROPEAN DEFENCE COMMUNITY (EDC). On 14 December 1953 Dulles said: 'If EDC should fail, the United States might be compelled to make an agonizing reappraisal of its basic policy.' This US threat to alter the STRATEGY for the DEFENCE of Western Europe recurred subsequently in US–European relations when transatlantic differences arose, not least in the context of BURDEN SHARING. In the event, the French National Assembly rejected the EDC, but the Federal Republic of Germany (FRG) was subsequently admitted to the NORTH ATLANTIC TREATY ORGANIZATION (NATO).

Agree to disagree A mutual understanding in negotiations that, on a specific topic under discussion, agreement has proved impossible, because of the diametrically opposed views of the parties concerned. In 1954, for instance, this term was used to sum up the position of the four occupying powers on the stalemate issue of German unification at the Berlin Conference.

Agrément This is the formal indication by one country to another that a diplomat to be sent to it by the other is acceptable. The *agrément* is a response to enquiries made by the sending STATE before the formal nomination of the diplomat being considered. It is a useful device to establish or reaffirm good relations between countries. Advance enquiries as to whether the nominee is going to be *persona grata* (acceptable) avoids embarrassment to either state.

AI See AMNESTY INTERNATIONAL.

AIC Advanced industrial country.

Aid Economic, cultural, social and military assistance given to a country or region by another government or international agency. Foreign aid is offered bilaterally by regional institutions and by global agencies under the UNITED NATIONS (UN).

Economic aid includes categories such as technical assistance, capital grants, development loans, food supplies, public guarantees for private investments and trade credits. Military aid includes transfer of hardware and support of military structures and establishments. The objectives of foreign aid include the support of allies, the rebuilding of war-shattered economies, promoting economic development, gaining ideological influence (as in the COLD WAR), obtaining strategic materials and rescuing countries or areas from economic collapse or national disasters.

AID, US See AGENCY FOR INTERNATIONAL DEVELOPMENT, US.

AIDS See ACQUIRED IMMUNE DEFICIENCY SYNDROME.

Ailleret Doctrine The idea, named after one of the Chiefs of Staff of French President Charles de Gaulle (1890–1970), that the French nuclear deterrent, the FORCE DE FRAPPE, was 'omnidirectional' – that it should be wholly independent of other countries and capable of being launched in any direction. It was a military expression of the President's independent foreign policy and his wish to reduce US influence in Europe. After the invasion of Czechoslovakia in August 1968 by the WARSAW PACT, it was succeeded by the Fourquet Plan (1969), which reverted to the idea of the USSR as the main target.

Air burst A term used to describe the detonation of a nuclear warhead in the air.

Air superiority The ability of an air force to dominate air space. It has two elements. First, it means being able to prevent enemy aircraft, especially bombers and reconnaissance planes, from operating over one's own lines or territory. This requires a significant interception or fighter force. Secondly, it implies the ability to fly missions over the enemy's lines, attacking troop concentrations and supply networks. For instance, the failure of the Luftwaffe to establish air superiority in 1940 was crucial to Britain's ability to continue the war against Nazi Germany. On the other hand, Allied air superiority by 1944 was essential to the success of D-DAY.

Alien A person who is not a citizen or a national of the STATE in which he or she is located. As a general principle of INTERNATIONAL LAW, states possess internal SOVEREIGNTY and are free to admit or exclude aliens as they choose. International Law recognizes distinctions between resident aliens who have established a home, and transient aliens. Greatly increased international mobility, a rise in the number of illegal immigrants and government responses to this, in particular in the form of exclusive immigration policies, have made the question of aliens a highly contentious one.

Aliya Hebrew word for 'ascent'. Jewish immigration to the Holy Land, Palestine and, latterly, the State of Israel from the DIASPORA. Settlement in the area has been a central tenet of ZIONISM. Significant immigration began at the end of the nineteenth century, particularly from EASTERN EUROPE. On 6 July 1950 the KNESSET, the parliament of Israel, passed the Law of Return granting every Jew the right of immigration into Israel. Within three-and-a-half years the Jewish population of Israel had more than doubled with 687,000 new immigrants.

All-source analysis A term in the assessment of INTELLIGENCE. It means the analysis of information on foreign targets from a range of separate sources. Such exercises are commonly coordinated by organizations such as the CENTRAL INTELLIGENCE AGENCY (CIA).

Alliance An agreement by STATES to support each other militarily in the event of an attack against any member, or to advance their mutual interests. Alliances may be bilateral or multilateral, secret or open, of short or long duration and be directed at preventing or winning a war. Many contemporary alliances have grown up into regional groupings. So, for example, the BRUSSELS TREATY (1948). The UNITED NATIONS CHARTER recognizes the right to COLLECTIVE SELF-DEFENCE in ARTICLE 51. While alliances may contribute to SECURITY and deter AGGRESSION, they may also contribute to international rivalry and the formation of counter-alliances, risking the widening of conflicts and producing ARMS RACES. For example, it is a moot question whether the alliances in Europe before 1914 stabilized the situation or increased tensions.

Alliance for Progress A US commitment in the 1960s to a long-term assistance programme to encourage economic growth, social modernization and democratization in Latin America. In a speech on 13 March 1961 President Kennedy (1917–63) pledged that the USA would work to satisfy the basic human needs of the Latin Americans. The programme was formally launched in August 1961 at Punta del Este, Uruguay, promising upwards of $20 billion in public and private investment. This so-called MARSHALL PLAN for Latin America reflected US fears that the region had become vulnerable to social revolution and Communist expansion, following the Cuban Revolution under Fidel Castro (b. 1926). The aid was reduced in the 1970s and came to a gradual end. Though it brought about some progress, there was a basic contradiction between its emphasis on social and agrarian reform and its anti-communism. The more anti-communist a Latin-American government was, the less likely it was that it would be willing to bring in social and agrarian reform; and the USA found itself intervening, as in Chile in 1973, to support non-democratic regimes.

Allied Control Council (1945–8) The government of Germany by the Allies after the Second World War. At a meeting on 5 June 1945 the Allies declared that the Council would function as a central government for Germany and would take whatever steps were necessary in Germany to secure PEACE and SECURITY. All Council decisions, dealing with such issues as DEMILITARIZATION, REPARATIONS, and denazification, were to be unanimous, and each commander would be supreme in his own zone of occupation. Irreconcilable difficulties soon emerged between the Soviet and Western representatives and the Council met for the last time in March 1948.

Alma-Ata Treaty (1991) The TREATY that replaced the former structure of the USSR with the COMMONWEALTH OF INDEPENDENT STATES (CIS).

Alsace-Lorraine The eastern provinces of France that were ceded to the new German Empire in 1871 after the Franco-Prussian War and then restored to France after the ARMISTICE of 1918. Between these dates these 'lost territories' were the object of strong French *REVANCHISM*. US President Woodrow Wilson stipulated their return in his FOURTEEN POINTS. This was effected in Article 2 of the Armistice, and later conceded by the German Weimar Republic in the LOCARNO TREATIES (1925). In May–June 1940 the provinces were reoccupied in the Western *BLITZKRIEG* and the Nazis expelled 70,000 French-speaking inhabitants from Lorraine. In February 1945, as the German armies retreated, French administration was restored.

Alternative world futures
The study of what the WORLD SYSTEM may look like in the future. The predictive method consists in extrapolating certain contemporary trends and projecting them into the future on the basis of certain working assumptions. This type of study has developed significantly over the years since the OIL CRISES of the 1970s, with growing popular concern over the population explosion, depletion of natural resources and destruction of the environment. It has been particularly illustrated by the work of such institutions as the CLUB OF ROME and the Hudson Institute, which emphasize the global scope and consequences of such problems and the inadequacy of seeking simply national, or even regional solutions.

Amazon Pact (1978)
A TREATY aimed at coordinating the development of the Amazon river basin and protecting the region's environment through the rational use of its resources. The signatories include Bolivia, Brazil, Colombia, Ecuador, Guyana, Peru, Surinam and Venezuela. It calls for: (1) careful use of the region's water resources; (2) the right of each country to develop its Amazon territory so long as it does not adversely affect other members' territories; (3) free navigation of all rivers; (4) improvement of health in the region and the construction of transport and communications; (5) encouragement of common research effort; (6) promotion of tourism. Its prime objective, to prevent the ecologically disastrous plundering of the resources of the Amazon, has not been achieved.

Ambassador
A diplomatic representative or agent of one sovereign STATE usually resident in another. As international relations implies a system of communications between states, the idea of an ambassador became one of its principal enabling figures. The modern practice of resident ambassadors began to appear in Italy in the fifteenth and sixteenth centuries, but the role became fully established as a vital institution in international relations at the VIENNA CONGRESS (1814–15) at the end of the Napoleonic Wars. The 1961 Vienna Convention on Diplomatic Relations reaffirmed the importance of the role of ambassadors.

America First Committee (1940–1)
A campaigning front by US isolationists, most notably, but not exclusively associated with Republicans from the Middle West, who lobbied to keep America out of the Second World War.

Americanismo
Evident from the early nineteenth century onwards, the idea of encouraging continental unity and, latterly, regional INTEGRATION among Spanish Americans. Simon Bolivar (1783–1830), for instance, envisaged a triple federation that would incorporate Mexico and Central America, the Spanish states of the northern part of the continent and, thirdly, the nations of southern South America. Later the USA encouraged it with a view to emphasizing the unity of the American hemisphere, and since the Second World War, as with MERCOSUR, there have been moves towards greater economic integration in South America.

Amnesty Amnesty clauses are frequently found in PEACE TREATIES and signify the willingness of the conflicting parties to apply the principle of *tabula rasa*, of a clean slate to past offences, which may also include WAR CRIMES. Amnesty may take a general or selective form. In the first case it will provide immunity for all wrongful acts done by the belligerents. One should distinguish between internal and external amnesties. The former are issued after CIVIL WARS, revolutions and upheavals and are political acts of clemency. The latter are provided for in peace treaties between STATES. Since the end of the First World War amnesty clauses have become increasingly rare. A post-Second World War example is the Évian Accord of 1962 between France and Algeria, which ended the war of Algerian independence, in which mutual amnesties were exchanged.

Amnesty International (AI) A leading NON-GOVERNMENTAL ORGANIZATION (NGO) for advocating and defending HUMAN RIGHTS. It was founded in the UK in 1961 and in 2002 has branches in more than 170 countries, with over 4,000 volunteer groups. It works for the release of political prisoners, other prisoners of conscience and victims of torture who neither use nor advocate violence, and issues annual reports on the status of human rights in different countries. Sustained by the belief that exposure to public view of such issues as the treatment of dissidents will persuade nation STATES to improve their record, Amnesty has pursued many campaigns, including those on behalf of the victims of major POWERS, such as the fate of dissidents in the USSR and in the People's Republic of China and of the victims of APARTHEID. Its annual reports have a precise focus and intent: to free prisoners of conscience, ensure prompt and fair trial for political prisoners, abolish the death penalty and torture and bring an end to all 'disappearances', such as occurred in the 1970s on a large scale in Argentina, and inhuman harassment of political opposition groups.

Amsterdam Treaty (1997) Treaty concluded during a marathon summit on 16–17 June at the end of an inter-governmental conference (IGC), which had lasted more than twelve months, and signed in Amsterdam on 2 October 1997. It was intended to make the EUROPEAN UNION (EU) more relevant to its citizens at a time of significant general disillusionment and to prepare the EU for the challenge of enlargement to include the countries of CENTRAL EUROPE and EASTERN EUROPE. It originated in a provision to revise the TREATY ON EUROPEAN UNION (TEU) and was supposed to emphasize, by improvement and institutional reform, the effectiveness of a range of EU policies and procedures. It appeared with six major headings: (1) 'Freedom, Security and Justice', (2) 'The Union and its Citizens', (3) 'An Effective and Coherent External Policy', (4) 'The Union's Institutions', (5) 'Closer Cooperation/Flexibility', and (6) 'Simplification and Consolidation of Treaties'. Its provisions are essentially modest and illustrate the frequent unwillingness of national governments to make concessions to the Community interest.

Anarchism A political philosophy that rejects the STATE and other forms of coercive authority and seeks their replacement by a social order based upon voluntary organization, cooperation and regulation. It developed from distinctive traditions, on the one hand, from extreme liberal individualism and, on the other, from cooperative communitarianism. In the nineteenth century it came to be associated with TERRORISM because of the activities of some of its groups. At the same time it influenced the development of some socialist ideas. From the 1960s onwards it has manifested itself as a key element in some PEACE MOVEMENTS and environmentalist groups.

Anarchy Analysts of international relations have commonly referred to the global order as an 'international anarchy' because there is no common or central world government or authority, or ultimate coercive body to resolve disputes between STATES, or groups of states.

ANC African National Congress.

Ancien Régime From the French for 'old order'. This refers to the political system in France, and across most of Europe, before the French Revolution of 1789 in which monarchs had (theoretically) absolute authority and the nobles and clergy enjoyed special privileges. It is sometimes used more loosely and ironically simply to describe an early political order.

ANF See ATLANTIC NUCLEAR FORCE.

Annexation The forcible acquisition of territory by one STATE at the expense of another. The population of the annexed territory become subjects of the new possessor state. Annexation may be made by FORCE or by TREATY. It involves an element of compulsion or threat. Examples include Nazi Germany's annexation of the SUDETEN-LAND in 1938 and that of ALSACE-LORRAINE in 1871. According to general INTER-NATIONAL LAW, the legality of annexation depends upon whether the use of force appears to be legitimate.

Anschluss (1938) From the German *anschliessen*, 'to connect'. This term is used to describe the Nazi takeover of Austria on 11 March 1938. This had a long preceding history, since Austria had been part of the HOLY ROMAN EMPIRE and had contributed materially to its defence. A common historical heritage and language resulted in a strong pro-German feeling among the majority of the Austrian population after the First World War. A union of Austria and Germany was specifically prohibited by the PARIS PEACE CONFERENCE (1919–20). Hitler (1889–1945), for whom this was his country of birth, and the Nazis regarded this takeover as an essential preliminary stage in their realization of a Greater Reich. The invasion followed an earlier abortive Nazi putsch in July 1934 in which the Austrian Chancellor Dollfuss (1892–1934) was assassinated. On 13 March 1938 Austria was designated a province of Germany, the 'Ostmark'. Article 4 of the AUSTRIAN STATE TREATY (1955) forbids a future Anschluss.

Antarctic Treaty (1959) This treaty was signed by twelve nations, including Britain, the USA, France, the USSR and Japan, providing for international cooperation and prohibiting military and nuclear activity of all kinds in Antarctica, and calling for mutual inspection. It was an outgrowth of the declaration by the UNITED NATIONS GEN-ERAL ASSEMBLY establishing 1957–8 as an 'International Geophysical Year' marked by global scientific cooperation relating to space, the oceans, weather and the Poles. Initially valid for thirty years, it was renewed in 1991, this time with forty nations signing the document, which also banned the exploitation of the continent's mineral resources for another fifty years.

Antarctic Treaty System (ATS) An arrangement for international cooperation between the STATES at the South Pole. It was established in 1961, originating from the ANTARCTIC TREATY of two years earlier and it was reaffirmed in 1991. Originally there were a dozen signatories. In 2002 there are more than forty. Antarctica counts for 10 per cent of the world's land surface and 30 per cent of the land in the Southern Hemisphere. ATS attempts to maintain the continent as a zone of peace, as a region open to all countries that wish to advance scientific discovery and join in its preservation, rather than as a region of exclusive jurisdictions and SOVEREIGNTY.

Anti-Ballistic Missile (ABM) System A system intended to locate, intercept and destroy BALLISTIC MISSILES and their separated warheads. It was in the early 1960s that the USSR and the USA started to study ways of destroying the other side's strategic ballistic missiles just after launch. The idea presented multiple difficulties, involving a very short reaction time, highly complex radars and interceptors and very high velocity missiles. The first ABM system to be deployed was GALOSH, to defend Moscow, in 1968.

Anti-Ballistic Missile (ABM) Treaty (1972) This was signed by the USA and the USSR on 26 May 1972, was part of the STRATEGIC ARMS LIMITATION TREATY (SALT I) and was intended to end any 'defensive' ARMS RACE. The TREATY limited the SUPERPOWERS to two ABM systems, each having no more than 100 interceptors. One could be used to defend the national capital and the other to protect INTER-CONTINENTAL BALLISTIC MISSILE (ICBM) sites. When US President Ronald Reagan (b. 1911) announced the STRATEGIC DEFENSE INITIATIVE (SDI) in 1983, the USSR and other powers claimed that this breached the ABM treaty. Furthermore, were such a system to be foolproof, it could be very destabilizing, conferring on its possessor FIRST-STRIKE CAPABILITY.

Anti-Comintern Pact (1930) A treaty originally concluded between Germany and Japan on 25 November 1930, its official title being 'Agreement against the Third International'. It was renewed in 1936 and again in 1941. Italy joined it on 6 November 1937; Hungary, Manchukuo and Spain in 1939. It obliged the parties to provide information to each other on the activities of the COMINTERN and to take counsel on defence measures. A secret supplementary clause bound the parties to NEUTRALITY in the event of either of them coming into conflict with the USSR. Although it was a defensive arrangement, it foreshadowed the formation of the Tripartite Pact of 27 September between Germany, Italy and Japan. During the Second World War, Croatia, Denmark, Finland, Romania, Slovakia and the pro-Japanese government of Wang-Ching Wei (1883–1944) acceded. It became void after the defeat of the AXIS, but outlasted the Comintern, which was dissolved in 1943.

ANZUS See AUSTRALIA, NEW ZEALAND AND UNITED STATES TREATY (1951).

Apartheid The term meaning 'apartness' in Afrikaans, the language of the former Dutch colonists in South Africa. Together with another concept, *baaskup*, meaning white supremacy, it meant racial segregation and underpinned the rule of the Nationalist Party in South Africa between 1948 and 1990. This policy resulted in the territorial separation of Europeans (18 per cent of the population) and non-Europeans and guaranteed the Europeans a monopoly of economic, political and social power. The black populations were confined to their own townships, or tribal 'homelands', were controlled by internal passports and denied political rights and representation in the national parliament. This system violated HUMAN RIGHTS both because of discrimination and because, among other things, of the system of arbitrary arrest and detention. As such it was the focus of international condemnation and SANCTIONS and was swept away after the release of Nelson Mandela (b. 1918), the leader of the African National Congress (ANC), in 1990, with nearly all the apartheid legislation being repealed by 1992.

Apatridos An international term for those without citizenship of any STATE.

APEC See ASIA-PACIFIC ECONOMIC COOPERATION.

Appeasement This term is historically most commonly associated with the policies of Britain and France towards Germany and Italy in the inter-war years, most particularly with the surrender of the SUDETENLAND in Czechoslovakia to Nazi Germany with the MUNICH AGREEMENT (1938). Since then a term, which earlier had signified magnanimous conciliation and a reasonable willingness to compromise and negotiate rather than confront and resist, has acquired derogatory overtones in both historical scholarship and common parlance. It has come to mean cowardice and the sacrifice of principle, such as the sovereign independence of small countries, for expedience, in this case placating a dictator, Hitler (1889–1945), and buying time. In the period since the Second World War it has been the subject of very great historical debate. It has also, more generally, become synonymous with weakness and a policy not to be repeated. 'No more Munichs' has been invoked time after time to justify policies of uncompromising firmness and rigidity in international relations – for instance, during the KOREAN WAR of 1950–3, the SUEZ CRISIS of 1956 and the GULF WAR in 1991. International relations theorists have not always shared the negative view. A number of those who have espoused REALISM have regarded appeasement, properly conducted, as an integral part of the process of the BALANCE OF POWER, and as necessary accommodation in the light of changing global circumstances to facilitate peaceful change.

Arab League This was initiated during the Second World War in September 1944 when delegates from Egypt, Lebanon, Transjordan, Syria and Iraq met in Alexandria to discuss ways of enhancing Arab cooperation. The subsequent Alexandria Protocol led to its creation on 22 March 1945 with the addition of North Yemen and Saudi Arabia. By the 1990s it had twenty-two members including the PALESTINE LIBERATION ORGANIZATION (PLO) and four African countries, Dijibouti, Mauritania, Somalia and Sudan. At one stage Egypt was expelled, though the headquarters returned to Cairo again. During the GULF WAR (1991) a majority voted to support the coalition expulsion of Iraq from Kuwait.

Arbitration A means of peaceful CONFLICT RESOLUTION, in which the contending parties select an impartial agent, an arbiter or court of arbitration to settle the conflict by compromise or through legal procedures, as agreed by the parties, who also agree to accept any decision as binding. A well-known case of arbitration was that arising from the claims of damages inflicted by the Confederate raider 'Alabama' made by the USA against Britain in the American Civil War, which was settled in the Washington Treaty of 1871. The first HAGUE PEACE CONFERENCE (1899) institutionalized the procedure by creating the PERMANENT COURT OF ARBITRATION. Both the LEAGUE OF NATIONS and the UNITED NATIONS (UN) have encouraged the procedure. It is, however, often difficult to persuade a STATE to entrust itself to a procedure whose results cannot be anticipated. Arbitration is likely to be used when the relations between the parties are generally good, where there is a common political culture and mutual respect for the rule of law.

Arcadia Conference (1941–2)   The Anglo-US conference held in December–January at which the two principals were US President Franklin D. Roosevelt (1882–1945) and the British Prime Minister Winston Churchill (1874–1965), following the Japanese attack on PEARL HARBOR on 7 December 1941 and the active entry of the USA into the Second World War. It was agreed that the Allies would defeat Germany first while undertaking holding action against Japan. The Allies also decided that they would try to prevent the Japanese capture of Hawaii, Alaska, Singapore, the Dutch East Indies, the Philippines, Rangoon and the land route from there to China. Churchill's suggestion of an invasion of North Africa won general approval. The conference established combined military planning – for instance, with Far East Command. The UNITED NATIONS DECLARATION was signed at the same time, on 1 January 1942.

Area bombing   The controversial strategy, otherwise known as the Strategic Bombing Offensive, or night-time blanket bombing, of urban centres and civilian populations, rather than simply military targets. It culminated in 1945 in the British bombing of Dresden and US attacks on Japanese cities. The strategy had its origins in the British air doctrine between the wars, which also had proponents in Europe and the USA, which emphasized the potential of large-scale bombing offences as a means of achieving victory independently of armies and navies. By the 1930s it was widely believed that mass long-range bomber raids were unstoppable and that they could deliver a knockout blow to a hostile power. This was also of considerable concern to British governments in the 1930s with a widespread fear that the 'bomber would always get through'.

Armed conflict   The clash of armed forces between STATES, the occupation of foreign territories by such forces with, or without resistance (international conflicts), as well as non-international clashes within borders. In 1970 the UNITED NATIONS GENERAL ASSEMBLY stipulated eight basic principles for the protection of civilians during armed conflict, including preservation of HUMAN RIGHTS discrimination between combatants and non-combatants, and the exemption of civilians from reprisals.

Armed propaganda   This is also known as 'propaganda by the deed', the terroristic and nihilistic use of FORCE to focus wide public attention on demands or protests. The emphasis is on the symbolic political importance of the action, rather than its practical effect. The attack on the World Trade Centre in New York on 11 September 2001 falls into this category; so, too, Basque desecration of the memorials of the SPANISH CIVIL WAR (1936–9), or the seizure of the US Embassy in Tehran during the Iranian Revolution of 1979.

Armistice A suspension, or temporary cessation, of hostilities by agreement between belligerent powers, such as the armistice between Germany and the Allied and Associated Powers on 11 November 1918, which concluded the First World War.

Arms control The term came into usage in the 1960s to describe the policy and processes for limiting the development, stockpiling and deployment of weapons. Its particular, though not exclusive, focus has been on NUCLEAR WEAPONS. It has been especially concerned with achieving stable DETERRENCE, averting accidents or use of arms by terrorist organizations, and limitation of PROLIFERATION. The major problem facing negotiators has been VERIFICATION, and this was especially so during the COLD WAR. Arms control differs from some of the advocacies of DISARMAMENT, since it assumes that arms will continue to exist and does not dispute their utility. Arms control negotiators have often argued that it is a more realistic way to SECURITY.

Arms race This term has been used since the 1850s to describe periodic competition between STATES or BLOCS by the modernization of weapons and increase in their numbers and destructiveness, with a view to increasing their SECURITY and gaining a specific level of comparative military strength or advantage. Examples include the Anglo-German naval rivalry before 1914 and the massive rearmament of the COLD WAR period. Simultaneous modernization of forces does not necessarily mean an arms race. At the same time, arms races need not be restricted to technological development and arms procurement. For example, the extension of CONSCRIPTION may be a significant element in an arms race. The situation in which an attempt to gain greater security by rearmament produces greater insecurity in the rival is called the SECURITY DILEMMA. An arms race in which increase is repeatedly met by increase is called the 'spiral model'. Arms races are so dependent upon economic resources that they must also be seen as a form of economic competition. Hence during the cold war the argument was commonly advanced in the USA that the Soviet economy would collapse under the pressure of the arms race, and this was offered as one of its justifications.

'Arsenal of Democracy' Speech (1940) The radio address by the US President Franklin D. Roosevelt (1882–1945) on 28 December 1940 in which he explained his LEND-LEASE programme. Arguing that Nazi ambitions included the domination of the Western Hemisphere, he stated that the USA must be 'the great arsenal of democracy' to supply Britain with munitions to keep it in the fight and 'to keep war away from our country and our people'.

Article X (LEAGUE OF NATIONS COVENANT) This was one of the most controversial articles in the Covenant in the USA because it invoked the idea of COLLECTIVE SECURITY to stop AGGRESSION. It led to a heated debate in the Senate. Opponents argued that it could drag the USA into conflicts not of its own choosing across the world. They also alleged that such a commitment would override the war-making powers of Congress. US President Woodrow Wilson (1856–1924) claimed the commitment would be moral rather than legal. The LODGE RESERVATIONS insisted that, were Article X to be accepted, Congressional approval would have to be granted before any act of implementation. In the event the US Senate refused to ratify the LEAGUE OF NATIONS.

Article 51 A key article in the UNITED NATIONS CHARTER (1945), which justifies the use of FORCE in self-defence and the creation of regional organizations for COLLECTIVE SELF-DEFENCE. It reads as follows: 'Nothing in the present Charter shall impair the inherent right of individual and collective self-defence if an armed attack occurs against a member of the United Nations, until the Security Council has taken measures necessary to maintain international peace and security. Measures taken by members in the exercise of the right of self-defence shall be immediately reported to the Security Council and shall not in any way affect the authority and responsibility of the Security Council under the present Charter to take at any time such actions as it deems necessary in order to maintain or restore international peace and security.'

Article 231 Otherwise known as the 'war guilt clause', it assigned all responsibility for the outbreak and conduct of the First World War to Germany and its allies in the VERSAILLES TREATY (1919). It became a hated symbol of Germany's post-war humiliation and played into the hands in particular of right-wing groups within Germany, most notably the Nazis, who exploited it to increase dissatisfaction with the Weimar Government. It also occasioned a long and continuing historiographical controversy over responsibility for the war.

Article 43 forces This term refers to Article 43 of the UNITED NATIONS CHARTER, which deals with the issue of UNITED NATIONS (UN) military FORCE in fulfilling the organization's resolutions. The Charter implies that the permanent members of the UNITED NATIONS SECURITY COUNCIL would provide the majority of the forces, if required. Though this happened in the KOREAN WAR of 1950–3 and during the Persian GULF WAR of 1991, most of the UN missions until the late 1980s used troops from other countries.

ASEAN See ASSOCIATION OF SOUTH EAST ASIAN NATIONS.

Asian dollars US dollars deposited in South Asian countries.

Asian Tigers The popular name for a group of Asian economies that have experienced dynamic economic growth patterns in the post-Second World War period and have come to be regarded as standard-bearers for economic liberalism and market economics. Hong Kong, Japan, South Korea, Singapore and Taiwan have been included in this category.

Asia-Pacific Economic Cooperation (APEC) This organization links countries on both sides of the PACIFIC RIM. It was set up originally in 1989 in Australia with twelve participants: Thailand, Malaysia, Singapore, Indonesia, Brunei, and the Philippines, the USA, Canada, Japan, South Korea and New Zealand. China, Hong Kong and Taiwan joined in 1991, followed shortly after by Mexico and Papua New Guinea, and by Chile in 1994. The combined economies of APEC total more than half of the world's gross domestic product (GDP). Its objectives are support for the principles of the WORLD TRADE ORGANIZATION (WTO) and it advocates 'open regionalism', favouring liberalization and avoiding preferential treatment.

Assertive multilateralism The idea particularly advanced by US governments that there should be international cooperation in upholding global SECURITY.

This idea is inherent in the UNITED NATIONS (UN), and the UNITED NATIONS SECURITY COUNCIL was given primary responsibility for maintaining the PEACE after the Second World War. It was evident, for instance, in the coalition against Iraq in 1990–1 after the invasion of Kuwait, in the interest of HUMANITARIAN INTERVENTION and in the coalition building against TERRORISM in 2001 after the destruction of the New York World Trade Centre. The idea very much depends on common resolve and widespread support and the belief that an action is to the common benefit rather than, for instance, serving simply the national interests of the USA.

Associated states An international term used in PEACE TREATIES to distinguish them from allied STATES. A well-known example is the USA during the latter part of the First World War. US President Woodrow Wilson (1856–1924) then proposed its inclusion in the VERSAILLES TREATY (1919), with those who had defeated the CENTRAL POWERS being described as 'Allied and Associated Powers'. The term is also used in organizations of economic INTEGRATION and cooperation. For instance, with the EUROPEAN UNION (EU) there are member states and associated states.

Association agreements These are agreements between the EUROPEAN UNION (EU) and neighbouring countries to develop close economic and political relations, possibly leading to eventual EU membership for the associated country. They are negotiated under Article 238 of the ROME TREATY (1957), which gives the EU the right to establish with non-member STATES 'association involving reciprocal rights and obligations, common action and special procedure'. The first such agreement was signed with Greece in 1961, followed by Turkey in 1964. Such agreements generally grant the associated country free access to the EU's market for most industrial products, and financial and technical aid. The associated country usually grants reciprocal concessions. The agreements also cover political cooperation with a view to promoting stability and democracy in the associated states. EUROPE AGREEMENTS are those association agreements with the states of CENTRAL EUROPE and EASTERN EUROPE post-1989 that stipulate eventual accession to the EU.

Association of South East Asian Nations (ASEAN) Formed in 1967 by Indonesia, Malaysia, the Philippines, Singapore and Thailand. Brunei joined in 1984 and Vietnam in 1995. ASEAN was originally an anti-communist alliance. In 2002 it is an organization for economic cooperation composed of the fastest-growing 'ASIAN TIGERS'. In 1992 it agreed to establish a FREE TRADE AREA within fifteen years.

Assured destruction A term used in nuclear STRATEGY. It has two meanings. As a capability, it refers to the technical potential of STATES to launch attacks against an adversary that lead to large-scale destruction of people and property. Before air power and NUCLEAR WEAPONS, such destruction was possible only via land invasion. The capability to achieve assured destruction is usually referred to as SECOND STRIKE CAPABILITY. As a policy, assured destruction is an example of what is termed in nuclear jargon 'counter-city targeting', which was particularly associated with US defence policy in the 1960s.

Asylum A quasi-legal process where one STATE grants protection to a national, or nationals, of another. In INTERNATIONAL LAW it can be challenged by a request for

EXTRADITION. It is sometimes said that asylum ends where extradition begins, but in the absence of a specific extradition TREATY there is no duty to extradite. Rights of asylum belong to states not to individuals, although Article 14 of the UNIVERSAL DEC- LARATION OF HUMAN RIGHTS (1948) does give individuals a right to political asylum. As the declaration took the form of a resolution of the UNITED NATIONS GENERAL ASSEMBLY, it is not legally (though it may be considered morally) binding on states.

Atlantic Charter (1941) The result of the meeting off Argentia, Newfoundland, between the US President Franklin Roosevelt (1882–1945) and the British Prime Minister Winston Churchill (1874–1965). The Atlantic Charter was signed on 14 August, four months before the Japanese attack on PEARL HARBOR. It was a declaration by the leaders of the principles on which they 'base[d] their hopes for a better future for the world' and has sometimes been described as an 'updated FOURTEEN POINTS'. The leaders rejected territorial aggrandizement, renounced the use of FORCE, upheld SELF- DETERMINATION of peoples, FREE TRADE and FREEDOM OF THE SEAS, specified DISARMA- MENT of the aggressor STATES and committed themselves to 'a wider and permanent system of general security'. Incorporating the FOUR FREEDOMS, the Charter provided an ideological basis for the subsequent GRAND ALLIANCE, was effective propaganda against isolationist sentiment in the USA and was formally endorsed by the UNITED NATIONS DECLARATION of 1 January 1942, which was signed by twenty-six countries.

Atlantic Community The idea advanced in particular since the Second World War of a partnership between Europe and North America, to solve common prob- lems. The Atlantic Council of the USA, based in Washington DC, and the NORTH ATLANTIC TREATY ORGANIZATION (NATO) are obvious embodiments of this idea, which has both produced great *RAPPROCHEMENT* and successes and led to transatlantic ten- sions. For instance, in the 1960s the French President Charles de Gaulle (1890–1970) strongly advanced both French nationalism and the notion of a 'Europe for the Europeans' with conspicuous defiance of the USA and an appeal for a reduction of its influence in Europe. During the COLD WAR the term incorporated Western Europe. With the fall of the BERLIN WALL and the transformation of EASTERN EUROPE, with several previously Communist states joining NATO, the concept has been extended, but this has not necessarily increased its credibility, since this to a great extent has depended on a perceived common threat from the EASTERN BLOC.

Atlantic Nuclear Force (ANF) A British defence proposal made in the early 1960s, which called for the nuclear guarantee provided by the NORTH ATLANTIC TREATY ORGANIZATION (NATO) to be shared by its member STATES. Offered as an alternative to the US MULTILATERAL FORCE (MLF) proposal, it came to nothing. It reflected two con- cerns, first the dependence of Western Europe on the US nuclear arsenal at a time when the USSR had effective means of retaliation against the USA, and, secondly, whether Britain in coming years could continue to have a viable nuclear deterrent.

Atlantic to the Urals An idea advanced by the French President Charles de Gaulle (1890–1970) in 1958 for an eventual coming-together of EASTERN EUROPE and Western Europe. At the time Europe was sharply divided by the IRON CURTAIN and separate socio-economic systems. The idea was associated with de Gaulle's aspirations for a 'Europe for the Europeans', a reduction of US influence over the Continent, for

DÉTENTE and a normalization of East–West European relations. The WARSAW PACT suppression of the PRAGUE SPRING in 1968 emphasized the current unrealism of the concept, but the dismantling of the BERLIN WALL in 1989 and events since then in CENTRAL EUROPE and EASTERN EUROPE have transformed perspectives.

Atlantic Wall Hitler's name for the chain of German field fortifications, stretching along the coastline from the Pyrenees to the Netherlands, a distance of 1,670 miles. It was constructed by forced labour between 1941 and 1944 and consisted of about 6,000 bunkers. The western bulwark of Nazi FORTRESS EUROPE, it was vacated by the Germans after D-DAY (1944).

Atlanticism A fundamental post-Second World War British international SECURITY policy stressing the priority of the NORTH ATLANTIC TREATY ORGANIZATION (NATO), of British links with the USA and the USA's commitment to defend Europe. It grew out of the wartime experience of the so-called SPECIAL RELATIONSHIP and evolved through the COLD WAR. It assumed that the security of Britain required the maintenance of a BALANCE OF POWER in Europe, that the USSR posed a military and ideological threat to Western Europe, and that neither Britian nor its European allies could, of themselves, defend Europe against a conventional or nuclear attack from the WARSAW PACT. Since 1989 and the fall of the BERLIN WALL, British governments have emphasized the continuing need for NATO and for US commitment. Some aspects of the policy of Atlanticism, particularly those involving the stationing of American bases and nuclear missiles in Britain, have created significant controversy, such as during the 1980s when Mrs Thatcher (b. 1925) was in power. She has been arguably the most Atlanticist of British prime ministers and described the British link with the USA as the 'extraordinary relationship'. Atlanticism as a policy option, particularly contrasted with Europeanism, has also been shared by those in other countries, not least in Germany. The word is sometimes now also used in Britain to indicate a preference for closer economic ties with the USA to closer integration with the EUROPEAN UNION (EU).

Atomic bomb The type of NUCLEAR WEAPON produced by the MANHATTAN PROJECT and used twice in August 1945 on Hiroshima and Nagasaki. The product of nuclear fission, rather than fusion, which is the cause of the HYDROGEN BOMB explosion. Its YIELD was under 20,000 tons of TNT equivalent. The explosion of the first Soviet atomic bomb in August 1949, several years before the West anticipated it, led the USA to develop the hydrogen bomb. This was to have explosive equivalence of millions of tons of TNT.

Atomic diplomacy This phrase has been used to describe any foreign policy stance that depends for its effect on a threat, either stated or implicit, of the use of NUCLEAR WEAPONS in the international order. It was used particularly widely in the 1950s and 1960s to describe the power politics of the nuclear age. In particular, there has been a debate among scholars as to the influence of monopoly possession of the ATOMIC BOMB between 1945 and 1949 on US foreign policy towards the USSR.

Atomic Energy Act (1946) Also known as the McMahon Act after Senator Brien McMahon (1903–52), this was the first law passed by US Congress with the purpose of controlling atomic energy. A five-man ATOMIC ENERGY COMMISSION (AEC) was made sole owner of fissionable material and given full control over atomic research. Three committees were also established, for military liaison, technical advice and a joint congressional committee. It outlawed any transfer of atomic secrets to any other powers. These included Britain, which had expected continuing partnership, and the Act was a major stimulus to Britain embarking on its own ATOMIC BOMB and HYDROGEN BOMB programmes.

Atomic Energy Commission (AEC) This was established by the first resolution adopted by the UNITED NATIONS GENERAL ASSEMBLY in 1946. It was composed of all the members of the UNITED NATIONS SECURITY COUNCIL plus Canada. In 1952 it was merged with the Commission for Conventional Armaments into a single Disarmament Commission with the same membership.

Atoms for Peace Plan (1953) A proposal presented to the UNITED NATIONS GENERAL ASSEMBLY that would provide for cooperation among the nuclear STATES and other nations in the peaceful development and application of atomic energy. It called for the establishment of an international agency under the UNITED NATIONS (UN) to encourage cooperation in the atomic field and it urged nuclear powers to divert fissionable materials from their weapons stockpiles to projects for atomic energy and to restrain the nuclear ARMS RACE. Subsequently, in 1957, the INTERNATIONAL ATOMIC ENERGY AGENCY (IAEA) was set up.

ATS See ANTARCTIC TREATY SYSTEM.

Attaché A person attached to an embassy or other diplomatic post in a specialist function – for instance, as a press officer, cultural or commercial attaché. Some are recruited by a STATE's foreign office, while others are recommended from other government agencies. The expanded use of attachés has been accompanied by numerous international accusations of espionage. Where a diplomatic officer is expelled from a country on grounds of espionage, it is common for the state from which he or she has come to retaliate by expelling one or more attachés of similar standing.

Attrition Means 'wearing out'. It is often, for instance, used to refer to the STRATEGY adopted by both sides during the First World War on the Western Front, which transformed the hope of a short WAR into one that lasted four years with massive casualties for small territorial gains. Wars of attrition are usually long, drawn-out affairs and place the entire range of a STATE's resources at the disposal of the military. A recent example of a very protracted war of attrition was that between Iraq and Iran between 1980 and 1989, which brought about almost total exhaustion on both sides.

Aussiedler German for 'emigrant'. As a political term it refers specifically to those ethnic Germans living outside Germany, the descendants of colonists of earlier times, in CENTRAL EUROPE and EASTERN EUROPE – for example, in the Volga region of Russia – who have settled or wish to settle in the Federal Republic of Germany (FRG). After 1948 they were given an unrestricted right to resettle, as distinct from other immigrants and asylum-seekers. Their numbers rose sharply after the fall of the BERLIN WALL in 1989, leading the German authorities to tighten the regulations by obliging potential emigrants first to submit an application in their country of residence.

Australia, New Zealand and United States Treaty (ANZUS)

(1951) The ANZUS Pact between Australia, New Zealand and the United States, signed on 1 September 1951, came into force on 29 April 1952. It provided for an indefinite defensive military ALLIANCE and committed the signatories to increase their military capabilities. It was designed to overcome Australia's and New Zealand's nervousness over Japanese revival, which was supported by the USA, and as part of the STRATEGY of CONTAINMENT against COMMUNISM at a time when Mao's victory in China (1949) and the outbreak of the KOREAN WAR (1950–3) caused widespread alarm. The pact also significantly reflected Britain's decline as a global power, with the USA assuming its protective role over these COMMONWEALTH countries. ANZUS was put under considerable stress in 1984 when the New Zealand government banned nuclear vessels from entering its ports. This led US President Reagan (b. 1911) the following year to declare that ANZUS was inoperative.

Austrian State Treaty

(1955) This ended the Allied occupation of Austria, which had begun ten years earlier. Having readily agreed to separate Austria from the unresolved question of a German peace settlement, the USSR in the Moscow Memorandum of April 1955 offered to sign a PEACE TREATY and remove occupation FORCES by the end of the year, release remaining prisoners of war and make certain economic concessions in return for Austria's pledge to remain neutral and pay $150 million for the remaining German assets in the country. The treaty was signed on 15 May, but the most important point, NEUTRALITY, was not put into the treaty itself but incorporated in the Austrian Constitution in October, after which Austria became a member of the UNITED NATIONS (UN). This treaty was one indication of the THAW after the death of Stalin and was one of the more effective early examples of conflict management in the COLD WAR. In the West it was perceived as something of a victory, since Western policy had been directed towards preventing Austria from becoming a Soviet satellite.

Autarky

Not to be confused with autarchy (self-rule), autarky means self-sufficiency. The term is most often used in international economics and has been particularly applied to the policies of self-sufficiency in Nazi Germany and the USSR.

Autonomy

The capacity to act independently; in the case of STATES, independently from the influence of other states or international organizations in the WORLD ORDER. The reality (or illusion) of autonomy has occasioned debates among theorists of international relations. Advocates of DEPENDENCY THEORY have claimed that the structural system of global CAPITALISM denies small developing states from exercising much autonomy, stating that they are to a considerable extent dependent on major interests in the industrialized world and such institutions as the INTERNATIONAL BANK FOR RECONSTRUCTION AND DEVELOPMENT (IBRD) (World Bank) and the INTERNATIONAL MONETARY FUND (IMF). Liberal theorists have argued from a different perspective, that the capitalist system, among other things, offering opportunities in a range of markets, creates greater autonomy.

Avis

This term is used to describe the statement issued by the EUROPEAN COMMISSION on whether or not the formal application of a country that wishes to join the EUROPEAN UNION (EU) is acceptable or not.

Avulsion An international term for territorial or border changes as a consequence of a river changing its course. One of the best-known examples of this is Chamizal, the Mexican border territory, which from 1864 until 1967 was the cause of a border dispute between the USA and Mexico, because the bed of the Rio Grande had changed and the USA had occupied the former river bed, in spite of a ruling by the International Arbitration Commission, which stated that it belonged to Mexico. The dispute was finally resolved in Mexico's favour in 1967, when the USA handed it back.

Axis A term first used by the Italian dictator Mussolini (1883–1945) on 1 November 1936 to describe the relationship between Fascist Italy and Nazi Germany that was established by the October Protocols of that year. Mussolini said of the 'Berlin–Rome line' that it was 'not a diaphragm but rather an axis'. Italy acceded to the German–Japanese ANTI-COMINTERN PACT on 25 November 1936 and on 22 May 1939 Germany and Italy entered a formal alliance, the PACT OF STEEL. On 27 September 1940 Germany, Italy and Japan signed the Tripartite Pact in Berlin. During the Second World War the term 'Axis Powers' was applied to those three countries plus the East European allies, Bulgaria, Hungary, Romania and Slovakia.

Azerbijan Crisis (1946) Also known as the 'Iranian Crisis', this was the first major post-Second World War crisis between the Western Powers and the USSR. In 1942 the USA, Britain and the USSR agreed to the joint occupation of Iran in order to prevent a German takeover of the oilfields. Though each ally had promised to withdraw its troops six months after the end of the war, Soviet troops still remained in Northern Iran in early 1946 and established the Autonomous Republic of Azerbijan. Iran appealed to the UNITED NATIONS (UN) and pressure from the powers persuaded the USSR to withdraw its forces in March 1946. The USSR simultaneously announced the formation of an Iranian–Soviet oil company, which the Iranian Parliament later rejected. The Crisis was a significant episode in the growth of the COLD WAR.

B

Baghdad Pact (1955) This TREATY was originally signed by Turkey and Iraq in February 1955 aimed against Kurdish groups. In November it was joined by Britain, Iran and Pakistan, becoming a Middle Eastern security organization to protect the region against Soviet pressure. It was opposed by Egypt and other Arab STATES, and after a coup in 1958 Iraq withdrew from the ALLIANCE. It was subsequently reorganized with the addition of the USA as the Central Treaty Organization (CENTO). It came to an end in 1979 following the Iranian revolution and the proclamation of non-alignment by both Iran and Pakistan.

Balance of payments This is the account of a country's international financial and commercial transactions with the rest of the world. Foreign currency receipts from the sale of goods and services are called exports and appear as a credit item on what is called the current account. Vice versa, foreign currency payments are called imports and appear on the debit side. The same applies to what is called the capital account – the inflows and outflows of capital, accounted as credits and debits. If receipts exceed spending, there is a balance-of-payments surplus; and vice versa, a deficit. A situation of uncorrected, continuing and unsustainable deficit is called a balance-of-payments crisis.

Balance of power The idea of the balance of power is based on the belief that PEACE is more likely to be preserved when an equilibrium of POWER exists among powers (particularly the major ones) as otherwise the strong will be tempted to attack the weak. The term can be used to refer both to how the international system operates and to how a STATE or ALLIANCE ought to conduct its external policy. Though the term (whose value has frequently been reduced by its use in a loose descriptive manner) has been used to describe circumstances from the period of Greek antiquity onwards, it has been of particular importance since the rise of the modern state system in Europe. The English international relations theorist Martin Wight (1913–72) specified nine separate understandings of the much-debated term: (1) an even distribution of power; (2) the principle that power should be evenly distributed; (3) the existing distribution of power; (4) the principle of aggrandizement of the strong powers at the expense of the weak; (5) the principle that one side ought to have a margin of strength in order to avert the danger of power becoming unevenly distributed; (6) a special role in maintaining an even distribution of power; (7) a special advantage in the existing balance of power; (8) predominance; (9) an inherent tendency in international politics to produce an even distribution of power. While the balance of power is widely seen as a process that regulates conflict and preserves national independence and the STATUS QUO, there has historically been much debate as to whether it preserves peace or leads to WAR. During the COLD WAR, during which the SUPERPOWERS were so dominant in their respective alliances, the terms BIPOLARITY and MULTIPOLARITY were introduced to describe the new order. So, also, with the NUCLEAR WEAPONS ARMS RACE after 1945 the term BALANCE OF TERROR came to be used.

Balance of terror A term coined in the COLD WAR to describe the stalemate produced by NUCLEAR WEAPONS, and the preservation of PEACE through DETERRENCE or MUTUAL ASSURED DESTRUCTION (MAD) as contrasted with the traditional BALANCE OF POWER. While the balance of power had to produce a recourse to WAR from time to time to preserve or recreate a balance, the balance of terror predicates the impossibility of a nuclear war because of the probability of utter destruction. Balance here does not imply absolute equality, but a situation in which the weaker power can still devastate the stronger to a completely unacceptable degree. The classical balance-of-power theory was based on MULTIPOLARITY while the balance of terror has referred to a situation of overwhelming bipolar nuclear strength between the two SUPERPOWERS. One of the major concerns of the USA and the USSR/Russia has been to prevent NUCLEAR PROLIFERATION, which, it is felt, can only encourage instability rather than balance.

Balance of trade This is the balance in visible trade over a specified period, the difference between a country's import of goods and services and its export of them. It is the most important element of the BALANCE OF PAYMENTS.

Balanced collective forces The requirement for balance in a military force comes from the consideration that all the elements should be complementary to one another so that it is constituted to fight with maximum effectiveness. By extension, this should also apply when a force not only comprises the various services but also extends to more than one nation. In an ALLIANCE the total strength and composition of the forces should likewise be arranged in the best 'balanced' way to achieve the objective of the mission.

Balfour Declaration (1917) The pledge, in the form of a letter, sent by the British Foreign Secretary Arthur Balfour (1848–1930) to Lord Rothschild (1868–1937) on 2 November 1917 supporting the aspiration of ZIONISM. Stating that the British Government viewed 'with favour the establishment in Palestine of a national home for the Jewish people', it promised that the British would use 'their best endeavours to facilitate the achievement of this object, it being clearly understood that nothing shall be done which may prejudice the civil and religious rights of existing non-Jewish communities in Palestine or the rights and political status enjoyed by Jews in any other country'. The declaration at once met with strong objections from the Arabs, who saw it as contradicting pledges to recognize the Arab leaders of the Arab Revolt of 1916 as rulers of Palestine. In particular, the Arabs saw the Hussein–McMahon correspondence as a promise that an independent Arab kingdom would include all of Palestine, though the British later argued that they had excluded the territory west of the river Jordan. However, the declaration was confirmed by the Allies for the British MANDATE over Palestine and endorsed by the LEAGUE OF NATIONS. With growing Jewish immigration, it became more and more difficult for Britain to reconcile its undertakings. Mounting tension, revolt, TERRORISM, British withdrawal and WAR, with Arab defeat, subsequently led to the emergence of the State of Israel in 1948.

Balfour Definition (1926) This clarified the nature of DOMINION status in the British Empire. The ex-prime minister Lord Balfour (1848–1930) was invited at the Imperial Conference of 1926 to chair a committee of dominion prime ministers and this issued a report defining the imperial relationship. According to this, the dominions constituted 'autonomous communities within the British Empire, equal in status, in no way subordinate to one another in any aspect of their domestic or external affairs, though united by a common allegiance to the Crown and freely associated as Members of the British Commonwealth of Nations'. This prepared the way for the 1931 STATUTE OF WESTMINSTER. The Balfour Report stressed that in matters of foreign affairs and defence the 'major share of responsibility rests, and must for some time continue to rest, with His Majesty's Government in Great Britain'.

Balkan Question An international term for disputes and conflicts in the Balkan Peninsula from the early nineteenth century. These resulted from the decline of the Ottoman and Hapsburg empires, from nationalist and ethnic uprisings and the rivalry between Austria-Hungary, France, Italy, Russia, Germany and Britain. The Sarajevo assassination of 28 June 1914 and the tension between Austria-Hungary and the South Slavs triggered the First World War. A serious problem after the WAR was the resettlement of the Turkish population from Greece. Subsequently, Fascist pressure exerted on Balkan STATES by Italy and Nazi Germany provoked military conflicts of Italy with Albania and Germany with Yugoslavia and Greece. With the disintegration of Yugoslavia in the 1990s the Balkans again became a prime focus of international concern and INTERVENTION.

Balkanization The fragmentation of a STATE or larger territorial unit into smaller, autonomous units. The word was coined in the early twentieth century to describe the disintegration of the Turkish Ottoman Empire, which produced chronic instability in the Balkans. It has subsequently been applied elsewhere, for example, to describe events in Russia since 1991, resulting from the mutual hostility of ethnic groups. Normally the term is used in a pejorative sense as something leading to, or reflecting, international upheaval. It is sometimes used to describe a deliberate policy of divide and rule.

Ballhausplatz The location in Vienna of the foreign affairs ministry of the Austro-Hungarian Empire. This term is sometimes used in describing Austro-Hungarian foreign policy – for example, in the years leading to the First World War. It is also the location of the present Austrian foreign ministry.

Ballistic missile From the V2s in the Second World War onwards, any missile that does not rely on aerodynamic surfaces to produce lift and that follows a ballistic trajectory when its thrust ends. With INTER-CONTINENTAL BALLISTIC MISSILES (ICBMS) most of the trajectory lies outside the atmosphere.

Baltic States During the inter-war years this term referred to Estonia, Latvia and Lithuania. After the Second World War, during which these STATES had been incorporated by the USSR, and during the COLD WAR the term came to be used more generally to refer to those states on the Baltic Sea.

Bamboo Curtain This phrase was used, analogously to the IRON CURTAIN during the COLD WAR, to refer to the wall of isolation developed by the communist People's Republic of China between 1949 under Mao-Zedong (1893–1976) and its opening to the West in the early 1970s.

Bandung Conferences (1955, 1985) (1) Held on 17 April 1955, with twenty-nine participating nations in Bandung, Indonesia, the first conference signalled the beginning of the NON-ALIGNED MOVEMENT (NAM), calling for NEUTRALITY between the SUPERPOWERS. The moving spirit here was the Indian Prime Minister Pandit Nehru (1889–1964). It was primarily concerned with the issues of world PEACE, specifically, the reluctance of the Western Powers to consult the developing nations regarding Asia, the tension between the People's Republic of China and the USA and the relationship of China to the rest of Asia. It also declared opposition to COLONIALISM throughout the world, and discussed the question of Indonesia's claim to New Guinea. (2) The second conference of African and Asian nations, held in 1985, reviewed the progress of the NON-ALIGNED MOVEMENT (NAM).

Bangkok Declaration (1993) This statement, signed by forty Asian governments, following a meeting between 29 March and 2 April, asserted that standards for HUMAN RIGHTS were not universal but determined by regional, cultural and other factors. While it stressed the 'universality, objectivity and non-selectivity of all human rights' it confronted the Western nations with the need to 'avoid double standards in the implementation of human rights'. As against the Western emphasis on civil and political rights, it drew attention to the need also to respect economic, social and cultural rights and the right to development.

Bank for International Settlements (BIS) With headquarters in Basel, Switzerland, this institution was set up on the basis of a proposal by the Young Committee in 1930, the body that moderated the REPARATIONS payable by Germany arising from the First World War. The original purpose was to enable the various national central banks to coordinate through their own bank the receipts and payments relating to these reparations. Hopes that it would develop significantly beyond this were frustrated when the INTERNATIONAL MONETARY FUND (IMF) was instituted at the end of the Second World War. More recently, however, the BIS has acted as a trustee for international government loans and carried out transactions for the IMF and the ORGANIZATION FOR ECONOMIC COOPERATION AND DEVELOPMENT (OECD).

Bantu Originally, this was the term for a wide range of languages in South Africa, but it came to have a political connotation under APARTHEID as a collective term for the African peoples of South Africa, as for instance in the Bantu Authorities Act (1951).

BAOR See BRITISH ARMY OF THE RHINE.

Bar Kochba Syndrome A theory relating to Israel's foreign and security policies named after the Jewish revolt against the Romans in AD 132–5, which led to the death of thousands. It was advanced in the early 1980s and argued that by, heroizing Bar Kochba, the Israelis were in danger of embracing an unrealistic and distorted view of Jewish and Israeli history, evidencing 'the admiration of rebelliousness and heroism detached from responsibility for their causes'.

Barbarossa (1941) The code name for the operation launched by Nazi Germany on 22 June 1941 in violation of the NAZI–SOVIET NON-AGGRESSION PACT of 1939. It was ordered by Hitler (1889–1945) in the 'B'-directive No. 21 of 18 December 1940 and was originally scheduled for 15 May 1941. In his briefing to the commanders of the WEHRMACHT he had stressed that the Russian campaign differed from that in the West because it was a life-and-death struggle between two ideologies and was above the restraints of INTERNATIONAL LAW – hence the 'commissar order' that exempted Soviet political officers from the protection of the GENEVA CONVENTIONS. Barbarossa was to serve the primary war aim of shaping EASTERN EUROPE to create *LEBENSRAUM*, 'living space', for the German people. Contrary to the Supreme Army Command's intention of waging the decisive battle before Moscow, Hitler had ordered operations in the Ukraine and north of Leningrad. Only at the end of November did the German divisions come close to Moscow. Then the offensive came to a halt, their forces being exhausted and short of supplies. On 5 December the Russian counter-offensive pushed the Germans back. Their defeat was due to an underrating of the Soviet Red Army, bad weather and the resistance of the Russian people.

Barcelona Declaration (1995) This was a pledge by the EUROPEAN UNION (EU) and twelve neighbouring Mediterranean states – Algeria, Cyprus, Egypt, Israel, Jordan, Lebanon, Malta, Morocco, Syria, Tunisia, Turkey and the Autonomous Palestinian Territories – at a conference in Barcelona on 28 November 1995 to establish a Mediterranean FREE TRADE AREA by 2010. This is the essence of the so-called European–Mediterranean Partnership and it is envisaged that this grouping will be linked through the EU to another free trade area with the countries of CENTRAL and EASTERN EUROPE.

Bargaining chip This phrase came to be used in ARMS CONTROL from the STRATEGIC ARMS LIMITATION TREATY (SALT) negotiations in the late 1960s. It meant any weapons system or forces that a negotiator is willing to surrender in return for specified concessions from the other side. For example, the Nixon administration in the USA called on Congress to approve the development of TRIDENT, the B-1 bomber and CRUISE as a bargaining chip in preparation for the SALT II negotiations. The tactic of developing weapons in order to trade them away in negotiations was criticized both on grounds of cost and, because, if it did not work, it would simply encourage the ARMS RACE.

Baruch Plan (1946) A US plan for internationalizing atomic energy that was submitted to the ATOMIC ENERGY COMMISSION (AEC) of the UNITED NATIONS (UN) by Bernard Baruch (1870–1965), at the time Chairman of the US Atomic Energy Commission, on 14 June 1946. He proposed a world atomic authority that would exercise control over all production of atomic energy and the mining of fissionable material. The plan assumed the cessation of the production of NUCLEAR WEAPONS by abolishing the rights of VETO on the UNITED NATIONS SECURITY COUNCIL on decisions of the proposed agency. The plan was rejected by the USSR.

Base currency This is the currency – for instance, the US dollar – against which the value of another currency is expressed. It is the other currency that is varied as the foreign exchange rate changes.

Basel programme (1897) The original official statement of the World Zionist Organization (WZO), at its first congress in Basel, Switzerland, which was convened by Theodor Herzl (1860–1904), author of *The Jewish State* published in 1896. 'Zionism', it stated, 'seeks to establish a home for the Jewish people in Palestine secured under public law'. The congress envisaged immigration into Palestine, a strong sense of Jewish national consciousness and lobbying of governments for support as all contributing towards the future foundation of an independent Jewish STATE. He argued that the construction of a Jewish state was the only effective response to anti-Semitism.

Basic Law In German the *Grundgesetz*, the constitution of the Federal Republic of Germany (FRG).

Battle of Britain (1940) The air offensive by Nazi Germany against Britain, initiated by the Luftwaffe on 15 December 1940 with the aim of wiping out the Royal Air Force to make possible the invasion of Britain, SEA LION. During the first phase, between 23 September and 6 October, there were daily attacks of around a thousand aircraft on airfields and naval bases, involving heavy losses without achieving the aim of the battle. On 7 October the Luftwaffe switched to night raids, particularly on London. The climax of the battle was on 15 October (Battle of Britain Day), when the Germans suffered record losses. The battle ended with a final raid on London on 11 May 1941.

Battlefield nuclear weapons See TACTICAL NUCLEAR WEAPONS.

Bay-of-Pigs invasion (1961) The abortive attempt to overthrow the revolutionary Cuban leader Fidel Castro (b. 1927) by about 1,500 Cuban exiles, trained by the CENTRAL INTELLIGENCE AGENCY (CIA), who landed on 17 April in the Bahia de Cochinos. Codenamed 'Operation Zapata', this amphibious landing was intended to spark off a revolt on the island. Its failure was perceived as a humiliation for US President Kennedy (1917–63), who had approved the invasion, though without endorsing official US involvement. It strengthened Castro's authority and substantiated his warnings about US intentions towards Cuba. The following year the introduction of Soviet nuclear missiles into Cuba provoked the most serious CRISIS of the COLD WAR.

Beggar-my-neighbour policy A policy of PROTECTIONISM in foreign trade that attempts to improve the domestic economy at the expense of foreign countries. It was particularly in evidence in the GREAT DEPRESSION and, more recently, in currency devaluations. Negative consequences are foreign retaliation and, if domestic industries are allowed to ignore foreign competition, inefficiency.

Beijing Spring This term has been used to refer to two movements for greater democratization in the People's Republic of China. The first is the so-called Democracy Wall Movement of 1978–9; the second, the pro-democracy campaign from April to June 1989, which ended with the large-scale massacre of protestors in TIANANMEN SQUARE on 3–4 June 1989.

Belligerency Formal acknowledgement of being in a state of WAR. When foreign STATES recognize that a condition of CIVIL WAR exists within a state, the effect of such recognition is to confer on the parties a *DE FACTO* recognition, and the rights and duties of legal warfare. Often this leads to external support to the insurgents. Recognition of belligerent rights also means acknowledgement that rebel forces have the right to govern the territory under their control.

Benelux An acronym for Belgium, the Netherlands and Luxembourg and the name of the CUSTOMS UNION (CU) between the three countries that came into existence in 1948. A new treaty of economic union was ratified in 1960. This regional grouping survives within the EUROPEAN UNION (EU) because the ROME TREATY (1957) allows such groupings provided they adhere to the rules and respect the objectives of the EUROPEAN COMMUNITY (EC), which in 2002 includes fifteen countries.

Benevolent neutrality The behaviour of a STATE when it departs from neutral impartiality during a conflict and gives support to one side.

Berlaymont This is the name of the building in Brussels that housed the EUROPEAN COMMISSION from 1969 and is frequently used as a synonym for the Commission.

Berlin Blockade (1948–9) This was a major CRISIS in the early COLD WAR arising from the isolation of the population of West Berlin over 100 miles within the Soviet occupation zone, when the USSR blocked road, rail and water routes. It lasted from June 1948 to May 1949 and was motivated by Soviet concern at the emerging unity of the Western zones and, more immediately, by a Western currency reform.

The USA and Britain met this challenge by organizing a continuous airlift, involving many thousands of flights, until the USSR lifted the BLOCKADE. They also hinted at further resolve if the airlift was disrupted by announcing the flight of planes to Britain that would be capable of carrying ATOMIC BOMBS. The effect of this crisis was to encourage, rather than to hinder, the emergence of the Federal Republic of Germany (FRG) and also to encourage the formation of the NORTH ATLANTIC TREATY ORGANIZATION (NATO), both in 1949.

Berlin Congress (1878)

The international conference that concluded the Eastern Crisis, convened by the German Chancellor Otto von Bismarck (1815–98) and held from 13 June to 13 July 1878. Its purpose was to re-establish a BALANCE OF POWER acceptable to the Great Powers. Among the results were the creation of an autonomous principality of Bulgaria (rejecting Russian domination over that territory), confirmation of the independence of Serbia, Montenegro and Romania and recognition of Russia's possession of the Caucasus and of Austria-Hungary's right to occupy Bosnia-Herzegovina. In the longer term it did not solve the EASTERN QUESTION. Russia was embittered by its reduced influence, for which it held Germany responsible and the Balkan populations remained discontented.

Berlin Crisis (1958–2)

Ten years after the BERLIN BLOCKADE (1948–9), this protracted and perilous crisis was precipitated by Soviet fears of West Germany's rearmament and especially the fear that it might acquire nuclear weapons. This ENCLAVE of CAPITALISM in the Soviet BLOC was, in any case, a significant, and destabilizing irritant for the USSR. The crisis was provoked by the insistence of their leader Nikita Khrushchev (1894–1971) that negotiations on European SECURITY, a nuclear-free Germany and the end of the four-power occupation of Berlin had to begin within six months or the USSR would conclude a separate PEACE TREATY with East Germany. This would have given the Communist German Democratic Republic (GDR) control over the access routes to West Berlin, which was over 100 miles behind the IRON CURTAIN, something wholly unacceptable to the West. This deadline was subsequently extended by stages until the end of 1961. Negotiations failed to bring a solution either in 1959 or at the PARIS SUMMIT (1960), where scheduled talks were sabotaged by the U-2 INCIDENT. The new US President John F. Kennedy (1917–63) discussed Berlin at the VIENNA SUMMIT (1961), but to no avail, and in August of that year the BERLIN WALL was erected to halt the massive emigration, particularly of skilled people, from the Communist state to the West, which threatened economically to bring the GDR to its knees. At considerable human cost, this nevertheless stabilized the situation.

Berlin Quadripartite Agreement (1971)

This was one of the key agreements associated with DÉTENTE and *OSTPOLITIK*. Signed by the USA, Britain, France and the USSR, the four POWERS renounced the use of FORCE to resolve their disputes and reaffirmed their responsibility for Berlin. The USSR guaranteed civilian transit traffic through the German Democratic Republic (GDR) to West Berlin, and the Western Powers declared that West Berlin had special ties to the Federal Republic of Germany (FRG) and that it would 'continue not to be a constituent part of the Federal Republic of Germany and not to be governed by it'. In April 1972 the two Germanys negotiated transit and visitation agreements relating to Berlin within the framework of the Four Power understanding.

Berlin Treaty (1971) See BERLIN QUADRIPARTITE AGREEMENT.

Berlin Wall (August 1961–November 1989) A key symbol of the East–West divide of the COLD WAR, the barrier that separated West Berlin from East Berlin and the Communist German Democratic Republic (GDR). Its speedy construction was begun on 13 August 1961 by the East German Government to prevent the flow of East Germans to the West through this loophole that threatened ruin to the GDR economy, not least since a significant proportion of the emigrants were highly skilled and qualified. In addition to the wall across Berlin, the 858-mile border between East and West Germany was strengthened with barbed wire, electrified fences, minefields, tank traps, electronic warning devices, watchtowers and bunkers. East German guards were instructed to capture or shoot anyone escaping. When the Wall was first built, the Western Powers did little more than make a verbal protest, including the claim that the action violated the Second World War agreements. It became symbolic of imprisonment under COMMUNISM, and of the seeming permanence of that system and the unfeasibility of West German hopes of reunification. At the same time it stabilized a dangerous situation over Berlin, which led at one stage to Soviet and US tanks advancing to within a couple of hundred yards of one another. On 9 November 1989 the East German Government announced that their citizens would no longer be prohibited from crossing over the border to the West. The Wall's subsequent breaching and dismantling became the symbol of the end of the COLD WAR and was followed by German reunification.

Bermuda Conference (1957) An Anglo-American Summit Conference between President Eisenhower (1890–1969) and the British Prime Minister Harold Macmillan (1894–1986). This re-established cordial relations between the two countries after the mutual recriminations of the SUEZ CRISIS of 1956 in which the US had condemned the military action by Britain and France, in collusion with Israel, to seize back the Suez Canal, which had just been nationalized by the Egyptian leader Nasser (1918–70). At Bermuda the USA agreed to supply Britain with 'Thor' guided missiles and to join the BAGHDAD PACT of 1955. Previously Britain had had to abandon its own guided missile project 'Blue Steel' because of economic constraints.

Big Brother This term was used sometimes in the West during the COLD WAR to describe the dominant relationship between the USSR and its satellite STATES.

Big Five (1) A term used after the First World War at the PARIS PEACE CONFERENCE (1919–20) for the Allied and Associated Powers, Britain, France, Italy, Japan and the USA. (2) After the Second World War it was used for the P5, the permanent members of the UNITED NATIONS SECURITY COUNCIL, USA, USSR, China, Britain, and France.

Big Four (1) The name applied to the Council of Four at the PARIS PEACE CONFERENCE (1919–20); (2) A diplomatic catchphrase during the Second World War. It refers to the USA, Britain, the USSR and Nationalist China and was first used in connection with the UNITED NATIONS DECLARATION of 1 January 1942, in which these nations stood at the head of the list of signatories.

Big stick diplomacy A term derived from the phrase used by US President Theodore Roosevelt (1858–1919) in a speech made in New York in 1912: 'Speak softly and carry a big stick and you will go far.'

Big Three The leaders of the major Allied POWERS during the Second World War, the US President Franklin D. Roosevelt (1882–1945), the British Prime Minister Winston Churchill (1874–1965) and the Soviet leader Joseph Stalin (1879–1953).

Bilateral agreements Agreements concluded between two parties. Until the nineteenth century they related usually to PEACE and trade, but since the VIENNA CONGRESS (1814–15) have come to cover ever more fields of cooperation. Since the second half of the twentieth century and into the twenty first, they have often been agreements between countries and international organizations.

Bilateral aid AID that is based on a direct arrangement between two countries. This greatly increased during the 1950s owing to DECOLONIZATION and the rivalry of the SUPERPOWERS during the COLD WAR. Large numbers of colonies became independent and many turned to their original colonial masters for economic assistance. A good example of this is Algerian relations with France after the granting of independence to the former in 1962. At the same time, aid has been used as a means of maintaining influence in territories formally under the control of the colonial powers, and in the struggle for influence in the THIRD WORLD of USSR/Russia, the People's Republic of China and the USA. Bilateral aid has become a permanent aspect of North–South relations.

Billiard ball model A metaphor used for the realist view of international relations, which emphasizes the primacy of the STATE (STATE-CENTRISM) in a WORLD SYSTEM where there is no overall political authority, but the constant interaction, and competition, of self-contained units.

Bi-multipolarity A term sometimes used to describe the configuration of STATES during the COLD WAR in which allies were grouped around the two poles of the USA and USSR, being in turn influenced by the SUPERPOWERS and also constraining them. It was an attempt to update the theory of the BALANCE OF POWER to the new global reality, but it was criticized on the grounds that in a worldwide ideological confrontation the influence of the lesser powers was probably not particularly restraining.

Bipartisanship In international relations, inter-party unity in foreign policy matters and/or agreement between institutions. The underlying assumption is that domestic party political rivalry should be suspended if a country is faced with a significant national danger from abroad, or challenge, and needs to present a united front. In the USA this would mean agreement both between the President and Congress and the Republican and Democratic parties. An example in Britain is the support given by the opposition parties to the Prime Minister Mrs Thatcher (b. 1925) in her determination to repossess the Falkland Islands after their invasion by Argentina in the FALKLANDS WAR (1982).

Bipolarity This is a term particularly associated with the East–West confrontation and BALANCE OF POWER during the COLD WAR. The commonest analysis of the period after 1945 was that there were now two overridingly dominant global powers, the USA and the USSR, in place of an international system with several great powers, as in the earlier CONCERT OF EUROPE. Bipolarity was the concept to fit this new situation. Some theorists were optimistic and believed that this could offer stability in a nuclear age of MUTUAL ASSURED DESTRUCTION (MAD). Others argued that the bipolar balance was doomed to break down – for instance, through the technological advance of one side in the ARMS RACE. In such circumstances there would be no adequately powerful third party that could, as during the earlier period, ally with the weaker power to cancel out any advantage gained by the stronger. Bipolarity is to be contrasted with MULTIPOLARITY and POLYCENTRISM, which are more appropriate models for the study of the global order since the 1960s.

BIS See BANK FOR INTERNATIONAL SETTLEMENTS.

Bismarckian After Otto von Bismarck (1815–98), the Prussian statesman, architect of German unification between 1862 and 1871 and subsequently (until 1890) Chancellor of the German Empire. His name is usually invoked in describing a policy of *REALPOLITIK* and, more specifically, in describing the belief that economic activities should serve the overall interests of STATE POWER and military capacity.

Black Monday (1987) A day – 19 October 1987– on which the world stock market suffered a dramatic fall, evoking fears of a repeat of 1929. In New York, for instance, the Dow Jones index fell by 23 per cent. The fears of a major global slump did not materialize.

Black Monday/Black Tuesday This refers to the collapse of the stock market on Wall Street on 28 and 29 September 1929. On the first day the crash reached full-blown proportions and on the Tuesday the bottom fell out of the market. These two days have become the symbol of the slump that affected the international market between 1929 and 1940.

Black September The name of an Arab terrorist organization formed after the Jordanian Civil War, which had begun in September 1970. Because the fighting resulted in the defeat and expulsion of Palestinians, it was given this name. Its most spectacular act was the killing of eleven Israeli athletes at the Munich Olympics in September 1972. Following criticism that it was harming the Palestinian cause, it was disbanded in 1974.

Black Wednesday (1992) A term referring to 16 September 1992 when currency speculation and international financial turbulence forced Britain out of the Exchange Rate Mechanism (ERM) of the EUROPEAN MONETARY SYSTEM (EMS). This debacle was a major contributor to Conservative electoral defeat in 1997.

Blitzkrieg German for 'lightning war'. This term describes the war doctrine put into effect by the Third Reich in the early stages of the Second World War, involving massed and unexpected air and armoured strikes. This brought speedy victories against Poland in 1939 and in Western Europe in 1940, but failed in conditions where there was no surprise and superior forces, as later against the USSR. It was based on the principle that the backbone of the army was armour, supported by air power.

Bloc In international relations, a political and/or economic grouping of STATES, which are often, but not necessarily bound together by TREATIES or ALLIANCES.

Blockade A form of limited warfare in which ports are blocked physically or by decree, such as during the Napoleonic Wars, so that vessels may be captured or destroyed. During the First World War Britain extended the notion of blockade by requiring ships from neutral ports to submit to search at designated ports. One reason for the development of submarines was as a means of circumventing blockade. Under INTERNATIONAL LAW blockades are acts of WAR. As such they must be declared and notification must be made to neutral countries. When, during the CUBAN MISSILE CRISIS (1962) the USA intercepted Soviet vessels travelling to Cuba, they described this action as a QUARANTINE rather than a blockade.

Blood and Soil (*Blut und Boden*) The Nazi German concept that the German race were bound by blood ties and rooted in their own territory. It was used in the racialist campaign against Jews and other nationalities, as was that of *LEBENSRAUM* ('living space').

Blue berets/helmets The term for armed forces of the UNITED NATIONS (UN), who, regardless of their national uniforms, all use blue berets or helmets as headgear.

Blue Streak An abortive project for a UK land-based INTER-CONTINENTAL BALLISTIC MISSILE (ICBM) with a range of 2,800 nautical miles. Its cost proved prohibitive for the UK and it never reached the stage of test-firing. Its cancellation (in 1960) was significant because it ended the attempt to have a STRATEGIC NUCLEAR WEAPON entirely independent of the USA. As a consequence the UK acquired POLARIS MISSILES following the NASSAU AGREEMENT of December 1962.

Blue Water Navy This term has been used since the late nineteenth century and means a navy capable of patrolling and fighting anywhere across the globe. This distinguishes it from the coastal protection fleets that many countries maintain instead of investing in long-range capability. A main focus of naval interest in the 1960s was the development of just such a fleet by the USSR.

Bluewater policy A term used to describe the traditional imperial British maritime STRATEGY of concentrating effort on the navy, colonial conquest and overseas trade. While Britain might also subsidize continental allies to carry on warfare, it meant the avoidance wherever possible of British continental military commitments.

BMD Ballistic Missile Defence.

Boat people A term coined in the 1980s for the Vietnamese REFUGEES fleeing by boat to Brunei, Indonesia, Malaysia, Singapore and Hong Kong. They were the subject of a special conference held in Bangkok and organized by the ASSOCIATION OF SOUTH EAST ASIAN NATIONS (ASEAN) in July 1988.

Boycott In international trade the refusal to buy products from a particular country or group of countries. It may be government sponsored or initiated by private groups or campaigns. As an instrument of trade, it may be motivated by economic, political and ideological interests or considerations of national SECURITY.

Brandt Reports (1980–3) The first report was entitled 'North–South: A Programme for Survival'. On the state of the world economy, it was produced by an international commission convened by the UNITED NATIONS (UN) between 1977 and 1979 under the chairmanship of Willy Brandt (1913–92), previously Chancellor of the Federal Republic of Germany (FRG). It recommended urgent improvement in trade relations between the developed countries of the northern hemisphere and the poor countries of the southern in the interests of both. The commission reconvened to produce a second report, 'Common Crisis: North–South Cooperation for World Recovery' (1983), which perceived 'far greater dangers than three years ago' and predicted 'conflict and catastrophe' unless the imbalances in global international finance could be addressed. A central recommendation was that the developed countries should annually give AID to the poorer countries equal to 0.7 per cent of Gross Domestic Product by 1985, rising to 1 per cent by the year 2000. With a few exceptions, the transfer of aid fell far short of these targets in following years.

Brest-Litovsk (1918) On 15 December 1917 an ARMISTICE was concluded at Brest-Litovsk between Germany and revolutionary Russia, where peace negotiations began a week later. They continued for several months without concrete results and with Trotsky (1879–1940), Commissar for External Affairs, holding out in the hope that revolution would spread to Germany and Austria. On 9 February 1918 the CENTRAL POWERS concluded a separate PEACE treaty with the Ukraine and on 18 February they resumed their military advance, persuading the Russian leader Lenin (1870–1924) to capitulate. On 3 March the Russians were forced to accept a dictated peace, by which the Baltic countries, Finland, the Caucasus and the Ukraine were separated from the former Russian Empire. The areas lost included 75 per cent of Russian heavy industry. In addition to this there were 6 billion gold marks to pay in REPARATIONS. The negotiations were continued in Bucharest. The Romanians were likewise humiliated. Besides the CESSION of the southern Dobrudja, the Central Powers claimed the Romanian oil and grain resources. The Treaty of Bucharest was signed on 7 May 1918.

Bretton Woods Conference (1944) Attended by forty-five STATES between 1 and 22 July 1944 in New Hampshire, the USA, this was the first United Nations Monetary and Financial Conference and resulted in the setting-up of the INTERNATIONAL MONETARY FUND (IMF) and the INTERNATIONAL BANK FOR RECONSTRUCTION AND DEVELOPMENT (IBRD) (World Bank). This was with a view to post-war reconstruction, stabilization and the expansion of world trade. It created a pool of common currencies, set rules for exchange-rate behaviour and made the IMF the world's 'lender of last resort'. It established an international monetary regime that lasted until 1971 and in which other countries fixed their currency parity against the US dollar. The term 'Bretton Woods' was used as shorthand to describe this system. A major reason for the ending of this system was the weakening of the American economy as a consequence of US involvement in the VIETNAM WAR.

Brezhnev Doctrine Named after the Soviet leader Leonid Brezhnev (1906–82), and also called the 'doctrine of limited sovereignty', the term that came to be applied in the West to the Soviet justification for the WARSAW PACT occupation of Czechoslovakia in August 1968. In a speech in that year he had said that a threat to COMMUNISM in any of the countries of the Soviet BLOC 'must engage the attention of all the Socialist States'. The doctrine arrogated to the USSR the right to prevent defection from the bloc and/or the overthrow of Communism in any of these states. Soviet acceptance under Mikhail Gorbachev (b. 1931) of the dismantling of the Soviet bloc in 1990–1 meant repudiation of the doctrine.

Brinkmanship A diplomatic catchword of the 1950s, described by the US SECRETARY OF STATE John Foster Dulles (1888–1959) as 'the ability to get to the verge without getting into war'. With this the USA would be willing to go to the brink in a nuclear age so that an adversary should clearly understand the consequences of not capitulating or seeking a compromise. This was linked to the contemporary doctrine of MASSIVE RETALIATION. Perhaps the most dramatic example of brinkmanship was the CUBAN MISSILE CRISIS (1962). Evidently the term, though coined at the height of the COLD WAR, can apply to other situations – for example, to Hitler's repeated defiance of the democratic powers over Austria, Czechoslovakia and Poland in the 1930s. The risks of nuclear war have posed the question as to whether an absolutely uncompromising adherence to the conception of NATIONAL INTEREST, such as brinkmanship suggests, is any longer a feasible policy.

British Army of the Rhine (BAOR) This was the title of the British army of occupation in Germany after 1945. Subsequently it has been the major commitment of British land forces to the NORTH ATLANTIC TREATY ORGANIZATION (NATO). During the COLD WAR its responsibility was to defend the northern section of the CENTRAL FRONT in any engagement with the WARSAW PACT. In the Paris Agreements of October 1954, which led to the rearmament of Germany, Britain promised to keep four divisions of troops on the Continent for fifty years. With the ending of the cold war a significant reduction in the size of the BAOR was agreed.

Brussels Because of the large number of institutions associated with the EUROPEAN UNION (EU), the word is commonly used to refer to the Union and its management.

Brussels Treaty (1948) A fifty-year defensive pact, signed on 17 March 1948 by Britain, France, the Netherlands, Belgium and Luxembourg, similar in form to the INTER-AMERICAN TREATY OF RECIPROCAL ASSISTANCE (1947) (the Rio Treaty). The pact was proposed by the US SECRETARY OF STATE George Marshall (1880–1959) and proved the willingness of Western Europe to contribute to its own defence in the COLD WAR. Soon after the signing, discussions were held with a view to including Italy, Norway, Denmark, Ireland and Portugal together with the USA and Canada. In June the VANDENBERG RESOLUTION was passed by 64–4 votes by the US Senate paving the way for the transatlantic NORTH ATLANTIC TREATY, signed in April 1949.

Buffer state A weak STATE located between, or on the borders of, stronger states that serve the security interests of the latter. Buffer states often exist only because their more powerful neighbours want a zone between themselves and their neighbours. Serving as they do the strategic and economic interests of their dominant neighbours, buffer states, historically, have contributed to the maintenance of the local and general BALANCE OF POWER, by reducing the chances of direct confrontation and conflict. As an example, for many years Afghanistan, Persia and Tibet served British imperial interests as buffers between Russia and the British Raj in India.

Buffer zone A delimited area controlled by a peacekeeping force, from which belligerents have been excluded. Such zones are created to prevent or reduce the possibility of future conflict. In some operations the UNITED NATIONS (UN) has referred to them as 'areas or zones of separation'.

Bundeswehr The German Federal Armed Forces. This was created following the Paris Agreements (1954). It is the largest NORTH ATLANTIC TREATY ORGANIZATION (NATO) land army in Europe and also contains a formidable air force and a small navy, which operates in the Baltic and North Sea. Following German reunification the Bundeswehr has undertaken the merging of professional soldiers from what was formerly East Germany with the Bundeswehr. An agreement made with the USSR in 1990 specified that this force would have a ceiling of 370,000 troops.

Burden sharing The issue of the respective expenditure on DEFENCE in the NORTH ATLANTIC TREATY ORGANIZATION (NATO) by the USA and the other NATO members. With the revival of West European prosperity, particularly that of the EUROPEAN COMMUNITY/UNION (EC/EU), there have been recurrent demands in the USA for European states to pay a higher proportion. At times some critics of NATO budget arrangements in the USA have been prepared to start withdrawing US troops from Europe in order to force European governments to increase their proportion of national expenditure on defence.

C

C3I Command, control, communications and intelligence.

Cairo Conference (1943) Second World War meeting between the US President Franklin Roosevelt (1882–1945) and the British Prime Minister Winston Churchill (1874–1965) and the Chinese leader Chiang Kai-Shek (1887–1975) between 22 and 26 November 1943. The resulting Cairo Declaration, issued on 1 December, gave specific detail to the principle of UNCONDITIONAL SURRENDER as relating to the Far East, and stated that 'Japan shall be stripped of all the islands in the Pacific which she has seized and occupied since 1914, and that all the territories Japan has stolen from the Chinese ... shall be restored to the Republic of China. Japan will also be expelled from all other territories she has taken by violence and greed.' It added, 'in due course Korea shall become free and independent'. Korea had been annexed to Japan after the Russo-Japanese War of 1904–5.

Calvo Doctrine Named after Carlos Calvo (1822–1906), an Argentinian jurist who in 1868 challenged the legitimacy of one STATE's INTERVENTION in the internal affairs of another to protect the rights of ALIENS. It was subsequently embodied in Article I of the Second Hague Convention at the HAGUE PEACE CONFERENCE (1907). It is a common feature of public contracts between Latin American governments and foreigners. Potentially raising conflicts between the idea of national SOVEREIGNTY and the standards of INTERNATIONAL LAW, it has been controversial.

Camp David Accords (1978) These were reached between the Israeli Prime Minister Menachem Begin (1913–92) and the Egyptian President Anwar Sadat

(1918–81) at the US presidential retreat on 17 September 1978, during the presidency of Jimmy Carter (b. 1924) and were intended to advance the peace process in the Middle East. The first concerned the status of the WEST BANK and the GAZA STRIP which Israel had occupied since the SIX DAY WAR of June 1967. It specified a transitional period of no more than five years in which Egypt, Israel and Jordan and 'representatives of the Palestinian people' would determine the final status of the territories based on the 'full autonomy' and 'self-governing authority', for the inhabitants of the two areas. The second arranged for a PEACE TREATY between Egypt and Israel. Phased withdrawal of Israeli forces from Sinai over three years and the dismantling of their settlements there was reciprocated by Egyptian willingness to open diplomatic and commercial relations with Israel.

Camp David Summit (1959) This was the first summit conference solely between the USA and the USSR. It was on the initiative of US President Eisenhower (1890–1969) and followed months of tension over the BERLIN CRISIS. It was held on 20–27 September. Eisenhower and the Soviet leader Nikita Khrushchev (1894–1971) agreed that a full summit should be held in 1960. Eisenhower hoped that Khrushchev would drop his threat to Berlin and that it might be possible to reduce the international tension of the COLD WAR. On substantive issues, however, such as Germany and DISARMAMENT, the two powers continued to differ.

Campaign for Nuclear Disarmament (CND) This movement was formed in 1958 in the UK 'to work for the abandonment of nuclear weapons and a substantial reduction in British defence spending'. It attracted wide attention in the 1960s through its annual marches from Aldermaston, the leading British nuclear arms centre, to London and its impact on the British Labour Party, whose party conference initially supported UNILATERALISM, but whose governments from 1964 onwards rejected it. A splinter group called the Committee of One Hundred was set up in 1962 under CND's president, the philosopher Lord Bertrand Russell (1872–1970), and engaged in civil disobedience. CND revived again with the EUROMISSILE controversy in the early 1980s. As the party of opposition, the Labour Party again embraced unilateralism as official policy in 1983, though its influence failed to dissuade the government from the deployment of CRUISE MISSILES.

Cantonization The division of a STATE into smaller units, as, for example, in Yugoslavia during the 1990s. The Swiss Confederation is constituted from cantons.

Capability A term used in the analysis of POWER in international relations, not least in military strength. In assessing a STATE's capability, for instance, of waging war successfully against another state, an analyst will be likely to consider not only actual military strength but the underlying economic resources for sustaining a WAR and other questions such as ideological conviction, nationalist sentiment, popular morale and the attitude of the people concerned towards its own government.

Capability analysis In international relations, this is the assessment that a STATE, ALLIANCE or other organization makes about its ability to achieve its objectives. Commonly, this will involve a range of considerations, military, political, diplomatic and economic, some significantly more tangible than others. Before taking a decision, for instance, to launch an invasion or intervene in a CIVIL WAR, a government will want to have appraised a range of options and to have calculated consequences. 'Capability' in this context is always relative, in relation to the abilities, strengths and weaknesses of the other ACTOR(S).

Cape to Cairo A slogan of British IMPERIALISM at the end of the nineteenth century at the time of the SCRAMBLE FOR AFRICA among the European powers. Cecil Rhodes (1853–1902) advocated the (unfulfilled) idea of a railway line from South Africa to the Mediterranean, the Cape–Cairo route with Britain controlling the territory the whole length of East Africa.

Capitalism The economic system based on private enterprise and private ownership, under which a major proportion at least of economic activity is carried out by profit-seeking organizations and individuals. It involves the use of markets and self-regulation rather than centralized planning to allocate resources, with the regulation of supply and demand through the price mechanism in a free market. As a theory, it assumes the free movement of capital, labour and trade and is to be contrasted with COMMUNISM, under which major economic decisions have to be taken collectively, with rigid state control over the economy and trade – the command economy. Capitalism has undergone many modifications, not least with the development of major international corporations, with the expanding role of the STATE and the increasing sophistication of financial systems and speed of transaction. Marxists and others have argued that Capitalism has been the dominant motive behind IMPERIALISM, leading to international rivalry and WAR, the thesis advanced by Lenin (1870–1924) in *Imperialism the Highest Stage of Capitalism* (1916). The theory is that the declining rate of profit at home has forced major capitalist countries and their entrepreneurs and investors to expand overseas, and that this has outlasted DECOLONIZATION, with the LESS DEVELOPED COUNTRIES (LDCS) in a dependency relationship on the industrialized world. Karl Marx (1818–83) in his critique envisaged capitalism as a specific stage in global economic development. However, the demise of the USSR and Communist regimes in EASTERN EUROPE, the opening of the economy of Communist China to market forces and GLOBALIZATION have affirmed not only the longevity of capitalism, but also its claim to be a WORLD SYSTEM.

Capitalist encirclement The idea advanced principally by the USSR that it was surrounded by hostile capitalist STATES committed to its destruction and that of the Communist system. It was lent credibility by the Allied intervention against the new revolutionary government between 1918 and 1921 and it became a dominant theme in Soviet foreign policy under Stalin (1879–1953), who used it as justification for ruthless suppression within Russia. After the Second World War, with the establishment of COMMUNISM in China and EASTERN EUROPE, the Soviet leader announced that capitalist encirclement had now been succeeded by a new reality of the 'two camps'. The two-camps doctrine posited the existence of a rough BALANCE OF POWER between the Communist and capitalist worlds, but with no abating of their antagonism.

Capitulations This term can be used in two senses: (1) in INTERNATIONAL LAW, conventions between armed forces that lay down specific surrender terms; (2) the grants of extraterritorial privileges by one STATE to the subjects of another, exempting them, for instance, from the jurisdictions of the courts in the countries in which they are residing. These, which were common in the nineteenth century, have disappeared with DECOLONIZATION and IRREDENTISM.

Captive Nations Resolution This was proposed in 1950 by the US Congress and required the President to denounce Soviet control of EASTERN EUROPE, calling on Americans to 'recommit themselves to the support of the just aspirations of these captive nations'. It was repeated through most of the COLD WAR, serving as a political concession to those who wanted the ROLLBACK of COMMUNISM. For their part, the EASTERN BLOC described it as illegitimate interference and incitement.

Cardenas Doctrine The statement by Lázaro Cárdenas (1895–1970), who was President of Mexico between 1934 and 1940, who in 1938 nationalized the largely US-owned oil refineries in his country, that a STATE could not act to protect its nationals in the territory of another state.

Caribbean Community (CARICOM) A British COMMONWEALTH regional body, which was established, as the Caribbean COMMON MARKET, by the Chaguaramas Treaty in Trinidad on 4 July 1973. It was originally seen as an extension of the CARIBBEAN FREE TRADE AREA (CARIFTA) and as a means of dealing with representatives of the EUROPEAN ECONOMIC COMMUNITY (EEC) in the negotiation leading to the LOMÉ CONVENTION of 1975. Six non-Commonwealth countries have observer status at CARICOM meetings, the Dominican Republic, Haiti, Mexico, Puerto Rico, Surinam and Venezuela. Its objectives of coordinating foreign policy and harmonization of economic and other policies have been only very modestly realized.

Caribbean Free Trade Area (CARIFTA) This was established by the countries of the British COMMONWEALTH in the Caribbean in 1968 to remove customs duties between member STATES. It was, though economically of negligible consequence, an important step towards the establishment of the CARIBBEAN COMMUNITY (CARICOM).

CARICOM See CARIBBEAN COMMUNITY.

CARIFTA See CARIBBEAN FREE TRADE AREA.

Carnegie Endowment for International Peace A US non-governmental institution devoted to the study of world affairs, founded by the industrialist and philanthropist Andrew Carnegie (1836–1919). It has encouraged the strengthening of INTERNATIONAL LAW, founding the Academy of International Law in the Hague, promoted conciliation and financed reconstruction projects. The endowment is used for a range of subjects, such as European SECURITY, global migration, study of economic problems, democratization and CONFLICT RESOLUTION. Its headquarters are in Washington DC and its Centre for Russian and Eurasian Programmes in Moscow, which was opened in 1993.

Cartel An agreement among countries or business organizations to restrict competition, based on a contractual understanding typically involving prices, production and the division of the market. During the GREAT DEPRESSION in the 1930s up to half of world trade was subject to cartel control. A post-Second World War example is the ORGANIZATION OF PETROLEUM EXPORTING COUNTRIES (OPEC), established in 1961.

Carter Doctrine This policy was announced by US President Jimmy Carter (b. 1924) in his State of the Union address to Congress on 23 January 1980. This was shortly after the Soviet invasion of Afghanistan and during the Iranian hostage CRISIS. He stated that 'an attempt by any outside force to gain control of the Persian Gulf region will be regarded as an assault on the vital interests of the United States of America, and such force will be repelled by any means necessary, including military force'. This was followed, among other initiatives, by the creation of the RAPID DEPLOY-MENT FORCE.

Cash-and-carry A US term first used in relation to the NEUTRALITY ACT of 1935, concerning arms embargo, trade quotas and a ban on loans. Cash-and-carry required that belligerents trading with the USA transport their goods in foreign vessels and pay for them in cash before they left American ports. It was adopted as part of the Neutrality Acts of 1937 and 1939, although a month after the outbreak of the Second World War it was limited to the North Atlantic area. It combined the objectives of keeping out of European entanglements, but at the same time helping Britain and France if war came, which it did in September 1939. By the new Act of 4 November 1939 Britain and France were permitted to purchase arms on a cash-and-carry basis.

Cassis de Dijon Case This resulted in a key judgment of the EUROPEAN COURT OF JUSTICE (ECJ). The case of *Rewe-Zentrale AG* v. *Bundesmonopolverwaltung für Brantwein* (1979) involved a German attempt to prevent the importation of this alcoholic drink from France on grounds of its low alcoholic content. The essence of this ruling was that any product lawfully produced and marketed in one member STATE must in principle be admitted to free circulation in the territory of another member state, subject to very limited exceptions. This precedent was used for the establishment of the SINGLE MARKET and abolition of NON-TARIFF BARRIERS (NBTS).

Casus belli A Latin term for a cause alleged by a STATE to justify it in declaring and making WAR on another state. For instance, the violation of Belgian NEUTRALITY by Germany in 1914 was provided as the *casus belli* for the British declaration of war. According to the UNITED NATIONS CHARTER, warlike measures are permissible, other than any authorized by the UNITED NATIONS SECURITY COUNCIL or the UNITED NATIONS GENERAL ASSEMBLY, only if made necessary by reason of individual or COL-LECTIVE SELF-DEFENCE against armed attack.

Casus foederis A Latin term for an event or situation that calls for an ALLIANCE obligation to be invoked. For instance, if one STATE agrees to come to the defence of another in the event of it being attacked by a THIRD PARTY and it is so attacked, a *casus foederis* has arisen.

Catalytic war A COLD WAR term for a small nuclear war, or the use of NUCLEAR WEAPONS by a lesser POWER that might lead to a conflict between the SUPERPOWERS. During the early years of the development of nuclear weapons there was considerable concern that a major nuclear conflict might occur by accident, through miscalculation, faulty detection and ESCALATION that could not be controlled.

CBMs See CONFIDENCE-BUILDING MEASURES.

CBW Chemical and biological warfare.

Ceasefire An agreement between hostile forces while efforts are made to negotiate a peace settlement. It does not mean that a peace settlement will necessarily follow. In some cases a ceasefire will remain in force for many years without formal conclusion of a WAR. In other cases, as in Yugoslavia in the 1990s, we see a succession of short-lived ceasefires before an agreement is reached or imposed.

CEES Central and East European States.

CENTO Central Treaty Organization. See BAGHDAD PACT (1955).

Central Europe See MITTELEUROPA. The term 'Central Europe' has been used flexibly and it is important to establish in which context and for which purpose it is being used. As an illustration of this point, the Disarmament Conference in Vienna in November 1973 defined Central Europe as Belgium, Czechoslovakia, the two Germanys, Holland, Luxembourg and Poland.

Central Front This term was used during the COLD WAR for the line of confrontation between the NORTH ATLANTIC TREATY ORGANIZATION (NATO) and the WARSAW TREATY ORGANIZATION (WTO), the border between the two German STATES. It was anticipated that war would break out here if rivalry between the USA and the USSR led to outright conflict and it was the focus of a great deal of strategic discussion. With the reunification of Germany in 1990, the disbanding of the WTO and the withdrawal of Russian troops from the territory of the old German Democratic Republic (GDR), the Central Front ceased to exist.

Central Intelligence Agency (CIA) Formed in 1947, along with the US NATIONAL SECURITY COUNCIL (NSC), by which it is supervised, and the Department of Defene as part of the National Security Act of that year. It superseded the individual service branch intelligence agencies and is responsible for foreign INTELLIGENCE gathering. Through the creation of a modern intelligence service the USA hoped to avoid another military debacle such as that which happened at PEARL HARBOR in 1941. The Central Intelligence Agency Act (1941) exempted the organization from all statutes concerning disclosure of its activities and gave its Director power to spend money without public accountability. This allowed COVERT ACTION on a large scale during the COLD WAR, and subsequently. These included the support of resistance movements to COMMUNISM, propaganda and involvements included the BAY OF PIGS INVASION (1961), help for the Contras in Nicaragua in the 1980s and counter-terrorism.

Central Powers The collective expression for Germany, Austria-Hungary, Bulgaria and Turkey during the First World War. The Central Powers, which were united by the monarchical principle, were linked by BILATERAL TREATIES. Though

Germany played a predominant part among them, it did not succeed in pressing its WAR claims upon its allies and they could never agree a common foreign policy. Their only coordinated appearance in public DIPLOMACY was the peace offer of 12 December 1916, which was rebuffed by the Allies and the negotiations for the BREST-LITOVSK TREATY of 1918.

Central war A term from the COLD WAR, it meant a direct major confrontation between the nuclear SUPERPOWERS. It assumed the probability that NUCLEAR WEAPONS would be used, but the term also covered head-on conventional armed confrontation. Another phrase, with nuclear connotation, is 'central strategic warfare'.

Centre A term used in DEPENDENCY THEORY to refer to the FIRST WORLD or the major industrialized countries in the global political economy.

Century Group This was named after the Century Association, a club in New York. It was founded in the Second World War in July 1940, after the fall of France and amid fears that Britain would also soon be defeated by Nazi Germany. It lobbied against ISOLATIONISM, calling for a prompt US declaration of war against Germany before US SECURITY was endangered.

Cession Cession is usually a formal procedure and is based on a TREATY. It is the handing over of territory and the SOVEREIGNTY over that territory, rather than forcible ANNEXATION without any formalities or attention to legalities. It may be effected by purchase (as, for instance, in the case of the US purchase of Alaska from Russia in 1867) exchange, gift or a voluntary merger. At the same time, cession can be as a consequence of the threat of FORCE, for example, the cession of the SUDETENLAND to Nazi Germany in 1938.

CFE See CONVENTIONAL FORCES IN EUROPE.

CFI Court of First Instance.

CFSP See COMMON FOREIGN AND SECURITY POLICY.

Chapultepec Conference See INTER-AMERICAN CONFERENCE ON PROBLEMS OF WAR AND PEACE (1945).

Chargé d'affaires Sometimes also referred to as 'Chargé d'affaires en titre', to distinguish the individual from being 'Chargé d'affaires ad interim', acting provisionally as head of a diplomatic mission. normally, they are assistants to AMBASSADORS and envoys. If the regular head of mission is recalled, the Chargé d'affaires heads the mission. This commonly reflects a downgrading or chilling of relations between the STATES concerned. A Chargé d'affaires is accredited from one foreign ministry to another, whereas an Ambassador is accredited from one head of state to another.

Charter 77 A movement in defence of HUMAN RIGHTS in Communist Czechoslovakia inspired by the HELSINKI ACCORDS (1975) of the CONFERENCE ON SECURITY AND COOPERATION IN EUROPE (CSCE). Signed in 1977, it appealed to the

Czech government to adhere to the UNITED NATIONS DECLARATION OF HUMAN RIGHTS and to the Final Act. Its supporters were persecuted and it became a symbol for the desire for freedom throughout the COMMUNIST BLOC, inspiring subsequent democratization after 1989.

Charter of Paris (1990) This was signed by the members of the CONFERENCE ON SECURITY AND COOPERATION IN EUROPE (CSCE) on 21 November 1990 and is generally considered to be the end of the COLD WAR, which followed the collapse of COMMUNISM in EASTERN EUROPE. It upheld the principles of the HELSINKI ACCORDS (1975) and transformed the CSCE into a permanent organization, the Organization for Security and Cooperation in Europe (OSCE).

Chatham House The Royal Institute of International Affairs, situated in St James's Square, London. It was originally founded in 1920 as the British Institute of International Affairs, assuming its new name in 1926. It was the first private organization set up in Britain comprehensively to study international relations, and among its many activities it publishes the journal *International Affairs*. Its conferences and discussions follow what are called the 'Chatham House Rules'. This means that the attribution to the contributor of views expressed is not to be revealed to the press.

Chauvinism Named after one Nicholas Chauvin, a prototype of a fanatically patriotic soldier fighting in the Napoleonic Wars. It means passionately displayed and uncritical NATIONALISM, which is often combined with XENOPHOBIA.

Checkpoint Charlie This separated East and West Berlin and became a famous focal point in the COLD WAR. After the BERLIN WALL was constructed in August 1961 by the government of the German Democratic Republic (GDR), US President John F. Kennedy (1917–63) ordered three checkpoints to be built in order that US forces could exercise their rights of access. It was removed at the end of the COLD WAR in 1990.

CHEKA 'The All-Russian Extraordinary Commission for Combating Counter-revolution and Sabotage', this organization was the security arm of the Communist revolution of 1917. It was established by decree in December of that year and charged with responsibility for rooting out all opposition to the new order. From the start it displayed a tendency to take over the political system and imposed severe repression. It was abolished at the end of the CIVIL WAR, but the use of terror as a principal instrument of government in the USSR, with the creation of a vast administrative apparatus and with prison and labour camps, was continued, and intensified, in the GPU, OGPU, NKVD and KGB, most dramatically in the purges under Joseph Stalin (1879–953).

Chemical and Biological Weapons (CBW) WEAPONS OF MASS DESTRUCTION, such as agent orange or sarin gas, which use poisonous agents or toxins. The Geneva Protocol of 1925 banned them from use in warfare, but it did not outlaw their production and STOCKPILING. A Convention on the Prohibition of the Development, Production and Stockpiling of Bacteriological (Biological) and Toxic Weapons and on their Destruction was signed on 10 April 1972 and since then nearly 100 nations have become signatories. However, work still continues on their development and there is particular fear in the international community at the potential for their use by terrorist organizations.

Chemical Weapons Convention (CWC) (1993) A multilateral agreement for the abolition of such weapons. Chemical weapons, notably poison gas, were banned after the First World War. This convention, though, bans all use of such weapons and also prohibits their development, production and stockpiling, or transfer. Monitoring was instituted with the Organization for the Prohibition of Chemical Weapons, which began work in 1996. Reports that Iraq had used such weapons against Iran and its own Kurdish minority led the UNITED NATIONS (UN) to demand the destruction of its chemical weapons factories. Particular concern has centred on the possession, or potential acquisition, of such weapons by ROGUE STATES or terrorist organizations.

Chernobyl catastrophe (1986) In the Ukraine, the worst accident in the history of nuclear power generation. During the night of 25–26 April safety precaution errors led to a chain reaction in the reactor core and the lid was blown off the reactor releasing large amounts of radioactivity into the atmosphere over a period of ten days, which was carried thousands of miles. 135,000 people had to be evacuated from the vicinity and the event strengthened the environmental lobby throughout the world that protested against nuclear power generation.

Chevaline The name for the modernization of the POLARIS nuclear missile system during the 1970s and 1980s by the British government. Its purpose was to maintain the ability of Polaris missiles to penetrate the Soviet anti-ballistic missile (ABM) system around Moscow (GALOSH) and maintain the so-called MOSCOW OPTION. Costing a billion pounds and regarded by the Labour Government of the time as controversial, this programme was not reported to Parliament until 1980, when Margaret Thatcher (b. 1925) was Prime Minister.

China card This phrase originated in the USA in the 1970s to describe the STRATEGY of its government of using improved relations with the People's Republic of China, as a consequence of DÉTENTE, to pressurize the USSR to be more amenable in international relations and, more particularly, with regard to ARMS CONTROL.

China Lobby A US network in the COLD WAR that lobbied strongly against the People's Republic of China from the end of the 1940s until the 1970s, against diplomatic RECOGNITION and against its being allowed to join the UNITED NATIONS (UN). At the same time it supported Chiang Kai-Shek (1887–1975) and the Chinese nationalist cause. Including a number of key figures in American life, it accused the Truman administration of the 'loss of China' (to COMMUNISM).

China White Paper (1949) This US DEPARTMENT OF STATE document, with an introduction by the US SECRETARY OF STATE Dean Acheson (1893–1971), was published to explain that nothing the USA could have done could have prevented the victory by Mao-Zedong (1893–1976) and the communists over the nationalists in China. With intense US concern in the early COLD WAR and the agitation of the so-called CHINA LOBBY over the 'loss of China', it generated considerable controversy.

Chinese Cultural Revolution (1966–76) Officially called the 'Great Proletarian Cultural Revolution', this was inaugurated in August 1966 when the Central Committee approved a resolution calling for a complete revolution in Chinese politics, society and culture. It amounted to a massive purge by the Communist leader Mao-Zedong (1893–1976) of the Communist Party, with Mao claiming that the 'officials of China are a class, and one whose interests are opposed to those of the workers and peasants.' The activists in this revolt were the Red Guards who were called on to extirpate the 'four olds', old ideas, old culture, old customs and old habits. Besides causing enormous disruption, the Cultural Revolution also led to the death of more than two million people. This violent episode has been consistently repudiated by the Chinese leadership since 1978.

Choke points A military term meaning places where transport or military material and personnel are concentrated and slowed down – for instance, a key strategic bridge. They are vulnerable points for a combatant since they provide easy targets for INTERDICTION and enemy strikes.

CHR See COMMISSION ON HUMAN RIGHTS.

Christian Aid This body was founded in 1949 by the British Council of Churches and some of its programmes are joint funded by the British government. It aims to assist development projects in places where human resources are inadequate to meet needs, particularly in Africa, Asia and Latin America, ranging from land reclamation and irrigation to medical support and training programmes.

CIA See CENTRAL INTELLIGENCE AGENCY.

CID See COMMITTEE OF IMPERIAL DEFENCE.

CIS See COMMONWEALTH OF INDEPENDENT STATES.

Civic nationalism See NATIONALISM.

Civil defence This term, used comprehensively, means all arrangements for reducing death, injury and damage in a territory inflicted through WAR or natural disaster. Modern wars have, more and more, involved civilians, and the measures taken, for instance, on the outbreak of war in 1939 – evacuation of population from cities, building of bomb shelters – are a classic illustration of civil defence, confronting TOTAL WAR. After the Second World War preparatory measures were taken and training provided for those who would be involved in trying to mitigate the effects of a possible nuclear conflict, or its immediate destruction and radioactive fall-out. The notion of civil defence against a nuclear strike became a subject of contention with supporters of the PEACE MOVEMENT from the 1950s onwards arguing that the idea of effective defence in such circumstances was nonsense. They further argued that mistaken public acceptance that civil defence could be effective in a nuclear war could lead to risk-taking by the nuclear powers.

Civil war A WAR fought within a country between the populations of different areas, different political groups, races or religions. It may involve the struggle between a people and its government or between groups contesting for POWER and LEGIT-IMACY. Civil wars are often greatly influenced or decided by external INTERVENTION, as, for instance, in the case of the SPANISH CIVIL WAR (1936–9). Civil war is only recognized in INTERNATIONAL LAW when both parties are recognized by other STATES. Hence there may be continuous or sporadic internal attacks within a country, as with Basque TERRORISM in Spain, without the situation becoming one of civil war.

Clash of civilizations The thesis advanced by the American Samuel Huntington (b. 1927) in an article in the US journal *Foreign Affairs* in 1993. It was heralded as a significant statement, equivalent to the famous X-ARTICLE in the same publication in 1946, which had articulated the idea of CONTAINMENT in the early COLD WAR. Huntington addressed the problem of the post-cold war conflicts of the early 1990s, in particular that between Western civilization and Islam. He made the following prediction: 'the fundamental sources of conflict in this new world will not be primarily ideological or primarily economic. The great division among humankind and the dominating source of conflict will be cultural. National states will remain the most powerful actors in world affairs, but the principal conflicts of global politics will occur between nations and groups of different civilizations. The clash of civilizations will be the battlelines of the future.'

Clausewitzian After Carl von Clausewitz (1780–1831), the Prussian General and author of *On War*, published posthumously in 1832, in which he presented WAR as a total phenomenon to be analysed in relation to the political and social background of which it is a part. He argued that there could be no 'purely military solution' to any military problem and that war was the continuation of policy by other means. He described war as a 'remarkable trinity', of which the essential elements were violence, the 'free play' of chance and intelligent political purpose. The ideas in this book, on the interaction of war and society, on TOTAL WAR, limited war and political purposes in relation to combat, make it a key text that has inspired much reflection, not least during the COLD WAR.

Client state A STATE, some of whose rights, for example, over the conduct of foreign relations or the management of its own finances, are subordinated to control by another state.

Clinton Doctrine The ideas guiding US foreign policy, particularly during the second term of US President Bill Clinton (b. 1946) between 1997 and 2001. The orientation of his policies reflected economic priorities, a stress on the expansion of free markets and the international competitiveness of the USA with 'export activism'. Together with this went emphasis on the spread of democracy and HUMAN RIGHTS. In the international crises of this period there was a policy of selectivity over intervention and retreat from any notion of automatic US commitment in problems across the world. During this period the benchmark of US military strength was defined as the ability to conduct and win two regional wars simultaneously.

Club of Paris The Club of Paris is an international forum for the negotiation, rescheduling or consolidation of debts given or guaranteed by official bilateral creditors. It was established in 1956 by a group of West European countries at that time seeking a multilateral trade and payments system for Argentina and its external debts, and was open to any creditor government willing to accept its rules. Private banks were excluded, handling their negotiations through the Club of London.

Club of Rome Formed at a meeting of politicians, industrialists, scientists, economists and administrators, which was held in Rome in 1968, this group set out to examine the relationship between economies, population, industrialization and the environment. Its best-known publication has been *The Limits of Growth* (1972). Since then it has, in particular, exercised influence in discussions of the problems of the environment.

CMEA See COUNCIL FOR MUTUAL ECONOMIC ASSISTANCE.

CMH See COMMON HERITAGE OF MANKIND.

Co-belligerency In WAR this describes a relationship short of a full military ALLIANCE, but one where the forces of one country cooperate with those of another.

Co-Decision Procedure A term used in the EUROPEAN UNION (EU), also known as the Conciliation Procedure. This legislative service, established by the TREATY ON EUROPEAN UNION (TEU) (1992), arranges for a Conciliation Committee for the COUNCIL OF MINISTERS and the EUROPEAN PARLIAMENT (EP) if they are unable to reach a common position. It enhances the authority of the EP by allowing it to block legislation if it was dissatisfied with the outcome of negotiations with the Council. The scope of this procedure has been broadened to cover other policy areas under the AMSTERDAM TREATY (1997).

Co-imperium The mutual agreement between two STATES that the right to administer state functions within a specified territory shall be jointly held by the two states. Co-imperium gives neither state the right to cede the territory.

Coercion of a state The application of FORCE or threat of use of force against a STATE amounting to compulsion. According to the Vienna Convention on the Law of Treaties of 1969, which codifies the principles embodied in the UNITED NATIONS CHARTER, a TREATY is void if it is extracted from a state by such coercion.

Coercive diplomacy Diplomacy by which a government will attempt to persuade an aggressor to reverse or halt actions already in train, which may include the threat to use military force in response. Governments down the ages have used 'carrot and stick' in their dealings with other powers. As describing a coherent, staged, STRATEGY, the term has been used since the 1960s. The key elements are that the aggressor/adversary is coerced to meet specified conditions, that a time limit for compliance is indicated, that punitive action will result from non-compliance and that inducement be offered to help persuade the adversary to follow the desired course of action. Such diplomacy was used to effect, for instance, during the CUBAN MISSILE CRISIS (1962), in that one of the inducements to settle the issue was the unannounced promise made to the USSR by the US President that the USA would withdraw its Jupiter missiles from Turkey.

Coexistence See PEACEFUL COEXISTENCE.

Cohesion Fund A term used in the EUROPEAN UNION (EU). This fund was instituted in 1993 under the TREATY ON EUROPEAN UNION with the purpose of reducing economic differences between the member STATES of the EU, by assisting the less well-off with project money for transport infrastructure and the environment.

Cold war The rivalry and conflict that were global in scope, territorial, economic and ideological, and that dominated international relations, and the interpretation of international relations, between 1945 and 1990. The two major protagonists were the USSR and the USA, each with its ALLIANCE system, and the origins of this East–West hostility date from the Russian Bolshevik Revolution of 1917. The collapse of Germany brought the two SUPERPOWERS, with a legacy of mutual suspicion and distrust, face to face, with sharply contrasted ideological world views, Communist and capitalist, and with mutual predictions that the opposing order would collapse. The contest was against the background of dramatic changes in the WORLD ORDER as a consequence of the Second World War, not least the pressure for DECOLONIZATION of the THIRD WORLD and the shrinking of European dominance. Another very important determinant was the invention of NUCLEAR WEAPONS, which led to a dramatic ARMS RACE and the BALANCE OF TERROR. The war was 'cold' only in the sense that there was not an all-out military conflict between the principal antagonists, but it involved continuous tension and numerous proxy wars, for instance, in the KOREAN WAR (1950–3), the VIETNAM WAR (1960–75) and the Middle East. Twice there were major crises over Berlin (in the BERLIN BLOCKADE of 1948–9 and the BERLIN CRISIS of 1958–62), and arguably the most dangerous confrontation of all was the CUBAN MISSILE CRISIS of 1962. The original political and economic tensions over issues such as free elections in EASTERN EUROPE, REPARATIONS from Germany and the MARSHALL PLAN soon led on to conspicuous military rivalry, and a pattern of ACTION–REACTION. The anxieties of the USA about Communist expansionism were particularly encouraged by the 'loss of China', the Soviet acquisition of nuclear weapons and the North Korean invasion of South Korea. From the late 1940s it embarked on the policy of CONTAINMENT through the NORTH ATLANTIC TREATY ORGANIZATION (NATO) and other regional organizations, to prevent the forcible imposition of COMMUNISM outside the COMMUNIST BLOC, which from 1949 included the People's Republic of China. In so doing it consolidated its position as leader of the West. Following the REARMAMENT of Western Germany in 1955, the USSR formalized its defence arrangements in the WARSAW PACT. The Communist Bloc was never the monolithic unity the West feared, or presented it to be. By the 1970s the USSR had achieved nuclear parity with the USA, and the USA was facing impasse and humiliation in Vietnam. At the same time the bitter SINO-SOVIET SPLIT mutually encouraged DÉTENTE, which did not end the East-West rivalry or lead to the rejection of long-term ideological ambitions by the superpowers, but reflected the view that the rivalry should be conducted at a lower level of risk; and produced important advances such as the HELSINKI ACCORDS (1975). There was also mutual concern between the superpowers at the prospect of PROLIFERATION of nuclear weapons among other countries. From the end of the 1970s until the mid-1980s there was a dramatic revival of East-West hostility, the so-called New Cold War, which included the Soviet invasion of Afghanistan, the suppression of SOLIDARITY in Poland and a massive rearmament programme on both sides, including the US proposals for the STRATEGIC DEFENSE INITIATIVE (SDI). With the advent of Mikhail Gorbachev (b. 1931) as Soviet leader, the superpowers quickly moved towards the resumption of arms agreements. Subsequently, the effective bankruptcy of the Soviet system, symbolized by the fall of the BERLIN WALL in November 1989, brought about the end of the cold war, which had, among other things, been a struggle between two economic systems. The origins and development of the conflict, not least the question of responsibility for it, and its impact on the WORLD ORDER, has attracted enormous interest among historians and students of international relations, and provoked considerable revisionist debate.

Cold warrior A US and British term current in the period between the 1950s and the 1990s and in historical analysis of East–West relations. It means an enthusiastic advocate of competition with, and resistance to, COMMUNISM and more particularly to the perceived ambitions of the USSR and the People's Republic of China in world affairs.

Collateral damage Any unintentional damage resulting from an armed attack. This term is most often used to refer to civilian casualties, though it may mean any damage that extends beyond an intended target. With the increasing destructiveness of weapons (and means of achieving high levels of accuracy) this consideration has become increasingly pertinent, not least because of the wish of governments to produce a moral justification for military action. It has also inevitably featured significantly in strategic debate over NUCLEAR WEAPONS. Though the term is new, the concept is not since, historically, discussions of the doctrine of the JUST WAR have also involved distinctions between legitimate and illegitimate targets.

Collective guilt In international relations this means the attribution of guilt to a whole people. This is something that it is difficult to substantiate or sustain from the viewpoints of INTERNATIONAL LAW or ethics. After the Second World War the German people were frequently, though not without strong objection to the claim, castigated for collective responsibility for the atrocities of the Nazi period.

Collective security Based on the idea that SECURITY is best achieved in the world by common commitment, the key to collective security is universality of participation and obligation. It rejects the notion of relying on the BALANCE OF POWER for the guarantee of PEACE. Ideally each STATE would guarantee the independence and security of every other state. Under these conditions an aggressor state would face the united opposition of the entire international community. This concept of collective security was at the heart of the LEAGUE OF NATIONS COVENANT and is perpetuated in UNITED NATIONS CHARTER. But the League was never a universal body and the UNITED NATIONS SECURITY COUNCIL may be vetoed by a single vote in its deliberations. This phrase is sometimes used inaccurately to describe regional or bloc security arrangements such as the NORTH ATLANTIC TREATY ORGANIZATION (NATO) or the INTER-AMERICAN TREATY OF RECIPROCAL ASSISTANCE (1947) (the Rio Treaty), which do not fulfil the criterion of universality and are examples of ALLIANCE systems and collective defence rather than collective security in the fullest sense.

Collective self-defence The right of a STATE or group of states to come to the DEFENCE of another state that is victim of an armed attack until the UNITED

NATIONS SECURITY COUNCIL has taken the measures necessary to restore international PEACE and SECURITY. The right of collective self-defence under ARTICLE 51 is most commonly accepted as the right of states to come to the rescue of a state whose situation meets the conditions of legitimate individual self-defence under the UNITED NATIONS CHARTER. There is no requirement that the states offering assistance should themselves be endangered. Collective defence is to be distinguished from the idea of COLLECTIVE SECURITY. The former has never been questioned by the UNITED NATIONS (UN). The NORTH ATLANTIC TREATY ORGANIZATION (NATO) as a regional organization, for instance, was explicitly based on the principle of collective self-defence.

Colonialism The rule of an area and its peoples by an external sovereign POWER. It has taken the form of emigrants from the mother country creating a new political community in another territory, or the establishment of rule over indigenous peoples. Colonies have been established throughout history to advance the military SECURITY, economic advantage and, more intangibly, the international prestige of the occupying countries or imperial power. As an issue in the rivalry of the GREAT POWERS, the colonies featured pre-eminently in the period between 1880 and 1914 when the Afro-Asian world was almost entirely brought under European dominance. The term is also used to describe the set of values and attitudes typical of colonizers, which have offered such justifications as 'civilizing mission', 'White Man's Burden' and MANIFEST DESTINY.

COMECON See COUNCIL FOR MUTUAL ECONOMIC ASSISTANCE.

COMINFORM The Communist Information Bureau, which was created in 1947, following the COMINTERN, which Stalin (1879–1953) had disbanded in 1943. A propagandist organization set up to promote international Communist harmony under the leadership of the USSR and to discredit socialist alternatives to COMMUNISM, and to counter the TRUMAN DOCTRINE and the MARSHALL PLAN, it originally consisted of the USSR, Bulgaria, Czechoslovakia, Hungary, Poland, Romania, Yugoslavia and in Western Europe the Communist parties of France and Italy. One of its first actions was the expulsion of Yugoslavia in 1948. It was formally dissolved by Nikita Khrushchev (1894–1971), in part as a gesture of Soviet reconciliation with that country.

COMINTERN The Communist International, also known as the Third International. It was formed in Moscow in 1919 and during the 1920s and 1930s coordinated Communist parties elsewhere in the world to meet the needs and interests of the USSR. The Soviet leader Stalin (1879–1953) formally dissolved it in 1943.

Comity A term for amicable gestures and courtesies extended from one STATE to another, without legal obligation. Comity is normally reciprocal and is based on the principle that sovereign STATES should treat each other as equals.

Commission See EUROPEAN COMMISSION.

Commission on Human Rights (CHR) Instituted by Article 68 of the UNITED NATIONS CHARTER, the Commission has been in the forefront of international action concerned with defining, promoting and protecting HUMAN RIGHTS. The Charter authorized the ECONOMIC AND SOCIAL COUNCIL (ECOSOC) 'to set up commissions in the economic and social fields'. The CHR has assisted in drafting a number of human rights instruments, including the INTERNATIONAL BILL OF HUMAN RIGHTS, and has been involved in fact-finding missions.

Committee of Imperial Defence (CID) From 1902 to 1914 and from 1919 to 1939 the Committee of Imperial Defence was the British government's main advisory body on every aspect of home and overseas DEFENCE. It played a major role in formulating the underlying principles of defence policy and prepared plans for the coordination of military effort in the event of WAR. At the end of 1916, in the middle of the First World War, the Secretariat was put at the disposal of the Cabinet as a whole and subsequently became the Cabinet Office. On the outbreak of the Second World War it was merged into the War Cabinet.

Committee of One Million This was formed by members of the US CHINA LOBBY in the USA in 1953, its full title originally being 'the Committee of One Million Against the Admission of Communist China to the United Nations'. Its aim was to secure a million signatures against this eventuality. The People's Republic of China (Communist China) was admitted to the UNITED NATIONS (UN) in October 1971.

Committee of Permanent Representatives (COREPER) This body comprises senior officials from the member STATES of the EUROPEAN UNION (EU), who examine draft legislation before it is examined by the COUNCIL OF MINIS-TERS. A proposal that has been agreed by COREPER becomes item A and is adopted by the Council without debate, whereas one that is designated item B is debated. COREPER I consists of Deputy Permanent Representatives, who are the ambassadors of the member states. Some 250 working parties report to COREPER.

Committee on the Present Danger This was a US lobby set up in December 1950, at a particularly acute phase of the COLD WAR, under Paul Nitze (b. 1907), who was the Director of the Policy Planning staff at the DEPARTMENT OF STATE. It supported the large defence spending programme envisaged in NSC-68 and the development of the HYDROGEN BOMB. It was disbanded in 1953. It was then revived many years later, in 1976, to oppose DÉTENTE and campaign for Ronald Reagan (b. 1911) as President.

Common Agricultural Policy (CAP) The policy of the EUROPEAN UNION (EU) towards agriculture. An obligation imposed by the ROME TREATY (1957), agreement was reached on its principles in 1962. Its purpose was to increase productivity, ensure a fair standard of living for farmers and guarantee a regular supply of food for consumers. The core of the CAP is a guaranteed price system, and it involves a common external tariff (CET). The policy has been contentious and controversial throughout the history of the EUROPEAN COMMUNITY/UNION (EC/EU) because of its PROTECTIONISM cost (by the 1980s this amouned to two-thirds of the budget of the EC) and over-roduction. Internationally, it has been problematic. The USA has frequently attacked it for its protectionism and many countries in the THIRD WORLD have found that it has damaged the development of their own agriculture, with the dumping of surpluses at cut prices on the world market. Reform of the system has been painfully slow.

Common European home A phrase associated with the last leader of the USSR, Mikhail Gorbachev (b. 1931), who used it on a variety of occasions in 1989–90 in discussions with Western leaders and in an address to the COUNCIL OF EUROPE. It reflected the dramatic changes in EASTERN EUROPE, the fall of the BERLIN WALL and the reduction of East–West hostilities, but it was used vaguely and rhetorically. It was unclear, for instance, whether the Soviet leader envisaged new Pan-European institutions, and in one speech in Bonn he said that it was a home 'in which the United States and Canada will also have a place'.

Common Foreign and Security Policy (CFSP) One of the three PILLARS of the EUROPEAN UNION (EU) as constituted by the TREATY ON EUROPEAN UNION (TEU) of 1992. It was established as an inter-governmental structure for cooperation between the member STATES and to supersede EUROPEAN POLITICAL COOPERATION (EPC) for the coordination of foreign policies. Additional emphasis was given in it to the issue of SECURITY with a view to the EU eventually developing a common DEFENCE policy. Direction of CFSP was given to the EUROPEAN COUNCIL with implementation through the COUNCIL OF MINISTERS.

Common Heritage of Mankind (CMH) This term refers to those resources that belong to humanity as a whole rather than individual STATES or groups of states. It has been used, for instance, in discussions about the distribution of global resources in relation to the North–South divide. It amounts to a claim for distributional justice, but does not have formal legal status in INTERNATIONAL LAW.

Common Market An economic agreement that takes cooperation a step beyond a CUSTOMS UNION to provide for the free movement of capital, labour and goods throughout the area bounded by the common external tariff (CET). The term became widely used after the late 1950s as an alternative name for the EUROPEAN ECONOMIC COMMUNITY (EEC). For instance, in the 1960s and 1970s in Britain the debate over membership frequently referred to the Common Market. More recently it is sometimes used by those who believe the EUROPEAN UNION (EU) should restrict itself to economic objectives.

Commonwealth of Independent States (CIS) The loose association of the former constituent republics of the USSR, excluding the BALTIC STATES, and intended to offer a framework for consultation. It was set up in December 1991 and joined by twelve STATES. Three of them, the Ukraine, Moldova and Turkmenistan refused to sign its charter of 1993 for a common economic and foreign policy.

Commonwealth of Nations Formerly known as the British Commonwealth of Nations, it was formalized as an organization by the STATUTE OF WESTMINSTER of 1931, which confirmed the status of the dominions as quasi-sovereign STATES bound by loyalty to the British Crown. It is composed of fifty-three former British colonies, with Cameroon and Mozambique being the newest members and South Africa being readmitted in 1994 after the ending of APARTHEID. It meets and consults on a regular basis to foster common links and coordinate mutual assistance, a small secretariat having been established in 1965. The great majority of its member states are poor and about 70 per cent of British state-to-state AID goes to Commonwealth countries.

Communal conflicts Conflicts within communities. These are frequently long-term and intractable, producing their own mythologies, as in Northern Ireland. Chronic conflicts may lead to CIVIL WAR and/or external INTERVENTION, as in the Middle East and Yugoslavia.

Communautaire This term is used in the EUROPEAN UNION (EU) to indicate an approach that is in the wider interests of the Union, rather than one that is simply pressing national or sectional interests within it. It is synonymous with the phrase 'good European'. In reality, it is often used rhetorically. A country or its representative will claim to be strongly 'communautaire', but will at the same time be very effectively pursuing a primarily national agenda and in other areas of EU policy not complying particularly well.

Communism Both a theory and a political movement, Communism also became a significant force in world affairs after the Bolshevik Revolution of 1917 in Russia. The term originated in Paris in the 1830s. Communism envisaged the overthrow of CAPITAL-ISM and a new social and economic order. Also called Marxism, its early classic statement was the *Communist Manifesto* of 1848, composed by Karl Marx (1818–83) and Friedrich Engels (1820–95), which included the advocacy of the abolition of private property. Communist parties emerged with the 1917 revolution under Lenin (1870–1924) with a commitment to authoritarian one-party control under a POLITBURO, so-called demo-cratic centralism. Single-party rule with a centrally planned economy became the dom-inating characteristics and, under his successor, Stalin (1879–1953), organized mass terror and the unprecedented elevation of the POWER of the STATE. With the COMINTERN other Communist parties were called on to obey the dictates of the USSR. In inter-national relations, Communism historically has attributed WAR and rivalry to IMPERIAL-ISM, appealing to PROLETARIAN INTERNATIONALISM against capitalism. Hope that international Communism would develop into a world system was dashed by POLYCEN-TRISM. The Soviet model was also challenged by EUROCOMMUNISM and underwent dis-solution after 1989. The word 'Communism' was used interchangeably by the USSR with 'Socialism'. When Moscow referred to the 'Socialist countries', the Soviet BLOC was meant. Outside the bloc it was usual to refer to them as 'Communist countries' and to reserve the word 'Socialism' to describe pluralist social democracy.

Communist Bloc Also called the 'Socialist Bloc'. A term that was widely used during the COLD WAR and in discussing its history, for the continuous Euro-Asian area ruled by Communist parties embracing the twelve aligned countries. These include Albania, Bulgaria, the People's Republic of China, Czechoslovakia, East Germany, Hungary, North Korea, Mongolia, Poland, Romania, North Vietnam and the USSR. The word 'bloc' has been used in spite of the fact that there were significant diver-gences within it, for instance the SINO-SOVIET SPLIT and the rift between the USSR and Yugoslavia. The term has also been used to denote all countries under Communist rule, including those outside the geographical area, such as Cuba.

Communist Information Bureau See COMINFORM.

Community method A phrase used in the EUROPEAN UNION (EU) to describe the development, since the 1950s, of INTEGRATION through its institutions, particularly the EUROPEAN COMMISSION, rather than through the means of inter-governmental processes.

Community of nations The idea that STATES are members of an international family that is recognized by its members. In joining the community of nations, a state is regarded as a sovereign entity with all the privileges and rights accorded the other members, but it agrees to accept also the duties and responsibilities involved in membership of the community, including adherence to its norms in INTERNATIONAL LAW.

Comparative advantage The concept in economics that countries specialize in the production of those goods and services that they produce most efficiently. Ideally, in a FREE TRADE environment, it is argued that the global specialization and division of labour resulting from this fact will lead to maximum overall productivity. This view has been contested by economists who have pointed to the inequality in the distribution of wealth, to dependency and retarded development in the THIRD WORLD.

Complex interdependence A term used in international relations theory that was coined by the US scholars Robert Keohane (b. 1941) and Robert Nye (b. 1937). It describes the range of links that connect societies in the contemporary world, a multifariousness of which inter-state relations are only one form. In this complexity of the transnational, economic relations are inevitably accorded more importance than in traditional realist analysis of the international system.

Concert of Europe This term was used for the notion of an understanding between the GREAT POWERS in the nineteenth century to resolve international problems by multilateral DIPLOMACY wherever a dispute threatened to involve them and disrupt the PEACE of Europe. It grew out of the Quadruple Alliance (1815) of Britain, Austria, Prussia and Russia and the VIENNA CONGRESS (1814–15). The Concert combined the idea of a BALANCE OF POWER with the concept of consultation among STATES. The participants agreed to meet in order to prevent violent conflict, to continue to discuss political problems of mutual interest and to submit minor disputes to international ARBITRATION. The notion of a Concert of Europe was still evident at the BERLIN CONGRESS (1878) and, though unsuccessfully, was invoked by some on the prelude to, and on the eve of, the First World War. It amounted to a HEGEMONY by the dominant powers and collapsed with the First World War. The pattern of the major powers being assigned central responsibilities for PEACE and SECURITY was repeated in the consultations of the LEAGUE OF NATIONS and the UNITED NATIONS (UN).

Conciliation A procedure by which a THIRD PARTY settles an international dispute. Unlike MEDIATION, conciliation is the task of an impartial commission, not of governments. It differs from ARBITRATION in that the conciliation report only suggests the terms of settlement whereas an award by arbitration is binding on the parties.

Conciliation Procedure See CO-DECISION PROCEDURE.

Concordat From the Latin *concordatum*, 'agreement'. A concordat is a diplomatic TREATY or agreement between the Pope, as Head of the Roman Catholic Church, and a STATE, normalizing relations between secular and church authorities. In most cases these have been introduced to terminate a state of hostility.

Conditio sine qua non A condition that must be fulfilled before anything else can be done.

Condominium The jurisdiction over a territory shared by two or more STATES, and formally defined. It may be shared either concurrently, at the same time, or sequentially. Such an arrangement typically allows for equal exercise of SOVEREIGNTY by the states concerned. As an example of such jurisdiction, Britain and Egypt had condominium over the Sudan from 1898 till 1953 to protect the headwaters of the River Nile.

Confederation A formal association of STATES, loosely tied together by TREATY, often establishing a central governing mechanism with certain powers over member states, but not directly over the citizens of those states. In a confederation the constituent states are sovereign and independent and enjoy the right of SECESSION. This is to be distinguished from a FEDERATION, or federal state, which forms one single subject of INTERNATIONAL LAW and exercises direct power over the citizens of the subordinate units.

Conference diplomacy The name given to large-scale multilateral diplomatic negotiations between STATES. It came into its own particularly in the nineteenth century with such peace conferences as the VIENNA CONGRESS (1814–15) and the BERLIN CONGRESS (1878). It was further widened and institutionalized in the LEAGUE OF NATIONS after the First World War, with the advocacy of open DIPLOMACY 'open covenants openly arrived at', and, after the Second World War, in the UNITED NATIONS (UN).

Conference for the Reduction and Limitation of Armaments (1932–4) Also known as the World Disarmament Conference, this conference was convened by the LEAGUE OF NATIONS, opening on 2 February 1932, and included non-members, among them the USA and the USSR. It was the largest international gathering since the PARIS PEACE CONFERENCE (1919–20) and involved lengthy discussions on the issues of 'equality' of armaments and categorization of what were and were not offensive weapons, its purpose being to produce a CONVENTION substantially limiting 'all national armaments'. During its deliberations Japan completed its conquest of Manchuria and the Nazi Party came to power in Germany. The VERSAILLES TREATY (1919) had prefaced the demand for German DISARMAMENT with the hope that this would make possible 'the initiation of a general limitation of the armaments of all nations'. The French insisted that a proper scheme of general SECURITY should precede disarmament. Hitler (1889–1945) withdrew Germany from the conference in October 1933 and, in the circumstances, this ruled out any agreement, since the German problem was the principal focus. Hitler went on to receive a 95 per cent endorsement by the German electorate of his action, which included withdrawal from the League, in November 1935.

Conference on Security and Cooperation in Europe (CSCE) This brought together representatives of thirty-three European STATES, together with those from the USA and Canada, in a series of negotiations in the 1970s and 1980s. The Final Act, signed in Helsinki on 1 August 1975, established certain principles that guided East–West diplomatic relations over Europe. They included the inviolability of frontiers, NON-INTERVENTION and respect for HUMAN RIGHTS. After the end of the COLD WAR the CSCE set up a permanent secretariat in Prague, a centre for conflict prevention in Vienna, an office for Democratic Institutions and Human Rights in Warsaw and an office for the National Minorities at the Hague. With the break-up of the USSR, Czechoslovakia and Yugoslavia in the 1990s, plus the accession of Albania, the membership increased to fifty-three states. In 1994 it was renamed the ORGANIZATION FOR SECURITY AND COOPERATION IN EUROPE (OSCE). Since then it has supervised elections, monitored ceasefires in EASTERN EUROPE and Russia and helped to ensure and advance human rights.

Confidence-building measures (CBMs) Agreements that are designed to establish, or increase, mutual trust. For example, such agreements were formulated by the CONFERENCE ON SECURITY AND COOPERATION IN EUROPE (CSCE) to help lay the basis for monitoring ARMS CONTROL and FORCE reductions.

Conflict prevention See PREVENTIVE DIPLOMACY.

Conflict resolution A problem-solving approach to conflicts that has proved particularly applicable in situations of communal strife. Conflict-resolution techniques involve persuading hostile parties to examine the points at issue from other angles and constructively to explore different non-conflictual ways of achieving their objectives.

Conflict-resolution theory This has developed since the Second World War with the increasing role of PEACEKEEPING and PEACE enforcement in international and inter-communal relations. It is concerned with the avoidance of hostilities and their recurrence, with improvement of communication between rivals and adversaries, and reconciliation. It involves, above all, impartial appraisal of the causes and circumstances of hostility and conflict, reviewed as comprehensively as possible, accounting for economic, political, cultural, psychological and sociological factors. Experimental studies in this field have concentrated particularly on communal conflicts.

Congress system The system established in 1815 to maintain the European PEACE after the Napoleonic Wars by regular diplomatic conferences between Britain, Austria, Russia and Prussia. These powers, the Quadruple Alliance, met at Aix-la-Chapelle (1818), Troppau (1820), Laibach (1821) and Verona (1822). However, Britain, increasingly critical of the interference of the POWERS in the internal affairs of other territories, absented itself from the final congress at St Petersburg in 1825.

Connally Resolution (1943) This was similar to the FULBRIGHT RESOLUTION of the same year. Passed by the US Senate on 5 November 1943 during the Second World War, it affirmed that the USA (1) would cooperate with other nations that had signed the UNITED NATIONS DECLARATION (1942) in waging the war, (2) would cooperate in securing the PEACE after, and (3) would cooperate in 'the establishment and mainten-ance of an international authority with power to prevent aggression and to preserve the peace of the world'.

Conscription The system by which citizens in a number of countries are recruited involuntarily on a national basis for their armed forces. The British intro-duced it only in the middle of the First World War and terminated it in the early 1960s. The USA replaced conscription, 'the draft', with an all-volunteer force after the VIETNAM WAR (1960–75).

Constructive engagement This term was used to describe the policy of the USA towards South Africa between 1981 and 1985, during the first administration of US President Ronald Reagan (b. 1911). It reversed the policy of his predecessor Jimmy Carter (b. 1924) of openly criticizing South Africa and calling for the respect for HUMAN RIGHTS in order to bring about the end of APARTHEID. Reagan was more con-ciliatory, emphasizing common cause against COMMUNISM, and Western strategic interests in the area. In 1985, though, the USA imposed limited SANCTIONS against South Africa.

Contadora Group An informal group, formed in 1983, which originally con-sisted of Colombia, Mexico, Panama and Venezuela. This was later joined by Costa Rica, El Salvador, Guatemala, Honduras and Nicaragua. In August 1987 the Contadora Group developed the 'Procedure for the Establishment of a Firm and Lasting Peace in Central America'. This opened the way for collaboration between the ORGANIZATION OF AMERICAN STATES (OAS) and the UNITED NATIONS (UN), which was to lead to the deployment of the UN Observer Group in Central America.

Containment The policy, associated pre-eminently with the USA for confining COMMUNISM to its existing boundaries after the Second World War, was a fundamen-tal element in the COLD WAR. It was originally articulated by George F. Kennan (b. 1904), the diplomat and sovietologist, and was the rationale behind the TRUMAN DOCTRINE of 1947. It was based on the conviction that, if Soviet and, later also, Chinese expansionism was blocked, Communism would sooner or later collapse as a consequence of its own internal weaknesses and contradictions. Originally, its major emphasis was on economic and political stabilization as with the MARSHALL PLAN (1947). By the end of the 1940s containment had also come to mean military ALLIANCES, as with the NORTH ATLANTIC TREATY ORGANIZATION (NATO), an arms pro-gramme that would allow the USA in its own words to 'negotiate from a position of strength', economic and military aid to non-Communist countries and military resist-ance as, later, with the KOREAN WAR (1950–3) and the VIETNAM WAR (1960–75). In the context of containment doctrine, much of the debate about STRATEGY during the COLD WAR was about the scope and nature of the Soviet and Chinese threat and its relation to unrest in the remainder of the world. With Vietnam, many came to see that the USA had overburdened itself. Others, from the early days, castigated containment for not being ambitious enough and called for ROLLBACK.

Contiguous zone The zone just beyond the TERRITORIAL WATERS of a coastal STATE within which it may take action to protect itself. It is common for states to extend their territorial waters to include the contiguous zone, and it is usually accepted (though some states have asserted a wider zone) to extend 12 nautical miles.

Continental shelf It is common for littoral STATES to claim control over their adjacent continental shelf, the land off their coasts before the steep decline to the oceans. It is defined in the Geneva Convention on the Continental Shelf of 1958.

Continental strategy A term used in British DEFENCE and SECURITY policy. Historically Britain has often concentrated on use of naval power and financial support to help allies on the Continent of Europe. Its Army was largely reserved for the defence of empire. Continental strategy means the commitment to be willing to fight a land WAR in Europe by the despatch of a British expeditionary force. This happened in both world wars. In 1954 with the Paris Agreements Britain committed itself to the BRITISH ARMY OF THE RHINE (BAOR), though there was, periodically, subsequent debate as to whether it should not concentrate its defence resources on the Navy and air support for troops in Europe. Since the 1990s it has contributed troops to the Balkans.

Continental system This was an attempt by the French Emperor Napoleon I (1769–1821) to exclude British trade from Europe after the Battle of Trafalgar (1805), which had defeated the French Navy. This was between 1806 and 1812 and he hoped that it would bring Britain to its knees, though British naval superiority forced its collapse and retaliation by Britain included seizure of neutral shipping. This term has subsequently been used in different contexts where there was a fear of exclusion, or isolation, of Britain from the Continent. It was argued, for instance, in the 1960s that, if Britain did not join the EUROPEAN COMMUNITY (EC), it would find itself facing a 'continental system' that would, perhaps, increasingly exclude British goods.

Continuity of states The principle that, where there is a change of SOVEREIGNTY, the rights and obligations of the STATE concerned remain unchanged.

Continuous Voyage Doctrine A principle applied in naval warfare whereby a belligerent has the right to seize and condemn neutral goods going from one neutral port ostensibly to another, if it can be proved that the particular goods have in reality an ultimate enemy destination, by sea or land. As such, it represents a significant limitation on the freedom of trade for neutral states.

Convention A binding international agreement concluded between two or more governments. The term tends to be applied to agreements of less formality than a TREATY.

Conventional Forces in Europe (CFE) Originally called the Conventional Stability Talks (CST), these were held in conjunction with the 1989 sessions of the CONFERENCE ON SECURITY AND COOPERATION IN EUROPE (CSCE) in Vienna. There were discussions between the NORTH ATLANTIC TREATY ORGANIZATION (NATO) and the WARSAW PACT on the reduction of conventional arms in Europe, concentrating on three issues, exchange of military information, asymmetric reduction to take account of superior Warsaw Pact levels and VERIFICATION. A TREATY was signed in 1990 that planned for a considerable arms reduction from the levels left by the COLD WAR.

Conventional war A WAR that does not involve NUCLEAR WEAPONS. A key concern of strategists since the Second World War, and in particular during the COLD WAR, has been that a conventional war might escalate into a nuclear conflict.

Conventional weapons This term usually means those weapons that are not nuclear. It can also be argued that the term should exclude chemical and biological weapons since they are not commonly used, and it is also used to mean weapons other than WEAPONS OF MASS DESTRUCTION.

Conventions on the rules of warfare See GENEVA CONVENTIONS (1949).

Convergence thesis This was a proposition, advanced first in the early 1960s in the West during the COLD WAR, which argued that, because of common technological developments, industrialization, urbanization and the common pursuit of affluence, the socio-economic systems of CAPITALISM and COMMUNISM would converge. There would also be increasing cooperation in technology, commerce and finance between East and West. The USSR rejected it as a denial of what they claimed would be an inevitable collapse of capitalism.

Convertibility The free exchange of a national currency into units of a foreign currency or gold. Convertibility is commonly restricted when a government seeks to protect a nation from serious imbalance in its international payments. After the Second World War, which had significantly weakened Britain's economic position, for instance, convertibility was not fully restored for thirteen years.

Coolidge Doctrine A statement in favour of INTERVENTION by US President Calvin Coolidge (1872–1933). It was made to Congress on 22 April 1922 and contradicted the CALVO DOCTRINE. Coolidge said: 'It is . . . well established that our Government has certain rights over and certain duties towards our own citizens and their property, wherever they may be located. The person and the property of a citizen are a part of the general domain of the nation, even when abroad.'

Cordon sanitaire French for a barrier to prevent the spread of disease. In international relations it was used to define the preventive measures taken to isolate France during the VIENNA CONGRESS (1814–15) after the Napoleonic Wars, and to contain the spread of revolutionary principles. It has been used subsequently, especially during the PARIS PEACE CONFERENCE (1919–20) after the Bolshevik Revolution, to describe the role of the SUCCESSION STATES in EASTERN EUROPE as a barrier against the spread of COMMUNISM.

Core A term used interchangeably with CENTRE in DEPENDENCY THEORY, meaning the major industrialized countries in the global political economy. It is also sometimes used to indicate the ruling interests in those countries.

COREPER See COMMITTEE OF PERMANENT REPRESENTATIVES.

Correlation of forces A significant and much-used term in the military and political thinking of Soviet COMMUNISM. It meant the USSR's capacity to compete with the West, its combined economic, military, diplomatic and ideological strength, in the COLD WAR. In a narrowly military interpretation, it described the capability and probability of achieving political objectives through force, echoing the famous statement of the Prussian Karl von Clausewitz (1780–1831) that war is 'nothing but the continuation of politics by other means'.

Council for Mutual Economic Assistance (CMEA/ COMECON) The organization for economic relations between the USSR and its allies in the COLD WAR. It was founded in January 1949 as a counter-move to the US MARSHALL PLAN (1947) and to begin with consisted merely of bilateral trade agreements and was intended largely to assist Soviet reconstruction. Subsequently, after the death of Stalin (1879–1953), it started to promote a division of labour in which countries specialized in particular sectors. It set out both to integrate the economies and to achieve self-sufficiency. External trade was discouraged and the currencies in the Soviet BLOC were non-convertible. Cuba and Vietnam joined in 1972 and 1978 respectively. It was formally dissolved in June 1991.

Council of Europe Based in Strasbourg, this was the result of the Hague Congress of May 1948 at which 600 leading representatives of sixteen countries discussed the future of Europe and pledged 'to achieve a closer union between its members in order to protect and promote the ideals and principles which constitute their common heritage and to further their economic and social progress'. The Council of Europe represented a disappointment to those who had argued for a federal Europe, who lost out to the so-called unionists who preferred an inter-governmental pattern. In the event, the Assembly of the Council of Europe has become a forum for the exchange of ideas and information on social, legal, educational and cultural matters. Its major contribution has been the EUROPEAN COURT OF HUMAN RIGHTS (ECHR). After the end of the COLD WAR its membership came to include almost every European country.

Council of Foreign Ministers This comprised the foreign ministers of the USA, Britain, France and China and was instituted in July 1945 at the POTSDAM CONFERENCE. It was intended to pave the way for a peace TREATY with Germany. This was an early victim of the emerging COLD WAR. In the event, a formal peace treaty with Germany was not signed until reunification in 1990.

Council of Ministers This is the key decision-making body of the EUROPEAN UNION (EU) representing the national governments of the member STATES. It consists of ministerial representatives from the states and its composition varies according to the subject on the agenda – hence, for example, with ministers of agriculture deliberating over the COMMON AGRICULTURAL POLICY (CAP). The issue of VETO has been, and continues to be, important. The LUXEMBOURG COMPROMISE (1966) confirmed the right of national veto, which significantly impeded further INTEGRATION. With the SINGLE EUROPEAN ACT (SEA) (1987) this obstacle was removed in some policy areas by the introduction of QUALIFIED MAJORITY VOTING (QMV). Direction of the Council is in the hands of the President and member states hold the Presidency in rotation, the office moving from state to state every six months.

Counter-force A term in nuclear arms STRATEGY, relating to targets. A counter-force target is, broadly, an enemy military target. Used more specifically, it means part of the enemy's own nuclear arms system.

Counter-insurgency The principles, STRATEGY and TACTICS for defeating GUERRILLA WARFARE. From the twentieth century this has particularly meant resisting such warfare that is motivated by revolutionary political, economic and social aims, both in the countryside and in cities. The Chinese Communist leader Mao-Zedong (1893–1976) pointed inadvertently to the problems of counter-insurgency when he commented: 'the guerrilla is the fish; the people are the water.' Robert Thompson (b. 1916), who conducted counter-insurgency in Malaysia and who subsequently was used as consultant on the subject by the USA in the VIETNAM WAR (1960–75), suggested five basic rules, which would avoid alienating the population. First, one must be seen to want a stable, democratic and prospering country. Secondly, one should avoid brutality and operate within the law. Thirdly, plans must be coherent. Fourthly, the priority should be the defeat of political subversion rather than the guerrillas. Fifthly, one should ensure that one's bases are secure before anything else. Counter-insurgency operations are also crucially dependent on good INTELLIGENCE and, as the USA found crucially to its cost in Vietnam, guerrillas should as far as possible be isolated from outside support.

Counter-intelligence Information gathered and activities conducted to protect against espionage and other INTELLIGENCE activities, sabotage, assassinations carried out by foreign governments, terrorist organizations or other agencies.

Counter-value In contrast to COUNTER-FORCE, a counter-value target in nuclear STRATEGY is any target that is not specifically a military one. Counter-value nuclear strikes would be directed against economic, industrial and political structures.

Coup d'état A swift and decisive seizure of POWER within a political system, often by a military group. It differs from a revolution in that it is not based on a popular uprising. Moreover, a *coup* is often presented as forestalling a possible revolution. Nor does it necessarily involve transformation of institutions or society, though these may follow it. It normally involves capture of existing leaders, of key communications, the media and government buildings. It has been a common occurrence in Africa and Latin America. But it is rare where there are accepted democratic procedures for governmental change and general acceptance of the legitimacy of a government.

Court of Auditors Since the RATIFICATION of the TREATY ON EUROPEAN UNION (TEU) of 1992, this has been formally the fifth institution of the EUROPEAN UNION (EU). It consists of one appointee named by the COUNCIL OF MINISTERS for each member STATE and examines all the accounts of revenue and expenditure for the EU institutions.

Court of First Instance (CFI) This was established in principle by the SINGLE EUROPEAN ACT (SEA) in 1987 and came into existence in 1989. It is based in Luxembourg and is a supporting institution to the EUROPEAN COURT OF JUSTICE (ECJ), assuming responsibility for some of the cases heard in the EUROPEAN UNION (EU), particularly those relating to the EUROPEAN COAL AND STEEL COMMUNITY (ECSC) and matters relating to EU employees.

Covert action The purpose of a covert action is to influence events abroad in the best interests of a nation's foreign policy. Such actions are SECURITY and INTELLIGENCE operations, often known to only a handful of people and are sometimes described as the 'third option' between DIPLOMACY and open conflict. Also known as the 'quiet option', covert actions have not always fitted that description, as was the case with the CENTRAL INTELLIGENCE AGENCY (CIA)-supported BAY OF PIGS INVASION of 1961, which involved humiliation for the USA. 'Special activities' carried out by intelligence agencies, if discovered, frequently invite controversy in democratic societies.

Credentials In DIPLOMACY documents that certify the POWERS conferred by a STATE on its diplomatic representatives. These documents are addressed to the sovereign to whom the representative is accredited.

Credibility Credibility is the essence of DETERRENCE. If an adversary believes that a deterrent threat is not a credible one, he is much less likely to resist a resort to AGGRESSION. There are two main elements to this, technical capability and political will, and what is crucial is to convince an opponent that, under specified and clearly stated conditions, a threat will be carried out.

Crimes against humanity These were included in the Charter of the International Military Tribunal for the NUREMBERG TRIALS (1945–7) at the end of the Second World War, which tried the Nazis, and have become part of the law of HUMAN RIGHTS. They were specified as 'murder, extermination, enslavement, deportation and other inhumane acts committed against any civilian population before or during (*a*) . . . war . . whether or not in violation of the domestic law of the country where perpetrated'. Since then the list has been extended to include, torture GENOCIDE, which fitted the category of 'other inhumane acts', and APARTHEID.

Crimes against peace One of the three categories of crimes specified at the NUREMBERG TRIALS (1945–7) at the end of the Second World War in the Charter of the International Military Tribunal set up to try the Nazis. Crimes against peace were defined as: 'planning, preparation, initiation or waging of a war of aggression, or a war in violation of international treaties, agreements or assurances, or participation in a common plan or conspiracy for the accomplishment of any of the foregoing'.

Crisis A decisive turning point, a severe conflict short of WAR, but one that encourages the belief that there could be a high probability of war and that may lead to one, such as the July Crisis of 1914. The causes of crises, their management, their resolution and comparisons between them have been very widely studied in international relations and international history, notably such crises as those that led to the two world wars, the repeated confrontations in the Middle East, such as the SUEZ CRISIS (1956) and the CUBAN MISSILE CRISIS (1962).

Crisis management As a skill, the management of a CRISIS, striking an appropriate balance between coercion and conciliation so as to maximize one's own interests and avoid military conflict. As a study, there has been a particular interest in this aspect of international relations evidenced in numerous publications since the 1960s. A key stimulus to this have been the crises of the COLD WAR, such as the BERLIN BLOCKADE (1948–9) and the CUBAN MISSILE CRISIS (1962). Avoidance of ESCALATION, clarity, precision and speed of communication are crucial aspects, as are awareness of when to stand firm, when to give ground and how to avoid miscalculation.

Crisis stability A situation of military balance. Crisis stability is achieved where a POWER or group of powers, because of this parity, is not afraid that its adversaries will consider it advantageous to mount a PRE-EMPTIVE WAR and therefore itself discounts the necessity of going to WAR.

Cruise and Pershing missiles The decision to deploy these intermediate-range missiles in Europe followed an agreement of 1979 by the NORTH ATLANTIC TREATY ORGANAZATION (NATO) partners. It was partly to counter the deployment of similar-range missiles being installed in EASTERN EUROPE and also to achieve the DUAL-TRACK POLICY of negotiating the elimination of such missiles. Their introduction led to significant political protest and a marked revival of PEACE MOVEMENTS, as with the Greenham Common protest. Having broken off arms talks, the USSR returned later to conclude the INTERMEDIATE-RANGE NUCLEAR FORCES (INF) TREATY (1987), under which the missiles were removed.

CSCE See CONFERENCE ON SECURITY AND COOPERATION IN EUROPE.

CU See CUSTOMS UNION.

Cuban Missile Crisis (1962) The most dangerous CRISIS and BRINKMANSHIP of the COLD WAR, between the USSR and the USA, which threatened WAR after the installation in Cuba of Soviet NUCLEAR WEAPONS. The Soviet leader Nikita Khrushchev (1894–1971) claimed the missiles were to protect Cuba from imminent American invasion, following the abortive BAY OF PIGS INVASION in 1961. President Kennedy learned of the missiles on 16 October through U-2 reconnaissance flights. Opinion in the Executive Committee of the NATIONAL SECURITY COUNCIL (NSC) was divided as to whether to recommend air strikes and/or a military invasion or some lesser measure. In the event a naval BLOCKADE (termed QUARANTINE) was imposed. The crisis was resolved on 28 October when Khrushchev, without consulting the Cuban leader Fidel Castro (b. 1927) agreed to dismantle the bases and Kennedy undertook that the USA would not invade Cuba, and privately gave the assurance that US Jupiter missiles would be withdrawn from Turkey. One of the immediate outcomes was the HOT-LINE AGREEMENT of 1963.

Cultural diplomacy The effort by a STATE to promote better knowledge about, and understanding of, its culture abroad. Examples include the British Council and the US Fulbright Programme. Such efforts have commonly been combined with other objectives, such as the promotion of Western values during the COLD WAR.

Cultural imperialism The imposition of cultural domination, languages, alien ideas and values on other peoples. It is to be distinguished from the voluntary assimilation of external influences, resulting from trade, travel and communications and other forces of GLOBALIZATION. Since the nineteenth century the cultural imperialism of Western nations has increasingly provoked reaction in the THIRD WORLD, as, for instance, with ISLAMIC FUNDAMENTALISM.

Curzon Line The frontier between the USSR and Poland after the Second World War. The line had first been suggested by the British Prime Minister David Lloyd George (1863–1945) and negotiations were handled by Lord Curzon (1859–1925), his Foreign Secretary. At the time Poland rejected it, but in 1939 it was used by Nazi Germany and the USSR as an agreed demarcation of their occupation zones. In 1945 Poland was forced to accept that the areas to the east of the line would remain Soviet territory.

Customs Union (CU) An economic association of STATES based upon an agreement to eliminate tariffs and other impediments to trade within the area of the union, but with a common external tariff (CET) on goods imported into the union. It is the common tariff that distinguishes it from a FREE TRADE AREA. The establishment of a customs union was the first objective of the ROME TREATY (1957), which established the EUROPEAN ECONOMIC COMMUNITY (EEC).

CWC See CHEMICAL WEAPONS CONVENTION (1993).

D

Damage limitation The principle that the main function and of military capability is to deny the forces of any enemy their opportunity to cause destruction, by seeking them out and destroying them. Less proactively, it can also refer to a whole range of measures, such as defence preparations, to deny an enemy its gains.

Danube Commission The international organization with headquarters in Budapest that regulates and controls navigation of the River Danube. It was established under the Belgrade Covention (1948), in which the STATES on the banks of the river agreed that the merchant ships of all states could navigate freely on it.

Danzig A FREE CITY established by Articles 100–8 of the VERSAILLES TREATY of 1919, in spite of its very large German population, to give Poland an outlet to the Baltic. From 1920 to 1939 it was under the protection of the LEAGUE OF NATIONS, which appointed a High Commissioner to administer it. The Senate was the supreme governing authority. In 1922 its economic life was integrated with that of Poland. In 1933 the German Nazi party gained the majority in Danzig, which became a source of continuous tension between Germany and Poland up to the outbreak of the Second World War. In September 1939 Danzig was conquered in the *BLITZKRIEG* and incorporated into the new province of Danzig-West Prussia. After the war the city, since then named Gdansk, reverted to Poland. It was subsequently a major centre of revolt against COMMUNISM during the SOLIDARITY movement.

Dayton Peace Accords (1995) The agreements, brokered by the USA under President Clinton (b. 1946) at an air force base in Dayton Ohio on 21 November 1995.

This brought an end to the Bosnian War, which had gone on for three years and had involved civilian massacres. In order to emphasize the transatlantic nature of the peace initiative, the Accords were formally signed by the presidents of Bosnia and Herzegovina, Croatia and Serbia in Paris on 14 December 1995.

D-Day (1944) The Second World War Normandy landings of 1944 by Allied forces known as 'Operation Overlord'. This began after long preparation on 6 June 1944 along a 50-mile stretch of the Normandy coast from the Cotentin Peninsula eastwards. The landing and subsequent engagements were costly in human life, but Paris was captured on 25 August and Allied troops crossed into Germany on 12 September 1944.

De facto **recognition** A provisional recognition by the government of one STATE that a particular regime exercise authoritative control over the territory of another state. It is extended often to see if the new regime establishes itself securely, or for practical considerations such as the maintenance of trade with the first country. The legality of the assumption of authority by the regime – when simply *de facto* recognition is involved – is immaterial; and such recognition is not necessarily a precondition for the establishment of *de jure* recognition and a formal diplomatic relationship.

De jure **recognition** Unqualified recognition of one government by another. *De jure* recognition always involves the establishment of normal diplomatic relations. This may either be 'express', when accompanied by a formal agreement to establish those relations, or 'tacit', when accompanied by an act that implies intention to recognize, such as a consular CONVENTION. If disputes subsequently occur between the STATES involved, diplomatic relations may be broken, but recognition is not withdrawn. As examples, the USA did not accord *de jure* jurisdiction to the USSR until 1933, sixteen years after the Russian Revolution. When Israel declared independence in 1948, the USA initially only recognized it *de facto*, while the USSR gave it *de jure* recognition from the outset.

De-Stalinization The hesitant process of selective liberalization in the USSR and most EASTERN EUROPEAN countries following the TWENTIETH PARTY CONGRESS of the Communist Party of the Soviet Union (CPSU) in February 1956, during which the Soviet leader Khrushchev (1894–1971) denounced Stalin's terror and personality cult. The measures were intended to reduce arbitrary rule and restore economic rationality. Censorship was somewhat relaxed, economic reforms introduced and many victims of Stalinist persecution were rehabilitated. Eastern European countries were accorded greater freedom to pursue their own path to COMMUNISM. This also led to the POLISH OCTOBER and HUNGARIAN REVOLUTION of 1956.

Death squads This term is usually applied to right-wing parliamentary or vigilante groups, as, notably, in Latin America, who murder their opposition, actual and potential, and not infrequently with the covert approval of the national government.

Debt crisis (1970s and 1980s) See INTERNATIONAL DEBT CRISIS.

Debt service The amount of money that a STATE must pay to public and private foreign lenders as interest on previous loans.

Decision In the EUROPEAN UNION (EU) this term is used to describe a legal instrument directly binding on the individual enterprise or person to which or whom it is applied.

Declaration on the Granting of Independence to Colonial Countries and Peoples (1960) See UNITED NATIONS DECLARATION ON THE GRANTING OF INDEPENDENCE TO COLONIAL COUNTRIES AND PEOPLES.

Declaration of Principles See OSLO ACCORDS (1993).

Declaratory policy In the language of nuclear STRATEGY, this term means the open statement of the circumstances in which a country would use its NUCLEAR WEAPONS, such as the US policy of MASSIVE RETALIATION. During the COLD WAR the UK advanced the so-called MOSCOW OPTION, though it did not detail the occasion of use, arguing that uncertainty increased the effectiveness of DETERRENCE.

Decolonization The process that has been dramatically in evidence since the end of the Second World War, which was strongly encouraged by the war, by which colonies become independent STATES possessing SOVEREIGNTY. The collapse of empires in the second half of the twentieth century saw POWER passing from the colonial powers, principally the UK, France, Belgium, Holland, Portugal, Japan and Russia, to indigenous peoples. The laws and often the bureaucracies of the departing powers remained. The boundaries drawn up by the colonialists often have not corresponded to ethnic divisions, leaving a legacy of intractable problems across the globe for the international community. Furthermore, the ending of imperial rule did not necessarily coincide with the achievement of full independence. Sovereign states were becoming more interdependent and it was hardly surprising that ex-colonies often to a considerable extent remained culturally and economically dependent on their former colonial states. NEO-COLONIALISM is the term used to describe this post-imperial condition of dependence.

Decoupling A concept relating to the LINKAGE between US nuclear forces and the defence of Western Europe during the COLD WAR. In the mid-1950s, particularly with the achievement by the USSR of thermonuclear CAPABILITY the NORTH ATLANTIC TREATY ORGANIZATION (NATO) decided that it could not match the CONVENTIONAL WEAPONS of the USSR and that it would be nuclear defence, first expressed as part of the doctrine of MASSIVE RETALIATION, that would effectively defend Western Europe. While this sent signals to the WARSAW PACT that nuclear retaliation would be the response to a conventional attack on Western Europe, this guarantee was never given in the form of an explicit commitment, but rather more as a tacit psychological assurance. This led to doubts as to whether the USA would resort to nuclear retaliation over Europe, a doubt openly voiced by the French President Charles de Gaulle (1890–1970) and underlined by the *FORCE DE FRAPPE*. With the development of discussions between the SUPERPOWERS in the 1960s and 1970s over DÉTENTE and ARMS CONTROL, these concerns became more widespread. Decoupling was the term used to indicate this fear that the US strategic force would not be available for the defence of Europe. This was one reason why the UK and Germany in 1977 persuaded the US President Jimmy Carter (b. 1924) to promise the deployment of EUROMISSILES.

DEFCON See DEFENCE CONDITION.

Defence What constitutes adequate defence in any given circumstances is subject to very subjective interpretations, depending on calculations of a potential adversary's power and intentions and of one's own capabilities and strength, which include not simply armed forces and weapons, but underlying economic strength and civilian morale. This has made DISARMAMENT and ARMS CONTROL problematic and complicated. With the rise of the modern STATE in competition with other states and with no overriding international authority, defence became the most prominent responsibility of governments. Historically, it has been construed in military terms and protection of national territory is historically its most conspicuous aspect. At the same time the concept includes defence of values and material prosperity. The advance of technology, particularly the invention of NUCLEAR WEAPONS, has transformed defence STRATEGY and intensified moral and ideological debates. For instance, the COLD WAR doctrine of MASSIVE RETALIATION and subsequent nuclear policies have introduced a new dimension, raising the whole issue of the relationship between defence and DETERRENCE. Since the end of the cold war, the perceived threat in the west of the USSR has been succeeded by a range of other threats. Traditional military defence concerns have been widened to embrace a more comprehensive agenda of SECURITY involving a range of risks, including such things as TERRORISM and environmental degradation.

Defence in depth This term denotes a system of ground defence based on successive lines or perimeters of defence. In linear defence, by contrast, all available forces are deployed in a single frontal system.

Defence condition (DEFCON) The US term for the stages of alert on which its forces are placed in an international CRISIS as WAR becomes more (or less) likely. The lower the number, the greater the state of readiness. DEFCON 5 is the normal peacetime level of readiness. DEFCON 1 is declared only if hostilities are imminent or conflict has already broken out.

Defence conversion The programme of DISARMAMENT that emerged as a consequence of the abating of the East–West COLD WAR confrontation after 1989. The transformation of war-making capabilities and instruments to peacetime uses was given high priority by the NORTH ATLANTIC TREATY ORGANIZATION (NATO) and the WARSAW PACT. In this context, NATO, for instance, organized the Allies and Cooperation Partners on Defence Conversion consultation group in 1992.

Delictum iuris gentium Latin for 'a crime against the law of nations'.

Delimitation The precise demarcation of two STATES or territories.

Demarcation A line establishing and delimiting by TREATY the border between two STATES or territories.

Démarche As a diplomatic term, démarche means a new initiative, as when negotiations are stalled and there is a will to find a resolution to a problem.

Demilitarization The obligation of a STATE under INTERNATIONAL LAW not to station military forces, and not to maintain military installations in specified areas or zones of its territory, including TERRITORIAL WATERS, rivers, canals and air space above the territory. The purpose is to prevent, or reduce, the possibility of the outbreak of WAR or conflict. An example is the demilitarization of the RHINELAND after the defeat of Germany in the First World War and, more comprehensively, that of Germany and Japan after the Second World War. Demilitarization has frequently been used to secure freedom of navigation on international waterways – for instance, the NEUTRALIZATION of the Black Sea after the Crimean War in the Paris Peace Treaty of 1856. In order to meet the challenge of modern weapons technology, the concept of demilitarization has been extended to cover ever larger regions in the period since the Second World War. Examples of this are the ANTARCTIC TREATY (1959) and the ban on NUCLEAR WEAPONS in Latin America in the TREATY FOR THE PROHIBITION OF NUCLEAR WEAPONS IN LATIN AMERICA (1967) (the Tlatelolco Treaty).

Demilitarized zone (DMZ) An area between two armies and/or STATES in a military confrontation in which it is agreed that it shall contain no troops or military installations. With the ARMISTICE that ended the KOREAN WAR (1950–3) in 1953, for instance, it was agreed to establish a zone two-and-a-half miles wide right across the country between North and South Korea.

Demographic deficit This phrase is commonly used to indict the EUROPEAN UNION (EU) for its absence of proper democratic accountability in its decision-making processes. This is both because of the legislative processes, the failure of national parliaments to be able adequately to scrutinize the EUROPEAN COMMISSION and the COUNCIL OF MINISTERS, and also because the EUROPEAN PARLIAMENT (EP), in spite of recent accretions of responsibility and power, is not yet a legislature in the traditional meaning of the word.

Demographic race This term describes the situation in which two or more ethnic or national groups are rivals within a given territory and where there is pressure, either official or implicit, to outbreed the other group to gain a higher proportion of the population.

Demontage A diplomatic term used in connection with WAR REPARATIONS. It means the dismantling of factories, industrial plant and other installations associated with the war potential of a defeated STATE, such as was demanded of Germany at the POTSDAM CONFERENCE in August 1945, and such as were transferred afterwards particularly to the USSR Demontage is insisted on as a necessary precautionary measure against future hostilities by the defeated state.

Denuclearization An agreement to prohibit NUCLEAR WEAPON in a specific zone, region or country. Antarctica and Latin America are two such areas. In 1987 the USA and USSR reached agreement to denuclearize EASTERN EUROPE and Western Europe by removing all Soviet and Western intermediate and short-range missiles and their nuclear warheads from the region in the INTERMEDIATE-RANGE NUCLEAR FORCES (INF) TREATY. Denuclearization and the creation of NUCLEAR FREE ZONES are related to such other ARMS CONTROL measures as bans on testing and limitations on the production of weapons-grade radioactive materials.

Department of State Since 1789 the official name of the US ministry of foreign affairs, the oldest department in the executive branch of US government, which is directly answerable to the President. It advises the President, formulates and puts into effect foreign policy, administers the foreign programmes assigned to it by Congress, provides for coordination of government agencies affecting foreign relations and promotes relations between the USA and other nations. During the COLD WAR, when security policy tended to dominate US actions in world affairs, many of its activities were transferred to the Department of Defense (see PENTAGON), the NATIONAL SECURITY COUNCIL (NSC) and the CENTRAL INTELLIGENCE AGENCY (CIA).

Dependency theory A concept that sets out to explain persistent poverty in Latin America and other parts of the DEVELOPING WORLD. Unlike theories of IMPERIALISM, this focuses on the history and development of the dependent countries themselves. Dependency theorists have criticized US policies, for instance, for the long-term as well as on-going consequences of dependency, military takeovers, continuing poverty and US resistance towards revolutionary change. In their view, not only have dependent countries not achieved wealth and development, but their poverty has been a consequence of the economic growth of dominant nations. Through dependent trade relations that linked the interests of local elites and their metropolitan counterparts, rich nations have extracted corporate profits, mineral resources and the value of inexpensive labour from dependent nations. Dependency theory gained a wide following in Latin America during the 1960s and 1970s.

Dependent state A member of the COMMUNITY of nations with qualified or limited status. A dependent STATE has a relationship with another state such that its freedom of independent action or SOVEREIGNTY is formally curtailed to such a degree that there is a dependency upon another state. This can range from colonial status to collaboration in international affairs. The status of dependency should not be confused with the universal condition of INTERDEPENDENCE in the global economy and world affairs. Historically, dependent states have often been alternatively referred to as vassal, semi-sovereign states or PROTECTORATES.

Derogation A temporary exemption from a treaty by a signatory. For example, in the EUROPEAN UNION (EU) derogations are often granted to new member STATES for periods of five or ten years under the terms of their respective accession agreement.

Desert Shield (1900–1) The US name for the build-up of coalition forces for the Persian GULF WAR (1991), following the Iraqi invasion of Kuwait. It began on 7 August 1990 and ended on 17 January 1991, when the air campaign against Iraq began.

Desert Storm (1991) The US name for the Persian GULF WAR (1991) after the beginning of the coalition air campaign. The WAR followed the Iraqi invasion and occupation of Kuwait. It began on 17 January 1991 and ended on 11 April 1991, when the ceasefire called for by the UNITED NATIONS SECURITY COUNCIL in Resolution 687 went into effect.

Destabilization The use of ideological, economic and military sabotage to prevent a STATE from providing SECURITY or necessities to its population. The goal is not always to take control of the country, but to destroy or cripple its economy, its infra-structure and thereby undermine popular support for the government. Destabilization seeks to render a country ungovernable, bringing about a collapse of the state from within. To appear legitimate, sabotage is often carried out by disaffected nations of the target country or by mercenaries, not by the army of the destabilizer. Distinct from COUNTER-INSURGENCY, destabilization is an assault against an established state while counter-insurgency tries to impede an incipient revolt. A major tactic in destabiliza-tion is the use of TERRORISM, as, in particular, in the Middle East.

Détente In its broadest usage a term employed since the mid-1950s to describe a lessening of tension in international relations, most particularly during the COLD WAR. In recent decades it has sometimes been used more specifically to refer to the moves and agreements that reduced antagonism between the SUPERPOWERS in the 1970s, and that was symbolized by the visit of US President Richard M. Nixon (1913–94) to Moscow, in 1972 and by the Helsinki Conference of 1975. A major achievement of this period was the negotiation and successful conclusion of the first bilateral STRA-TEGIC ARMS LIMITATION TALKS (SALT I) (1969–72). Détente did not mean either of the superpowers foreswearing their long-term aims or an end to global rivalry between them, and each had a different conception of it. To the extent that it was real, it related less to military agreements than to the recognition that there did exist both a certain stalemate and a certain degree of mutual economic INTERDEPENDENCE and common interest, because of the costs of DEFENCE, in agreeing to a degree of ARMS CONTROL. The term has also been used to refer to the relations between the superpowers from the mid-1980s onwards, during which further arms agreements, the fall of the BERLIN WALL and the ending of Soviet HEGEMONY over EASTERN EUROPE transformed the international agenda.

Deterrence In its broadest sense deterrence means any STRATEGY of policy that is intended to persuade a potential enemy not to attack. In some ways, deterrence has always been the role of all military forces except those specifically intended for wars of conquest. In the nuclear age deterrence can be seen as a policy for protecting against AGGRESSION by making the direct cost of retaliation greater than any benefit that can be gained, as with the doctrine of MASSIVE RETALIATION. The major difficulty with theories of deterrence, as opposed to defensive strategy, is that they run into problems of CREDIBILITY with widespread doubts that a NATION attacked in a particular way would necessarily carry out its earlier threat. Its importance in military theory since 1945 also derives from the perceived 'lesson' of the Second World War, that the Western democracies had neglected adequately to confront the AXIS powers with the consequences of AGGRESSION. Deterrence is not to be confused with compellance, which means using force or threats to get another to do something, or persuasion via reward.

Development decades Since 1961 the UNITED NATIONS GENERAL ASSEMBLY has specified successive decades for the achievement of objectives in development, including percentages for economic growth, eradication of poverty and fairer distri-bution of wealth. The goals have normally outstripped the achievements.

DG Director/Directorate-General (EUROPEAN UNION (EU)).

Diaspora A term of Greek origin, meaning 'scattering' and referring to the disper-sion of the Jews after the Babylonian Exile of 586 BC and to the communities so dis-persed. While, historically, it has been applied to the Jews living outside Palestine, more recently it has come to be used generally to describe other peoples who have been scattered, such as the Armenians after the First World War, or the Palestinians after the Arab–Israeli war of 1948–9.

Diplomacy Formal activity of a STATE vis-à-vis other states, including exchange of ambassadors and other diplomatic agents, correspondence between heads of state and so on. It can be traced to Ancient Greece, flourished with the development of the modern state system from the fifteenth century onwards and was formalized and regu-larized as a consequence of, and following, the VIENNA CONGRESS (1814–15), which ended the Napoleonic Wars. The basic role of diplomacy is representation of, and rec-onciliation by negotiation between, national interests.

Diplomatic bag Documents and other items may be carried from an embassy abroad to its home government without interference. Under INTERNATIONAL LAW the diplomatic bag should be exempt from customs scrutiny and its contents remain con-fidential. There have, however, been cases of interference by governments, and also cases of abuse by the embassies concerned in which the diplomatic bag has been used for carrying arms or even for kidnap.

Diplomatic immunities and privileges The customary protection and benefits granted to members of a diplomatic mission by the HOST STATE.

Diplomatic recognition See RECOGNITION.

Direct effect A principle that underpins the legal system of the EUROPEAN UNION (EU). By declaring that the ROME TREATY (1957) established individual rights that national courts in the member STATES had to protect, the EUROPEAN COURT OF JUSTICE (ECJ) promulgated the doctrine of direct effect (in the Van Gend en Loos judgment of 1963). The primacy of Community legislation was confirmed in the fol-lowing year in the *Costa* v. *ENEL* case. These rulings transformed the Community's preliminary ruling system (whereby national courts might ask the ECJ for a ruling on a point of EC law) into a mechanism to challenge the compatibility of national law with EC law. Direct effect and supremacy have enabled individuals to involve the ECJ in national policy debates and imposed an obligation for national courts to set aside laws and policies that violate European Community law.

Directive Within the EUROPEAN UNION (EU) a directive is a legislative instrument addressed to member STATES. It is binding with regard to the result to be achieved, but allows the member states flexibility of means to achieve that result.

Directorate-General An organizational unit equivalent to a Civil Service department in the EUROPEAN COMMISSION, COUNCIL OF MINISTERS or EUROPEAN PAR-LIAMENT (EP) Secretariat in the EUROPEAN UNION (EU).

Disarmament A key aim of PEACE MOVEMENTS. The idea of preventing WARS by destroying weapons has become particularly prevalent since the nineteenth century, notably since the Crimean War of 1854–6. This is a consequence of the technological developments of warfare, with the construction of weapons whose sole purpose was mass death and destruction, and of the rising proportion of civilian victims in modern wars. In the period between the two world wars disarmament and peace movements tended to distinguish between general disarmament and weapon-specific disarmament. The latter referred to weapons deemed to be particularly dangerous. With the experience of the First World War in mind, there was particular emphasis on military aircraft, bombing and chemical weapons. Since the 1950s the focal point has been nuclear disarmament. The major problem that arms, once invented, cannot be disinvented has meant that governments have tended to go, in preference, for policies of ARMS CONTROL.

Disarmament decades Since the 1970s the UNITED NATIONS GENERAL ASSEMBLY has habitually named succeeding decades as 'disarmament decades', even though, as early as the 1980s, 'the Second Disarmament Decade', there was a dramatic increase in armaments, not least in WEAPONS OF MASS DESTRUCTION. This is one of several devices of the General Assembly, reflecting the apprehensions of many POWERS, particularly the middle-ranking and smaller ones, for focusing world attention on the need for reducing the burden of armaments and their dangers.

Disengagement The withdrawal of potentially hostile military forces from positions of direct confrontation. For instance, during the COLD WAR almost one hundred plans were put forward in the 1950s and 1960s, of which the best known was the RAPACKI PLAN (1957), for neutralizing and demilitarizing CENTRAL EUROPEAN areas. Supporters of such proposals here, as elsewhere, have argued that disengagement and the establishment of a neutral zone would reduce the threat of a major conflict erupting from border tensions and incidents and could even lead to wider DISARMAMENT. NORTH ATLANTIC TREATY ORGANIZATION (NATO) critics of Soviet proposals claimed they would weaken the forces of the West in Europe and the USSR rebutted Western counter-proposals on the grounds that these would undermine Soviet influence and Communist control in EASTERN EUROPE. In 1989 the IRON CURTAIN was breached and, with the CONVENTIONAL FORCES IN EUROPE (CFE) TREATY of 1990, the Conventional Forces in Europe agreement of two years later and the dissolution of the WARSAW PACT, this situation has dramatically changed.

Disinformation False INTELLIGENCE information or propaganda planted by a government or agency to mislead opposing intelligence services and to shape public opinion. It usually involves the use of double agents and is commonly mixed with enough legitimate intelligence to make the false information believable.

DM See DEMILITARIZED ZONE.

Do-something syndrome The pressure on governments and other agencies, when confronted with grim situations, as for example with the CRISIS and massacres in Bosnia in the 1990s, to try to rectify them. This raises the question of whether, in particular, under pressure from public opinion, outside powers or institutions should intervene or not.

DOD The US Department of Defense.

Dollar diplomacy A phrase that became current during US President Taft's administration (1909–13). It denoted the American Policy of lending to favoured governments to enhance US political and economic influence. This policy was pursued most vigorously in Central America, the Far East and Liberia.

Domestic analogy The comparison between the internal order of STATES and societies and relations between states in the global order. The argument advanced is that international relations could benefit from emulating the internal order of states under a sovereign authority. In his classic analysis of SOVEREIGNTY, the English philosopher Thomas Hobbes (1588–1679) had called for a 'common power' to provide order and security. Absence of government, by contrast, is the defining feature of international society, which has sometimes been described as the 'INTERNATIONAL ANARCHY'. Such an aspiration could only be met by a WORLD GOVERNMENT.

Domestic change agents Those factors and developments within STATES, political, economic, social and cultural, that cause changes within the international system.

Domestic jurisdiction Those matters that fall within the jurisdiction of a STATE and are subject solely to its own law. This is an attribute of national SOVEREIGNTY and equality. Article 2(7) of the UNITED NATIONS CHARTER, for instance, precludes the UNITED NATIONS (UN) from intervening in matters essentially within a state's domestic jurisdiction. The scope of this jurisdiction, however, is increasingly challenged by HUMANITARIAN INTERVENTION, support for the right of SELF-DETERMINATION, or HUMAN RIGHTS. The self-sufficient integrity of domestic jurisdiction is also called into question by greater global INTERDEPENDENCE and worldwide environmental concerns.

Dominion A self-governing territory, formerly with colonial status, enjoying free association with the UK. The word was first used with the designation SOVEREIGNTY in the case of Canada in the British North America Act of 1867. The relationship between the autonomous COMMONWEALTH communities and the UK was clarified in the STATUTE OF WESTMINSTER of 1931.

Domino theory A term derived from the comments made by US President Dwight D. Eisenhower (1890–1969) at a press conference on 7 April 1954 when he gave his reasons for US commitment to a non-communist Vietnam. He declared that, if COMMUNISM was not blocked there, a domino effect would occur: 'You have a row of dominoes. You knock over the first one, and what will happen until the last one is the certainty that it will go over very quickly. So that you have the beginning of a disintegration that could have the most profound influences.' Combined with the theory of CONTAINMENT, the domino theory encouraged the belief that Communism should be resisted at all costs and that negotiations would mean APPEASEMENT. Through the early and middle stages of the COLD WAR, no presidential administration challenged these tenets. They regarded them as a test of US CREDIBILITY in the world and did not wish to be accused of letting any other country – as President Truman's administration had in the case of China in 1949 – be lost to Communism.

Drago Doctrine The proposition that STATES cannot use FORCE in the recovery of debts incurred by other states. It holds that a state's defaulting on its public debt owed to foreigners or another state does not give that state the right to intervene militarily to collect the debt. It is named after the Argentinian foreign minister Luis Drago (1859–1921), who proposed it in 1902 as a consequence of the British–German–Italian naval BLOCKADE of Venezuela, which had defaulted on its debts. The doctrine received immediate support from the USA and the other states of Latin America. The Second HAGUE PEACE CONFERENCE in 1907 discussed the issue and the outcome was Hague Convention III, the so-called Porter Convention, which upheld the Drago Doctrine with the significant stipulation that NON-INTERVENTION need not apply in those cases in which the state refuses to negotiate or abide by an arbitral decision. In 1936 the Pan-American Conference in Buenos Aires adopted the Drago Doctrine as a fundamental principle for the Americas.

Drang nach Osten German for 'drive to the East', a phrase describing the historic area of German expansionism. From the early Middle Ages the boundary between Germans and Slavs had shifted from generation to generation. During the thirteenth and fourteenth centuries the Teutonic Knights had pushed north-east, encouraged by the temporary decline of the Kingdom of Poland. In the eighteenth and nineteenth centuries, when the Turkish Empire was in decline, there were further drives into Poland and the south-east. German expansionism under Kaiser William II (1859–1941) included a proposed railway from Berlin to Baghdad. Hitler (1889–1945) sought *LEBENSRAUM* ('living space') in EASTERN EUROPE to create a vast self-sufficient empire, a 'thousand-year Reich'.

Drawing rights The right of members of the INTERNATIONAL MONETARY FUND (IMF) to acquire foreign currency from the Fund in return for their own, to an extent proportional to the size of their quota. After 1970 these were extended by the creation of Special Drawing Rights, which enabled members to obtain further amounts. Governments use these to settle BALANCE OF PAYMENTS deficits.

Dual-capability system A defence system capable of delivering either CONVENTIONAL WEAPONS or NUCLEAR WEAPONS. These systems may be missiles, aircraft or artillery.

Dual-key system An arrangement by which the USA shares control of a NUCLEAR WEAPONS system with the country in which it is based, or the national military service primarily responsible for operating it. An early example was the DEPLOYMENT of the intermediate ballistic missile Thor in the UK during the late 1950s and early 1960s. Thor missiles were provided by the USA and operated by the RAF, but could not be launched without the consent of both governments. Dual-key authority became an issue in the 1980s in the controversy over the deployment of CRUISE MISSILES, which did not have the system for UK joint control.

Dual-track policy Also known as 'twin-track policy', a policy adopted by the NORTH AMERICAN TREATY ORGANIZATION (NATO) in December 1979 to deploy 572 medium-range missiles under US control in Western Europe, while at the same time seeking bilateral negotiations between the USA and the USSR with a view to fixing an overall ceiling on the number of such missiles deployed by both sides in Europe. There were thus to be two tracks to NATO policy in responding to the targeting of Soviet SS-20 missiles on Western Europe. Deployment of these missiles was scheduled for December 1983. Though arms talks were opened in Geneva on 30 November 1981, failure to reach agreement led to the deployment of CRUISE MISSILES in Europe in 1984. Subsequent discussions brought about the INTERMEDIATE-RANGE NUCLEAR FORCES (INF) TREATY in December 1987, which led to the withdrawal of such missiles from Europe, which was claimed by NATO as a victory for the dual-track approach.

Dumbarton Oaks conference (1944) A meeting of representatives of the USA, the USSR, the UK and Nationalist China in Washington DC between August and October 1944 to draft proposals for the constitution of a general international organization to preserve PEACE after the Second World War, the UNITED NATIONS (UN). Its results, published as 'Proposals for the Establishment of a General International Organization', specified its purposes and membership and the objectives of global peace and SECURITY and the promotion of international economic and social cooperation. Some issues remained to be resolved at the YALTA CONFERENCE (1945), notably the voting procedure on the UNITED NATIONS SECURITY COUNCIL. Dumbarton Oaks, nevertheless, laid the substantive foundation of the UNITED NATIONS CHARTER, which was subsequently adopted at the SAN FRANCISCO CONFERENCE in October 1945.

Dunkirk (1940) Second World War battle and rescue operation. German troops reached the Channel on 20 May 1940, but the advance was temporarily halted on 24 May. The Luftwaffe, the German air force, planned an offensive against the Allied Forces but failed to prevent the rescue of 338,226 people from the northern French beach by vessels of all descriptions by 4 June. Vast quantities of equipment had to be abandoned. Otherwise known as 'Operation Dynamo', the evacuation gave a significant boost to civilian morale and determination. The term 'Dunkirk spirit' is used to describe patriotic resistance.

Dunkirk Treaty (1947) A fifty-year SECURITY pact concluded by Britain and France in 1947 calling for consultation and joint action against any renewal of German AGGRESSION. In 1948 it served as the nucleus for the creation of the BRUSSELS TREATY organization, which expanded the bilateral security guarantee to include Belgium, the Netherlands and Luxembourg. In 1955 the Brussels Treaty organization was renamed the WESTERN EUROPEAN UNION (WEU). Germany and Italy were added as members and the objective of the pact was changed from deterring German aggression to providing for joint action in the event of an attack by the USSR. The WEU led in turn to the expansion of the NORTH ATLANTIC TREATY ORGANIZATION (NATO) through the admission of West Germany.

E

Earth Summit See UNITED NATIONS CONFERENCE ON ENVIRONMENT AND DEVELOPMENT (UNCED) (1992).

East of Suez The policy adopted by the British Labour Government in 1966–7, which greatly reduced Britain's military commitments in the Far East and Southern

Asia. In 1967, a year in which he had to devalue sterling, the Prime Minister Harold Wilson (1916–95) announced that a complete withdrawal east of Suez would take place by the early 1970s, justifying it on grounds of economic necessity. It displeased the USA, which at that time was deeply involved in the VIETNAM WAR (1960–75). It was applied erratically, however. The successor government of Edward Heath (b. 1916) between 1970 and 1974, for instance, deployed forces in Singapore, the Indian Ocean and the Persian Gulf. And subsequently, concentration of British defence resources in Europe and the Atlantic did not preclude interventions elsewhere, as during the GULF WAR of 1991.

Eastern Bloc The former Communist STATES of EASTERN EUROPE, including the member countries of the WARSAW PACT plus Albania and Yugoslavia.

Eastern Europe During the COLD WAR with the division of Europe following the defeat of Nazi Germany in 1945, this term had a political as well as geographical connotation. It meant those countries that fell within the Soviet SPHERE OF INFLUENCE, including the European part of the USSR. In all of these countries single-party Communist government was established. This area, historically, has been dominated by empires with supranational and dynastic ideologies. The territories themselves have contained a mixture of races and religious affiliations and been riven by political particularism. Each STATE, with nineteenth- and twentieth-century demands for SELF-DETERMINATION, as for instance, in Czechoslovakia and Yugoslavia, has had to deal with substantial minorities and with the claims of IRREDENTISM.

Eastern European Mutual Assistance Treaty See WARSAW PACT (1955).

Eastern Front A term used for both world wars to describe the battle front between Germany and Russia/the USSR.

Eastern Question The dominant question in international relations in the nineteenth century, which arose from the many problems caused by the decline of the unreformed Ottoman Turkish Empire, 'the sick man of Europe', and the rivalry of the GREAT POWERS, notably Britain and Russia over this area. The main concern, from the late eighteenth century onwards, was over the threat of Russian expansionism, and fears for the British Empire, particularly India, which led to direct conflict in the Crimean War of 1854–6, in which Russia was defeated by Britain and France. Until the end of the century, when its attention moved to Egypt, Britain sought to bolster the Turkish position as a means of preventing Russia gaining control over Constantinople and the Straits. Instability in the Balkans and growing PANSLAVISM led to Austro-Russian rivalry, which subsequently brought about the First World War and the collapse of the Turkish Empire. The Eastern Question in the traditional sense ended with the emergence of modern Turkey and the LAUSANNE TREATY (1923). The area, nevertheless, remained strategically crucial, as can be seen during the COLD WAR.

East–West conflict A phrase describing the dominant issue of the COLD WAR in international relations between 1945 and 1989, which ranged from proxy wars and dangerous crises to covert competition for influence in the world. The two poles were the USSR and the USA.

EBRD See EUROPEAN BANK FOR RECONSTRUCTION AND DEVELOPMENT.

EC See EUROPEAN COMMUNITY.

ECE See ECONOMIC COMMISSION FOR EUROPE.

ECJ See EUROPEAN COURT OF JUSTICE.

Economic and Monetary Union (EMU) The creation of a common monetary system for the EUROPEAN UNION (EU), including coordination of monetary policies and the creation of the EUROPEAN CENTRAL BANK (ECB) and the adoption of a single currency. The idea of EMU has been on the agenda of the EUROPEAN COMMUNITY/UNION (EC/EU) since the Hague Summit of 1969 and the Werner Report of 1970. In 1979 the intermediate arrangement, the EUROPEAN MONETARY SYSTEM (EMS), was instituted. In 1989 the Delors Report outlined a three-stage sequence for the achievement of full EMU. The TREATY ON EUROPEAN UNION (TEU) (1992) committed the EU to establish full EMU by 1999. Not all EU members have committed themselves to this process by 2002. Britain, for instance, is non-participant. The issue of membership has generated considerable political and economic controversy, not least in Britain. A key issue in this debate has been the question of the further loss of SOVEREIGNTY and subordination to the ECB.

Economic and Social Council (ECOSOC) This is one of the major organs of the UNITED NATIONS (UN), whose purpose is to advance economic and social welfare throughout the world, especially in the developing countries. It directs research, issues reports and coordinates the work of dozens of international agencies in the field.

Economic Commission for Europe (ECE) This body was set up in 1947 by the ECONOMIC AND SOCIAL COUNCIL (ECOSOC) of the UNITED NATIONS (UN) to help revive and strengthen the European economies. Its scope extends also to environmental policies and membership includes Canada and the USA as well as the European countries.

Economic nationalism This is characterized by extensive government control of trade and the subjection of economic matters to overriding considerations of political or military policy. As opposed to a multilateral trading system with a free flow of trade and free CONVERTIBILITY of currencies, economic nationalism involves a nation seeking prosperity or correcting financial disequilibrium by protecting the home market and/or opening up foreign markets through unilateral or bilateral government action. Techniques employed include austerity programmes, barter arrangements, currency depreciation, imposition of quotas and tariffs among other means. Pursuit of economic nationalism has frequently invited and resulted in retaliation by other STATES, as witnessed, dramatically, in the GREAT DEPRESSION of the 1930s.

ECOSOC See ECONOMIC AND SOCIAL COUNCIL.

ECSC See EUROPEAN COAL AND STEEL COMMUNITY.

ECU See EUROPEAN CURRENCY UNIT.

EDC See EUROPEAN DEFENCE COMMUNITY.

EEA See EUROPEAN ECONOMIC AREA.

EEC See EUROPEAN ECONOMIC COMMUNITY.

EEZ See EXCLUSIVE ECONOMIC ZONE.

Effectiveness principle A criterion for diplomatic RECOGNITION, determining whether a new government should be regarded as legitimate by other STATES. This principle argues that, if a new government is able to exercise power within, and maintain it over, the population of a territory, it should be so recognized.

EFTA See EUROPEAN FREE TRADE ASSOCIATION.

EIB See EUROPEAN INVESTMENT BANK.

Eisenhower Doctrine (1957) An elaboration of the US doctrine of CONTAINMENT, formulated by the US SECRETARY OF STATE John Foster Dulles (1888–1959). The President was authorized to provide up to $200 million in economic AID and to despatch forces to any Middle Eastern STATE requesting assistance against 'overt armed aggression from any other nation controlled by international Communism'. In April 1957 the threat of its implementation helped prop up the Jordanian government and in May 1958 5,000 US troops were sent to Lebanon to avert a revolution that did not take place. It was open to the criticism that it confused Arab NATIONALISM with international COMMUNISM, and before the end of 1958 Eisenhower (1890–1969) was emphasizing accommodation with Arab nationalism rather than military intervention as a means of containing the USSR in the Middle East.

ELINT Electronic intelligence.

Elysée The Elysée Palace is the official residence and seat of power at the heart of Paris of the French President.

Elysée Treaty (1963) See TREATY OF FRIENDSHIP.

Empty Chair Crisis The period from June 1965 to January 1966 when France boycotted meetings of the COUNCIL OF MINISTERS of the EUROPEAN COMMUNITIES apart from those dealing with minor or routine business. This was the result of the opposition of the strongly nationalist French President Charles de Gaulle (1890–1970) to proposals that would have strengthened SUPRANATIONALISM in the EUROPEAN COMMUNITY (EC). The argument was resolved by the LUXEMBOURG COMPROMISE, which effectively impeded further political integration until the SINGLE EUROPEAN ACT (SEA) (1987).

EMU See ECONOMIC AND MONETARY UNION.

Encirclement This term was in particular invoked by Wilhelmine Germany in the years leading up to and during the First World War, claiming that Britain, France and Russia, which were joined in the Triple Entente, were blocking its legitimate ambitions. The accusation was first prominently voiced by the German Chancellor Prince Bulow (1849–1929) in a speech to the Reichstag in 1906. After 1918 it featured in the historical debate over responsibility for the war and ARTICLE 231. It has been used in other contexts too – for instance, in the Communist charge of capitalist encirclement from 1918 onwards.

Enclave The territory of one STATE surrounded by the territory of another – for example, the Republic of San Marino enclosed by Italy. The most significant enclave in international relations after 1945 until the reunification of Germany was West Berlin, linked to West Germany and under the occupation of the USA, Britain and France, but situated over 100 miles inside Communist East Germany.

Enigma The enciphering machine for radio transmissions, invented in the 1920s and adopted for military purposes by Germany in the Second World War, being used by all their armed services. This was copied by Polish cryptoanalysts and provided the key to the most important intelligence breakthrough, the British deciphering of ULTRA. This British codebreaking was crucial in the conduct of the war, not least for the Battle of the Atlantic, the Mediterranean campaign and the preparation for D-DAY.

Enlargement The continuing process of accepting new member STATES into the EUROPEAN UNION (EU). The first enlargement to the then EUROPEAN COMMUNITY (EC) was in 1973 with the accession of Britain, Denmark and Eire. During the 1980s Greece, Spain and Portugal joined, and in 1995 Austria, Finland and Sweden. There are a significant number of states waiting to join, not least those in EASTERN EUROPE, previously under the HEGEMONY of the USSR.

Enosis The Greek word for 'union'. The idea of having a greater Hellas, or Greece, including all Greeks under foreign rule was an ancient aspiration. This term has been used specifically after the Second World War to express the wish of Greek Cypriots to be united with Greece. With the Dodecanese islands going to Greece in 1947, only Cyprus remained outside, though 80 per cent of its population were Greek. Between 1955 and 1959 Greek Cypriots in the form of EOKA (acronym for 'National Organization of Cypriot Fighters') mounted a guerrilla war against British authority. The movement only died down with the failed *COUP D'ÉTAT* against Archbishop Makarios III (1913–77), which led to the Turkish invasion of northern Cyprus and the partition of the island. Since the Turkish invasion of Cyprus in 1974 and subsequent occupation of the north-eastern part of the island, the term 'dual enosis' has appeared to define the idea of a Greek part in union with Greece and a Turkish part in union with Turkey.

Entente French for an 'understanding'. The word was used, for instance, to indicate the *RAPPROCHEMENT* between Britain and France in the 1840s and then, when a specific *entente* was signed between those powers in 1904, settling colonial differences. Subsequently, together with Russia, the Triple Entente came into existence. It is to be distinguished from ALLIANCE, in that the latter usually has more formal commitments, while *entente* can be vaguer.

Entente cordiale The name applied to periods of Anglo-French cordiality, common interest and cooperation in foreign affairs. The phrase was coined in the 1840s. It was later of great significance in the period between the Anglo-French Entente of 1904 and the outbreak of the First World War during which Britain, France and Russia formed the Triple Entente, which faced the CENTRAL POWERS during the WAR.

EPC See (1) EUROPEAN POLITICAL COMMUNITY (2) EUROPEAN POLITICAL COOPERATION.

EPU See EUROPEAN PAYMENTS UNION.

Equality of states The doctrine that all STATES are judicially equal and enjoy the same rights and the capacity to exercise them.

ERM See EXCHANGE RATE MECHANISM.

ERP European Recovery Programme (1948–52). See MARSHALL PLAN.

Escalation In modern STRATEGY escalation is an issue both in planning analysis and in actual policy. Using the analogy of a ladder, military strategists think of potential conflict in terms of a series of steps from minimum to maximum exercise of FORCE. A major concern of the period since 1945 has been the potential for the escalation of CONVENTIONAL WAR into nuclear conflict.

ESDI See EUROPEAN SECURITY AND DEFENCE IDENTITY.

Estrada Doctrine Named after Genaro Estrada (1887–1957), Mexican Secretary of Foreign Affairs, who advanced it in 1930. It is otherwise known as the Effectiveness Doctrine. It lays down that a STATE should not apply subjective considerations when it comes to recognizing a new government. It posits that the only test of RECOGNITION should be whether or not the government is in effective control of the machinery of state and the population of the country.

Ethnic cleansing This term gained common currency in the 1990s during the conflict in Yugoslavia to describe the planned, forcible expulsion of populations through terror on grounds of their ethnicity, religion and culture. As in Yugoslavia, this is often accompanied by massacres. Other modern examples include the Nazi HOLOCAUST and the mass extermination in Cambodia in the years 1975–8 by the Khmer Rouge, the persecution of the population of East Timor after 1975, or, again in the 1990s, the GENOCIDE in Rwanda. Though the term is new, the phenomenon is as old as history. It violates every norm of HUMAN RIGHTS. The EUROPEAN CONVENTION ON HUMAN RIGHTS states that 'no one shall be expelled, by means either of an individual or collective measure from the territory of which he (or she) is a national'. Article 4 of Protocol IV also rules that 'collective expulsion of aliens is prohibited'.

Ethnic conflict Conflict between groups that are culturally distinctive but that inhabit the same or adjacent lands. The potential for such conflict exists where populations and territories are not coterminous, as in the lands that previously composed the Austro-Hungarian Empire. Where minorities are denied proper representation or are discriminated against, tensions inevitably arise, with demands for SELF-DETERMINATION sometimes leading to SECESSION. The most dramatic recent manifestations of ethnic conflict have been in the Balkans, in particular the area that was previously Yugoslavia, a multi-ethnic STATE created after the First World War.

Ethnic nationalism See NATIONALISM.

Ethnocracy A government under which ethnic and racial affiliation and not citizenship of the STATE determines the distribution of public resources, rights and privileges. In such a political order the dominant ethnic group uses the state apparatus to push its own interests and claims at the expense of other groups.

EU See EUROPEAN UNION.

EURATOM See EUROPEAN ATOMIC ENERGY COMMUNITY.

Euro The new currency in the EUROPEAN UNION (EU). The decision to call it the Euro was taken by the EUROPEAN COUNCIL in December 1995. It ruled that the currency would be used in daily transactions from the beginning of 2002 at the latest. One Euro would equal one ECU, and the transition from national notes and coins within the Euro-zone, or member STATES accepting the new currency would be completed by the start of July in the same year.

Eurocommunism The name given to the reconstituted COMMUNISM that emerged in particular in the Italian, French and Spanish Communist Parties in the 1970s. It was a response to events in EASTERN EUROPE, DÉTENTE, the SINO-SOVIET SPLIT and the changing nature of the electorate in Western Europe, with rising prosperity and the decline of the old working class. Eurocommunists rejected the Soviet model, renounced Soviet HEGEMONY over the international Communist movement, encouraged internal debate within the Communist Party, advocated reforms rather than revolution, and plural democratic politics as the way to POWER. In Italy the Eurocommunists even attempted what they called a 'historic compromise' with the Christian Democratic Party, which would, if successful, have ended their exclusion from power.

Eurocorps This was created in November 1993 as a Franco-German rapid reaction brigade, based in Baden-Wurttemberg, and became operational in 1995. With 50,000 troops in 2002, it contains additional units from Spain, Belgium and Luxembourg. It illustrates the wish of some members of the EUROPEAN UNION (EU) for greater European DEFENCE INTEGRATION and identity.

Eurogroup The informal association of the defence ministers of European member STATES of the NORTH ATLANTIC TREATY ORGANIZATION (NATO), which meets to review developments and initiatives that are of specifically European concern within the organization and to encourage defence cooperation between these states.

Euromissile A journalistic term from the 1980s used to describe those NUCLEAR MISSILES that were part of nuclear modernization, the key focus of ARMS CONTROL negotiations and the object of considerable controversy and opposition by the PEACE

MOVEMENT, the CRUISE AND PERSHING MISSILES, which were deployed in Western Europe.

Europe à la carte A term used in the EUROPEAN UNION (EU) to describe the selection of policies by member STATES on an optional basis so that there is not completely uniform progress towards INTEGRATION. A good example is the TREATY ON EUROPEAN UNION (TEU) (1992), where Britain opted out of both a firm commitment to EUROPEAN MONETARY UNION (EMU) and the Social Chapter, though later it signed up to the latter.

Europe Agreements These are the Association Agreements (the earliest being signed in 1991) between the EUROPEAN UNION (EU) and the CENTRAL EUROPEAN and EASTERN EUROPEAN STATES. They have reflected both the commitment of the EU to these states because they wish to join it and the desire to assist them with their economic and political transition from COMMUNISM. They have been negotiated by the EUROPEAN COMMISSION under Article 238 of the ROME TREATY (1957), which gives the EU the right to establish with non-member states 'association involving reciprocal rights and obligations, common action and special procedures'.

Europe des patries French for Europe of the nation states. This phrase is commonly associated with the European vision of President Charles de Gaulle (1890–1970), though the phrase was first used by his Prime Minister, Michel Debré (1912–96). In opposing a federal Europe, as advocated by some of the leading figures in the EUROPEAN COMMUNITY (EC), de Gaulle and those who followed him stressed the priority of the nation state and the need for cooperation between the culturally diverse states of Europe in a looser organization. Such a European order was clearly explicit in the French FOUCHET PLAN of 1961.

European Atomic Energy Community (EURATOM) This was established at the same time as the EUROPEAN ECONOMIC COMMUNITY (EEC) to promote the development of nuclear energy for peaceful purposes. After the MERGER TREATY (1965), which took effect in 1967, responsibility for it passed to the EUROPEAN COMMISSION, which can call for the coordination of national atomic programmes and recommend concentration on particular research programmes. It has been charged with creating a COMMON MARKET in nuclear materials, products, investment and expertise, and establishing safety standards. It has not developed its full potential because of past failure in the EUROPEAN COMMUNITY (EC) to develop a common energy and the tendency of member STATES to resort to national solutions for their energy problems.

European Bank for Reconstruction and Development (EBRD) This EUROPEAN COMMUNITY (EC) initiative was approved by the EUROPEAN COUNCIL in December 1989 a month after the fall of the BERLIN WALL. It was set up to assist the economic reconstruction of EASTERN EUROPE in the transition from COMMUNISM. Members include a range of countries outside Europe, including Canada, the USA, Australia, Israel and Japan among others, though the EUROPEAN COMMISSION and the EUROPEAN INVESTMENT BANK (EIB) have a 51 per cent stake in it. Much of its lending has gone to create effective infrastructures for the developing market economies of these post-Communist states.

European Central Bank (ECB) This institution came into operation with the implementation of Stage 3 in the plan for ECONOMIC AND MONETARY UNION (EMU) as laid down by the TREATY ON EUROPEAN UNION (TEU) (1992). It is located in Frankfurt in Germany, is an independent body and is entrusted with responsibility for the monetary policy of the EUROPEAN UNION (EU). Its executive body consists of six people appointed for eight years. The Governing Council, which makes policy, includes the governors of the national central banks as well.

European Coal and Steel Community (ECSC) This was the first EUROPEAN COMMUNITY, established in 1952 to create a COMMON MARKET for the coal and steel industries of France, West Germany, Belgium, Holland, Luxembourg and Italy. It followed the Schuman Plan of 1950 and was placed under the direction of a single authority, the 'High Authority'. It also had a Council of Ministers representing governments, an Assembly and a Court of Justice. The major inspiration behind it was Jean Monnet (1888–1979), who, between 1952 and 1955, was its first President. The ECSC applied the COMMUNITY METHOD and was the first successful example of SECTORAL INTEGRATION, which prepared the way for the subsequent incorporation of other areas of the economy in the EUROPEAN ECONOMIC COMMUNITY (EEC). A decision to merge the executives of the ECSC, the EEC and the EUROPEAN ATOMIC AGENCY COMMUNITY (EURATOM) came into effect on 1 July 1967.

European Commission The highest administrative organ and one of the two executive institutions of the EUROPEAN UNION (EU). It was created to represent the supranational element, collectively to identify and promote the common interest of this regional organization. It produces policy proposals, mediates within the COUNCIL OF MINISTERS, executes the latter's decisions and is guardian of the treaties. The term 'Commission' is used to refer both to the administration in Brussels and to the body of Commissioners. The latter are appointed from the member countries, nominated by governments and appointed by the Council of Ministers. Commissioners are appointed for a four-year renewable term and have to swear an oath of loyalty to the EU, and of independence from any national government or other body. Where decisions are not implemented, the Commission can submit a complaint to the EUROPEAN COURT OF JUSTICE (ECJ). The Commission is also generally responsible for the financial management of the EU.

European Communities There are three European Communities, which collectively are known as the EUROPEAN COMMUNITY (EC) and that form the first PILLAR of the EUROPEAN UNION (EU). They are the EUROPEAN COAL AND STEEL COMMUNITY (ECSC), the EUROPEAN ATOMIC AGENCY COMMUNITY (EURATOM) and the EUROPEAN ECONOMIC COMMUNITY (EEC).

European Community (EC) Since November 1993, when the TREATY ON EUROPEAN UNION (TEU) (1992) or Maastricht Treaty came into effect, the term European Community has been the collective name for the three communities that make up the first PILLAR of the EUROPEAN UNION (EU). The term European Community continues unofficially to refer to the EUROPEAN ECONOMIC COMMUNITY (EEC).

European Convention on Human Rights Its fuller title is the European Convention for the Protection of Human Rights and Fundamental Freedoms. It was the first initiative undertaken by the COUNCIL OF EUROPE. Signed in Rome in November 1950, it came into operation in September 1953. Rather than being a statement of principles, it set down detailed definitions of specific rights. Its watchdog is the associated European Commission of Human Rights, with the ultimate arbiter being the EUROPEAN COURT OF HUMAN RIGHTS. Not all the signatories of the convention have recognized the right of individuals to lodge complaints with the Commission, nor the compulsory jurisdiction of the Court. Observance of its principles has been taken by the Council of Europe as the essential criterion which applicant countries must meet.

European Council The official name for the summit meetings of the heads of state and government of the member STATES of the EUROPEAN UNION (EU). This intergovernmental forum was originally proposed in the early 1970s by the French President Valéry Giscard D'Estaing (b. 1926). It was officially recognized in the SINGLE EUROPEAN ACT (SEA) (1986). From the late 1970s it came to be widened to include the President of the EUROPEAN COMMISSION and the foreign ministers of the member states.

European Court of Human Rights (ECHR) This body, not to be confused with the EUROPEAN COURT OF JUSTICE (ECJ), is the final arbiter of the EUROPEAN CONVENTION ON HUMAN RIGHTS and is elected by the Assembly of the COUNCIL OF EUROPE. Members of the Court serve for nine years. Complaints of violations of HUMAN RIGHTS are referred to it only after the EUROPEAN COMMISSION has examined them and been unable to arrive at a 'friendly settlement'. The Court is based in Strasbourg.

European Court of Justice (ECJ) The judicial court of the EUROPEAN UNION (EU). It is located in Luxembourg and was originally created with the EUROPEAN COAL AND STEEL COMMUNITY (ECSC) in 1952. It gives opinions on international TREATIES to which the EU is a party, handles matters referred from national courts and deals with disputes between the member STATES and the EU, the institutions themselves and individuals and corporate bodies. Its decisions are binding and have precedence over national laws.

European Currency Unit (ECU) This was an artificial currency used to maintain parities and indicate divergencies in the Exchange Rate Mechanism (ERM) of the EUROPEAN MONETARY SYSTEM (EMS), which came into existence in 1979. After the TREATY ON EUROPEAN UNION (TEU) (1992), effective from November 1993, and with the introduction of the ECONOMIC AND MONETARY UNION (EMU), it was replaced by the EURO.

European Defence Community (EDC) An attempt in the early 1950s, suggested by the Pleven Plan, to rearm the West Germans without arming Germany. The idea was a European Army to counter the USSR's superiority in conventional armed strength. After the outbreak of the KOREAN WAR (1950–3), US pressure mounted for the Federal Republic of Germany (FRG) to contribute directly to the defence of Western Europe. At the same time, there was apprehension in Europe at the prospect of German rearmament, which might pose a future threat of revived MILITARISM. The EDC was agreed by France, Germany, Italy and Benelux on 26 May 1952.

It was to have a single defence minister accountable to the European Assembly and the Council of Ministers of the EUROPEAN COAL AND STEEL COMMUNITY (ECSC). In the event, though, it was defeated in the French National Assembly on 30 August 1954, having been the focus of protracted political controversy. In the same October under the Paris agreements Germany was admitted to the NORTH ATLANTIC TREATY ORGAN-IZATION (NATO) and the WESTERN EUROPEAN UNION (WEU), but with guarantees to gain French acceptance. Among them Britain made a formal long-term commitment to the Continent with the BRITISH ARMY OF THE RHINE (BAOR).

European Economic Area (EEA) This comprises the territory of the EURO-PEAN UNION (EU) and the EUROPEAN FREE TRADE ASSOCIATION (EFTA). These organ-izations signed an agreement in 1992 (which came into effect on 1 January 1994) for the free movement of capital, goods, services and workers. EFTA agreed to accept over 80 per cent of the rules relating to the SINGLE MARKET. Switzerland voted by referen-dum not to participate. In January 1995 three of the EFTA members, Austria, Finland and Sweden, joined the EU as full members.

European Economic Community (EEC) This is commonly known as the EUROPEAN COMMUNITY (EC). It was established on 27 March 1957 and came into operation on 1 January 1958, with proposals for INTEGRATION across all economic sec-tors including agriculture, for a CUSTOMS UNION with a common external tariff and development of a common trade policy. Of the three communities, it has been by far the most important.

European Free Trade Association (EFTA) The 'Seven', established when the STOCKHOLM CONVENTION (1959) came into force in 1960, initially included Austria, Britain, Denmark, Norway, Portugal, Sweden and Switzerland, countries that were not at that stage willing or able to join the EUROPEAN ECONOMIC COMMUNITY (EEC). Finland became an associate member in 1961 and Iceland a full member in 1970. It was partly an attempt to broaden the EEC into a more extensive FREE TRADE AREA and was primarily motivated by Britain, which preferred a free trade area arrangement to a CUSTOMS UNION. It planned to eliminate tariffs on most industrial goods within seven years, but, unlike the EEC, it was not to extend to agriculture. In size of market it could not compete with the EEC. By 1995 only Iceland, Norway and Switzerland had not entered the EUROPEAN UNION (EU).

European Investment Bank (EIB) This was established in 1958 as part of the EUROPEAN ECONOMIC COMMUNITY (EEC) under the ROME TREATY of 1957, though with a separate legal identity. Its capital is provided by the member STATES of the EUROPEAN UNION (EU). It finances major regional capital investments within the EU, but also in territories previously colonies of the member STATES. Funds have also been allocated to projects in EASTERN EUROPE.

European Monetary System (EMS) This regulated exchange rate system was established by the EUROPEAN COMMUNITY (EC) in March 1979 to stabilize the currencies of the member STATES and to prepare the way for a common monetary system and a common currency. Its two key elements were the Exchange Rate Mechanism (ERM) and the EUROPEAN CURRENCY UNIT (ECU). It helped to reduce currency fluctuation and bring down inflation in the 1980s, and bringing about a higher degree of cooperation between central banks, though, subsequently, intense currency speculation in 1992–3 disrupted it. Particularly precipitate was the departure of Britain and Italy from the ERM on BLACK WEDNESDAY (16 September 1992). The EMS prepared the way, following the Delors Report and the TREATY ON EUROPEAN UNION (TEU) (1992) for ECONOMIC AND MONETARY UNION (EMU).

European North Atlantic Treaty Organization (European NATO) The European members of the NORTH ATLANTIC TREATY ORGANIZATION (NATO). Of these France has been a partial member since 1966. In discussions of DEFENCE and SECURITY this is normally used in indicating the specifically common concerns of the European members, or 'pillar', which may not necessarily fully be shared by the USA and Canada.

European Parliament (EP) The directly elected assembly of the EUROPEAN UNION (EU), which had its origins in the advisory Assembly of the EUROPEAN COAL AND STEEL COMMUNITY (ECSC). Direct elections were introduced in 1979 to take place on a quinquennial basis and with seats allocated according to national populations. It has been charged with supervising the EUROPEAN COMMISSION and the COUNCIL OF MINISTERS and with participating in the budgetary and legislative processes. Its plenary sessions are held in Strasbourg, though most of its committees convene in Brussels.

European Payments Union (EPU) This was established in September 1950 in association with the MARSHALL PLAN under the auspices of the Organization for European Economic Cooperation (OEEC), which preceded the ORGANIZATION FOR ECONOMIC COOPERATION AND DEVELOPMENT (OECD), to facilitate credits for trade and transfers of funds between the central banks of sixteen West European countries. It helped with the reconstruction and revival of war-damaged economies, in particular by easing problems over BALANCE OF PAYMENTS and exchange controls. It also provided the countries concerned with good experience in cooperation. It was dismantled in December 1958 with the introduction of full currency CONVERTIBILITY, to be replaced by the European Monetary Agreement.

European Political Community (EPC) The proposal of the French Premier René Pleven (1901–93) for a EUROPEAN DEFENCE COMMUNITY (EDC) was accompanied by the idea of a political authority, the EPC, to oversee it. The second proposal was drafted by the Assembly of EUROPEAN COAL AND STEEL COMMUNITY (ECSC), and, if it had come into effect, would have had significant implications for the SIX, not least in respect of national SOVEREIGNTY. In the event it failed to materialize, together with the rejection of the EDC by the French National Assembly in August 1954.

European Political Cooperation (EPC) The predecessor to the COMMON FOREIGN AND SECURITY POLICY (CFSP) of the EUROPEAN UNION (EU), the EPC reflected the efforts of EUROPEAN COMMUNITY (EC) members from the early 1970s further to advance West European INTEGRATION and to strengthen the collective Community identity in world affairs. In October 1970 it adopted the Davignon Report calling for greater foreign policy cooperation and coordination between the member STATES. It had the most success in presenting EC foreign policy in other international fora such as the UNITED NATIONS (UN). It was brought under the aegis of the ROME TREATY (1957) in Title III of the SINGLE EUROPEAN ACT (SEA) (1986), which amended that Treaty. The weakness of the EPC, as an inter-governmental body with discordant voices, became very obvious during the GULF WAR (1991).

European Recovery Programme (ERP) (1948–52). See MARSHALL PLAN.

European Security and Defence Identity (ESDI) The TREATY ON EUROPEAN UNION (TEU) (1992) included ESDI and suggested that it should involve a revived WESTERN EUROPEAN UNION (WEU) linked to the COMMON FOREIGN AND SECURITY POLICY (CFSP) of the EUROPEAN UNION (EU). The idea of such an identity raises crucially the issue of its relation to the NORTH ATLANTIC TREATY ORGANIZATION (NATO), and more particularly, of continuing US commitment to European DEFENCE and SECURITY. In 1994 NATO gave its support to the strengthening of the European pillar of the Alliance with the WEU and the EU as its main elements, and to the idea that the European allies would be able to take more responsibility for managing their security and defence.

European Union Originally the heart of this was the COMMON MARKET, or EUROPEAN ECONOMIC COMMUNITY (EEC), set up by the ROME TREATY (1957) for France, Germany, Italy, Belgium, the Netherlands and Luxembourg. In 2002 this consists of fifteen states, with the accession of Britain, Denmark and Eire (1973), Greece (1981), Spain and Portugal (1986) and Austria, Finland and Sweden (1995). In 1980 it became known as the EUROPEAN COMMUNITY (EC). In fact, it began with three 'communities': the EUROPEAN COAL AND STEEL COMMUNITY (ECSC) (1952) and, founded concurrently with the EEC, the EUROPEAN ATOMIC AGENCY (EURATOM), in addition to the EEC. The title of this major regional organization and ACTOR in world affairs was changed to EUROPEAN UNION (EU) in November 1993 as a consequence of the RATIFICATION of the TREATY ON EUROPEAN UNION (TEU) (1992). The Rome Treaty committed the EEC to 'ever closer union'. As a concept rather than a title, the term 'European Union' has been frequently invoked, but with different interpretations, from full eventual political INTEGRATION to something much looser. The term has been associated with specific initiatives, such as the Draft Treaty on European Union of 1984, and used simply rhetorically. The EU, with its three 'pillars', is preparing for the accession of a number of other STATES.

Eurosclerosis This term came into use in the late 1970s and 1980s to describe the growing uncompetitiveness in the global economy of the EUROPEAN COMMUNITY (EC), with stagnation, inflation and sharply rising unemployment, and also the slowing of momentum towards greater European INTEGRATION. The background to this was the OIL CRISES following the YOM KIPPUR WAR (1973) and the Iranian Revolution (1979). The member STATES had reacted individually and in a protectionist way, rather than collectively, to the consequences of the dramatic rise in the cost of oil. A key response to Eurosclerosis in the 1980s was the commitment to the SINGLE MARKET with the elimination of NON-TARIFF BARRIERS (NTBS).

Ex aequo et bono Latin for 'on the basis of fairness and justice'. Article 38 of the State of the INTERNATIONAL COURT OF JUSTICE (ICJ) rules that a decision may be

reached in a case on these grounds rather than strictly by reference to what is laid down in TREATIES and customs. However, the tribunal can reach a decision on this basis only if the parties concerned agree to it. STATES are rarely willing to surrender such powers of deliberation to an international tribunal.

Exchange Rate Mechanism (ERM) See EUROPEAN MONETARY SYSTEM (EMS).

Exchange rates The system by which the currency of one country is convertible at an agreed rate of exchange into currencies of other countries. Between 1945 and 1971 the exchange rates between West European countries, for instance, were regulated by the BRETTON WOODS CONFERENCE.

Exclave An exclave is usually a relatively small part of a STATE, administratively part of it, but separated from it by the territory of another state.

Exclusive economic zone (EEZ) A coastal STATE's adjacent maritime area, usually 200 nautical miles in breadth, over which the state claims exclusive right to the economic resources, with powers relating to pollution, control and freedom of passage and overflight.

Executive agreement An obligation based on agreement between heads of government and/or STATE without legislative sanction. For instance, in the USA this is if the President or his representative makes an agreement without RATIFICATION by Senate. Examples of executive agreements are those that were reached by the BIG THREE at the YALTA CONFERENCE in 1945. A series of congressional hearings in the late 1960s and 1970s revealed the existence of a whole number of executive agreements involving DEFENCE and INTELLIGENCE operations that had been concluded on executive authority and been kept quiet.

Expatriation The deprivation by a STATE of the rights of citizenship vis-à-vis certain groups or classes of its citizens, or individuals. Though such citizens lose their rights under municipal law (that is, the law of their own country), they remain nations of their home STATE for purposes of INTERNATIONAL LAW.

Export of revolution This phrase was commonly used during the COLD WAR by the West in accusing Communist regimes, particularly those of the USSR and China, of instigating and encouraging revolutionary movements and subversion in the non-Communist world. Earlier Leon Trotsky (1879–1940), with his doctrine of permanent revolution, had been the most prominent advocate of, and believer in, the spread of Communist revolution. From the 1960s Cuba in particular was also accused by the USA of participating in attempts to overthrow governments in Latin America. An implicit, though not usually observed, condition of PEACEFUL COEXISTENCE was that the SUPERPOWERS should desist from exporting revolution or, on the Western side, counter-revolution.

Extended deterrence A nuclear STRATEGY term from the COLD WAR. It means where one nuclear power deters attacks not only against itself but also against its allies. The term NUCLEAR UMBRELLA was frequently used to describe it in relation to the NORTH ATLANTIC TREATY ORGANIZATION (NATO). In other words, an attack by the Soviet Union and its allies in the WARSAW PACT against Western Europe could have led to central strategic warfare between the USA and the USSR.

Extra-territoriality The process, common in the nineteenth century, but rare today, where the subjects or citizens of one country are exempt from the legal jurisdiction of the country in which they are living. Based on international custom and treaty provision, it was applied most frequently in China. Since the Second World War the USA and most European STATES have abandoned it. Today the term is used primarily to refer to DIPLOMATIC IMMUNITY, the exclusion of the territory occupied by a foreign agency/embassy from the jurisdiction of the state where it is located. It is also used to define the jurisdictional position of the armed forces of one state present in the territory of an ally, as with NORTH ATLANTIC TREATY ORGANIZATION (NATO) STATUS OF FORCES AGREEMENTS (SOFAS).

Extradition The judicial, or in some cases administrative, procedure by which a fugitive from justice found in one STATE is delivered to the state where the violation occurred. It is initiated by a formal request from one state to another and is governed by the specific obligations of extradition TREATIES. Where surrender of a fugitive takes place in the absence of such a treaty, it is called rendition. Normally the offence must satisfy the criterion of 'double criminality' – that is, a crime in both states. Very often states are not willing to extradite for political offences.

Eyeball to eyeball A phrase from the COLD WAR describing the highest level of international tension between the SUPERPOWERS with the clear possibility of the outbreak of all-out war. It originated with the most dramatic confrontation of the post-war years, the CUBAN MISSILE CRISIS (1962). During this the US SECRETARY OF STATE Dean Rusk (1909–94) commented: 'We're eyeball to eyeball and I think the other fella just blinked.'

F

Failed nation state This term is used to describe those STATES that are unstable, riven by ETHNIC CONFLICT and unable to provide SECURITY and other basic necessities for their peoples. It features most commonly in relation to such states in the THIRD WORLD, for instance, in sub-Saharan Africa. In the 1990s, though, the failed nation state that attracted most international attention was Yugoslavia.

Fait accompli In international relations an act by one or several STATES that creates a new situation vis-à-vis another state or group of states. Following a *fait accompli*, the other state finds its options reduced to doing nothing or reacting to the altered situation. Hence it can produce a situation of considerable risk and important consequences. Both Hitler's invasion of the RHINELAND in 1936 and the construction of the BERLIN WALL by the German Democratic Republic (GDR) in 1961 confronted Western powers with a *fait accompli*. The Soviet introduction of nuclear missiles into Cuba in 1962 presented the USA with a *fait accompli*, which, nevertheless, in the outcome of the CUBAN MISSILE CRISIS (1962) was reversed.

Falklands War (1982) This followed the capture of the South Atlantic Falkland Islands (in Spanish 'Las Islas Malvinas') and South Georgia on 2 April 1982 by Argentina. Britain has occupied the islands continuously since 1833, defending its possession on grounds of SOVEREIGNTY (contested by Argentina) and on those of the SELF-DETERMINATION of the inhabitants who wish to remain under the British flag. In 1965 the UNITED NATIONS (UN) had appealed in Resolution 2065 for a peaceful settlement of the sovereignty dispute, but protracted negotiations were stalled over the issue of the wishes of the islanders. The Argentinian JUNTA under General Galtieri (b. 1926) had calculated because of the British announcement of naval cuts, including the Endurance in South Atlantic waters, that the government of Mrs Thatcher (b. 1925) would not resist an invasion and that the USA, which had been assisted by Argentina against the Sandinistas in Nicaragua, would at least remain neutral. In the event, the USA led the UNITED NATIONS SECURITY COUNCIL in passing a resolution for immediate Argentinian withdrawal and the EUROPEAN COMMUNITY (EC) imposed SANCTIONS. The USA attempted to resolve the CRISIS with the SHUTTLE DIPLOMACY of SECRETARY OF STATE Alexander Haig (b. 1924) but sided with Britain with invaluable INTELLIGENCE and material support. At the same, Britain had despatched an armada, the Taskforce, to retake the islands. The Argentinian forces surrendered on 14 June 1982 and the Junta subsequently fell from POWER, replaced by a freely elected government.

Fascism An authoritarian revolutionary ideology that emerged in the early twentieth century, originally came to prominence in Italy and, then, in a more extreme and racialist version, in Nazi Germany. The term came from *fasces*, the insignia of the consuls of ancient Rome. Fascism was present elsewhere in Europe to a greater or lesser degree. Its characteristics were extreme NATIONALISM, MILITARISM, RACISM, IMPERIALISM, anti-Communism, the rejection of liberal individualism and democracy, strong emphasis on the role of the leader (in Germany the *Führerprinzip*) and economic AUTARKY. With this went an out-and-out rejection of INTERNATIONALISM and PACIFISM. Since the end of the Second World War the term FASCIST has been used widely and often unspecifically as a pejorative. However, there have been a number of postwar movements both in Western Europe and, after 1989, in EASTERN EUROPE that have been referred to as 'neo-Fascist', in which extreme nationalism, XENOPHOBIA and racialism are the most prominent aspects.

Fatah Arabic word for conquest and the acronym for the Palestine National Liberation Movement. This was the Syrian branch of the PALESTINE LIBERATION ORGANIZATION (PLO), which became the most powerful group in the movement after the SIX DAY WAR (1967). During the 1960s and 1970s it advocated GUERRILLA WARFARE and armed struggle against Israel. Since the 1980s it has also embraced pragmatism and moderation and approved the OSLO ACCORDS (1993).

Fatwa An Islamic legal opinion issued by a Muslim spiritual leader or mufti, on matters domestic or foreign relating to Islamic law.

Fedayeen Arabic for commandos or guerrilla fighters.

Federal Reserve System The system established in the USA in 1913, which is under a Board of Governors in Washington, and carries out the function of a central bank, providing regulatory control over the commercial banks. It comprises twelve federal reserve banks. The system is responsible for currency issue, is lender of last resort and is responsible for monetary management and policy and, in conjunction with the US Treasury, for exchange rate policy and external monetary policy. While its officers are appointed by the US President, the system has generally maintained considerable independence in its policy decisions.

Federalism A federal system of government involves a central or 'federal' government, as in the USA, existing alongside STATE or provincial governments. Its purpose is to reconcile unity and diversity. It may be a description, as of Switzerland, which has twenty-three cantons and three major linguistic groups, French, German and Italian, or an aspiration and potential process, as with those who would like to see the regional economic INTEGRATION of the EUROPEAN UNION (EU) evolve into a full federation. Based on a written constitution, powers are divided between the two tiers of government (not simply delegated down from the centre). Each tier is sovereign in particular fields of responsibility and each tier has its own source of revenue. In addition, a constitutional court must act as arbitrator between the different authorities. The issue of federalism becomes a prominent one in international relations in two sets of circumstances, when, as has happened in, for instance Africa and the Caribbean after DECOLONIZATION, parts have wished to secede, or where an attempt is made to replace a loose CONFEDERATION with a more centralized federation.

Federation See FEDERALISM.

Fifth Column A subversive movement to weaken a government's defensive efforts during a CIVIL WAR or an attack by another nation. The term originated during the SPANISH CIVIL WAR (1936–9), when the rebel Nationalist forces of General Franco (1892–1975) attacked the Loyalists in Madrid with four columns, proclaiming that a fifth existed within the city to aid their cause. The action of the QUISLING group of traitors in Norway during the Nazi attack in 1940 offers an example of the decisive role that a fifth column may play in sabotaging government resistance.

Final Act In DIPLOMACY the document that sums up the work of an international meeting, often including a TREATY or other agreement or principles that the meeting has drafted. An example of this is the Final Act in the HELSINKI ACCORDS (1975).

Finlandization The term expressed the fear during the COLD WAR of Soviet pressure on Western Europe, which would lead the latter increasingly to come under the influence of the USSR. It was based on an analysis of Finnish relations with the USSR, which saw the Finns after the Second World War as trimming their policies and political system to suit the needs of the latter, even by subservient anticipation. The argument of those who used this term tended to be: Finland today; Europe tomorrow. An early usage was with regard to Austria in the early 1950s, where some argued that it would truckle to the USSR in order to regain its unity and formal SOVEREIGNTY. It was also a term used by critics of DÉTENTE in the 1970s.

First Indochina War See INDOCHINA WAR (1946–54).

First-strike capability The ability to launch a successful nuclear attack without fear of MASSIVE RETALIATION. The USA had this capability in the late 1940s and early 1950s, when it had first a monopoly of the ATOMIC BOMB (until August 1949) and then a lead in the production of NUCLEAR WEAPONS and their means of delivery. Subsequent parity between the USA and the USSR was to create the so-called BALANCE OF TERROR.

First Tier A term for those countries that are stable democracies and have wealthy, technologically advanced market-based economies.

First World This term is used, collectively, to describe the advanced industrial countries (AICs) – a UNITED NATIONS (UN) abbreviation for North America, Western Europe, Japan and Australasia. These countries are also referred to as the NORTH.

Five Principles of Peaceful Coexistence These were first specified in an agreement signed by the People's Republic of China and India in April 1954. They were incorporated by the Declaration of the BANDUNG CONFERENCE (1955) and endorsed in the Chinese Constitution of 1975. The principles were: mutual respect for each other's national territory and SOVEREIGNTY, non-aggression, non-interference in each other's internal affairs, equality and mutual benefit and PEACEFUL COEXISTENCE. The idea of peaceful coexistence between East and West was advanced by the Soviet leader Nikita Khrushchev (1894–1971) at the TWENTIETH PARTY CONGRESS of the Communist Party in February 1956.

Flexible response A US military doctrine that argued that the USA should enable its forces to match any act of AGGRESSION from a Communist STATE at an appropriate level of response, from nuclear WAR to COUNTER-INSURGENCY. It replaced the NEW LOOK policy. It was, in particular, adopted by the NORTH ATLANTIC TREATY ORGANIZATION (NATO) from 1967 to replace MASSIVE RETALIATION in the event of a Soviet attack on Western Europe. The background to this was the lack of credibility of massive retaliation and apprehension as to whether the USA would risk a thermonuclear attack on itself for Europe. Flexible response involved the strengthening of conventional forces and the idea of controlled ESCALATION in the event of conflict, with a selective use of NUCLEAR WEAPONS to indicate intent, to be devised by the recently instituted NUCLEAR PLANNING GROUP (NPG).

Floating exchange rate A market-determined exchange rate of a currency that may change continuously as it is not pegged to another currency, or group of currencies, or to gold by a central bank. Under a free or floating exchange rate the rate adjusts itself until the supply and demand for currencies are brought into balance. After the ending of the US dollar standard established by the BRETTON WOODS CONFERENCE (1944) in August 1971, a number of West European currencies, for example, were floated, generating considerable uncertainty in currency markets. The instability in the 1970s among other things encouraged the creation of the EUROPEAN MONETARY SYSTEM (EMS).

Flottenpolitik The expansionist German naval policy introduced by Kaiser William II (1859–1941) and Admiral von Tirpitz (1849–1930) in the 1890s, which precipitated sharp rivalry with Britain and growing pressure on the budgets of both countries. The campaign in Germany for a strong navy to meet the requirements of a growing world power with colonial interests was launched in 1895. The first Navy Law followed in 1898 and a succeeding one, which projected a doubling of the number of battleships by 1916, was passed in 1900. In 1906 Britain began the construction of Dreadnoughts, to be followed by Germany the next year. The navy race became the most visible cause of tension between Britain and Germany in the years leading to the outbreak of the First World War.

Foggy Bottom The nickname of the US STATE DEPARTMENT, which is responsible for foreign relations. It is located in a low-lying foggy area in Washington DC.

Food weapon Sometimes this is referred to as 'food power' or as 'food as a political tool'. This term followed the suggestion in a CENTRAL INTELLIGENCE AGENCY (CIA) report that the agricultural abundance of the USA in 1974, combined with increasing worldwide grain shortages, would give the USA a measure of POWER and influence it had not had before. The food trade was one of the elements, for instance, in negotiating DÉTENTE with the USSR in the 1970s.

Force In international relations this is usually with reference to force of arms, though this is not necessarily the case and may refer to other forms, such as economic force. The UNITED NATIONS CHARTER declares in Article 2 (4): 'All members shall refrain in their international relations from the threat or use of force against the territorial integrity or political independence of any state, or in any other manner inconsistent with the purpose of the United Nations.' International relations have often been described as an 'anarchy' for the reason that there is no global authority capable effectively of outlawing the use of force among STATES.

Force de frappe The original name for the French STRATEGIC NUCLEAR WEAPON, which was first deployed in the form of forty medium-range bombers between 1964 and 1966, during the Presidency of Charles de Gaulle (1890–1970). It was very much emphasized by the President that this was a national WEAPON OF LAST RESORT and was a significant element in his DIPLOMACY. Since then the French have developed a three-part structure of nuclear strategic forces, consisting of air force bombers, land-based INTER-CONTINENTAL BALLISTIC MISSILES (ICBMS) and their SUBMARINE-LAUNCHED BALLISTIC MISSILE (SLBM) fleet.

Force majeure The French for 'greater force'. Used between one power and another in international relations, whether in terms of diplomatic pressure or military threat, it is often cited as the reason why the weaker power cannot fulfil its obligations. The weaker power pleads that it is not in a position to resist.

Formosa Resolution (1955) One of the broadest discretionary grants of war powers made by Congress to a President of the USA, in this case to Dwight D. Eisenhower (1890–1969). The background to this was the COLD WAR CRISIS over Formosa (now Taiwan) between Communist China and the Chinese Nationalists under Jiang Jieshi, the latter based on Formosa. By the end of 1954 Communist China was attacking the Nationalist-controlled islands of Jinmen and Mazu in the Formosa

Straits. The resolution authorized the President 'to employ the armed forces of the United States as he deems necessary' to defend Taiwan and the offshore islands. As a consequence of this, Congress established a powerful precedent, reducing its control over the question of declaring WAR. This pattern was repeated and the EISENHOWER DOCTRINE (for the Middle East) announced in 1957 was echoed in the TONKIN GULF RESOLUTION (1964) during the VIETNAM WAR (1960–75). This authorized the US President to 'take all necessary steps, including the use of armed forces' to prevent further Communist aggression in South East Asia.

Fortress Europe (1) A Second World War Nazi slogan. It was issued as a warning from the autumn of 1942 (as plans for Allied invasion of the Continent matured) that an attack would meet with an impenetrable wall. In 1944–5, the Soviet advance into CENTRAL EUROPE and D-DAY revealed it for the vain boast that it was. Moreover, as US President Franklin Roosevelt (1882–1945) pointed out, with reference to the Allied bombing of Germany, the 'fortress' had no roof. (2) A term used in discussions about the role of the EUROPEAN UNION (EU) in the global economy, to express the fear that, while extending full FREE TRADE within its borders, the EU might follow a policy of PROTECTIONISM externally. This fear was voiced particularly at the time of the creation of the SINGLE MARKET, not least in the USA. A particular focus of controversy has been the COMMON AGRICULTURAL POLICY (CAP).

Forty-Ninth Parallel The boundary between the USA and Canada across more than 3,000 miles, this is the longest undefended frontier in the world. It was formally defined in the Webster–Ashburton Treaty (1842).

Fouchet Plan (1961) This was the draft TREATY for a 'union of states' with which the French President Charles de Gaulle (1890–1970) proposed a coordination of the foreign policies of the SIX under French leadership, while as far as possible retaining national SOVEREIGNTY. Its rejection encouraged the division between France and the other members who wanted to give priority to ENLARGEMENT of the EUROPEAN COMMUNITY (EC), which, for his part, de Gaulle refused. It was an informal grouping in conception rather than federal, expressing the French President's belief in a EUROPE DES PATRIES.

Founding Treaties This is the collective term for the three agreements that established the EUROPEAN COMMUNITY (EC). These are the Paris Treaty (1951) which set up the EUROPEAN COAL AND STEEL COMMUNITY (ECSC) and the two ROME TREATIES of 1957 which respectively established the EUROPEAN ECONOMIC COMMUNITY (EEC) and the EUROPEAN ATOMIC ENERGY COMMUNITY (EURATOM).

Four Freedoms (1) The Second World War proclamation by US President Franklin D. Roosevelt (1882–1945) in the course of his Annual Message to Congress in 1941, rallying the American people against accepting what he called a 'dictator's peace'. These were followed by the ATLANTIC CHARTER in August 1941. The freedoms were: (1) of speech and expression, everywhere in the world; (2) the freedom of every person to worship God in his own way, everywhere in the world; (3) freedom from want, which, 'translated into world terms, means economic understandings that will secure to every nation a healthy peacetime life for its inhabitants everywhere in the world'; 4) freedom from fear, which, translated into world terms, means a worldwide reduction of armaments to such a point and in such a thorough fashion that no nation will be in a position to commit an act of physical aggression against any neighbour anywhere in the world. (2) This term is also used in the EUROPEAN UNION (EU) for the free movement of goods, persons, services and capital as laid down by Article 3 of the ROME TREATY (1957).

Four Policemen Concept

This idea was first advanced by US President Franklin D. Roosevelt (1882–1945) at the TEHRAN CONFERENCE (1943) with reference to a post-war global international organization. As part of such an organization, he proposed that a body composed of the USA, Britain, China and the USSR would police the rest of the world to prevent and combat AGGRESSION. Subsequently this idea came to be assimilated into the UNITED NATIONS (UN), with the select permanent membership of the UNITED NATIONS SECURITY COUNCIL.

Fourteen Points (1918)

The principles announced by US President Woodrow Wilson (1856–1924) to explain the US rationale for entering the First World War and the purposes that should govern the peace settlement and the maintenance of PEACE generally following the war. The Fourteen Points included the call for open DIPLOMACY, FREEDOM OF THE SEAS, DISARMAMENT, removal of economic barriers, international supervision of colonies, peaceful change based on SELF-DETERMINATION and the creation of an association that would guarantee the political independence and territorial integrity of great and small STATES alike. This last objective was to find expression in the LEAGUE OF NATIONS.

Fourth World

A term categorizing the LEAST DEVELOPED NATIONS (LDCS) as a group of those countries needing specially supportive treatment in AID and development projects. Many of the populations that live in the Fourth World live in conditions described by the economists of the INTERNATIONAL BANK FOR RECONSTRUCTION AND DEVELOPMENT (IBRD) (World Bank) as below the income level that provides the bare essentials of food, clothing and shelter. By contrast many countries in the THIRD WORLD have managed continuous economic growth and demonstrated increasing economic viability. Fourth World countries are so impoverished that they are unable to develop the resources and technical capabilities to reach the stage of self-sustaining economic growth. The FIRST WORLD and the THIRD WORLD STATES have concluded a number of arrangements and agreements such as the LOMÉ CONVENTIONS and these provide preferential access to Western markets, but often at the expense of the Fourth World.

France of the East

This description was sometimes applied to Romania during the COLD WAR, particularly in the 1960s on account of its independent stance in foreign policy. Like France, not only is Romania a Romance country, but it also defied the USSR in the COUNCIL FOR MUTUAL ECONOMIC ASSISTANCE (CMEA/COMECON) and the WARSAW PACT, as France, under General de Gaulle (1890–1970) in particular, defied the USA in the NORTH ATLANTIC TREATY ORGANIZATION (NATO). In 1967 France withdrew from the integrated military structure of NATO and in 1968 Romania refused to participate in the Warsaw Pact invasion of Czechoslovakia after the PRAGUE SPRING (1968).

Francophonie A term coined by the President of Senegal Sedar Senghor (b. 1906) to define a cultural community with France of those nations influenced by the French language and culture. The African states of the Organisation Commune Africaine et Mauricienne (OCAM) started to convene conferences, the first taking place in Niger in 1969, with a view to the permanent cooperation among these STATES, then numbering about 300 million people. The hope of the participants was, in part, that such an organization would promote economic and technical aid, but also that it would encourage French language and culture and help to enhance France's role on the international scene.

Free city A city singled out as having its own international statutes governing its relations with the STATE in which it is an ENCLAVE and with other states and international organizations. A well-known example in history is DANZIG (now Gdansk). After the First World War the Allied Powers attempted to resolve the problem of its affiliation to Germany or Poland by granting it the statute of a free city under the LEAGUE OF NATIONS. It later became a *CASUS BELLI* of the Second World War.

Free trade The idea according to which governments should not regulate, tax or otherwise interfere with international commerce, in which there should be no tariffs, subsidies on exports or imports and no quotas or other restrictions. This was advanced in opposition to the earlier policy of MERCANTILISM by Adam Smith (1723–90) in *The Wealth of Nations* (1776) and in *The Principles of Political Economy and Taxation* (1817) by David Ricardo (1772–1823). The major argument put forward in favour of free trade has been that it encourages each country to specialize in the production of those goods in which it has the greatest COMPARATIVE ADVANTAGE. As a policy it can be applied unilaterally or multilaterally. Free trade has always been most strenuously advocated by major countries with trade surpluses, such as Britain in the nineteenth century and the USA in the twentieth. Historically, proponents of free trade have also often argued that it would lead to PEACE and INTERNATIONALISM.

Free trade area A group of independent STATES with FREE TRADE among them, but not necessarily with a joint trade policy for the rest of the world. It must apply to a substantial proportion of trade, but some sectors such as agriculture may be exempted from it. A free trade area is to be distinguished from a CUSTOMS UNION, in that the latter also has a common external tariff (CET).

Free world The term used in the West during the COLD WAR collectively to describe the non-Communist countries of the world.

Free world military forces This term was used to describe those nations, the USA and its allies, that provided assistance to the Republic of Vietnam (South Vietnam) between 1959 and 1975. Forty countries provided military and/or economic aid. At the peak of the conflict the USA contributed 540,000 troops to the conflict.

Freedom of the Seas A customary norm formulated in the seventeenth century by the Dutch jurist Hugo Grotius (1583–1645) in his study *Mare Liberum* (1608) and a subject of the Second Geneva Convention on the High Seas of 1958. It is the principle that the HIGH SEAS, outside TERRITORIAL WATERS, are free and not subject to the SOVEREIGNTY of any STATE. In modern law it is accepted that no part of the High Seas may be appropriated by state or person and that people of all nations have liberty of navigation, of fishing outside countries' exclusive areas, of laying submarine cables and pipelines, and of flying over High Seas. Earlier in the century two important political declarations supported this freedom, the second point of US President Woodrow Wilson's FOURTEEN POINTS (1918), which affirmed freedom of the seas in PEACE and WAR as one of his aims and Article 7 of the ATLANTIC CHARTER (1941), which proclaimed that peace should make the seas free to all.

French Union An association created in 1946 under the Constitution of the French Fourth Republic, which attempted to redefine the relationship between France and its colonies. Black African representatives in the French Constitutional Assembly accepted the Union because it pointed the way to equality before the law and the recognition of indigenous cultures, ending the attempt made under the Third Republic to assimilate the colonized into French culture. The first significant change in the status of colonies came in 1956 with the drafting of the administrative framework that paved the way for the decentralization of powers. By the early 1960s twelve former French colonies had become independent and entered the UNITED NATIONS (UN). In retrospect the French Union marked a transitional phase that allowed the majority of France's African colonists to take a more or less peaceful path to independence, without the violence and horror of the Algerian War.

Friendly fire A contemporary euphemism for casualties accidentally inflicted on military personnel by their own side, or their coalition partners, a hazard not totally avoidable in modern warfare even with clear markings on vehicles.

Friends of the Earth An international environmental pressure group, with many thousands of members worldwide, which was founded in 1969. It has concerned itself with a range of issues such as industrial pollution, the GREENHOUSE EFFECT and alternative sources of energy and has been influential in the GREEN MOVEMENT.

FTA Free trade area.

Fulbright Resolution (1943) A resolution adopted by the US House of Representatives in the middle of the Second World War. It called for the creation of a post-war international organization for the maintenance of world peace. This and a similar Senate resolution indicated US encouragement for the creation of what subsequently emerged as the UNITED NATIONS (UN).

Fulfilment Policy The term used to denote the policy of implementation of the obligations of the VERSAILLES TREATY (1919), as initiated by the German government of the Weimar Republic in 1921 when it attempted to prove to the Allies its capacity for paying REPARATIONS. Within Germany this term was applied as an indictment by the right-wing opposition, which denounced the acceptance of Versailles and subsequently the LOCARNO TREATIES (1925). Prominent among the critics were the Nazis. Critics not only emphasized national pride, but also blamed inflation and economic weakness on the policy.

Functionalism In international relations, a theory of INTEGRATION that argues that, since many problems tend to be worldwide in scope, common social and economic needs lead to the formation of international agencies that encourage further cooperation and progressive evolution of international consensus. The best-known early proponent of functionalism was the economist David Mitrany (1888–1975), whose influential *A Working Peace System* appeared in 1943 as minds were turning towards the construction of a durable post-Second World War international order. The functionalist hope was that enhanced social and economic integration would overcome the objection to supranational institutions and head towards international government in the longer term. Habits of cooperation acquired in economic and social fields could be transferred to growing political integration within the world community. Though the intended scope was global, functionalism, nicknamed 'federalism without tears', found early application in the process of West European integration.

Fundamentalism A word originating in the USA in the 1920s. A fundamentalist movement is one that emphasizes the absolute truth of what are perceived to be fundamental aspects of a religious, or secular political, belief. It is, for instance, used for those who interpret scriptures in a literal way. Increasingly, it has become associated with political movements, conservative, nationalist or radical, and those in which religion and politics, national and international, are closely intertwined, as with ISLAMIC FUNDAMENTALISM.

G

G5 See GROUP OF FIVE.

G7 See GROUP OF SEVEN.

G10 See GROUP OF TEN.

G20 See GROUP OF TWENTY.

G77 See GROUP OF SEVENTY-SEVEN.

Gaither Report (1957) The official name of this US document was 'Deterrence and Survival in the Nuclear Age'. It was prepared for US President Dwight D. Eisenhower (1890–1969) and recognized that the USSR was now a military rival of the first order. It predicted that in two years Soviet INTER-CONTINENTAL BALLISTIC MISSILES (ICBMS) would be able to destroy the whole of the US STRATEGIC AIR COMMAND (SAC). It alerted the President to the possibility of what later became known (though it was a false alarm), as the MISSILE GAP.

Galosh The name given by the NORTH ATLANTIC TREATY ORGANIZATION (NATO) to the Soviet ANTI-BALLISTIC MISSILE (ABM) SYSTEM designed to defend Moscow, which was deployed in the 1960s.

Game theory A branch of mathematics that concentrates on the study of independent decision making and the exercise of rationality in the face of choices. It has been applied to a range of real situations, including ARMED CONFLICT, the ARMS RACE and environmental policy. It can be used in any situation in which there are two or more decision-makers (called 'players'), each with the choice of two or more courses of action, (called 'strategies').

GATT See GENERAL AGREEMENT ON TARIFFS AND TRADE.

Gaullism The ideas associated with Charles de Gaulle (1890–1970), leader of the Free French in the Second World War and founder of the Fifth Republic in 1958, and with those of the Gaullist Party. In French history it has three meanings. Between 1940 and 1945 it described the attitude of those who rejected the ARMISTICE signed with Germany. Between 1946 and 1958 it involved opposition to the Fourth Republic. Thirdly, it means the ideas identified with de Gaulle and those who have declared themselves to be his heirs during the Fifth Republic. De Gaulle envisaged history and international politics in terms of the rivalry of nations and of the primacy of the nation state. To enable France to fulfil its international role, the first imperative was to free it by DECOLONIZATION. The NATION should also be able to guarantee its national independence without resorting to alliances with powers whose interests might not coincide with those of France. In the contemporary world for France this also involved the possession of the independent nuclear FORCE DE FRAPPE. The term has acquired something of a general connotation with reference to NATIONALISM and resistance to the tutelage of the SUPERPOWERS. It has often involved anti-Americanism. In domestic politics it infers a mixture of presidentialism, plebiscitary democracy, strong leadership and a centralized STATE.

Gaza Strip The area along Israel's south-west border and the Mediterranean, and controlled by Israel. The population is substantially Palestinian and the area has been a problematic one in Arab–Israeli relations.

GCHQ See GOVERNMENT COMMUNICATIONS HEADQUARTERS.

GENERAL AGREEMENT ON TARIFFS AND TRADE (GATT) An

agency established in 1947 under the auspices of the UNITED NATIONS (UN) to work out a set of rules for the conduct and growth on international trade and set up a framework for negotiations on the reduction and elimination of trade barriers. Its main objective was to establish non-discrimination. To begin with several areas of trade including agriculture and textiles were excluded, though from 1963 it was agreed to incorporate agriculture, services and copyright. Its principles served as guidelines for a succession of rounds of negotiation, including among others the KENNEDY ROUND (1964–7), the TOKYO ROUND (1973–9) and the URUGUAY ROUND (1986–94). GATT was replaced by the WORLD TRADE ORGANISATION (WTO) as from 1995.

General Assembly See UNITED NATIONS GENERAL ASSEMBLY.

Generalized System of Preferences (GSP) A means by which industrialized STATES agree to aid developing economies. It was first proposed by the UNITED NATIONS CONFERENCE ON TRADE AND DEVELOPMENT (UNCTAD) in 1968 to replace the practice of industrial countries giving preference to exports from only some

developing countries. One of the most important GSPs is that adopted by the
EUROPEAN COMMUNITIES (EC) in 1971 and applied to countries not otherwise formally
associated with the EC. GSPs are of limited value to the extent that these THIRD WORLD
countries gain preference over only a handful of non-European industrialized states.

Geneva Accords (1954) The collective term for the series of agreements on
Indochina at the GENEVA CONFERENCE of 1954. These included a ceasefire for Vietnam
with a provisional demarcation line at roughly 17 degrees north latitude, provisions
for French withdrawal from the South, limitations on the presence of foreign troops
in Vietnam and a prohibition on the entry of new troops. They further specified a
ceasefire and troops withdrawal for Laos and Cambodia, the establishment of an
International Supervisory Commission to implement the ceasefire and provision for
unification elections in Vietnam in July 1956.

Geneva Conference (1954) The GENEVA ACCORDS were the main outcome of
this conference, which met from 8 May to 21 July. Attending were delegates from the
USA, the USSR, the People's Republic of China, Britain, France, India, the Republic of
Vietnam, the Democratic Republic of Vietnam, Laos and Cambodia. The conference
also discussed Korea, but attempts to reach the unification of that country reached an
impasse in June.

Geneva Conference (1961–2) This was called in early 1961 to settle the complexities of the Laos Crisis (1960–2). Delegates from fourteen nations issued an agreement on the Declaration of the Neutrality of Laos. Under a coalition government,
headed by Prince Souvanna Phouma (1901–84), Laos would be a neutral STATE, joining no ALLIANCES, permitting no construction of foreign military bases and separating
itself from the protective guarantees of the SOUTH EAST ASIA TREATY ORGANIZATION
(SEATO). The participants also pledged that any foreign troops would be withdrawn
within seventy-five days. The final declaration was signed on 21 July 1962, guaranteeing the NEUTRALITY of Laos and creating an International Control Commission.

Geneva Conventions (1949) These are four treaties that represent agreements, updates and codifications of international humanitarian law, reflecting the
rule that HUMAN RIGHTS must not be suspended in time of WAR, for the protection of
war victims, including prisoners of war and civilians. Sometimes called the 'Red Cross
Conventions', they were drafted under the aegis of the INTERNATIONAL COMMITTEE OF
THE RED CROSS (ICRC) and approved then by some forty-eight countries on 12 August
1949. Since then most NATIONS have ratified them. They followed earlier Conventions
dating back to 1864. In 1977 further protocols were added relating to non-combatants
and victims of CIVIL WAR.

Geneva Protocol (1924) Its full title was Protocol for the Pacific Settlement of
International Disputes. It was an abortive agreement proposed among the members
of the LEAGUE OF NATIONS in 1924 that the League's Council should submit disputes
to the PERMANENT COURT OF INTERNATIONAL JUSTICE (PCIJ). If the Council could
not agree on whether a dispute was submissible, the matter would be passed to a committee of arbitrators for a binding decision. The Protocol also, significantly, provided
that matters of domestic jurisdiction, formerly outside the LEAGUE OF NATIONS

COVENANT were to be reconciled under Article XI, and that a DISARMAMENT conference would meet in June 1925, after which the other provisions in the protocol would take effect. Intended to strengthen the League, it was nullified when Britain rejected it in March 1925.

Geneva Summit Conference (1955) This reflected the hope, following the death of Stalin (1879–1953) and events indicating a growing mood of conciliation such as the end of the KOREAN WAR (1950–3), the AUSTRIAN STATE TREATY (1955) and the resolution of the Trieste dispute between Italy and Yugoslavia, that East–West relations might be improved by a face-to-face meeting with the Soviet leader's successors. The British Prime Minister Sir Winston Churchill (1874–1965) had, in particular, encouraged the holding of such a meeting. It was held from 18 to 23 July with delegations from the USA, Britain, France and the USSR. They discussed the issue of German reunification, European SECURITY, DISARMAMENT and East–West contacts. A major stumbling block was the Soviet insistence that the NORTH ATLANTIC TREATY ORGANIZATION (NATO) should be dismantled before any agreement on German reunification could be reached. The US President Dwight D. Eisenhower (1890–1969) declared that the USA would never wage aggressive WAR and called for OPEN SKIES aerial reconnaissance. It was followed by a meeting of foreign ministers in the same year in October and November, but this produced deadlock on all issues.

Geneva Summit Conference (1985) Held between 19 and 21 November 1985, this was the first of four summit conferences held between the US President Ronald Reagan (b. 1911) and the Soviet leader Mikhail Gorbachev (b. 1931). The initiative came from the President and was accepted by Gorbachev to strengthen his own political position and to assess the US attitude towards ARMS CONTROL. Both agreed to a future summit, though President Reagan avoided any commitment on arms reduction or the STRATEGIC DEFENSE INITIATIVE (SDI).

Genocide The mass, systematic slaughter of a people, for example, of the Jews by Nazi Germany in the HOLOCAUST (1941–5), of the Armenians by the Ottoman Turks in 1915, during the First World War, of the population of East Timor by the Indonesians, and the massacres in Rwanda. It was the reaction to the Nazi atrocities that prompted the UNITED NATIONS (UN) to adopt the GENOCIDE CONVENTION (1948), as the gravest possible violation of HUMAN RIGHTS.

Genocide Convention (1948) This was largely prompted as a reaction to the HOLOCAUST (1941–5) of the Jews by Nazi Germany. Its full title is the Convention on the Prevention and Punishment of the Crime of Genocide. It defines genocide as 'acts committed with intent to destroy, in whole or in part, a national, ethnic, racial or religious group' and was approved and opened for RATIFICATION by the UNITED NATIONS GENERAL ASSEMBLY. Several charges have been made since then. Among the most flagrant have been the ETHNIC CLEANSING in the former Yugoslavia and the massacres of Tutsis and Hutus in Rwanda and Burundi.

Gentlemen's agreements In international relations, agreements between statesmen and diplomats that are not legally binding but to be performed on the basis of good faith. Because the commitment is only a political one or a moral one, without legally enforceable claim to specific performance, it rests on trust and mutual goodwill alone.

Geopolitics An approach to international relations and foreign policy that stresses the dependency of national policy on geography. Commonly, it is now used to describe political geography considered in terms of the structure of the world. The term was coined by the Swedish political scientist Rudolf Kjellen (1864–1922), who defined the STATE as a 'geographic organism in space'. It has, however, a more controversial aspect. Geopolitics was encouraged by Nazi Germany to legitimate the idea of LEBENSRAUM ('living space'). There its most prominent exponent was Karl Haushofer (1869–1946). Another key figure was the British geographer Sir Halford Mackinder (1869–1947), who had developed the HEARTLAND THEORY at the beginning of the twentieth century, which argued that the power that was able to control the Eurasian land mass would be able to control the world.

Glasboro' Summit (1967) The only summit between leaders of the USA and the USSR between 1961 and 1972. The Soviet Prime Minister Kosygin (1904–80) met US President Johnson (1908–73) on 23 and 25 June shortly after the Arab–Israeli SIX DAY WAR (1967). The major questions on the agenda were the situations in the Middle East and Vietnam, on which the SUPERPOWERS differed, with the USSR calling for Israeli withdrawal from the territories they had just taken over and criticizing the US role in Vietnam. The encounter did not produce any positive effect.

Glasnost A Russian word meaning 'openness' associated particularly with the Soviet leader Mikhail Gorbachev (b. 1931), used by him first in a Party Congress speech in February 1986. He insisted that, if the USSR was to be effectively 'restructured' and made more competitive, the Communist Party and system had to become less bureaucratic and secretive. In international relations this was to involve greater freedom of contact between the USSR and the West, and of expression in the media. It subsequently contributed to the weakening of Gorbachev's authority and the disintegration of the USSR.

Global commons A term used to describe the common resources of the environment, and across the world, that are shared by populations. They included the oceans, major rivers, forests and the Arctic and Antarctic Poles. This term is used in particular when national economic interests result in depletion of valuable resources and destruction of the environment, as with that of parts of the Amazon rainforest, and those concerned with the future of the planet, and its peoples wish to draw attention to the common responsibilities of humanity.

Global governance This is not to be confused with the idea of WORLD GOVERN-MENT, which implies a single authority or FEDERALISM. It means the cooperation of STATES and other agencies or ACTORS in addressing common problems across the world. Examples of issues in which it is appropriate to use this term, among others, are North–South relations, SUSTAINABLE DEVELOPMENT, and HUMANITARIAN INTERVENTION.

Globalism This term, on the one hand, can be used to mean an international approach to an issue in the sense that it is a global problem, for instance, fossil-fuel pollution of the atmosphere. Here it infers that national, inter-state or regional efforts will not be adequate to resolve it. In a second sense it has been and continues to be used to describe the hegemonic influence and outreach of the SUPERPOWERS, involving contrasting world views and INTERVENTION across the globe.

Globalization This term is commonly used, often fairly imprecisely, to denote widespread and far-reaching economic, cultural and social change in the contemporary world. In particular, it describes the interpenetration of economies and decline of national control over them, the move towards a world economy that is no longer based on autonomous national economies, but rather on a consolidated global market place. Finance capital has, in particular, become highly mobile and multinational enterprises move from country to country, aided by deregulation. INTERDEPENDENCE is intensified, with the encouragement of communications, travel and the Internet. There has been a marked move towards REGIONALISM, as with the EUROPEAN UNION (EU). At the same time, political and environmental issues such as HUMAN RIGHTS and nuclear safety are being addressed at the global level.

GNP Gross National Product.

Golan Heights A strip of land between Jordan and Lebanon, thirty miles from Damascus, Syria. Israel occupied these heights in the SIX DAY WAR (1967). On 14 December 1981 the Israel parliament, the KNESSET, passed the Golan Heights Law, which officially formalized the annexation of the area. Israel then built thirty-five settlements there. Syria made the total Israeli withdrawal from the Heights and its return to Syrian SOVEREIGNTY a condition of peace.

Gold standard A currency system in which all money is convertible into gold on demand. This was common in Europe and the USA before the outbreak of war in 1914. It meant keeping a reserve of gold large enough to meet all demands to back the issue of notes. The British return to the gold standard in 1925 was at a too high rate of exchange and the level became unsustainable during the slump of 1929–31, with Britain being forced to abandon it in 1931. Though direct CONVERTIBILITY with gold has been abandoned, the level of reserves in gold still has a part to play underpinning international credit arrangements and individual currencies.

Golden triangle In the EUROPEAN COMMUNITY (EC) and EUROPEAN UNION (EU) this phrase has been used to describe its core, the area including France, Germany and Northern Italy, which before the mid-1970s enjoyed high levels of economic growth, by contrast, for instance, with Britain.

Good neighbour policy This relates to a phase in US–Latin American DIPLOMACY between 1930 and 1945, during the US presidencies of Herbert Hoover (1874–1964) and Franklin Roosevelt (1882–1945). It amounted to a formal renunciation of US INTERVENTION and a call for the recognition of equality among American republics and of their collective and individual responsibilities. Its formal inauguration was the signature by US SECRETARY OF STATE Cordell Hull (1871–1955) in 1933 of the Convention on the Rights and Duties of States. This declared that no STATE had the right to intervene in the affairs of another. The policy was of benefit during the Second World War when most Latin American nations cooperated with US hemispheric DEFENCE measures.

Good offices One of the methods for the peaceful settlement of disputes. In the exercise of good offices a third neutral party offers to be a means of communication between the disputants. This does not involve it in proposing terms for a settlement of the dispute in question.

Gorbachev Doctrine A term coined by the Western media to refer to the new initiatives in cooperation between the SUPERPOWERS in Soviet foreign policy under the last Soviet leader, Mikhail Gorbachev (b. 1931). His reappraisal of policy led to the INTERMEDIATE-RANGE NUCLEAR FORCES (INF) TREATY, withdrawal of Soviet forces from Afghanistan, liberalization in EASTERN EUROPE, with the abandonment of the BREZHNEV DOCTRINE and essential agreement with the West in the GULF WAR (1991).

Government Communications Headquarters (GCHQ) The British electronics intelligence agency, based in Cheltenham, Gloucestershire, which works closely with the US NATIONAL SECURITY AGENCY (NSA). This partnership was formally established in 1947 with the British exchange of ENIGMA intelligence in return for US electronic intelligence. The British operation has been directly responsible for monitoring radio and telegraph, telex and telephone traffic to and from Britain, China, the Middle East and Australasia. In addition to monitoring electronic traffic, the staff also develops and breaks codes and works on new methods of electronic surveillance.

Government-in-exile A government established outside its territory, as, for instance, among other examples, the Polish Government-in-exile in London during the Second World War. Such a government may have been the *de jure* government of a country from which it has had to flee, or been expelled, with its removal being regarded as temporary, or it may be created as a new government. In the second case, the government-in-exile must be recognized by other STATES before it has the proper authority to represent the state. As such it is anticipating that one day it will become *de facto* and *de jure* the government of the state.

Governor-General The Head of State in the nations of the COMMONWEALTH, excepting Britain. They are proxies of the British monarch and are guided by the conventions of constitutional monarchy.

GPU The Russian acronym for Chief Political Directorate. It replaced CHEKA and in 1923 was renamed OGPU (Unified Chief Political Directorate). In 1926 Stalin (1879–1953) began to use the secret police against his inner-party opposition, leading to arrests, imprisonment and executions. In 1934 it was renamed the NKVD, acronym for the People's Commissariat of Internal Affairs.

Graduated deterrence This term is used to describe the maintenance of a defensive posture capable of deterring attack at the level of conventional, tactical nuclear, intermediate-range and strategic nuclear levels. It is closely tied to the policy of FLEXIBLE RESPONSE and is also sometimes used to include DETERRENCE at the political level.

Grand Alliance A description of the far-reaching cooperation between the USA, Britain and the USSR against the AXIS, after the Nazi German invasion of the USSR on 22 June 1941. It involved key summit meetings, large-scale American and British military and economic aid to the USSR. Propaganda in the West emphasized the Russian struggle for freedom against German tyranny and soft-pedalled criticisms of COMMUNISM, while Stalin (1879–1953) dissolved the COMINTERN in May 1943. There were, however, significant tensions between the powers, not least over the SECOND FRONT and developments in EASTERN EUROPE and the Grand Alliance soon broke down in the rivalry of the COLD WAR.

Great Depression The world economic crisis triggered by the Wall Street crash on 24 October 1929, which was followed by the collapse of several major banks. It ended the post-war boom of the 1920s, forced the West off the GOLD STANDARD, created mass unemployment and, with the rise to power of the Nazis, helped to bring about the Second World War.

Great Game Called also the 'Great Game in Asia'. This term was popularized by the English writer Rudyard Kipling (1856–1936) to describe the competition between Russia and Britain over lands such as Afghanistan, lying between their respective colonial territories. During the nineteenth century Russia extended its power further and further into Central and Eastern Asia. Britain wanted to block Russia's expansionist ambitions, for instance, to gain access to the warm-water ports of the Persian Gulf or extend its influence into India. This rivalry and distrust between the leading sea power and the greatest land power developed in the century after the battle of Waterloo (1815) and became one of the most salient aspects of international relations.

Great Leap Forward A disastrous episode, between 1958 and 1960, in the Chinese People's Republic, where the attempt was made to achieve COMMUNISM at one fell swoop through mass mobilization. The attempt was made to rely on the creative enthusiasm of the masses and China's massive supply of manpower as a substitute for the severe lack of capital goods to bring about dramatic increases in both agricultural and industrial production. It produced a major economic and demographic disaster, with mass starvation. Maoist experiments in the countryside, with such initiatives as rural backyard steel furnaces and close planting of rice, helped to produce a famine that cost upwards of thirty million lives.

Great Patriotic War The Soviet and Russian name for the Second World War in the period from 22 June 1941, the Nazi German invasion of the USSR, BARBAROSSA, to 2 September 1945, the defeat of Japan.

Great Powers This classification became popular following the VIENNA CONGRESS (1814–15), which ended the Napoleonic War. In the nineteenth century it included the Austrian Empire, France, Germany, Britain and Russia. After the First World War it consisted of France, Britain, Italy, the USA and Japan. After the Second World War the classification included China, Britain, France, the USA and the USSR, with the last two also described as SUPERPOWERS.

Greater East Asia Co-Prosperity Sphere The idea of Pan-Asianism in Japan dated back to the Meiji period of the nineteenth century, but in November 1938 the Japanese government announced its intention to build a NEW ORDER in East Asia, which would consist of Japan, China and Manchukuo (before the Japanese takeover of 1931–3, Manchuria). This concept was later extended to incorporate other countries in South East Asia; and in August 1940 the Japanese Foreign Minister first spoke of Japan's wish to build a 'Greater East Asia Co-Prosperity Sphere'. This was described as an economically self-sufficient sphere of 'co-existence and co-prosperity' under Japanese leadership. It was envisaged as including the British, Dutch and French colonies in East and South East Asia and was later extended to cover the Philippines. While it was projected as Asia for the Asians, the concept was presented as a justification for Japanese IMPERIALISM.

Green currencies National currencies used in managing the COMMON AGRICULTURAL POLICY (CAP), introduced by the EUROPEAN COMMUNITY (EC) in the late 1960s. In order to preserve the common price structure agreed in 1962 at a time when the fixed exchange rate financial system instituted at the BRETTON WOODS CONFERENCE (1944) was breaking down, when currencies were fluctuating and prices unstable, the EC decided to retain the CAP prices at their original level. These values, expressed in notional currencies, were the green currencies. To effect adjustments the EC introduced a compensation system of Monetary Compensation Awards (MCAs).

Green Line The border of Israel before the SIX DAY WAR (1967). This was drawn on the maps (with a green marker) after the Arab–Israel War of 1948, specifying the areas under Jewish control in Palestine.

Green Movement The protest, which assumed electoral form from the 1970s, against the adverse effects of economic growth and technological modernization. Green issues primarily concern the environment, including climatic change, pollution, nuclear hazards, excessive use of pesticides and so on. Environmental protection, however, has often been part of a broader agenda including DEFENCE policy, the PEACE MOVEMENT and civil rights. By the late 1980s the Greens had secured parliamentary representation in several states, notably West Germany, and in the EUROPEAN PARLIAMENT (EP).

Greenhouse effect The warming of the atmosphere as a result of industrial pollution with the emission of gases that prevent the escape of heat from the earth's surface. The main cause of these emissions are fossil fuels, and scientists and environmental experts have speculated on the impact of climate change with rising sea levels and such a very high proportion of the world population living in coastal regions. A Framework Convention on Climate Change, initiated by the UNITED NATIONS GENERAL ASSEMBLY in 1991, was signed by 153 nations and by the EUROPEAN COMMUNITY (EC) at the UNITED NATIONS CONFERENCE ON ENVIRONMENT AND DEVELOPMENT (UNCED) (1992) (the Earth Summit). It has become a contentious issue in international politics, with countries frequently failing to meet the reduced targets for emissions.

Greenpeace An environmental protest organization, which can be traced back to a group in Vancouver, Canada, in 1969 who launched a campaign of protest against the testing of NUCLEAR WEAPONS over the Aleutian islands. Founded in 1971, it describes itself as 'an independent, campaigning organization, which uses non-violent, creative confrontation to expose global environmental problems, and to force the solutions which are essential to a green and peaceful future'. Its campaigns have covered a range of issues, from pollution to protection of whales, and one of its most memorable involvements has been against French nuclear testing in the Pacific.

GRIT The acronym stands for Gradual and Reciprocated Initiatives in Tension Reduction. It used to describe plans for arms reduction where each side reduces its arsenal by a small amount and urges the other side to do likewise.

Grotian This refers to the views and influence of the Dutch jurist Hugo Grotius (1583–1645), one of the most important figures in the development of INTERNATIONAL LAW. He was the author, among other things, of *De Iure Belli ac Pacis* (1625) and argued, against contemporary sceptics, that there could be universal moral standards that might be applied in judging the rights and wrongs of international conflicts. He stressed two fundamental principles. Self-preservation was always legitimate. Injury inflicted wantonly (not in self-defence) was always illegitimate.

Grosse Politik An abbreviation of *Die grosse Politik der Europäischen Kabinette 1871–1914*, a collection of diplomatic records from the German Foreign Ministry (Auswärtiges Amt). The collection appeared from 1922 to 1927 and was the first official comprehensive publication of documents by the government of a GREAT POWER covering the period from the foundation of the German Empire to the outbreak of the First World War. It provided material for research on the question of responsibility for the outbreak of the war, which had been provoked by ARTICLE 231.

Ground burst The detonation of a nuclear device at, or below, ground level.

Group of Five (G5) The following leading industrial countries: the USA, Britain, France, the Federal Republic of Germany (FRG) and Japan.

Group of Seven (G7) The seven leading industrial nations, the USA, Japan, Germany, France, Britain, Italy and Canada, which from the 1980s have met on a regular basis to discuss common economic problems.

Group of Seventy-Seven (G77) A lobby group of the LESS DEVELOPED COUNTRIES (LDCS), which presses for changes in the international order.

Group of Ten (G10) Belgium, Canada, France, the Federal Republic of Germany (FRG), Italy, Japan, the Netherlands, Sweden, Britain and the USA, which meet to discuss international monetary arrangements.

Group of Twenty (G20) The Group of Ten plus Argentina, Australia, Brazil, India, Indonesia, Iraq, Morocco, Mexico, Switzerland and Zaire, a grouping established by the INTERNATIONAL MONETARY FUND (IMF) to recommend improvements to its operations.

GSP See GENERALIZED SYSTEM OF PREFERENCES.

Guerrilla warfare Irregular warfare, fought by small bands against an invading army or in rebellion against an established government. The success of such warfare largely depends on the support the fighters receive from the local population, in providing food and havens and supplies and not cooperating with the anti-guerrilla forces. An outside source of supply is often the key to success and a major strategy for anti-guerrilla forces is to cut off these lines. A major example of successful guerrilla warfare was the WAR in Vietnam in the 1960s and 1970s, where Vietcong guerrillas, later joined by regular forces from North Vietnam, eventually gained the upper hand over the forces of the Republic of Vietnam, the USA and allied states.

Gulf War (1991) Sometimes called the 'Second Gulf War' to distinguish it from the previous long Iraq–Iran conflict, this followed the invasion of Kuwait by Iraqi forces on 2 August 1990. The USA and Britain immediately demanded Iraq's withdrawal and obtained strong international backing as reflected in a series of resolutions by the UNITED NATIONS SECURITY COUNCIL. Resolution 678 authorized the use of FORCE and coalition forces, of which the US military formed by far the largest contingent, launched a successful counter-attack from 17 January 1991, consisting of a forty-day air campaign followed by a four-day land campaign. This was the first major military conflict in the post-COLD WAR period, as it was not obstructed by the USSR. The key considerations for the coalition were the potential threat of the Iraqi ruler Saddam Hussein (b. 1937) to the SECURITY of Saudi Arabia and the Gulf Region. Subsequently, stringent SANCTIONS have been maintained against Iraq and anti-government revolts were repressed by Saddam, with Iraq continuing to be considered a major ROGUE STATE. The war, in addition to numerous casualties on the Iraqi side, also saw the displacement of two million people in the region and devastating environmental damage.

Gunboat diplomacy The use, or threat of the use, of naval FORCE to obtain concessions. The history, in particular, of the British Navy, which was the dominant marine force in the nineteenth century, provides many examples. The most famous of these is the Don Pacifico incident (1850), in which Lord Palmerston (1784–1865) threatened to bombard Athens if compensation were not paid to a Gilbraltarian merchant who was a British citizen.

Gymnich Meetings Informal meetings of the foreign ministers of the member STATES of the EUROPEAN UNION (EU), which are held once during each Council Presidency (each Presidency lasting six months). They are named after the first such meeting held in 1973 under the Presidency of Germany in 1973.

H

Hague Peace Conferences (1899, 1907) These were convened at a time of significant rearmament on the part of the GREAT POWERS by the Tsar of Russia Nicholas II (1868–1918). The first conference, attended by twenty-six STATES, concluded an agreement on ARMS CONTROL and other measures for maintaining PEACE. It codified international ARBITRATION procedures into its Convention for the Pacific Settlement of International Disputes (later revised in the Second Hague Conference) and established the PERMANENT COURT OF ARBITRATION. It also codified many of the accepted practices of land warfare. Forty-four states participated in the Second Conference, which sought conventions on the PACIFIC SETTLEMENT OF DISPUTES and other issues. It revised the 1899 convention concerning the rights and duties of belligerents and of neutral states and persons. It failed, however, to achieve its ambition of reducing arms levels. The Second Conference was notable for significantly increased participation by the smaller states and by non-European countries.

Hallstein Doctrine The policy of the Federal Republic of German (FRG) (West Germany) of withholding diplomatic relations from STATES that recognized the German Democratic Republic (GDR) (Communist East Germany), with the exception of the USSR. It was named after Walter Hallstein (1901–82), the State Secretary in the West German Foreign Ministry under Chancellor Adenauer (1876–1967), who was later to become the first President of the EUROPEAN COMMISSION, and was announced in 1955 with a view to isolating the GDR. It reflected Adenauer's priority of binding West Germany economically and in terms of security to the West over the commitment to German reunification. The policy persuaded a significant number of THIRD WORLD countries to boycott the GDR. After a decade the doctrine was becoming obsolescent and inconvenient for the FRG. Chancellor Kiesinger (1904–88) indicated that he was prepared to accept *DE FACTO* RECOGNITION of the regime of the GDR, thereby giving the GDR some diplomatic LEGITIMACY, and proceeded to recognize Czechoslovakia and Yugoslavia in 1967 and 1968 respectively. The Hallstein Doctrine was finally discarded in the *RAPPROCHEMENT* of West Germany with EASTERN EUROPE under Chancellor Willy Brandt (1913–92), the so-called *OSTPOLITIK*, in particular in the Basic Treaty (*Grundvertrag*) of 1972.

Hamas The Arabic acronym for the 'Islamic Resistance Movement'. This is a non-state revolutionary group devoted to the destruction of the State of Israel and the creation of an Islamic Palestinian STATE. Though Hamas is a separate organization from the PALESTINE LIBERATION ORGANIZATION (PLO), it sought to cooperate with other Palestinian groups conducting the INTIFADA uprising that began in December 1987. Hamas regards the entire territory of the former Palestine MANDATE as 'an inviolable Islamic trust' and rejects the idea of a secular state altogether.

Hard currency A currency that has a continuous high level of demand relative to supply in the foreign exchange markets. Currencies of stable industrialized countries can usually be included. Such currencies retain a high value, usually because of favourable balance of payments, such as with the Swiss Franc. They are used widely for the financing of international trade, a prime example being the US Dollar.

Harmel Report (1967) A paper commissioned by the NORTH ATLANTIC TREATY ORGANIZATION (NATO), named after the Belgian Foreign Minister Pierre Harmel (b. 1911), with the title 'The Future Tasks of the Alliance'. Adopted in December 1967, it reflected significant rethinking of the role of NATO in the light of the DEFENCE and SECURITY challenges of the 1960s. The report proposed that NATO combine DETERRENCE with DÉTENTE in its relations with the USSR and its allies and committed it to attempting to achieve a more stable relationship that would assist in resolving political issues between NATO and the WARSAW PACT.

Harmonization In international relations, close coordination where STATES agree to achieve greater conformity in their policies. Normally states agree to this in specific areas. Where institutions are created to supervise this process, they are often international rather than supranational. Harmonization ought to be distinguished from INTEGRATION, though it may lead to it. Examples of agents of harmonization are those bodies such as the ORGANIZATION OF ECONOMIC COOPERATION AND DEVELOPMENT (OECD) after the Second World War that attempted to bring about economic recovery on a regional basis by encouraging FREE TRADE and CONVERTIBILITY.

Havana Charter (1948) The agreement that set up the International Trade Organization (ITO) in 1947–8. It sought to promote balanced economic growth by the abolition of exchange controls, trade barriers (with the exception of protection for infant industries) and discrimination. It advocated full employment throughout the world and was signed by most Western countries (though Czechoslovakia was the only East European country to do so). All signatories had to grant MOST-FAVOURED-NATION (MFN) STATUS to the others.

Haves and Have-Nots 'There are in the world two families only, the Haves and the Have-nots.' This famous comment by the Spanish writer Cervantes (1547–1616) is used to describe the disparity between STATES and populations, for instance between the industrialized NORTH and the SOUTH. E. H. Carr (1892–1982) in his book *The Twenty Years' Crisis* on inter-war international relations discussed the Haves and Have-Nots in the context of peaceful change and the relations between STATUS QUO powers and the REVISIONISM of other powers.

Hawks and doves Terms from the COLD WAR, describing respectively those who favour forceful actions and words and those who take a softer line. The 'hawks', for instance, during the CUBAN MISSILE CRISIS (1962), wanted to take immediate military action against Cuba and the Soviet missile emplacements there. The terms originated in the USA and have international currency.

HD See HUMAN DIMENSION.

Heartland Theory The theory in GEOPOLITICS developed by the British geographer Sir Halford Mackinder (1869–1947), originally in his paper 'The Geographical Pivot of History' (1904), that the STATE that could control the human and physical resources of the Eurasian land mass between Germany and central Siberia would be in a position to control the world. The theory emerged from his detailed study of the relationship between land and sea power. He expressed his idea in this way: 'Who rules East Europe commands the Heartland. Who rules the Heartland commands the World Island. Who rules the World Island commands the World.' This theory was widely interpreted as a rationalization and justification for the traditional British policy of preserving a BALANCE OF POWER in Europe and resisting German or Russian ambitions for HEGEMONY there. The idea endured to influence the Western policy of CONTAINMENT of Soviet and Communist expansion during the COLD WAR.

Hearts and minds This phrase was coined by Sir Gerald Templer (1898–1979) during the British colonial Malaysian Emergency of 1948–60 to express the essence of COUNTER-INSURGENCY. Templer expressed it as follows: 'The shooting side of the business is only 25 per cent of the trouble and the other 75 per cent lies in getting the people of the country behind us.' He argued that the authorities should not only provide the population with protection from intimidation by the insurgents, but also provide them with positive reasons for supporting the authorities rather than the insurgents.

Hegemonial Stability Theory A theory that was developed in the 1970s in the USA and that argued that stable regimes depend upon a hegemonial power to establish rules. This particularly relates to the stability of international economic relations, and the need for a HEGEMONY to sustain a liberal world economic order. It is argued that other STATES rely on the hegemonial power not being effectively challenged by powers that wish to upset the STATUS QUO. The most obvious examples of such hegemonial stabilizers are the PAX BRITANNICA in the period of FREE TRADE and the USA between the end of the Second World War and the breakdown of the arrangement established at the BRETTON WOODS CONFERENCE (1944) in 1971.

Hegemony In international relations the extension by a STATE of preponderant influence or control over another state or states. It is a term found in Thucydides' fifth-century BC *History of the Peloponnesian War*. Study of hegemonies helps to explain the relations between dominant states and their clients or satellites, the creation of SPHERES OF INFLUENCE, and stability, or upheaval, in the WORLD ORDER. Interest in hegemony has been particularly stimulated by the respective roles of the USA and the USSR in the COLD WAR, and by the HEGEMONIAL STABILITY THEORY, which posits that hegemony is necessary to a liberal economic world order.

Helsinki Accords (1975) On 1 August 1975 in Helsinki, Finland, thirty-five STATES adopted the Final Act of the CONFERENCE ON SECURITY AND CO-OPERATION IN EUROPE (CSCE). Signatories included all the countries of Europe, with the exception of Albania, plus the USA and Canada. The Act was an expression of the DÉTENTE of the 1970s, seen both in the *RAPPROCHEMENT* by the SUPERPOWERS during the US Presidency of Nixon (1913–94) in the early 1970s and in the German *OSTPOLITIK*. In return for a Western recognition of the post-war division of Europe, the USSR and its allies showed themselves willing to discuss SECURITY and cooperation on a Pan-European basis. Of particular importance was the inclusion of Principle VII, 'Respect for Human Rights and Fundamental Freedoms', and Basket III, 'Cooperation in Humanitarian and other Fields'. The significance of this was that now HUMAN RIGHTS became a major issue in relations between East and West. At subsequent meetings, respectively in Belgrade (1977–8), Madrid (1980–3) and Vienna (1989), the SOVIET BLOC was called on to improve its record in human rights. Helsinki, by drawing attention to human rights, also gave encouragement to dissent in EASTERN EUROPE.

Helsinki Summit (1990) This was held on 9 September and was convened hastily following the invasion of Kuwait by the Iraqi leader Saddam Hussein (b. 1937). This was the third summit between US President George Bush Sr (b. 1924) and the Soviet leader Mikhail Gorbachev (b. 1931) and was proclaimed the first 'post-Cold War summit'. Both sides insisted on Iraqi withdrawal from Kuwait and there was full agreement on the enforcement of economic SANCTIONS against Iraq. But, while the

USA was ready to consider military FORCE and was supported in this by the British government, the USSR was very keen to achieve a diplomatic solution. The USSR also kept military advisers in Iraq and wanted assurances from the USA that its forces would leave Saudi Arabia after the CRISIS was over.

High Authority The High Authority of the EUROPEAN COAL AND STEEL COMMUNITY (ECSC) was the supranational institution responsible for formulating a COMMON MARKET in coal and steel and for such related issues as pricing, competition and investment. The Frenchman Jean Monnet (1889–1979), the inspiration behind the Schuman Plan (1950), which proposed the ECSC, was the High Authority's first President, between 1952 and 1955. The High Authority as such ceased to exist when the institutions of the EUROPEAN COMMUNITIES (EC) were integrated in the MERGER TREATY (1965), which came into force on 1 July 1967.

High Commissioner A term used specifically by the STATES of the COMMONWEALTH to refer to AMBASSADORS or heads of mission sent by one member country to another. The use of this term rather than ambassador indicates the special relationship considered to exist between the member states of the Commonwealth.

High Contracting Parties Term for parties to an international agreement.

High Seas All the world's oceans and seas that lie outside the national TERRITORIAL WATERS of coastal STATES. The High Seas are open to commerce and navigation by all countries. States may extend jurisdiction to vessels flying their flags on the High Seas, but not to the seas themselves. Under the 1958 Geneva Convention on the High Seas, 'No state may validly purport to subject any part of them to its sovereignty.' By INTERNATIONAL LAW, all states have equal rights to engage on the High Seas in fishing, laying of submarine cables and pipelines, and overflight by aircraft. The exercise of the freedom of the seas is qualified by the general requirement that, in the exercise of their freedom to use the High Seas, reasonable regard is due to the interests of other states.

Highway of Death (1991) Also known as the 'Highway to Hell'. The seven-mile length of the Basra–Kuwait City road on which Coalition forces trapped a convoy of some 1,500 vehicles with retreating Iraqi soldiers in the last stages of the GULF WAR (1991). Television coverage was particularly graphic, shocking public opinion, and this event reportedly contributed to the decision by US President George Bush Sr (b. 1924) to halt the campaign against Saddam Hussein (b. 1937) when he did.

Hinterland Doctrine This colonial doctrine argued that, in newly occupied territories, the possession of the coastline by the colonizing power carried with it the right to colonize the hinterland. It was openly advanced by Imperial Germany in Africa in the years before the First World War. It meant that no other country had the right to block access to the interior.

Hitler–Stalin Pact See NAZI–SOVIET NON-AGGRESSION PACT (1939).

Hoare–Laval Plan (1935) This was proposed by Sir Samuel Hoare (1880–1959), British Foreign Secretary, and his opposite number in France,

Pierre Laval (1883–1945), to end the conflict between Fascist Italy under Mussolini (1883–1945) and Ethiopia, which posed a challenge to the LEAGUE OF NATIONS. If implemented, it would have handed Italy 60,000 square miles of territory in Africa and economic control over the southern half of Ethiopia, including the most fertile parts of the country. The fact that partial dismemberment of Ethiopia was discussed after Italy had committed an ACT OF WAR contradicted the apparent commitment of the British and French governments to the principle of COLLECTIVE SECURITY under the League. The plan was leaked by a Paris newspaper and Hoare was forced to resign. In May 1936 Ethiopia fell to the Italians. This plan has been described as the death warrant of the League.

Hobbesian A view of life that is similar to that presented by the English thinker Thomas Hobbes (1588–1697), whose political writings reflected the dilemmas of the Civil War. His best-known book is *Leviathan* (1651), in which he strongly advanced the necessity for strong effective central control and the concept of SOVEREIGNTY as the only alternative to chronic insecurity and ANARCHY. His ideas have been applied to the analysis of international relations in the 'INTERNATIONAL ANARCHY' to support REALISM. In this view, international SECURITY rests more on POWER and the BALANCE OF POWER than law or other rules and norms. Hobbes claimed that there was one fundamental law of nature, 'the liberty each man hath, to use his own power, as he will himself, for the preservation of his own nature'; and one fundamental law, that 'every man ought to endeavour peace as far as he has hope of obtaining it, and when he cannot obtain it . . . he may seek and use all helps and advantages of war'.

Holocaust (1941–5) The systematic GENOCIDE of European Jewry by Nazi Germany during the Second World War. Extermination, also called the 'Final Solution', followed systematic persecution in the preceding period, from the assumption of power in 1933 by Hitler (1889–1945). At the NUREMBERG TRIALS of the Nazis, the number of those Jews killed was estimated at six million. The Holocaust led to the extension of INTERNATIONAL LAW to include CRIMES AGAINST HUMANITY. It was also a crucial factor in the encouragement of ZIONISM and its ambition for a Jewish STATE, and international sympathy for this objective, which led to the creation of the State of Israel in 1948.

Holy Alliance (1815) The loose alliance of European STATES (except Britain, Turkey and the Papal States) created by Tsar Alexander of Russia (1777–1825), Francis I of Austria (1768–1835) and Frederick William III of Prussia (1770–1840) in September 1815 at the VIENNA CONGRESS (1814–15). The idea of this association was conceived of by Alexander I and it was directed against the rising liberal movements in Europe. Officially, it was to promote Christian principles in international relations, but in practical terms it was to preserve the order established at Vienna after the final defeat of the French Emperor Napoleon (1769–1821), and was identified with repression and autocracy. It was ruptured by the Crimean War (1854–6), which isolated Russia. In a different context this was to some extent recreated by the German Chancellor Bismarck (1815–98) in his League of Three Emperors.

Holy Roman Empire (962–1806) An empire of west central Europe. In AD 800 Charlemagne (*c.*742–814), King of the Franks, revived the imperial title. From the coronation of Emperor Otto I (912–73) in 962 the Empire was always associated with the German Crown, even after it became a Hapsburg title in the fifteenth century. In 1530 King Charles I of Spain was crowned as the Holy Roman Emperor, as Charles V (1500–58). His empire included Spain, Germany, the Netherlands, Sardinia and Sicily, together with the newly conquered territories of the Americas. In 1806 the imperial crown was surrendered to the French Emperor Napoleon (1769–1821) and the Empire was not revived after his downfall.

Holy See The juridical international person of the Roman Catholic Church with its physical location at the Vatican in Rome and its sovereign, the Pope. The Holy See (sometimes used interchangeably with the Vatican) is a subject of INTERNATIONAL LAW and as such exchanges diplomatic representatives with other STATES, enters into bilateral TREATIES (Concordats) and is a party to multilateral treaties. Though its territory, granted it by the Lateran Treaty of 1929, encompasses only a hundred acres, it sends agents abroad, papal nuncios, with the same status as ambassadors.

Hoover Moratorium (1931) Announced during the GREAT DEPRESSION on 20 June 1931 by the US President Herbert Hoover (1874–1964), this allowed a one-year suspension of all inter-governmental payments, including debts and REPARATIONS, subject to the agreement of the other nations. France, which stood to lose a considerable amount in reparations payments, resisted, but finally agreed on 6 July. Designed to help Germany out of its depression-induced financial crisis, the moratorium led to another agreement in July 1931 for a standstill on German short-term debts and led to the Lausanne Conference of 1932, where the delegates agreed to reduce the total amount Germany owed by about 90 per cent, dependent upon the USA making proportionate reductions in the amount Britain and France owed in war and reconstruction loans.

Horizontal proliferation The acquisition and development of NUCLEAR WEAPONS by non-nuclear states. The INTERNATIONAL ATOMIC ENERGY AGENCY (IAEA) and the nuclear powers have adopted strict guidelines to try to prevent the spread of nuclear missiles and technology for military purposes, a very major SECURITY concern in the contemporary world.

Horn of Africa The area occupied by Ethiopia, Somalia and Djibouti. The conflicting territorial claims and the national and tribal conflicts here made it a region of conspicuous instability in the twentieth century. Its strategic position on the oil route through the Red Sea also meant that it was a point of significant tension in East–West relations and the COLD WAR, notably from the 1960s.

Hossbach Protocol (1937) The minutes of a conversation between Adolf Hitler (1889–1945), his foreign minister, Neurath (1873–1956), Blomberg (1878–1946), *Reichswehr* minister, and the supreme commanders of the three branches of the German forces on 5 November 1937, and named after Hitler's adjutant, who kept the minutes. The memorandum recorded the Nazi leader's intention to secure *LEBENSRAUM* ('living-space') for the German people by military conquest. He envisaged the outbreak of WAR not later than 1943–5, possibly earlier if France was crippled by internal crisis. The first blow by Germany was to be struck against Austria and Czechoslovakia. Poland was also to be eliminated, while the USSR was kept in check by Japan. The memorandum demonstrates that Hitler never gave up the aims formulated in his book *Mein Kampf* and expected his policy to lead to war, in spite of APPEASEMENT by the Western powers.

HOST STATE (or NATION) A STATE that allows military forces and equipment from allied countries and organizations such as the NORTH ATLANTIC TREATY ORGANIZATION (NATO) to be located on, or pass through, its territory.

Hostages Hostage taking for political or financial gain has become common, not least in international crises, such as during the GULF WAR (1991). The first international conventions explicitly to prohibit the taking of hostages were the four GENEVA CONVENTIONS of 1949. A common provision (Article 3) prohibited the taking of hostages during non-international armed conflicts within the territories of the signatories. It is also prohibited by the International Convention of the Taking of Hostages adopted by the UNITED NATIONS GENERAL ASSEMBLY, which came into force on 3 June 1983. It describes hostage taking as 'an offence of grave concern to the international community', and calls on all parties to it to do all they can to secure the release of hostages within their own territory. Alleged offenders must be placed in custody for trial or EXTRADITION. If they are not extradited, they must be prosecuted.

Hot pursuit The crossing of international frontiers by security forces in pursuit of guerrillas who are using another STATE as a refuge. The most successful guerrilla movements in recent decades have been those with just such a refuge in a HOST STATE, for instance, during the VIETNAM WAR (1960–75), when the North Vietnamese strengthened their forces in South Vietnam through infiltration via Laos and Cambodia. The violation of Cambodian NEUTRALITY by the USA in pursuit of these forces created an international outcry, which graphically illustrates the difficulties that can arise through hot pursuit. As an international legal doctrine, hot pursuit allows the arrest over the HIGH SEAS of vessels and aircraft suspected of having violated national laws within national territorial jurisdiction. Under INTERNATIONAL LAW hot pursuit must be (1) begun within the jurisdiction of the offended state, (2) undertaken only by the public vessels or aircraft of the territorial sovereign, (3) continuous until the pursued vessel is arrested, or (4) broken off when the vessel has passed into the territorial waters of another state.

Hot-line agreements Agreements between the USA and the USSR to provide, and later to improve on, a direct and highly reliable channel of communication between Moscow and Washington. The first was signed in June 1963 with the intention of preventing diplomatic crises escalating into WAR. It was the CUBAN MISSILE CRISIS of October 1962 that compelled the two nuclear SUPERPOWERS to set up the hot line. At the time of that CRISIS it took more than six hours for messages to be delivered through diplomatic channels between the Soviet leader and the American President. It was designed for communication through the written word, primarily to reduce chances of a faulty translation and to give the leaders more time to consider decisions. In 1984 a subsequent agreement arranged for fax capability to be added and in 1987 a further one to establish nuclear risk reduction centres in Moscow and Washington. The hot line has been activated during tense moments in international relations, such as the SIX DAY WAR (1967). The US terminal is located in the National Military Command Centre at the PENTAGON, from which a direct line leads to the WHITE HOUSE. Both Britain and France have similar lines with Russia, established in the 1960s.

House Un-American Activities Committee (HUAC) A US

Congressional Committee of the House of Representatives, which was active from 1938 until 1975. It was instituted 'for the purpose of conducting an investigation of (1) the extent, character and object of un-American propaganda that is instigated from foreign countries or of a domestic origin and attacks the principle of the form of government as guaranteed by the Constitution, and (2) all other questions in relations thereto that would aid Congress in any remedial legislation'. It was especially active in the early years of the COLD WAR in its campaign against real and alleged Communists, whether government officials, academics or figures from the world of entertainment. It was particularly associated with MCCARTHYISM. The Committee was redesignated the Internal Security Committee in 1969 and finally abolished by the House in January 1975.

House–Grey Memorandum (1916) An agreement made on 22 February

1916 between Colonel Edward M. House (1858–1938), adviser to US President Woodrow Wilson (1856–1924) and Lord Grey (1862–1933), British Foreign Secretary. At the time the USA was still neutral in the WAR with Germany. The agreement now stated that the USA should cooperate with the Allies against the CENTRAL POWERS, with FORCE if necessary, to end the war and create a new WORLD ORDER. It reflected House's pro-British and pro-democratic position but also the negative calculation of the likely impact of a German victory on US SECURITY interests.

HUAC See HOUSE UN-AMERICAN ACTIVITIES COMMITTEE.

Human dimension One of the defects of the HELSINKI ACCORDS (1975) was the

absence of effective means of monitoring, or ensuring compliance with, the elements of the accords that related to HUMAN RIGHTS. The Vienna meeting of the CONFERENCE ON SECURITY AND COOPERATION IN EUROPE (CSCE) introduced what was called the Human Rights Dimension Mechanism (or Vienna Mechanism). It involved four proposals: (1) exchange of information, (2) bilateral meetings to discuss specific issues, (3) a procedure allowing STATES to bring human rights situations and cases to the attention of other countries, (4) convening of a future meeting of the ORGANIZATION FOR SECURITY AND COOPERATION IN EUROPE (OSCE). In 1991 an additional proposal in the form of the Moscow Human Dimension Mechanism for on-site investigation of alleged human rights abuse by independent experts.

Human rights An international term that refers to certain moral and legal

entitlements that all human beings are said to possess. In international relations the issue of human rights has grown significantly in importance since the Second World War, as can be seen, for instance, in the UNIVERSAL DECLARATION OF HUMAN RIGHTS (UDHR) (1948), the HELSINKI ACCORDS (1975) and recent justifications for HUMANITARIAN INTERVENTION, as, for example, in Bosnia. The rights to which everyone is entitled include civil and political rights such as the right to life, liberty, security of person, equality before the law, privacy, thought, conscience and religion, nationality and freedom of movement and residence. They also include economic, social and cultural rights, including the right to food, housing, health care, employment, education and participation in the cultural life of the community. In world affairs there is a growing acceptance of the idea that the international community (however defined) has an obligation to ensure that governments recognize and respect human rights within their own territories and that infringements of human rights should not be defended by reference to national SELF-DETERMINATION.

Humanitarian intervention One of the more jealously protected norms of international life is that of NON-INTERVENTION. That is, STATES as sovereign entities generally claim the right to exclusive authority over what takes place within their own borders and regard any external INTERVENTION as a denial of the right of SELF-DETERMINATION. At the same time each state under the norms of HUMAN RIGHTS is obliged to protect the rights of all persons under its jurisdiction. Humanitarian intervention is the doctrine under which one or more states may take military action inside the territory of another state in order to protect those who are expecting serious human rights persecution up to and including GENOCIDE. The period since 1990 provides several high profile examples of this, in particular the action by the UNITED NATIONS (UN) on behalf of the Kurds and Marsh Arabs in Iraq after the war of 1991 and in the former states of Yugoslavia.

HUMINT Human intelligence, espionage.

Hungarian Revolution (1956) An unsuccessful popular revolt in Hungary from 23 October to 14 November 1956 against Soviet political, military and economic dominance and the rigid pro-Soviet communist regime. It began with a student uprising in Budapest demanding the reinstatement of the liberal communist leader Imre Nagy (1896–1958), the removal of Soviet troops from Hungary and a changeover to a multi-party system of government. The firing by police on the demonstrators led to a general strike until Soviet troops left the country. On 30 October a socialist coalition government was formed under Nagy, who appealed to the UNITED NATIONS (UN) to guarantee Hungary NEUTRALITY upon its withdrawal from the WARSAW PACT. The USSR denounced the revolt as a counter-revolution and suppressed it with significant loss of life. Nagy was subsequently executed and control was reimposed under János Kádár. These events caused widespread indignation in the non-communist world, though public opinion was also aroused at this time, and distracted from these events, by the SUEZ CRISIS (1956).

Hydrogen bomb Now more frequently referred to as the thermonuclear bomb, this was the second, and vastly more powerful, development in the field of NUCLEAR WEAPONS, after the ATOMIC BOMB. Unlike its predecessor, which depended on the splitting of the atom, it relies on nuclear fusion, in which two light atoms combine to form a heavier element. There was initially some doubt in the USA as to whether it should proceed with what it called 'the superbomb'. In August 1949, however, a matter of years before the West anticipated this would happen, the USSR exploded its first atomic weapon, dramatically boosting the ARMS RACE, and this swept away military reservations. By 1953 not only the USA but also the USSR had the hydrogen bomb. In 1957 Britain successfully tested it, too.

Hypernationalism Extreme NATIONALISM, a term coined in 1990 by the US international relations theorist John Mearsheimer and defined as the belief that 'other nations or nation states are both inferior and threatening'. This, for instance, was particularly characteristic of Nazi Germany and Fascist Italy, in which MILITARISM was glorified. WAR with other NATIONS was regarded both as inevitable, as the result of evolutionary forces and racial dominance, and as the ultimate expression for the goals and values of the nation.

I

IAEA See INTERNATIONAL ATOMIC ENERGY AGENCY.

IBRD See INTERNATIONAL BANK FOR RECONSTRUCTION AND DEVELOPMENT.

ICBM See INTER-CONTINENTAL BALLISTIC MISSILE.

ICJ See INTERNATIONAL COURT OF JUSTICE.

IDA See INTERNATIONAL DEVELOPMENT ASSOCIATION.

Idealism In the study of international relations, this term refers to an approach that stresses the importance of moral and legal norms and INTERNATIONALISM, and stresses the necessity for effective international organizations. This is in contrast to emphasis on POWER, considerations of NATIONAL INTEREST and the sovereign independence of the STATE; indeed, idealists see the independence of the latter in the 'INTERNATIONAL ANARCHY' as the basic cause of WAR. The term came into wide use in the 1920s in the context of WILSONIANISM, the establishment of the LEAGUE OF NATIONS and the KELLOGG–BRIAND PACT (1928) with the hope that such initiatives might guarantee PEACE throughout the world by the general acceptance of the principle of COLLECTIVE SECURITY. In addition to advancing universalism, the belief in the achievability of durable peace, the idealist approach has also, more and more, come to include environmental concerns.

Ideology A set of ideas and system of thought, or belief, explaining the human condition. The term was first used in 1796 meaning 'science of ideas', coming to acquire a more specific meaning, that of a set of ideas reflecting a particular group, which may also be a programme. Hence one refers to 'Fascist ideology', 'Communist ideology', 'Islamic ideology' and so on. Marxists have, for instance, identified it with the dominant class, hence 'bourgeois ideology' or 'proletarian ideology'. It is a term most commonly used by people describing other systems of ideas or beliefs than their own and normally assumes that the system described is one among a number of systems. Hence, a devout Christian is unlikely to refer to 'Christian ideology'. The study of international relations necessarily involves an appreciation of the role of ideologies, most obviously in examining such issues as the COLD WAR.

IGC Inter-Governmental Conference (EUROPEAN UNION (EU)).

IGO International governmental organization. An organization where membership is composed of STATES – for instance, the UNITED NATIONS (UN).

ILO See INTERNATIONAL LABOUR ORGANIZATION.

IMF See INTERNATIONAL MONETARY FUND.

Imperial overstretch A term popularized following the publication of *The Rise and Fall of the Great Powers* (1987) by the British-born US history professor Paul Kennedy (b. 1945). In this book he argued that 'the historical record suggests that if a particular nation is allocating over the long term more than ten percent (and in some cases – when it is structurally weak – more than five percent) of GNP to armaments, that it is likely to limit its growth rate'. As new powers developed in the world, they were likely to burden themselves with increasing military expenditure. 'If, however, too large a proportion of the state's resources is diverted from wealth creation and allocated instead to military purposes, then that is likely to lead to a weakening of national power over the long run.' Examples of this include the British Empire and the USSR.

Imperial Preference The system by which Britain and its overseas dependencies have granted preferential trade treatment to one another. It originated in 1919 when Britain had no general tariff, as an arrangement whereby members of the Empire granted Britain economic preference in return for protection by the British fleet. The system was extended in 1932 when Britain adopted a general tariff, against the background of the world depression. The OTTAWA AGREEMENTS (1932) arranged special terms for the Dominions to trade their primary products to Britain in return for granting British manufactured goods preference in their markets. Imperial preference proved a major difficulty in British efforts to enter the EUROPEAN ECONOMIC COMMUNITY (EEC) in 1961. In particular, France, wishing to protect its agriculture, insisted on Britain relinquishing preferential arrangements. After entry in 1973, special trade agreements with many Commonwealth countries were concluded by the EUROPEAN COMMUNITY (EC).

Imperialism A relationship of dominance of one government or people over another government or people; the expansion of a STATE beyond its own frontiers with the aim of dominating other states or societies. This term was originally coined to criticize the Napoleonic conquests. As an extension of POWER through conquest and the pursuit of global influence, it reached its height between 1870 and the outbreak of the First World War in 1914, the period of dramatic competitive expansionism overseas, to secure colonies and SPHERES OF INFLUENCE – the so-called new imperialism that saw, among other acquisitions, the 'SCRAMBLE FOR AFRICA' of the European powers. This period also saw the economic analysis of imperialism, most notably by Lenin (1870–1924), who, in *Imperialism as the Highest State of Capitalism* (1916), argued that imperialism (the state of CAPITALISM characterized by accumulation on a world scale) was an economic necessity for capitalism in order to overcome the falling rate of profit in domestic markets. This also, in his view, led to 'imperialist war', which was his diagnosis of the First World War. Imperial ambitions have been motivated by the need for commercial expansion or territory, by the desire for military glory or diplomatic advantage, because of strategic calculations and for cultural, ideological reasons. Historically, imperialism has generally assumed a racial, intellectual and cultural superiority on the part of the newcomers. Explanations of this phenomenon have stimulated a long historical and theoretical debate, including much discussion of 'informal empire' such as Britain enjoyed in the hey-day of FREE TRADE. It has also become a much-used and abused slogan, especially in the COLD WAR, in which both East and West indicted the other for imperialist INTERVENTION, subversion and influence. A survey conducted in the 1960s concluded that the term was employed worldwide in at least one in ten of every political broadcasts. In the twentieth century, following the Second World War, which gravely undermined the dominance of the European powers, the great majority of colonies achieved independence and DECOLONIZATION. The term NEO-IMPERIALISM is sometimes used to describe certain (usually economic policies) of the developed world in relation to the THIRD WORLD.

Indian Independence Act (1947) This major act of DECOLONIZATION became effective on 15 August 1947. It confirmed the partition of the subcontinent and DOMINION status for both India and Pakistan.

Indochina War (1946–54) This is sometimes referred to as the 'First' Indochina War, to distinguish it from the later VIETNAM WAR (1960–75). French control over this colony was challenged by the Vietminh, a nationalist and Communist movement led by Ho Chi Minh (1890–1969). Guerrilla attacks on the French colonialists culminated in a conventional battle at Dien Bien Phu in 1954 in which France was defeated. By this time the USA was already paying 80 per cent of the French war liabilities. Peace terms were agreed at the subsequent GENEVA CONFERENCE (1954), which provided for French withdrawal, the division of Indochina into the separate countries of Cambodia and Laos, and the *de facto* division of North and South Vietnam. With both the north and south claiming to represent Vietnam, the scene was set for the later conflict.

INF See INTERMEDIATE-RANGE NUCLEAR FORCES TREATY (1987).

Informal empire A term used to describe a type of IMPERIALISM by which the imperial or 'metropolitan' power does not rule the colonized territory directly, but leaves it formally independent while in practice controlling it indirectly through economic power, exploitation or other international influence. Historians have debated at length, for instance, the informal commercial empire of the British in the eighteenth and nineteenth centuries and its relationship to formal empire and the so-called 'new imperialism' at the end of the nineteenth century and beginning of the twentieth.

INGO International non-governmental organization. An organization whose membership is composed of private individuals or groups – for instance, AMNESTY INTERNATIONAL.

Innocent passage The right of foreign vessels to cross the TERRITORIAL WATERS of another STATE without interference by that state. Passage is 'innocent' provided it does not prejudice the PEACE, good order, or SECURITY of the coastal state. It includes stopping and anchoring, but only when incidental to ordinary navigation or made necessary by superior force or distress. Under INTERNATIONAL LAW, vessels in innocent passage are subject to normal rules of transport and navigation and to the laws of the coastal sovereign. In return, the vessels of all states are allowed to use the most expedient route. Under these same conditions the Geneva Convention of 1958 on the territorial waters and the CONTIGUOUS ZONE recognizes the right of innocent passage for warships.

Insurgency An internal uprising that is aimed against an existing government, usually with the goal of replacing or overthrowing it.

Integration As an economic process, this means the abolition of discrimination and the HARMONIZATION of economies, as, for example, with the member states of the EUROPEAN UNION (EU). In degrees of deepening, there are four stages: FREE TRADE AREA, CUSTOMS UNION, COMMON MARKET and economic union. In the case of total economic integration, one needs the unification of monetary, fiscal, social and trade policies and the setting-up of a supranational authority. The extent to which the EU should proceed to integration is highly controversial, raising political and economic issues of the first order.

Intelligence Information that is gathered covertly or openly by a government or agency about another country or alliance's intentions and capabilities. Strategic and military intelligence are concerned with discovering a range of things: the disposition and strength of military forces, weapons' development, plans, alliances and agreements, the capability and morale of military forces and civilian opinion. Effective intelligence gathering requires the wider appreciation of political, economic and social data, of a country's underlying strength or potential responses. Quite frequently, excellent military intelligence is not balanced with political intelligence analysis of the same quality. Since the Second World War intelligence gathering (or its failure) has been of particularly crucial importance, particularly where an element of surprise has been involved, for instance as with the SIX DAY WAR (1967), the YOM KIPPUR WAR (1973), or the FALKLANDS WAR (1982). The history of intelligence, which was often referred to as the missing dimension of international relations, has attracted growing scholarly attention in recent decades.

Inter-American Conference on Problems of War and Peace

(1945) Also known as the Chapultepec Conference and the Mexico City Conference, this took place between 21 February and 8 March 1945 in Mexico City and established the principle of regional self-defence, pending action by the UNITED NATIONS (UN). That is to say, an attack on one of the participant countries was to be considered an attack on all. The Chapultepec Act served as the basis for ARTICLE 51 of the UNITED NATIONS CHARTER, authorizing regional security arrangements, and for the INTER-AMERICAN TREATY OF RECIPROCAL ASSISTANCE (1947) (the Rio Treaty). The conference included all the Western Hemisphere nations that had cooperated in the Second World War (all but Argentina, which had been accused of pro-Nazi sympathies). Subsequently, Argentina joined the agreement on the basis that it accepted the results of the conference, which also discussed US economic cooperation with, and assistance for, Latin America.

Inter-American Treaty of Reciprocal Assistance (1947) Also known

as the Rio Treaty, this resulted from the INTER-AMERICAN CONFERENCE ON PROBLEMS

OF WAR AND PEACE (1945) and deals with American SECURITY and provides that any attack on an American NATION will be considered an attack on all and will be countered by collective SANCTIONS, political, economic and/or military, according to ARTICLE 51 of the UNITED NATIONS CHARTER. 'Attack' is also taken to include subversion. The area guaranteed by the Treaty, and upheld by the ORGANIZATION OF AMERICAN STATES (OAS), also incorporates Canada and the remaining European dependencies in the Western Hemisphere. It served as a model for the NORTH ATLANTIC TREATY of 1949.

Inter-Continental Ballistic Missile (ICBM) Developed in the ARMS RACE of the COLD WAR, this means any land-based, rocket-propelled missile capable of delivering a nuclear warhead (or warheads) to a distance more than 3,000 nautical miles. The 1972 STRATEGIC ARMS LIMITATION TALKS (SALT I) further defined an ICBM as a strategic ballistic missile capable of ranges in excess of the shortest distance between the north-eastern border of the continental USA and the north-western border of the continental USSR.

Inter-Continental Ballistic Missiles (ICBMs) Missiles with a range of up to 10,000 miles. The first were deployed by the USSR in 1958–9, though by the time of the CUBAN MISSILE CRISIS (1962) the USA had very significantly more than the USSR. The first generation had single warheads. Subsequently, multiple warheads, MULTIPLE INDEPENDENTLY TARGETED RE-ENTRY VEHICLES (MIRVS) were introduced.

Interdependence This term has been used increasingly in international relations since the 1960s to describe the mutual dependency of state interests. This has been particularly so with reference to the COLD WAR and North–South relations, for instance, with the BRANDT REPORTS of 1980 and 1983. It has often been seen as leading to greater cooperation, not least in addressing global problems. It has also been pointed out, however, that it may lead to conflicts. The US international relations theorist Kenneth Waltz (b. 1924), for instance, has argued that it may precipitate trouble because nations inherently wish to regain independence and freedom from foreign influence and control.

Interdiction Interdiction means the use of military force to prevent transportation of supplies, equipment or troops past a particular point or along some route. Typically, in modern warfare it refers to the use of air power to destroy bridges, major railway junctions and other CHOKE POINTS well inside enemy territory, thus preventing both supplies and reinforcements from reaching the battlefield.

Intergovernmentalism In theories of INTEGRATION, such as those applied to the EUROPEAN UNION (EU), intergovernmentalism refers to the dominance of national governments in the integration process over supranational or other ACTORS.

Intermediate-range ballistic missile (IRBM) A missile with a range of between 1,500 and 3,000 nautical miles. It was the stationing of Soviet IRBMs in Cuba in 1962 that sparked off the CUBAN MISSILE CRISIS (1962).

Intermediate-Range Nuclear Forces (INF) Treaty (1987) An important DISARMAMENT TREATY between the USA under President Ronald Reagan (b. 1911) and the USSR under Mikhail Gorbachev (b. 1931) for the elimination of their immediate range and shorter-range nuclear missiles, signed in Washington on 18 December 1987. The treaty required the destruction of the two SUPERPOWERS' ground-launched ballistic and CRUISE MISSILES with ranges of between 500 and 5,000 kilometres, their launchers and associated support structures and equipment within three years after the Treaty entered into force in 1998.

Intermestic Issues and concerns that are of both international and domestic significance. Frequently they will involve a range of ministries and agencies, as, for instance, with major environmental questions.

Internal colonialism This phrase was originally used by revolutionaries in Russia during the nineteenth century to describe the exploitation of peasants by the urban classes. Since the 1960s it has been used (in radical critiques) to describe regions and territories that are simultaneously economically relatively disadvantaged and culturally distinct and that tend to support nationalist political movements. Discussions, for instance, of Welsh and Scottish NATIONALISM and their motivations have made use of this term, in relating them to English governmental and economic dominance.

Internal peacekeeping Internal peacekeeping involves an operation attempting to help settle an internal conflict within a country, an INTERVENTION within a CIVIL WAR situation. International organizations have often found these the most difficult missions to manage owing to the nature of the conflict, since frequently more than two belligerent parties are involved in civil wars, and to reach arrangements among all parties is very difficult.

International anarchy A phrase used to denote a world consisting of independent sovereign STATES, acknowledging no political superior, whose relationship is ultimately regulated by rivalry, conflict and WAR.

International Atomic Energy Agency (IAEA) An agency of the UNITED NATIONS (UN) established in 1957 to foster cooperation among nations in developing atomic energy for peaceful purposes. It was first proposed by US President Eisenhower (1890–1969) in his ATOMS FOR PEACE proposals before the UNITED NATIONS GENERAL ASSEMBLY in 1953. It was created to reduce the threat of WAR by encouraging cooperation, especially between the atomic powers and developing STATES. It seeks to raise living standards in the world by developing cheap power sources and by teaching the new technology to the scientists of the underdeveloped countries. Its creators hoped that it would eventually provide the means for international inspection and control.

International Bank for Reconstruction and Development (IBRD) Also known as the World Bank, this was established in 1946 together with the INTERNATIONAL MONETARY FUND (IMF) as an outcome of the BRETTON WOODS CONFERENCE of 1944. It was originally created to help with economic reconstruction consequent on the Second World War. Now much of its attention is directed to the THIRD WORLD as provider of funds and economic advice, largely for infrastructural projects. It is funded by quota subscriptions of member countries. Membership of the

IMF is required before joining the World Bank. In 1980 the Bank introduced a new policy under its Economic Structural Adjustment Programme by which it makes loans to ease the BALANCE OF PAYMENTS problems of developing countries. This is conditional on free market economic policies specified by the Bank.

International Bill of Human Rights This is a collective term for four HUMAN RIGHTS documents, which together form the core of the universally attested rights humans should enjoy. They are the UNIVERSAL DECLARATION OF HUMAN RIGHTS (UDHR), the International Covenant on Economic Social and Cultural Rights, the International Covenant on Civil and Political Rights, and the Optional Protocol to the International Covenant on Civil and Political Rights.

International Brigade The approximately 60,000 volunteers from fifty-three countries who went to fight in the SPANISH CIVIL WAR (1936–9) on the Republican side against General Franco (1892–1975) and the supporters of his insurgent Nationalist cause. The idea originated in Paris and was backed by the COMINTERN. They regarded this as an anti-fascist crusade and a high percentage were Communists. Unable to make Spain 'the tomb of Fascism', many of them went on to fight in various armies and resistance movements against Germany and Italy.

International Committee of the Red Cross (ICRC) One of the oldest institutions in existence concerned with HUMAN RIGHTS, founded in 1863. It was started by Henri Dunant (1828–1910), who began campaigning for more humane treatment for the wounded after first-hand experience of the Battle of Solferino (1859) and the first Geneva Convention inspired by it was adopted in 1864. With branches all over the world, it works on behalf of prisoners of war, the wounded and other victims of ARMED CONFLICT.

International Court of Justice (ICJ) Also called the World Court, this is the name given to the supreme judicial body of the UNITED NATIONS (UN). It is located in The Hague, Holland, and has the competence or legal authority to hear any case brought to it by parties to a dispute that have accepted its jurisdiction. It can also provide advisory opinions on any legal matter referred to it by STATES or the organs and agencies of the UN. In reaching its decisions the Court applies general principles, treaties and the judgements of authorities in the field of INTERNATIONAL LAW. It can also take decisions *EX AEQUO ET BONO* (according to what is just and fair), as well as by the tenets of existing International Law. The ICJ has fifteen judges and operates by a majority vote, which cannot be appealed.

International debt crisis (1970s and 1980s) This was caused by rising oil prices after 1973, a worldwide recession including a drop in commodity prices, and a tightening of US monetary policies leading to higher interest rates. It first attracted significant public attention in 1982 when Brazil and Mexico nearly defaulted on their external debt. One estimate was that the sum total of medium and long-term debt owed by the LESS DEVELOPED COUNTRIES (LDCS) rose from $86 billion in 1971 to $606 billion in 1983. Two-thirds of the debt was held by twenty countries, with Brazil and Mexico as the largest debtors. Much of the money loaned came from US commercial banks. The US government and the INTERNATIONAL MONETARY FUND (IMF) played an important role in resolving the crisis, providing emergency assistance and debt rescheduling.

International Development Act (1949) See POINT FOUR PROGRAMME.

International Development Association (IDA) An affiliate of the INTERNATIONAL BANK FOR RECONSTRUCTION AND DEVELOPMENT (IBRD) (World Bank). It was set up in 1960 in order to provide loans on easier terms than the World Bank to the poorest or LEAST DEVELOPED COUNTRIES (LDCS), the forty lowest-income economies. Approximately half its loans go to sub-Saharan Africa. Its organizational structure is similar to that of the World Bank, though it is legally and financially separate from it.

International Labour Organization (ILO) A specialized agency of the UNITED NATIONS (UN), originally established by the VERSAILLES TREATY of 1919 with the LEAGUE OF NATIONS to improve working conditions and living standards in member countries. This had subsumed the International Labour Office established at the turn of the twentieth century, concerned with such issues as the eight-hour day and restricting child labour. It was affiliated with the League of Nations and in 1946 became the first of the specialized agencies associated with the UN. It has promoted improved labour conditions and workers' rights through the adoption of the International Labour Code, consisting of more than 350 conventions, covering such issues as workers' health, social security, migration and unemployment. Its conference meets annually at the ILO headquarters in Geneva. It has increasingly directed its efforts to the THIRD WORLD and to assisting developing STATES.

International Law Also referred to as the Law of Nations, the body of legal rules considered binding upon STATES and under which individuals now also have rights recognized. It is founded primarily upon TREATIES and customs, as well as general principles of law recognized by civilized nations. Since 1945 the EUROPEAN CONVENTION ON HUMAN RIGHTS and the UNITED NATIONS (UN) UNIVERSAL DECLARATION ON HUMAN RIGHTS have gone some way to committing states to providing a wider range of HUMAN RIGHTS. The evolution of International Law has been strongly influenced by natural law traditions, but in modern times there has been a strong preference for convention, by which treaties create International Law and bind their signatories. Those who emphasize the INTERNATIONAL ANARCHY and the use of FORCE in international relations have frequently expressed scepticism about the efficacy of International Law in the world as the world actually is. Nevertheless, even though International Law has not eliminated WAR, it has extended its own role considerably, covering such issues as slavery, the conduct of war and the treatment of civilians. International Law is sometimes categorized into universal, general and particular International Law. Universal refers to those norms that are considered to be binding on all states because they are so fundamental or basic to the COMMUNITY OF NATIONS, whether or not they have consented to them. General International Law is often used to describe norms derived from law-making treaties by a large number of states. Particular International Law refers to the norms created by treaties among a limited number of states.

International Monetary Fund (IMF) This organization was established in 1947 with the purpose of providing additional liquidity in and confidence behind the international monetary system. It seeks to encourage the liberalization of cross-border currency and settlement activities. In practice its role is that of lender to member countries that are facing trade payment difficulties. The IMF also publishes useful surveys of international developments and forecasts.

International regime A system of rules, duties, obligations and rights established to promote better relations between nation STATES, either in relation to a specific subject, or more generally.

Internationalism An approach to world affairs that emphasizes universal and transnational interests rather than NATIONALISM and concerns of STATE power. In international relations it is evident in ideas of world society, INTERNATIONAL LAW, concepts of a common humanity, PEACE, and universal HUMAN RIGHTS. Both the LEAGUE OF NATIONS and the UNITED NATIONS (UN) have attempted to embody internationalist principles. Recently, the growth of concern over the global environment and the disparity between affluence and poverty, between the industrialized countries and the THIRD WORLD has given internationalism additional salience.

Interposition force Also known as a 'barrier force', this is a traditional form of peacekeeping in which a neutral military unit places itself physically between two or more belligerents. A DEMILITARIZED ZONE (DMZ) is normally established in the process, within which the peacekeepers place themselves.

Intervention The coercive interference by a STATE or group of states in the domestic jurisdiction of another state. It is particularly controversial because the emergence of the modern state system also involved the development of state SOVEREIGNTY, which implies the contrary principle of NON-INTERVENTION in the internal concerns of other states. Legitimate exceptions have been argued to the general principle, such as for self-defence, counter-intervention, intervention to assist SELF-DETERMINATION and HUMANITARIAN INTERVENTION. Well-known examples include the intervention of Germany, Italy and the USSR in the SPANISH CIVIL WAR (1936–9) and those of the SUPERPOWERS in their respective SPHERES OF INFLUENCE after 1945.

Intifada This is the name for the popular uprising or 'shaking-off' in the OCCUPIED TERRITORIES in Palestine that began in December 1987 and lasted until 1993. Demonstrations, strikes and an embargo on Israeli goods had as their objective the end of Israeli occupation and the establishment of Palestinian independence. More than a thousand died and 40,000 were arrested as a consequence of these disturbances. After this pressure was exerted on the PALESTINIAN LIBERATION ORGANIZATION (PLO) to engage in peace talks with Israel to advocate a two-state solution, and to renounce TERRORISM. Since 2000 there has been an acute revival of terrorist violence and Israeli repression in the area.

IPE International Political Economy.

IR International Relations.

Iran-Contra Affair A tangled US political scandal during the second administration of President Ronald Reagan (b. 1911). It involved the diversion to the Contra rebels in Nicaragua of funds that had been collected from secret arms deals with Iran. It became public in November 1986. The purpose of the arms dealing had been to secure the freeing of US HOSTAGES in the hands of Islamic militants in the Middle East. The assistance to the Contras contravened a ban passed by Congress in October 1984.

Iranian Crisis (1946) See AZERBIJAN CRISIS.

IRBMs See INTERMEDIATE-RANGE BALLISTIC MISSILES.

Iron Curtain A phrase from the COLD WAR to describe the barrier to communications and travel set up by the COMMUNIST BLOC after the Second World War, of which the most visible element (erected sixteen years later in 1961) was to be the BERLIN WALL. The term is commonly attributed to Sir Winston Churchill (1874–1965), who first publicly used it in his famous 'Iron Curtain Speech' in Fulton Missouri on 5 May 1946, designed to alert the West. In fact it had been previously used in 1945 by the Nazi Propaganda Minister Joseph Goebbels (1897–1945); and even earlier in 1930 in the USSR, when the West was accused of having erected an iron curtain to prevent the 'fire of Communism' spreading to the capitalist world.

Iron Triangle A term used for a key strategic area in the VIETNAM WAR (1960–75), twenty miles north of the capital of South Vietnam, Saigon. It was the scene of major US military offensives in 1967–8, involving a scorched-earth policy to root out Viet Cong infiltration.

Irredentism A term derived from the Italian Risorgimento, the nineteenth-century movement for Italian unification. *Italia irredenta*, 'unredeemed Italy', referred to Fiume, Trento and Trieste, those areas that lay outside the physical control of the Italian STATE. It is now used as a general term in international relations to indicate the desire of a people in a particular state to annex those adjoining territories of another country inhabited by the linguistic and/or cultural minorities of the first state. It can occur whenever a political boundary does not coincide with ethnic or linguistic boundaries, as when former imperial powers have mapped their boundary lines with scant concern for the communal integrity of the people inhabiting those states, and has often been used to justify territorial aggrandizement. Well-known examples include the Nazi German claim on the Czech SUDETENLAND and Iraq's on Kuwait as its nineteenth province, which led to the GULF WAR of 1991.

Islamic fundamentalism A term coined by the Western world to describe political terrorist movements led by Muslims who claim justification for their behaviour in Islamic practice, if not scripture. The term is used loosely and somewhat indiscriminately to denote the ideologies of numerous radical Islamic groups, as well as the regimes of some Muslim countries prone to commit acts of terror. What is new about contemporary Islamic fundamentalists is the development of movements that advance a political project based on Islam. By contrast, more traditional Islamic fundamentalists are more concerned with personal ethics and spirituality. Both are often united in their criticism that official corruption in their own countries is a result of Western influences, and therefore reject Western values.

Isolationism A doctrine that views the national interest of a country as best served by insulating it from the political entanglements of the international community. It has particularly been used to describe the stance of the USA, as, for example, in the inter-war years, such as its refusal to join the LEAGUE OF NATIONS and its subsequent NEUTRALITY ACTS. Proponents of isolationism there have based their arguments on the concept of the geographical, ideological and cultural separateness of the USA. Over more than two centuries the USA has practised various degrees of non-involvement in international affairs, but has never been isolated. Nor has it implemented the principle of non-involvement in Pacific and Far Eastern affairs to the extent that it did in Europe.

J

Jackson Amendment (1972) Introduced by US Senator Henry Jackson (1912–83) as an amendment to the East–West Trade Relations Act, which was one of the initiatives in the policy of DÉTENTE under President Richard Nixon (1913–94). This act proposed to grant the USSR MOST-FAVOURED-NATION (MFN) status. Jackson claimed that the USSR should improve its record in HUMAN RIGHTS, particularly with regard to the Jewish REFUSENIKS. The amendment denied the USSR this economic status so long as it imposed 'more than a nominal tax . . . on any citizen as a consequence of emigration'.

Japanese–American Security Treaty (1951) A bilateral DEFENCE pact that provides for joint consultations if the SECURITY of Japan is threatened. The TREATY was signed in a revised form in 1960 and reaffirmed in 1995. Under its terms the USA retains the right to maintain land, sea and air forces in Japan, which may be used (1), without prior consultation, to maintain PEACE and security in the Far East, or (2), following consultation, to defend Japan against an armed attack. The Treaty specifies that military operations conducted from Japanese bases outside 'shall be subject to prior consultation with the Government of Japan'. US acceptance of primary responsibility for the security of Japan was necessitated by the Japanese Constitution of 1947, which provided for the renunciation of WAR and MILITARISM. The 1960 Treaty, however, encouraged Japanese rearmament.

JCS Joint Chiefs of Staff.

Jerusalem Programme (1951) A restatement of the objectives of ZIONISM, which was adopted by the 23rd Zionist Congress. The original BASEL PROGRAMME (1897) was felt to be no longer adequate after the creation of the State of Israel in 1948. The Jerusalem Programme stated: 'The task of Zionism is the strengthening of the State of Israel, the ingathering of the exiles in Eretz Israel (Palestine), and the fostering of the unity of the Jewish people.' There were subsequent modifications to this in 1961 and 1968.

JHA Justice and Home Affairs (EUROPEAN UNION (EU)).

Jihad Originally, in the militant interpretation of this term, this was the doctrine of the struggle against unbelievers and unbelief for the expansion and protection of

Islam. In the colonial era wars against external forces were often regarded in this light, as is that of the Mahdi (1848–85) in the Sudan against the British and French between 1881 and 1885. Islamic fundamentalists, whether fighting the USSR in Afghanistan in the 1980s, against Israel, or against the USA, as guerrilla warriors or, as increasingly in recent decades, through TERRORISM have considered themselves as fighting a Holy War to which they are compelled by sacred duty. Jihad, though, can also have moral and non-aggressive connotations.

Jingoism Chauvinistic IMPERIALISM. 'Jingoists' originated as a nickname for those who supported the plan by the British Prime Minister Benjamin Disraeli (1804–81) to send a fleet into Turkish waters to check the advance of the Russians in the Russo-Turkish War of 1877–8. The term came from the music hall song: 'We don't want to fight | But by jingo if we do | We've got the ships, we've got the men | We've got the money too.'

Johnson Doctrine (1965) Announced by US President Lyndon B. Johnson (1908–73) on 2 May 1965, this represented an extension of the ROOSEVELT COROLLARY (1904) of the MONROE DOCTRINE (1923). It accompanied his decision to send US marines into the Dominican Republic, which had been plunged into CIVIL WAR, and stated that 'the American nations will not permit the establishment of another Communist government in the Western Hemisphere'. It was supported by a vote in the House of Representatives on 20 September 1965.

Johnson–Mann Doctrine (1963) A principle of US foreign policy in Latin America, formulated by the administration of President Lyndon B. Johnson (1908–73) and issued to US ambassadors by the Under-Secretary of State for Latin-American Affairs to the effect that the KENNEDY DOCTRINE of support solely for repre-sentative governments in Latin-America formed through general elections would be superseded by the offer to support any Latin-American government whose interests were compatible with those of the USA.

Junta The Spanish word for a council. Originally juntas were set up in Spain dur-ing the Napoleonic Wars to conduct the campaign against the French Army. Now it is commonly used to describe a group of officers taking legislative and executive powers to control a country or region. Typically, a junta comes to power following a *COUP D'ÉTAT*, as the Greek Colonels did in 1967. Under such a regime, civilians are com-monly excluded from key government posts and political parties are banned.

Jupiter missiles A class of INTERMEDIATE-RANGE BALLISTIC MISSILES (IRBMS), which were developed by the US Army in the mid-1950s. Under agreements signed in 1959, thirty Jupiter missiles were deployed in Italy and fifteen in Turkey, close to the border with the USSR The unannounced agreement by US President Kennedy (1917–63) to remove these missiles from Turkey in return for the Soviet withdrawal of missiles from Cuba during the CUBAN MISSILE CRISIS (1962) helped to end that CRISIS.

Jus ad bellum Latin for the law/justification for going to WAR, a phrase used in particular with reference to the theory of the JUST WAR. It is to be distinguished from the *jus in bello*, which concerns the conduct of war.

Jus cogens A norm of general INTERNATIONAL LAW from which STATES cannot escape. For a norm to be *jus cogens* it must be accepted and recognized by the international community of states as a whole. The most explicit expression of it in contemporary international relations is Article 53 of the Vienna Convention on the Law of Treaties (1969), where it is stated that: 'A treaty is void if, at the time of its conclusion, it conflicts with a peremptory norm of general International Law.' The rules against GENOCIDE and AGGRESSION are the two peremptory rules of International Law enjoying general practice.

Jus gentium The Latin term for the Law of Nations. Originally this described the body of law used in ancient Rome to settle disputes between Roman citizens and foreigners, or between foreigners alone. The term is now used to denote the body of rules common to the legal systems of all civilized STATES.

Jus in bello See LAWS OF WAR.

Jus sanguinis Latin term, 'law of blood'. This is the principle by which individuals obtain citizenship of a particular country on the basis of the nationality of their parents.

Jus soli Latin term, 'law of the place of one's birth'. This principle allows individuals to obtain citizenship in a particular country on the grounds that they have been born in it.

Just War The distinction between just and unjust WAR was historically defined and refined by the Christian Church. Canon Law (Church law) drew a distinction between *JUS AD BELLUM* (justifiable cause in the reasons for fighting) and *JUS IN BELLO* (justice in the course and conduct of a war – an idea later materializing in the GENEVA CONVENTIONS (1949)). The great medieval theologian St Thomas Aquinas (1226–74), developing earlier ideas from the Church Fathers, specified, for instance, that it was necessary that the person waging war had sufficient authority, that there was just cause and that the war was fought for PEACE and for the good. Other criteria of the Just War emphasized that FORCE should be the last resort and that it should be proportional. The idea of the Just War presents a number of problems. For instance, how does one define legitimate authority? Is it not possible to fight a just war in a thoroughly unjust way? The Dutch jurist Hugo Grotius (1583–1645) did more than anyone else to establish this doctrine in INTERNATIONAL LAW in his *On the Laws of War and Peace* (1625). In his view, war was just if it was: (1) in self-defence; (2) enforcing legitimate rights; (3) to exact just REPARATIONS, and (4) imposing justified punishment. The Just War Doctrine laid the basis for the idea of limited war. After the Second World War the idea attracted revived attention, providing an underpinning to the limitations imposed by the LEAGUE OF NATIONS COVENANT (1919) upon the resort to war, the KELLOGG–BRIAND PACT (1928) and the UNITED NATIONS CHARTER. The phrase 'Just War PACIFISM' has been coined to indicate selective opposition to war.

Justiciable and non-justiciable disputes Justiciable disputes are those that lend themselves to legal settlement by ARBITRATION or ADJUDICATION. Non-justiciable disputes are those to which techniques of political settlement are applied by bilateral DIPLOMACY, through GOOD OFFICES, MEDIATION, inquiry or conciliation. The idea of peaceful settlement through arbitration experienced a considerable vogue during the opening decades of the twentieth century, as evidenced, for instance, by the creation of the Permanent Court of Arbitration in 1899. The distinction between legal and political disputes, though, arose because STATES wanted to exempt from the finality of legal settlement those matters touching on national independence and vital interests, as so interpreted by themselves. That states may not wish to settle disputes by law does not mean that there is no law applicable to the dispute under consideration.

K

Kantian After the Prussian philosopher Immanuel Kant (1724–1804), who claimed that 'true politics cannot take a single step without first paying homage to morals'. This extended to international politics, and one of his major advocacies was the preservation of perpetual PEACE. As he put it in *Metaphysical Elements of Justice*: 'Moral-practical reason within us pronounces the following irresistible veto: There shall be no war, either between human beings in the state of nature, or between separate states, which although internally law-governed still live in a lawless condition in their external relationships with one another. For war is not a way in which anyone should pursue his rights . . . '. He regarded the creation of a republican constitution as a first step towards the elimination of WAR, since republics, in his words, were 'incapable of bellicosity'. He called for an ALLIANCE of republican STATES that would resolve all disputes by peaceful means.

Katyn Forest Massacre (1940) Katyn near Smolensk, Russia. Here in April or May 1940 about 4,800 Polish officers were shot by the Soviet NKVD. They were only some of those who had been taken prisoner (and could not be accounted for) in the September campaign of 1939, when eastern Poland was incorporated by the USSR. The graves were discovered by the advancing German army in March 1943. The Soviet leader Stalin (1879–1953) accused the Polish Government in Exile of collaborating with Nazi propaganda when it called for the INTERNATIONAL COMMITTEE OF THE RED CROSS (ICRC) to investigate the crime on the spot; and used this as a pretext to break off links with it. During the war the US and British governments regarded the maintenance of the GRAND ALLIANCE with the USSR as the highest priority and, for diplomatic reasons, were unwilling openly to admit the manifest evidence of Soviet guilt. Privately, though, it aroused grave apprehensions as to possible Soviet intentions after a German defeat.

Kellogg–Briand Pact (1928) An international agreement to replace WAR by CONFLICT RESOLUTION. It was signed on 27 August 1928 by the leaders of fifteen nations. Within a few years sixty-two nations had signed it, including the USA, Britain, France, Germany, Italy, Japan and the USSR. It was named after the French Foreign Minister Aristide Briand (1862–1932) and the US SECRETARY OF STATE Frank B. Kellogg (1856-1937). The signatories stated that they were persuaded the time had come 'when a frank renunciation of war as an instrument of national policy should be made' and pledged to settle 'all disputes and conflicts of whatever nature or of whatever origin . . . by pacific means'. The treaty did not incorporate powers of enforcement; nor did it prescribe definite responsibilities. It also said nothing about wars of self-defence. International leaders openly interpreted the pact to be null and void if their nations were invaded. While the Second World War put the agreement conclusively to rest, the ideal of resolving conflicts through international relations rather than war remains.

Kennedy Doctrine A principle of US foreign policy in Latin America, openly formulated by President Kennedy (1917–63) in a speech on 5 July 1961 to a conference of the ALLIANCE for Progress in Punta del Este. It stated that the US government would give economic and military assistance only to those countries of the region that had democratic representative governments established through general elections.

Kennedy Grand Design Under this name US President Kennedy (1917–63) on 4 July 1962 announced a plan for a transatlantic commonwealth, in which one pillar would comprise the USA and Canada and the second the collective European states in the EUROPEAN ECONOMIC COMMUNITY (EEC) and the EUROPEAN FREE TRADE ASSOCIATION (EFTA). In a subsequent speech in January 1963 by the US Secretary of State Christian Herter (1895–1966), this proposed commonwealth was called 'Atlantica'. He specified four aims, that it should: (1) maintain close political ties between the countries of Western Europe and North America; (2) strengthen economic and military ties; (3) foster the political affiliation of all free nations; and (4) form a common political front against Communist aggression. This conception was opposed by the French President Charles de Gaulle (1890–1970) with his notion of 'Europe for the Europeans', with the reduction of American influence in Western Europe.

Kennedy Round International tariff negotiations between 1963 and 1967. It was the sixth session of such negotiations under the procedures laid down by the GENERAL AGREEMENT ON TARIFFS AND TRADE (GATT) and followed the passage of the US Trade Expansion Act (1962), which reflected growing American concern over the rising economic strength of the EUROPEAN ECONOMIC COMMUNITY (EEC). The negotiations traded increased exports to the EEC in return for greater European access to US markets through the mutual reduction of tariffs. Negotiations among fifty-three nations concluded with a reduction in the range of 35–39 per cent, affecting a total of $40 billion of trade. The Kennedy Round also concluded a joint agreement to supply 4.5 million tons of wheat per year as food AID and drafted an international code to help standardize anti-dumping practices.

KGB The acronym for the Committee of State Security, the last of a succession of names for the Soviet secret police. It was created in March 1954 and styled itself 'the punishing sword of the Party'. Its First Department dealt with international intelligence gathering. In 1991 it was renamed the Agency for Federal Security of the Russian Republic.

King Cotton Diplomacy A phrase used to describe the DIPLOMACY of the Confederacy during the American Civil War. Because Britain and France depended on cotton from the Southern States, the Confederacy reasoned that they would resist the BLOCKADE being imposed by the North and give RECOGNITION and support. The South attempted to impose an embargo and resorted to burning its own cotton. The STRATEGY failed for several reasons. Britain had stockpiled cotton before the war, was importing it also from India, and was profiting from other industries and not as dependent on cotton as the Confederacy believed. In addition, it did not want to go to war with the North.

Knesset The Parliament of the State of Israel. It is elected for four-year terms on the basis of universal suffrage and according to rules of proportional representation.

Korean War (1950–3) The early COLD WAR conflict that followed the invasion of South Korea by North Korea on 25 June 1950. The fact that the USSR was at this time boycotting the UNITED NATIONS SECURITY COUNCIL permitted a United Nations (UN) resolution to form a multinational force to combat the AGGRESSION. US President Truman (1884–1972) was determined to resist any further extension of COMMUNISM, particularly after the victory of Mao-Zedong (1893–1976) in China the previous year. When this force reached the Chinese border, occupying most of North Korea in October 1950, China invaded with over a million soldiers, producing a stalemate. An ARMISTICE was signed on 27 July 1953 and a DEMILITARIZED ZONE instituted between North and South Korea, patrolled by the UN. This was one of a number of indications of a lessening of international tension following the death of Stalin (1879–1953). Though three million died in the course of the conflict, it did not lead to the wider conflagration that some feared, with recourse to use of the ATOMIC BOMB, or invasion of China. In essence it remained a limited conflict.

Kreminology A word coined during the COLD WAR to describe the interpretation of the policies and intentions of the USSR. Faced with a closed society and the secrecy of Soviet decision making, its practitioners relied on reading between the lines of public declarations, decoding allusions and making inferences. A leading figure in Kreminology was George F. Kennan (b. 1904), one of the early proponents of the doctrine of CONTAINMENT of the USSR and COMMUNISM.

Kremlin The Moscow citadel, the locus of government offices, churches and the former palaces of the Tsar. It was used to refer to the government of the USSR and now refers to that of the Russian Federation.

L

Landlocked states STATES without a coastline. They have been particularly vulnerable to economic warfare since controlling access to the sea can be used to apply pressure to the landlocked state and BLOCKADE its economy. The territorial arrangement of the Polish Corridor up to DANZIG (now Gdansk) after the First World War, though it created significant tension with Germany, was contrived to allow Poland maritime access. The revision by the LAW OF THE SEA CONFERENCE (UNCLOS) in 1982 attempted to extend the landlocked states some maritime rights, especially concerning resources of the seabed under the COMMON HERITAGE OF MANKIND (CHM) doctrine. However, this has not been universally ratified.

Lausanne Treaty (1923) The revised peace settlement between Britain, France and Turkey after the First World War. It followed Greece's defeat in Anatolia and the repudiation of the Sèvres Treaty (1920) by the Turkish leader Kemal Ataturk (1881–1938). Turkey gained Smyrna, Eastern Thrace and the islands of Imbros and Tenedos from Greece. It also led to a compulsory exchange of minorities, affirmed Turkey's territorial integrity and SOVEREIGNTY and ended the Greek dream of uniting Anatolian Greeks in an enlarged Greek state.

Law of Nations See INTERNATIONAL LAW.

Law of the Sea Conferences (UNCLOS I, II and III) (1958, 1960, 1973–82) The general principles of the Law of the Sea are that STATES should be able to use the HIGH SEAS without interference and that it is the responsibility of states to maintain law and order on the sea. The 1958 conference produced four conventions, respectively on the CONTINENTAL SHELF, the TERRITORIAL WATERS or sea, the CONTIGUOUS ZONE, the High Seas, and fishing and conservation of the living resources of the High Seas. All of these agreements had entered into force by 1966. The second conference concentrated on the issue of the breadth of the territorial sea and the proposal failed by one vote. The third conference set out to develop a comprehensive TREATY taking into account changes since 1958, and these negotiations dragged on for nine years, with the most prominent of the opponents being the USA, which objected most to provisions relating to deep-sea mining. The primary unresolved issues related to the nature of control to be exercised over this and other forms of exploitation of sea resources beyond the 200-mile national exclusive economic zones. However, the USA took the view that much of the rest of the proposed treaty was already binding as part of customary INTERNATIONAL LAW.

Laws of War The rules governing the conduct of ARMED CONFLICT and the protection of victims of WAR.

LDCs See (1) LESS DEVELOPED COUNTRIES; (2) LEAST DEVELOPED COUNTRIES.

League of Arab States See ARAB LEAGUE.

League of Nations An association of NATION STATES rather than a supranational body, the League was founded on 24 April 1919 at the PARIS PEACE CONFERENCE (1919–20) following the First World War, with a constitution, the LEAGUE OF NATIONS COVENANT, consisting of twenty-six articles. It was incorporated in, and therefore subsequently identified with, the PEACE TREATIES. With headquarters in Geneva, it was an institutional attempt to achieve COLLECTIVE SECURITY and DISARMAMENT, binding its members to respect the territorial integrity of other STATES and to preserve them against AGGRESSION. International disputes were to be referred to it for ARBITRATION and SANCTIONS were to be applied against non-compliant states. A leading and conspicuous defect was that it never had universal membership. Most notably, in spite of its championship by US President Woodrow Wilson (1856–1924) (it was heralded in the last of the FOURTEEN POINTS), the USA rejected it. The only GREAT POWERS to be members throughout its existence were Britain and France. Germany was not allowed to join until 1926 and left after the rise to power of Hitler (1889–1945) in 1933. Japan left after the conquest of Manchuria, in 1933, and Italy after the defeat of Abyssinia, in 1937. The USSR did not join until 1934 and was expelled for invading Finland in 1939.

The League did not possess an army and the half-hearted application of sanctions against Italy in 193–6 proved the decisive test of its CREDIBILITY. After this it was discredited as a peacekeeping institution and effectively bypassed during the CRISES leading to the Second World War. In other work, however, for instance, with MANDATES and REFUGEE resettlement, it was more successful. Its responsibilities were transferred to the UNITED NATIONS (UN) in 1946.

League of Nations Covenant A document with twenty-six articles that provided the constitution for the LEAGUE OF NATIONS and was included in the VERSAILLES TREATY (1919). The first seven articles established the constitutional basis of the League. The purpose of the organization was to promote international cooperation, PEACE and SECURITY achieved through DISARMAMENT, the pacific settlement of disputes, the use of SANCTIONS and the collective guarantee of one another's independence. The core was ARTICLE X, under which members agreed to preserve each other's territorial integrity and political independence against external AGGRESSION. Articles XI–XVI specified the procedures for resolving international conflicts.

Least Developed Countries (LDCs) An international term introduced in the 1980s by the UNITED NATIONS CONFERENCE ON TRADE AND DEVELOPMENT (UNCTAD) to describe the forty poorest and most economically backward countries in the world. The majority of these countries are in Africa, though they also include Afghanistan, Nepal, Samoa and Yemen. The present classification emphasizes income rather than development.

Lebensraum German for 'living space'. An essential part of the programme of German National Socialism, providing for the expansion of the German people. It was preceded by PAN-GERMANISM, which the doctrine of *Lebensraum* combined with the Aryan racial doctrine: in the framework of a 'new world order' the predestined German master race was to gain living space at the cost of the Slavs and Jews. The creation of the Greater German Reich led to the temporary acquisition of land in the east as in 1918 with the BREST-LITOVSK TREATY. The failure of Operation BARBAROSSA and the defeat of Nazi Germany in 1945 reversed the process and led to the expulsion of millions of Germans from EASTERN EUROPE.

Legal War The conduct of formal hostilities among nations permitted by INTERNATIONAL LAW under the LEAGUE OF NATIONS COVENANT to resort to WAR after complying with certain conditions. Under the UNITED NATIONS CHARTER, self-defence, as specified in ARTICLE 51, is the only justification for war.

Legation This term has two senses in international relations. First there is the right of legation, which is the right of a recognized independent STATE to accredit envoys to other states and receive them in return. Only states that are fully sovereign can exercise the right of legation. Secondly, legation can mean a diplomatic establishment that ranks below that of an embassy.

Legitimacy The implication of the existence of right, as when a government is said to have, or to have been granted, a right to govern based on such criteria as its popular acceptance, or the legal and constitutional processes that brought it to, and maintain it in, a position of authority. The German sociologist Max Weber (1864–1920) described three general bases, historically, for legitimation, or justification, of authority: tradition, charisma, such as messianic leadership, and rational legal authority. Significant problems arise when the authority exercised is not accepted as legitimate, where, for instance, populations do not accept territorial boundaries, in divided societies, and particularly where there are questions of national minorities. This, for instance, led in the 1990s to the disintegration of Yugoslavia.

Lend-Lease The Second World War US programme to provide economic and military assistance to countries fighting the AXIS. Originally designed in 1940–1 to support Britain in its resistance to Nazi Germany, it later developed into a programme to assist all of America's allies at war. Arguing that the USA must become an 'ARSENAL OF DEMOCRACY', President Franklin D. Roosevelt (1882–1945) first proposed Lend-Lease in December 1940 as a means of overcoming Britain's inability to pay for war supplies. The Lend-Lease Act was passed in March 1941 and by the end of the war $50 billion dollars in total in assistance had been disbursed to thirty-eight countries, including China and the USSR Its abrupt termination after the war caused international tension, particularly with the USSR.

Less developed countries (LDCs) A term referring to economic development normally used to describe the THIRD WORLD of Africa, Asia and Latin America. These countries are generally recipients of AID and dependent on the advanced industrial countries. They are also sometimes described as 'SOUTH' in the characterization of the North–South divide.

LIC See LOW-INTENSITY CONFLICT.

Limited Nuclear Test-Ban Treaty (1963) See PARTIAL TEST-BAN TREATY.

Limited Nuclear War See LIMITED STRATEGIC WAR.

Limited sovereignty A doctrine advanced both by the USA and the USSR during the COLD WAR. It was proposed in the USA in 1947 as a corollary of the TRUMAN DOCTRINE (1947) and argued that, where the USA had accepted the responsibility of protecting a country against COMMUNISM, the country concerned should accept US control of its external and internal policies to the extent that this was relevant to SECURITY. The doctrine was widely discussed in the West during the cold war and was notably rejected by France. This argument was advanced, on the other side, in the WARSAW PACT, especially in the USSR with the BREZHNEV DOCTRINE.

Limited strategic war The concept of WAR in which nuclear strikes are used, but with calculated restraint as to the number and power of warheads and the nature of targets, so they may be combined with bargaining and communication with the enemy. Many have argued that it would, in fact, be very hard to limit nuclear ESCALATION. The notion of limited nuclear options first became public knowledge in 1974 when President Nixon's Secretary of Defence James Schlesinger (b. 1929) announced the SCHLESINGER DOCTRINE, a new STRATEGY moving away from ASSURED DESTRUCTION.

Limits of growth A report published in 1972, commissioned by the CLUB OF ROME. It was a significant contribution to a growing debate about global resources, unrestrained industrialization and the environment. It predicted that, if current trends continued, within 100 years or less the world would see mass starvation and death due to pollution. While alerting its readers to the depletion of resources, it also predicted a growing gap between rich and poor if growth continued unchecked.

Linkage The dependence of one question, or policy, on another. In international relations this term can refer to bargaining concessions in diplomatic/economic negotiations in one field for those in another. For instance, this might be the lifting of SANCTIONS in return for improvement in provision of HUMAN RIGHTS, or the granting of trade concessions and credits in return for a commitment to ARMS CONTROL. Linkage as a diplomatic ploy was, for example, particularly used in DÉTENTE by the US SECRETARY OF STATE Henry Kissinger (b. 1923) in the early 1970s. Conceptually, the term 'linkage' is used to describe the pluralist theoretical perspective in international relations, emphasizing interaction between domestic and foreign policies and between national developments and international events.

Lisbon force goals A decision taken by the NORTH ATLANTIC TREATY ORGANIZATION (NATO) in Lisbon in 1952. It proposed to increase conventional NATO forces to a level such that they would be able to repel a Soviet invasion of Western Europe. European members were reluctant to commit themselves to the doubling of forces in two years that it involved and the costs that would be diverted from investment and social welfare. The incoming US administration under President Eisenhower (1890–1969), which came into office in 1953, was apprehensive about the inflationary consequences of such rearmament and the goals were abandoned. NATO then switched to an emphasis on nuclear defence with the adoption of the doctrine of MASSIVE RETALIATION in 1954.

Littoral states States bordering on water. Israel and Egypt, for instance, are littoral states of the Red Sea.

LNOs Limited nuclear options.

Localization In world affairs this term is used to describe the reaction against GLOBALIZATION, seen, for instance, in ethnic NATIONALISM, demands for greater popular participation and environmental movements. Within countries it means demands for devolution and the mobilization of local opinion against national policies.

Locarno Treaties (1925) A series of agreements for the stabilization of Europe and RAPPROCHEMENT between Germany and its neighbours signed in December 1925. They comprised five separate documents, four of which were conventions for ARBITRATION between Germany and its neighbours, France, Belgium, Czechoslovakia and Poland. The fifth, and best-known (the 'Rhineland Pact'), was a multilateral TREATY. The first part was a treaty of non-aggression by which the powers situated on the Rhine, Germany, France and Belgium, agreed not to attack, invade or resort to WAR against each other. Secondly, by a treaty of mutual assistance, the Western European countries, Britain, France, Germany, Belgium and Italy, agreed to respect the DEMILITARIZATION of the RHINELAND, to defend the existing borders and to give military assistance to any power that fell victim to the treaty's violation. In spite of pressure from France for an 'eastern Locarno', reassuring EASTERN EUROPE, such guarantees were not forthcoming and Germany felt free later to challenge those boundaries. The so-called spirit of Locarno was short lived and in 1936 Hitler (1889–1945) reoccupied the Rhineland as the first of his territorial moves that subsequently led to the Second World War.

Lodge   Corollary   (1911) Named after US Senator Henry Cabot Lodge (1850–1924), this added an amendment to the MONROE DOCTRINE (1823). It arose from the projected sale of land in California to Japanese investors, including a harbour. The corollary stated that such strategic places could not be sold to a foreign country whose government might make military use of them against the USA. The Senate endorsed this on 2 August 1912 by a vote of 51–4 and the land sale never took place.

Lodge   Reservations These were named after Senator Henry Cabot Lodge (1850–1924), Chairman of the US Senate Foreign Relations Committee, who was the leading congressional opponent of President Woodrow Wilson (1856–1924). The most important of fourteen reservations was the second, which stipulated that an act or joint resolution of Congress be required for any US action under ARTICLE X of the LEAGUE OF NATIONS COVENANT, which was attached to the VERSAILLES TREATY (1919). For the President, these reservations, of which eight were passed, nullified the Treaty, which was subsequently rejected by the USA on 19 March 1920. As a consequence the USA did not join the LEAGUE OF NATIONS.

Logistics The military science relating to the supply, storage and delivery of all the necessities of an army, from ammunition, fuel, reinforcements and weapons to clothing, food and medicine. With the pace, mobility and destructiveness of modern warfare, these require much planning, calculation and manpower. Logistics can be subdivided into strategic and tactical: the first covering the acquisition, stocking and transport of supplies to the theatre of WAR or battlefield; and the second their distribution within it.

Lomé   Conventions These four conventions, respectively in 1975, 1979, 1984 and 1989, defined the economic relationship and established terms of trade between the members of the EUROPEAN COMMUNITY (EC) and the AFRICAN, CARIBBEAN AND PACIFIC (ACP) countries, which were mainly ex-European colonies. The Lomé agreements have exempted ACP from industrial and the great majority of agricultural, tariffs. They also concern development AID in grants and low-interest loans.

LON See LEAGUE OF NATIONS.

Long Peace A phrase coined by the US historian of the COLD WAR John Lewis Gaddis (b. 1941) in a book published in 1987 with that title and subtitled *Inquiries into the History of the Cold War*. He stressed the stability of the East–West balance during the period since the Second World War: 'Without anyone having designed it . . . the nations of the post-war era locked into a system of international relations that, because it had been based upon the realities of power, has served the cause of order – if not justice – better than one might have expected.'

Low-intensity conflict (LIC) Hostilities that fall short of full-scale WAR. LIC includes a range of military interventions: in particular, PEACEKEEPING, anti-terrorism, commando action and support for foreign law-enforcement agencies, assisting other governments to maintain order. With the growth of international TERRORISM since the 1960s, as in Northern Ireland and the Middle East, and the extension of covert AID in particular by the SUPERPOWERS, low-intensity conflict and planning for it have become a growing concern for armed and security forces.

Luxembourg Compromise Sometimes nicknamed the 'agreement to dis-agree'. This arrangement, reached by the six members of the EUROPEAN COMMUNITIES in January 1966, resolved the six-month dispute of the 'EMPTY CHAIR CRISIS' between France and its partners. It dealt with the rights of STATES within the EC COUNCIL OF MINISTERS. Since it stated that the representatives of individual STATES had a right to veto proposals where they believed their own national interests might be adversely affected, it marked a victory in the dispute for the French President Charles de Gaulle (1890–1970). It strengthened the position of national governments vis-à-vis the Commission and stalled further developments in European INTEGRATION for twenty years.

Luxembourg Declaration (1984) A joint statement issued by the EUROPEAN COMMUNITIES (EC) and the EUROPEAN FREE TRADE ASSOCIATION (EFTA) committing them to close economic cooperation. Subsequently, in 1990, the two organizations agreed to establish the EUROPEAN ECONOMIC AREA (EEA).

Luxembourg Treaty (1970) This was the first significant amendment to the ROME TREATY (1957). It was signed by the six member states of the EUROPEAN COM-MUNITY (EC), France, Germany, Italy, Belgium, the Netherlands and Luxembourg, in April 1970. Its most important innovation was to introduce a new budgetary method of funding the organization.

Lytton Commission (1932) This was formed at China's request by the LEAGUE OF NATIONS and headed by the second Earl of Lytton (1876–1947) following the occupation of Manchuria by Japan and its transformation into the PUPPET STATE of Manchukuo, which was also to include part of Mongolia. The Commission's report condemned Japan for its AGGRESSION in China and rejected claims that Manchukuo was an independent STATE. It recommended that the territory be governed by an autonomous administration under Chinese SOVEREIGNTY, which at the same time made special provision for Japan's economic interests in the region. Japan consoli-dated its hold over Manchukuo and left the League.

M

Maastricht Treaty See TREATY ON EUROPEAN UNION (TEU) (1992).

Machiavellianism After Niccolò Machiavelli (1469–1527), the Renaissance Florentine official, diplomat and scholar who, in his most famous tract *The Prince* (1513), described and advocated the pursuit and maintenance of POWER untroubled by moral scruples. The word came to describe the acceptance of RAISON D'ÉTAT and pursuit of self-interest as overriding all other considerations. Presuming human self-ishness to be the key motivating force in humanity, he regarded strong-arm government as the only answer to the disorder and corruption of Italian public life in his own day.

Machtpolitik German for power politics. In international relations it refers particularly to negotiations under an implied threat of FORCE.

MAD Mutual Assured Destruction. See ASSURED DESTRUCTION.

Maghreb From the Arabic for 'western'. That part of north-west Africa that includes Algeria, Morocco and Tunisia.

Maginot Line The construction during the 1930s of a fortified barrier in north-east France to protect against German invasion. It was named after André Maginot (1877–32), Minister of War. While intended to provide SECURITY, it has also usually been taken as a symbol of French unwillingness to engage in offensive military planning after the LOCARNO TREATIES (1925), which guaranteed the Franco-German border. Crucially, the Maginot Line through reasons of finance and DIPLOMACY was not extended from the Ardennes to the North Sea. This ensured that, when the German BLITZKRIEG hit France in May 1940, it came through the Belgian Ardennes.

Maginot mentality This phrase was used by some critics of the NORTH ATLANTIC TREATY ORGANIZATION (NATO) STRATEGY in Europe during the COLD WAR. They claimed that the fixed forward DEFENCE along the entire line of the frontier between East and West Germany was repeating the French mistake that had helped to bring France to defeat in May 1940. The main argument was that fixed defence ceded the WARSAW PACT the initiative. The criticism was misplaced. The Maginot Line had not been completed and was circumvented by Nazi Germany. Moreover, defence of the frontier was necessary to retain German faith in NATO.

Malthusianism The influential and controversial theory expounded by the English Rev. Thomas Malthus (1766–1834) in his *Essay on the Principle of Population* first published in 1798. He argued that human population would always adjust upwards to an increase in the means of subsistence, food increasing in arithmetical progression and population in geometrical progression. Hence food would always be scarce in relation to population.

Mandates The LEAGUE OF NATIONS instituted mandates under Article XXII of the LEAGUE OF NATIONS COVENANT, by which territories formerly held by Germany and Turkey were placed under the guardianship of one of the victorious allies in the First World War. This was to be until such time as the territory was ready to take its place as an independent STATE in the COMMUNITY OF NATIONS. Like the subsequent TRUST TERRITORIES under the UNITED NATIONS (UN), mandates fell under no state's SOVEREIGNTY. Each mandatory power was responsible to the League. The system had three categories, relating to their stage of development. Class A consisted of Arab territories formerly under the Ottoman Empire (Iraq, Lebanon, Palestine, Syria and Transjordan). B mandates were the former German possessions in Africa, the

Cameroons, Rwanda Urundi, Tanganyika and Togoland. Class C included South-West Africa, Samoa, Nauru, the Carolines, the Marianas and the Marshall Islands.

Manhattan Project The research project established by the US Department of War in 1942 during the Second World War to develop the world's first ATOMIC BOMB. A special laboratory, Los Alamos, was constructed in New Mexico. Some scientists argued that international controls be instituted before the bomb was used, but their appeals failed to persuade the officials in the US administration. Following a test in July near Alamogordo, atomic bombs were dropped on Hiroshima on 6 August 1945 and three days later at Nagasaki. The war in the Far East ended on 14 August.

Manifest Destiny A phrase that came to be used commonly in the 1840s and 1850s in the USA by expansionists. It was first used in an article in the *Democratic Review* in 1845 in which the editor wrote that it was the 'manifest destiny' of US citizens 'to overspread the Continent allotted by Providence for the free development of our yearly multiplying millions'. By the end of the nineteenth century this was coming to be advanced as justification for US acquisition of territories overseas, such as Hawaii.

Marshall Plan (1947) The proposal for an extensive programme of US aid to assist and stimulate economic reconstruction and recovery in Europe after the Second World War, announced by General George Marshall (1880–1959), US SECRETARY OF STATE. It was rejected by the USSR and EASTERN BLOC countries, and the distribution of funds over a four-year period to Western Europe was instigated by the European Recovery Programme (ERP), providing in total $13.2 billion. Its purpose was to prevent destabilization and the spread of COMMUNISM, to encourage the US economy by enabling Western Europe to purchase American goods, and to provide humanitarian support. By 1952 industrial production overall in Western Europe had reached 35 per cent above its pre-war level. The plan also optimistically envisaged greater European economic INTEGRATION, accompanying the stabilization and rising prosperity, than at this stage occurred.

Martial Law Normally the temporary control by military authorities of civilian populations, such as during wartime occupations or in times when major civil disturbances threaten, or appear to threaten. A major example in recent times is the suppression of SOLIDARITY in Poland in December 1981 by the so-called Military Council of National Salvation (WRON) under General Jaruzelski (b. 1923).

Marxism See COMMUNISM.

Masada Complex A term that has been applied to Israeli political thinking in relation to its hostile Arab neighbours. Masada was the fortified castle above the Dead Sea in which 960 Jewish Zealots held out against Roman forces. In the end, when the Romans broke through in 73 AD, all but two women and five children had committed suicide rather than surrender. This term has been used to sum up the view that a fight to the bitter end is preferable to surrender of Israeli statehood, with the slogan 'Masada shall not fall again!'

Massive Retaliation A global strategic doctrine adopted by the USA and the NORTH ATLANTIC TREATY ORGANIZATION (NATO) in 1954. It suggested that the USA would rely on the deterrent power of NUCLEAR WEAPONS as a primary means of conducting foreign policy. It would enable the USA and NATO to negotiate from a position of strength and help the US administration achieve a balanced budget. Regarded as cost-effective DEFENCE, massive retaliation would mean a large-scale nuclear response against Soviet territory. In Europe the failure to achieve the LISBON FORCE GOALS indicated that the cost of matching the conventional strength of the USSR and its allies was more than the NATO STATES were willing to bear. In practice, it limited policy options, offering the choice between TOTAL WAR and inaction. In particular, it raised doubts in Europe as to whether the USA would be willing to risk nuclear retaliation for a Soviet attack in Europe. It was later superseded by the doctrine of FLEXIBLE RESPONSE.

MBFR   See MUTUAL AND BALANCED FORCE REDUCTION.

McCarthyism   The witch-hunting named after Republican Senator Joseph R. McCarthy (1909–57) of Wisconsin. During the early 1950s he mounted highly publicized campaigns for the exposure of Communists in American public life, exploiting the tensions of the early years of the COLD WAR, following the Soviet acquisition of the ATOMIC BOMB, the victory of COMMUNISM in China (both in 1949) and the invasion of South Korea by North Korea in 1950. Under senatorial immunity he made repeated unsubstantiated allegations, particularly against officials in the DEPARTMENT OF STATE. The term has been applied more widely to cover other cases where concern over national SECURITY has been manipulated for political purposes and demagogues have made false accusations and abused legislative investigatory powers.

McMahon Act (1946)   See ATOMIC ENERGY ACT.

Measures Short of War   Actions undertaken by one STATE against another to protect its rights and retaliate without formal declaration of WAR. It may include such measures as breaking off diplomatic relations, RETORSION or BLOCKADE, among others. Under both the LEAGUE OF NATIONS COVENANT and the UNITED NATIONS CHARTER the idea has been that members should have recourse to procedures for the peaceful settlement of disputes rather than resorting to measures short of war, or conflict.

Megaphone diplomacy   This term was first applied to the hostile verbal exchanges between the USA and the USSR in the early 1980s at a time of high tension in the COLD WAR. A particular example was the denunciation of the USSR as the 'evil empire'. Since then the term 'megaphone diplomacy' has been used more generally.

Mediation   The involvement of a third party in the settlement of a dispute. This differs from GOOD OFFICES in that the mediator not only offers to be an impartial channel of communication between the parties but assists them by making suggestions and proposals, attempting to reconcile and ameliorate relations, and actively negotiating.

Megaton   A term used to indicate the YIELD of a NUCLEAR WEAPON, measured in terms of the amount of a conventional explosive, such as TNT, which would have to be exploded to produce the same energy release. A megaton explosion is equivalent to exploding a million tons of TNT (a kiloton being equivalent to the detonation of a thousand tons).

MEP Member of the EUROPEAN PARLIAMENT (EP).

Mercantilism Historically, the mercantilist system was a product of the emergence of the early modern STATE with its centralized administration and standing army, though, as a term, it was largely unknown until the publication of *The Wealth of Nations* (1776) by Adam Smith (1723–90), which advocated FREE TRADE. The main goal of mercantilism was to increase national wealth through a favourable BALANCE OF TRADE which would increase a country's stock of gold, silver and specie (bullionism). To achieve this end countries promoted industries that made them self-sufficient by excluding foreign production as much as possible from the domestic market through such means as monopolies and tariffs. Currently the term may be used to describe the belief in the merits of BALANCE OF PAYMENTS surpluses and advocacy of PROTECTIONISM.

Mercosur The regional economic organization linking Argentina, Brazil, Paraguay and Uruguay, which was established by the Treaty of Asunción in 1991. In 1996 Chile gained associate status. A FREE TRADE AREA with between 200 and 300 million, it is the second most important economic bloc in the Americas after the signing of the NORTH AMERICAN FREE TRADE AGREEMENT (NAFTA).

Merger Treaty (1965) This treaty established a single COUNCIL OF MINISTERS and a single EUROPEAN COMMISSION for the three EUROPEAN COMMUNITIES, the EUROPEAN ECONOMIC COMMUNITY (EEC), the EUROPEAN COAL AND STEEL COMMUNITY (ECSC) and the EUROPEAN ATOMIC ENERGY COMMUNITY (EURATOM). It came into force on 6 July 1967.

Messina Conference The meeting in June 1955 of the foreign ministers of the SIX, the member states of the EUROPEAN COAL AND STEEL COMMUNITY (ECSC), which subsequently (through the report produced by the Belgian Foreign Minister Paul-Henri Spaak (1899–1972)) resulted in the ROME TREATIES (1957), which set up the EUROPEAN ECONOMIC COMMUNITY (EEC) and the EUROPEAN ATOMIC ENERGY COMMISSION (EURATOM).

Metaconflict A conflict over the nature of a conflict.

Mexico City Conference (1945) See CHAPULTEPEC CONFERENCE.

MFN Most favoured nation. See MOST-FAVOURED-NATION STATUS.

MIC See MILITARY–INDUSTRIAL COMPLEX.

Micro-states The UNITED NATIONS (UN) and the COMMONWEALTH OF NATIONS define micro-states as those with under one million inhabitants. There are forty of these STATES, some of them occupying strategically important locations, such as Malta. The US invasion of Grenada drew particular attention to this kind of state and how it may assume an international importance bearing no relation to its size.

Middle powers Those states able to play only a restricted role in regions other than their own. The British international relations scholar Martin Wright (1913–72) defined a middle power in *Power Politics* (1978) as follows: 'a power with such military strength, resources and strategic position that, in peacetime, the great powers bid for its support, and wartime, while it has no hopes of winning a war against a great power, it can hope to inflict costs on a greater power out of proportion to what the great power can hope to gain by attacking it.' Such powers may also be classified as 'secondary powers' or sometimes 'regional great powers'.

Militarism This term came into existence in the mid-nineteenth century to characterize, among other things, the ascendancy of Prussia and the pretensions of the French Second Empire. It has normally been used with a pejorative intention. A society is in the grip of militarism when there is an excessive influence of military institutions, personnel and values over civilians. It was described by Alfred Vagts in his *History of Militarism* (1938) as 'a domination of the military over the civilian, an undue preponderance of military demands, and emphasis on military considerations, spirit, ideals and scales of values, in the life of states'. Militarism was rampant, for instance, in Nazi Germany and Fascist Italy and more recently the term has been used by critics of the immense defence build-up and ARMS RACE that characterized the COLD WAR and of the propaganda that accompanied it.

Military–industrial complex This phrase was used by US President Dwight D. Eisenhower (1890–1969) in his farewell address on 17 January 1961. During the Second World War the USA had organized itself to fight a WAR in which the military expanded enormously. The network of military, industrial and bureaucratic links had developed further as national infrastructure in the COLD WAR to sustain the policy of CONTAINMENT against COMMUNISM and the USSR and China in particular, supported by an anti-Communist consensus in public opinion. At various times – for example, during the VIETNAM WAR (1960–75) – the institutions and activities of this dominant interest have been challenged and, from the point of view of governments, justified by new emergencies and threats, real or perceived.

Military Necessity Doctrine The doctrine according to which in cases of extreme military emergency and necessity the LAWS OF WAR lose their binding force. This is rejected by CONVENTIONS from the HAGUE PEACE CONFERENCES (1899, 1907), which state that the belligerents' right to adopt means of injuring the enemy is not unlimited and that this rule does not lose its binding force in cases of military necessity.

Military Operations Other Than War (MOOTW) A US term to describe military operations engaged in with the object of resolving conflicts, preventing the outbreak of wars and supporting governments in crisis.

Minimum deterrence A term from the COLD WAR. Minimum deterrence is what is believed to be just enough to deter an enemy from mounting a FIRST STRIKE. The British and French nuclear capabilities have been regarded as minimum deterrents. For instance, although Britain's capability was greatly inferior to the US arsenal, it was argued that it could inflict enough damage on the USSR, the MOSCOW OPTION, to dissuade the latter from attacking.

Minority clauses Clauses in treaties between STATES that provide for the protection of national minorities. They were incorporated, for instance, in the inter-war years into those treaties between the Allied and Associated Powers and certain East European and Balkan states such as Hungary, Bulgaria and Turkey, providing for the protection of their racial, religious and linguistic minorities. An attempt to protect and enhance HUMAN RIGHTS, they were hard to sustain in the face of the rise of the dictatorships and failure of COLLECTIVE SECURITY.

Minority treaties A series of agreements between the victorious Allied Powers after the First World War and the countries of CENTRAL and EASTERN EUROPE. These were guaranteed by the LEAGUE OF NATIONS and obliged the STATES to respect the rights of their ethnic minorities. They were not always reciprocal. An example of this is the TREATY with Poland, which included protection of the German minority, while the Polish minority in Germany was not offered protection by any such treaty. Polish public opinion regarded the treaty as a limitation of national SOVEREIGNTY by the League and interference with internal affairs. From 1934 Poland consequently refused to cooperate with the League in minorities issues.

MIRVs See MULTIPLE INDEPENDENTLY TARGETED RE-ENTRY VEHICLES.

Missile gap The illusion in the USA in the late 1950s that the USSR had a far larger arsenal of nuclear missiles than it in fact had and that the USA was vulnerable to a FIRST STRIKE. Soviet defence advances had been a series of shocks. In the first place, it had expected its first ATOMIC BOMB years before the USA anticipated that it would be able to. Not least, also, the USSR had been the first country successfully to launch a satellite, SPUTNIK I, in 1957. The allegation that the Republican administration under Dwight D. Eisenhower (1890–1969) had allowed the USSR to steal a march in the nuclear ARMS RACE featured prominently in the 1960 presidential election campaign in which the Democrat candidate John F. Kennedy (1917–63) was successful. By the time of the CUBAN MISSILE CRISIS (1962), with much-improved US INTELLIGENCE gathering, it was clear that the USSR was very significantly behind.

Mission civilisatrice The French for 'civilizing mission', this term has been used since the nineteenth century to justify and commend French colonial expansion and global influence.

Mitteleuropa German for CENTRAL EUROPE. This concept first developed in the nineteenth century in the German-speaking areas of the Hapsburg Empire to describe an area possessing an identity distinct from both Prussian and Slav traditions. It was popularized in the first half of the twentieth century by German nationalists in general and, latterly, by the Third Reich to mean an enlarged area of German economic HEGEMONY and dominance. Since 1989 it has been taken up by previously Communist STATES in EASTERN EUROPE to assert their independence and regional identity.

MLF See MULTILATERAL FORCE.

MNC Multinational corporation, sometimes also called transnational corporation.

Mobilization In WAR, the preparation of a NATION. During the First and Second World wars this meant very significant government economic and social intervention as well as calling up forces and reserves to active military duty and arming them. Government controls were placed over manpower, resources, production and prices. In the major combatant nations, TOTAL WAR meant precisely that, with considerable attention also paid to sustaining the morale of populations.

MOD British Ministry of Defence.

Molotov–Ribbentrop Pact See NAZI-SOVIET NON-AGGRESSION PACT (1939).

Mondialisme Term for the foreign policy associated with French President Valéry Giscard d'Estaing (b. 1926), motivated by the belief that France should maintain a worldwide presence and practise an assertive role in world affairs. It was a modified continuation of the policy of *grandeur* of President de Gaulle (1890–1970) and involved a number of initiatives in the THIRD WORLD, not least in Francophone Africa and, in particularly close association with West Germany, encouraged important developments in the EUROPEAN COMMUNITY (EC) such as the EUROPEAN COUNCIL and the EUROPEAN MONETARY SYSTEM (EMS).

Monnet method Named after Jean Monnet (1888–1979), a key figure in the process of West European INTEGRATION in the years that led to the ROME TREATIES of 1957. It has been described as the approach of 'integration by stealth', promoting SPILLOVER from one economic sector to another (beginning with coal and steel in the EUROPEAN COAL AND STEEL COMMUNITY (ECSC)), and from market integration to political unity.

Monroe Doctrine (1823) The propositions contained in the annual message of US President James Monroe (1758–1831) to Congress on 2 December 1823 and the general tenet of US foreign policy since then. The original propositions were: (1) the 'American Continents, by the free and independent condition which they have assumed and maintained, are henceforward not to be considered as subjects for future colonization by European Powers'; (2) in 'wars of European powers in matters relating to themselves we have never taken part, nor does it comport with our policy to do so', and (3) we 'owe it . . . to candour . . . to declare that we should consider any attempt on their [European Powers'] part to extend their system to any portion of this hemisphere as dangerous to our peace and safety'. The Monroe Doctrine has been raised as a barrier to European INTERVENTION in Central and Latin America, but also, through the ROOSEVELT COROLLARY (1904) as a justification for US intervention in that area. An article of faith in the USA, as a defence of the new society, it subsequently also assumed a hegemonic aspect as defining the rights of the USA within its own SPHERE OF INFLUENCE. So, for instance, it was invoked during the COLD WAR, such as in the CUBAN MISSILE CRISIS (1962) to justify the QUARANTINE of Cuba and in other interventions to prevent COMMUNISM spreading in Latin America.

Monrovia Group Formally known as the Inter-African and Malagasy States Organization of African Unity. This was the group of twenty African STATES that attended a summit meeting in Monrovia, Nigeria, in May 1961, which affirmed the equality of all African states, and laid the basis for the ORGANIZATION OF AFRICAN STATES (OAS).

Mood Theory This term refers to the role of public opinion in the formulation of, or constraint on, foreign policy. It was coined by the American Gabriel Almond (b. 1911) in his book *The American People and Foreign Policy*, published during the VIET-NAM WAR (1960–75) in 1966. It was argued in this work that public opinion is not passive, but neither is it innovative. Mass public opinion holds international issues in vague focus, is impressionistic and not well informed about them. However, certain attitudes based on past experience exercise an influence, for instance, the 'Never Again' sentiment after the carnage of the First World War, or the subsequent alleged effect of the VIETNAM SYNDROME on US attitudes to foreign military intervention after 1973.

MOOTW See MILITARY OPERATIONS OTHER THAN WAR.

Moratorium A pause, for example, in negotiations, pending the agreement of a TREATY; or suspension, for a period, of debt repayments.

Moscow Conference (1960) A Communist summit conference held in November 1960 with the purpose of addressing the growing split between the USSR and the Chinese People's Republic, which at this stage was not plainly visible to the outside world. China criticized the USSR under Nikita Khrushchev (1894–1971) for its policy of PEACEFUL COEXISTENCE with the West and spoke out strongly in favour of WARS OF NATIONAL LIBERATION. A common statement issued on 6 December on peaceful coexistence did not succeed in preventing growing hostility, which was to lead even to limited military clashes in the late 1960s, between Soviet and Chinese forces.

Moscow Declaration (1943) Issued by the foreign ministers of the USA, Britain, the Soviet Union and China in October 1943, this was the first clear commitment to the early establishment of a general international organization for the maintenance of PEACE and SECURITY, which should be an improvement on the LEAGUE OF NATIONS. Final agreement was reached on the foundation of the UNITED NATIONS (UN) at the SAN FRANCISCO CONFERENCE between April and June 1945.

Moscow Line A term from the COLD WAR, it denoted the orientation of those Communist parties that supported the Communist Party of the Soviet Union (CPSU) as the guide, leader and interpreter of Marxist-Leninism on an international scale.

Moscow Option A strategic rationale for the British possession of NUCLEAR WEAPONS during the COLD WAR, this was sometimes also called the 'Moscow Criterion'. From the 1960s the argument was advanced that the threat that Britain posed to the USSR in terms of its nuclear capability was the ability to destroy Moscow in retaliation for a Soviet strike against Britain. The target was chosen for two reasons for its deterrent effect – because Moscow was the capital of the USSR and because, with its destruction, Soviet state power would be paralysed.

Most-favoured-nation (MFN) status Although this term implies the granting of special favours, it in fact means that all members of a trading system will receive the same advantages granted to the STATE most favoured. The purpose is to avoid discrimination in international trade and to encourage MULTILATERALISM. According to this principle, if one state makes a trading concession to another, this must automatically be extended to all other members. MFN is stated in Article 1 of the GENERAL AGREEMENT ON TARIFFS AND TRADE (GATT) and its successor, the WORLD TRADE ORGANIZATION (WTO).

Mujahideen The Arabic for 'those who engage in struggle for the sake of God'. It is a general designation for Muslims engaged in 'Holy War' or JIHAD. It is also applied, specifically, to various Muslim political and paramilitary groups – for instance, the Afghan Mujahideen following the Soviet invasion of Afghanistan in 1979.

Mukden Incident (1931) The destruction in September 1931 of a small section of the South Manchurian Railway (SMR) near the town of Mukden in Manchuria. The railway was run by the Japanese and protected by Japanese troops, who claimed that the Chinese were responsible for the damage, a claim not supported by the evidence. This issue led to the Japanese occupation of Manchuria and a major challenge of CREDIBILITY of the LEAGUE OF NATIONS, as the upholder of PEACE and INTERNATIONAL LAW.

Multilateral aid Aid in money or kind given by one group of countries collectively or through an international agency to another group of countries. The INTERNATIONAL BANK FOR RECONSTRUCTION AND DEVELOPMENT (IBRD) (World Bank) and the INTERNATIONAL DEVELOPMENT ASSOCIATION (IDA) are the largest sources of multilateral aid.

Multilateral Force (MLF) A proposal by the US President John F. Kennedy (1917–63) made in 1961. It called for the creation within the NORTH ATLANTIC TREATY ORGANIZATION (NATO) of international units staffed by nations of all the NATO member states. By the late 1950s the USSR had INTER-CONTINENTAL BALLISTIC MISSILES (ICBMS) capable of striking the USA, and Europeans were becoming progressively concerned with the nuclear ARMS RACE that the USA might not be prepared to use its nuclear capability in the event of a Soviet attack on Europe. Alternatively, and this became credible at the time of the CUBAN MISSILE CRISIS in October 1962, the SUPER-POWERS might plunge Europe into a nuclear war. This particular attempt to reassure the other NATO countries and to prevent nuclear PROLIFERATION was jettisoned by President Lyndon B. Johnson (1908–73) in 1974. The USA was unwilling to accept a power of VETO over strategic decisions from its partners and the French were unwilling to give up nuclear independence.

Multilateralism As a term in disarmament, as opposed to UNILATERALISM, the view that disarmament, in particular, nuclear disarmament, can become a reality only when all the countries involved are prepared to negotiate it. It is also applied to other issues where negotiation requires to be on a worldwide scale – for example, multilateral trade bargaining in the WORLD TRADE ORGANIZATION (WTO).

Multiple Independently Targeted Re-Entry Vehicles (MIRVs) A
set of warheads carried by a single missile, which can be directed with great accuracy.

These were introduced in the 1960s and meant a significant ESCALATION in the nuclear ARMS RACE, and increase in the destructive capability of the SUPERPOWERS. Not least, also, their introduction complicated the problems of ARMS CONTROL, making it harder to calculate the respective nuclear capability of the superpower arsenals.

Multipolarity An international situation in which there are several poles, or major powers, the situation, in fact, of the classic BALANCE OF POWER in which powers will group and ally to prevent HEGEMONY, as with the traditional GREAT POWERS in Europe. At the end of the Second World War the scale of resources and the military strength of the USA and the USSR dictated the BIPOLARITY of the COLD WAR. Following the re-emergence of China, with the great economic power of the EUROPEAN UNION (EU) and Japan and the end of the cold war, some prefer to analyse the global order today as multipolar, although the USA is so much the most dominant power.

Munich Agreement (1938) Agreed on 29 September 1938 between Britain, France, Germany and Italy, it forced Czechoslovakia to cede the SUDETENLAND, which contained three and a quarter million ethnic Germans, to Germany – to be accomplished in ten days. It followed the Nazi incorporation of Austria, the *ANSCHLUSS* (1938) and persistent threats by Hitler (1889–1945). It was the major act of APPEASEMENT by Britain under Neville Chamberlain (1869-1940) and France under Daladier (1884-1970) and a classic example of GREAT POWER DIPLOMACY at the expense of small nations. Chamberlain announced it as 'peace in our time', but this was illusory. The promised guarantee for the continued existence of Czechoslovakia never materialized and World War II broke out less than a year later with the invasion of Poland. Debate still continues, though, as to whether the year's delay was of more benefit to the Allies or Germany. Chamberlain was later to claim that Hitler had 'missed the bus'.

Munich analogy This term relates to the so-called 'lessons of Munich', the APPEASEMENT of Nazi Germany by Britain and France in September 1938 with the CESSION of the SUDETENLAND in Czechoslovakia. The argument that the failure to resist Hitler (1889–1945) encouraged further AGGRESSION leading to the Second World War has been invoked frequently in international crises since then, including the SUEZ CRISIS (1956), the VIETNAM WAR in the 1960s and 1970s and the GULF WAR (1991). This is to advocate a policy of military strength rather than concession or negotiations. The rhetorical cry of 'no more Munichs' has often been heard in circumstances that bear little or no comparison with the events of 1938.

Muscovites More generally, inhabitants of Moscow, this term had a specific political connotation in the years immediately after the Second World War. It was specially applied to those non-Soviet Communists who had spent the greater part of the war in the USSR. They returned to their home countries with the Red Army. Whether in EASTERN EUROPE, North Korea or China, their line tended to conflict with that of national Communists. The tension between the USSR and 'national Communism' first became sharply apparent in the rift with Yugoslavia in 1948.

Muslim Brotherhood A non-state ISLAMIC FUNDAMENTALIST group that seeks to replace existing secular governments in the Muslim world by regimes in which religious and political affairs would be governed by Islamic law, the Shariah. This name has been applied to several organizations – for instance, those of Egypt and Syria.

Mutual and Balanced Force Reduction (MBFR) These were a series of abortive attempts between 1973 and 1989 to agree a limitation of ground forces in Europe between the NORTH ATLANTIC TREATY ORGANIZATION (NATO) and the WARSAW PACT. They foundered on disagreements over the actual number of troops deployed and problems of VERIFICATION and enforcement. The meetings were reconvened, and this time successfully, in Vienna as the CONVENTIONAL FORCES IN EUROPE (CFE) forum in 1989.

Mutual Assured Destruction (MAD) See ASSURED DESTRUCTION.

Mutual Defence Assistance Act (MDAA) (1949) This followed the ratification of the NORTH ATLANTIC TREATY ORGANIZATION (NATO) by the US Senate. President Harry Truman (1884–1972) requested Congress to authorize financial support to help it meet its obligations of mutual defence. It was passed during a period of high international tension with the news that the USSR had just exploded its first ATOMIC BOMB. The Act was signed on 6 October 1949. Of the $1.314 billion initially provided, $1 billion were earmarked for the allies of the USA in NATO.

N

N+1 problem The formula by which N equals the number of STATES possessing NUCLEAR WEAPONS and +1 represents the problems posed by the addition of another state with nuclear arms.

NAC See NORTH ATLANTIC COUNCIL.

NACC See NORTH ATLANTIC COOPERATION COUNCIL.

NAFTA See NORTH AMERICAN FREE TRADE AGREEMENT.

NAM See NON-ALIGNED MOVEMENT.

Nansen Passport This was named after the Norwegian explorer Fridtjof Nansen (1861–1930), who was appointed High Commissioner of Refugees by the LEAGUE OF NATIONS in 1922. The passport, which carried his name and photograph, was recognized as valid identification for stateless and displaced persons throughout Europe. Nansen's work laid the basis for subsequent refugee initiatives and the creation of the United Nations High Commissioner for Refugees after 1945.

Narco-terrorism This term refers to two different phenomena. First, it is a form of revolutionary TERRORISM in which those involved use the production of narcotics to finance their revolutionary activities, or deliberately use drugs to undermine the social fabric of a country. Secondly, it is a form of entrepreneurial terrorism in which the drug traffickers themselves use terrorism in order to keep governments and police forces from interfering with their operations and profits.

Nassau Agreement (1962) An agreement between the US President John F. Kennedy (1917–63) and the British Prime Minister Harold Macmillan (1894–1986) at Nassau in the Bahamas on 18 December 1962, following strong pleading by the latter. It confirmed that the USA would provide POLARIS MISSILES for the British navy operating under the command of the NORTH ATLANTIC TREATY ORGANIZATION (NATO). This was used a month later by the French President Charles de Gaulle (1890–1970) as one of the reasons for justifying his rejection of the UK's application to join the EUROPEAN ECONOMIC COMMUNITY (EEC), enabling him to argue Britain's transatlantic dependence and lack of convincing commitment to Europe.

Nation A population with a common identity. A nation coterminous with STATE boundaries is referred to as a nation state, though the terms 'nation', 'state' and 'nation state' are often used synonymously. It is possible to be a nation without a single state. For instance, the Kurdish people form a non-state nation, divided between several states. States that contain more than one nation are usually referred to as multinational states or empires.

National Declaration on the League of Nations and Armaments See PEACE BALLOT.

National interest The concept of the SECURITY and well-being of the STATE, used, among other things, in the formulation of, and justification for, foreign policies. A national interest approach to foreign policy demands 'realistic' handling of international problems based on the use of POWER in international relations. Historically the doctrine of national interest evolved as *RAISON D'ÉTAT*. This approach is commonly contrasted with moral and utopian approaches to international affairs.

National liberation wars See WARS OF NATIONAL LIBERATION.

National Security Agency (NSA) The USA's electronic intelligence-gathering operation, which officially came into existence in 1952. By the 1980s it had the capacity to intercept every form of communication. It is responsible for breaking foreign codes and developing new American codes and electronic surveillance equipment for use in the field by the CENTRAL INTELLIGENCE AGENCY (CIA) and other agents.

National Security Council (NSC) The US agency that was created by the National Security Act (1947) to advise the US President on the coordination of foreign, domestic and military policies related to NATIONAL SECURITY. Its role is to study DEFENCE issues and make recommendations. In the years of the COLD WAR its influence sometimes rivalled that of the DEPARTMENT OF STATE. Its permanent membership includes the President, the Vice-President, the Secretary of State, the Defence Secretary, the Chairman of the Joint Chiefs of Staff and the Director of the CENTRAL INTELLIGENCE AGENCY (CIA).

National security Issues dealing with the survival, protection and welfare of a STATE and its subjects.

National self-determination See SELF-DETERMINATION.

Nationalism A belief, sentiment, IDEOLOGY and dominant force in the development of the modern world. Originating in Europe, it spread throughout the THIRD WORLD in the course of the twentieth century. Going beyond patriotism, it affirms that a STATE should be founded in a NATION and that a nation should be constituted as a sovereign nation state, that the political unit should be co-extensive with the national unit. Historically, it developed, to a significant extent, as a consequence of the French Revolution of 1789 and in reaction to the subsequent Napoleonic conquests and through the nationalist movements of the nineteenth century with their mixture of economic, linguistic, cultural and racial motivation. It was further encouraged by the commitment to SELF-DETERMINATION after the First World War and by DECOLONIZATION, in which nationalism in the Third World emerged in anti-colonial movements. Nationalism is a historical process that has resulted in the emergence of modern nation states, a political doctrine, the activity of political parties and a condition of mind in which allegiance to one's state or people predominates. Recent analysis of this phenomenon has emphasized, among other things, the process of nation building and the functional interpretation in terms of modernization and the transition from agrarian societies. The impact of nationalism can be gauged by the multiplication of the nation states over the last two centuries and its resurgence in post-Communist Europe, among other things. Its potential for extremism can be seen, for instance, in the Fascist movements of the years after the Second World War and the violent ethnic eruptions that have followed the end of the COLD WAR. It is now customary to make a distinction between civic nationalism, in which membership of the nation is equated with citizenship and regarded as a political and legal category, and ethnic nationalism, in which membership is based on race and ancestry and is believed to be an inherent characteristic.

Nationality An individual's membership in a nation state, for which he or she will receive protection in return for acceptance of obligations. The UNIVERSAL DECLARATION OF HUMAN RIGHTS (UDHR) proclaims the right to a nationality in Article 15 as follows: (1) everyone has the right to a nationality; (2) none shall be arbitrarily deprived of his nationality nor denied the right to change his nationality. Those without nationality are described as stateless.

Nation state See STATE.

NATO See NORTH ATLANTIC TREATY ORGANIZATION.

Naturalization The legal process by which a government may extend citizenship of its country to individuals, such as REFUGEES, who cannot claim it by the nationality of their parents or place of birth.

Nazi–Soviet Non-Aggression Pact (1939) Also called the Hitler–Stalin Pact, or the Molotov–Ribbentrop Pact. This NON-AGGRESSION PACT was concluded on 23 August 1939, a week before the outbreak of the Second World War and was signed by the foreign ministers of Germany and the USSR, Joachim Von Ribbentrop (1893–1946) and Vlacheslav Molotov (1890–1986). It stated that the two countries would not support any third power in the event that it attacked either of the two signatories, that they would consult with each other on matters of common interest, and that each would refrain from associating with any groupings of powers aimed at the other. A secret PROTOCOL (which was made public in 1948) divided EASTERN EUROPE into German and Soviet spheres of influence, and each signatory was given territorial gains, along a line following the northern frontier of Lithuania and the CURZON LINE for Poland. It was followed by several economic agreements and was to have been in force for ten years, but was repudiated with the Nazi invasion of the USSR, BARBAROSSA, in June 1941.

Near Abroad States The former republics of the USSR, Latvia, Estonia, Lithuania, Belarus, the Ukraine, Moldova, Georgia, Armenia, Azerbaijan, Uzbekistan, Turkmenistan, Kazakihstan, Tajikistan and Kyrgystan. The Russian use of the term 'Near Abroad States' also indicates the importance of these STATES to the SECURITY of the Russian state and the priority of that concern to the government in Moscow. This designation in addition suggests Moscow's right to intervene in the internal affairs of these states if its security is threatened.

Necessary peace This phrase is sometimes used to describe the stabilization in military competition between the SUPERPOWERS, the USA and the USSR, during the COLD WAR, which is said to have resulted from the mutual fear of all-out nuclear war.

Neo-colonialism A term used to describe the post-colonial situation in which, it is argued, the former colonial powers still dominate, or control, their former colonies. They do this economically because of control of the markets in which the ex-colonies need to sell their goods and in which the latter (new STATES with a much lower standard of living) need to buy the technological products only made by the former colonial powers. Political control also takes place as a result of constant interference by the former colonial powers in the affairs of the THIRD WORLD.

Neo-functionalism A theory of INTEGRATION that has been applied particularly to Europe, associated most prominently with the work of the US theorist Ernst Haas (b.1924), for example, in his book *The Uniting of Europe* (1958). He argued that, once integration got underway, it gained momentum through SPILLOVER. In the first place, those groups pressing for integration would wish it to continue and to extend any benefits from it. Secondly, new transnational or supranational authorities would emerge, like the HIGH AUTHORITY in the EUROPEAN COAL AND STEEL COMMUNITY (ECSC), and they would wish to further the process. There is a particular interest in this approach with institution building. The hope that SECTORAL INTEGRATION and the spillover effect would lead automatically over the longer term to political integration was to be frustrated, among other things by the LUXEMBOURG COMPROMISE (1966) and the continued resilience of NATIONALISM.

Neo-imperialism Also called 'informal imperialism'. The economic exploitation of poor countries by rich ones without direct military INTERVENTION or formal state control. This term has been used in particular by Marxist writers to describe a situation in which the resources of developing countries are controlled after political independence by multinational companies from the advanced countries, in particular the previous imperial powers.

Neo-isolationism A term current from the late 1960s and 1970s, related then in particular to the question of US withdrawal from Vietnam. It involves in general reduced commitments, particularly military ones, in other parts of the world. Neo-isolationists would assert that the USA no longer has the capability nor should feel it is its duty to police the rest of the world. This term has often been used, too, in describing calls for troop withdrawals from Europe.

Neo-realism Also called 'structural realism', this school of thought has further developed the tradition of REALISM in international relations. The best-known exponent is the US international relations thinker Kenneth Waltz (b. 1924), whose book *Theory of International Politics* (1979) has been particularly influential. Neo-realists have adapted realism to new international agendas, to meet the arguments of those who affirm the growth of INTERDEPENDENCE and TRANSNATIONALISM with a novel emphasis on the overall structures in the international order. While accepting the dominant importance of the STATE and of considerations of POWER, they have set out to show how different structures produce different patterns in world politics and condition the behaviour of states.

Neutralism A policy of non-involvement in conflicts between STATES or POWER blocs. Many states in the THIRD WORLD, for instance, took up a neutralist position during the COLD WAR.

Neutrality This differs from NEUTRALISM in that it is an international legal position in a situation of 'hot war'. Under INTERNATIONAL LAW, STATES can claim rights that warring states should respect.

Neutrality Acts These were passed in 1935, 1936, 1937 and 1939 in the USA, reflecting US anxieties to avoid becoming involved in a future war and underlining American ISOLATIONISM, which was particularly strong in the Middle West. More specifically, they reflected a belief held by a number of prominent figures that the USA had been drawn into the First World War because of loans to, and trade with, the Western Allies, Britain and France. The 1935 Act banned munitions exports. That of 1936 banned loans to belligerents and that in the succeeding year extended these provisions to cases of CIVIL WAR. The act of 1939 was passed two months after the outbreak of the First World War. It prohibited US ships from carrying goods and passengers to belligerent ports but allowed belligerents to purchase goods on a 'CASH AND CARRY' basis – payment in advance and the goods carried in the belligerent's own ships.

Neutralization The act of excluding by TREATY a designated area of a STATE's territory from an ARMED CONFLICT, in which any military action is illegal.

New Commonwealth The term used to describe the former British colonies that became members of the COMMONWEALTH following their post-Second World War independence. This was to contrast them from the 'old' White Commonwealth Dominions of Australia, Canada, New Zealand and South Africa.

New Eastern Policy A phrase sometimes used for *OSTPOLITIK*, the West German policy from the 1960s of RAPPROCHEMENT with the STATES of EASTERN EUROPE, particularly the German Democratic Republic (GDR).

New Frontier A phrase used by J. F. Kennedy (1917–63) during the US presidential candidate nomination at the Democrat's National Convention in 1960. It expressed the energy and optimism of his term of office between 1961 and 1963. The initiatives included a civil rights programme, space exploration, the ALLIANCE FOR PROGRESS, the formation of the PEACE CORPS and encouragement of global tariff reductions. This ambitious programme was slowed down by Congressional opposition and the grave international issues, particularly the BERLIN CRISIS (1958–62) and the CUBAN MISSILE CRISIS (1962).

New International Economic Order (NIEO) This phrase was coined at a special session of the UNITED NATIONS GENERAL ASSEMBLY in 1974, which dealt with the subjects of the export of raw materials and economic development, at a time of growing debate over North–South relations. There were proposals for a larger annual transfer of resources from affluent to poor STATES, a better balance between the prices of imported and exported goods, a reform of the international monetary system and encouragement of trading opportunities for developing countries. One principle advanced asserted that each STATE had an absolute right to control its wealth and natural resources, including the right to nationalize or expropriate foreign property. This was strongly opposed by the representatives of the developed market economies, who have since made few of the concessions requested by the LESS DEVELOPED COUNTRIES (LDCs) in the spirit of the NIEO.

New Look The US nuclear arms policy associated with the Presidency of Dwight D. Eisenhower (1890–1969). It was published in NATIONAL SECURITY COUNCIL (NSC) policy paper NSC 162/2 of 1953 entitled 'Basic National Security', which supported the STRATEGY of MASSIVE RETALIATION in response to a Soviet attack. Reliance on NUCLEAR WEAPONS was also considered less burdensome than major conventional rearmament for the taxpayer. The phrase 'New Look' was sometimes used also to refer to the support for WAR FIGHTING in the Reagan administration, during the 1980s.

New Manifest Destiny A US phrase from the 1890s to describe the American expansionist spirit of the time. It was motivated in part by the economic recession in this period. The idea of MANIFEST DESTINY that had referred to the development of the USA itself in the nineteenth century was now advanced as a projection of POWER and influence overseas, particularly towards Latin America and the Far East. It involved a belief in Anglo-Saxon racial superiority, in a US 'civilizing mission' and, though less blatantly, in a degree of rivalry for influence in the world with the other Anglo-Saxon powers, Britain and Germany.

New Order An expression denoting the Nazi concept of a Europe integrated under centralized German political and economic control. Nazi propaganda during the Second World War attempted to persuade people that such a system would be to the benefit of all Europe rather than merely provide the economic resources to enrich Germany. The phrase 'New Order in Asia' was the plan for Japanese expansion into South East Asia. Announced by the Japanese Prime Minister Konoe (1891–1945) in November 1938, this envisaged a coordination of military, political and economic activities under Japanese leadership in China and Manchukuo (Manchuria). After the outbreak of the Second World War, he called for a 'New Order in Greater East Asia', the region now expanded to include much of South East Asia.

New World Order This phrase was used by US President George Bush Sr. (b. 1924) in a speech to a joint session of both Houses of Congress on 11 September 1990 soon after the Iraqi invasion of Kuwait. 'Out of these troubled times,' he said, 'a new world order can emerge: a new era – freer from the threat of terror, stronger in the pursuit of justice and more secure in the quest for peace, an era in which the nations of the world, East and West, North and South, can prosper and live in harmony'. The purpose was to evoke the idea of a new commitment to COLLECTIVE SECURITY in the aftermath of the fall of the BERLIN WALL and the possibility of a new start in East–West relations. More immediately, Bush was keen that any INTERVENTION in the Gulf be seen as an international act.

NIC Newly industrialized or newly industrializing countries.

Nice Treaty (2001) This was concluded following a meeting of the heads of government of the EUROPEAN UNION (EU) in December 2000 at Nice, France, and was signed on 26 February 2001. Agreement was reached on a reform of the EU institutions to provide for the prospective ENLARGEMENT of the EU. A compromise was reached on QUALIFIED MAJORITY VOTING (QMV) and the post-enlargement composition of the EUROPEAN PARLIAMENT (EP), which generally strengthened the position of the larger STATES, though from 2005 these states Britain, France, Germany, Italy and Spain would have only one Commissioner each. Thirty additional policy areas were transferred from being under the system of national VETO to QMV. It was also agreed that 'enhanced cooperation' would be permissible for any group of eight or more states wishing to pursue greater INTEGRATION in particular spheres.

NIEO See NEW INTERNATIONAL ECONOMIC ORDER.

Nixon Doctrine This, the policy of VIETNAMIZATION, was announced by US President Richard Nixon (1913–94) to journalists in Guam on 25 July 1969 at the height of the VIETNAM WAR (1960–75), when the US government was facing mounting domestic and international pressure and protest. While committing the USA to the protection of South East Asia and Japan by the NUCLEAR UMBRELLA, he indicated that Asian soldiers rather than Americans would have to carry the burden of land warfare in Vietnam in future. The Nixon Doctrine would not, he promised, modify any regional undertakings to the SOUTH EAST ASIA TREATY ORGANIZATION (SEATO) or any bilateral commitments in the area. Anti-war critics castigated it as a continuation of the policy of CONTAINMENT. It was also argued that, since it made the USA more dependent on its Asian allies, it would make it more vulnerable to instability in the area.

NKVD Acronym for the People's Commissariat of Internal Affairs. This was responsible for the internal SECURITY of the USSR and was in charge of the secret police, the border guards, the army security division and the concentration camps. It existed from 1917 to 1924, and from 1934 to 1946. It carried out the great purges under Stalin (1879–1953) in 1936–8 and was subsequently involved in the executions and deportations of other peoples from areas occupied by the USSR during the Second World War, such as the KATYN FOREST MASSACRE (1940).

No first use This usually refers to the policy of guaranteeing that a power will not initiate the use of NUCLEAR WEAPONS in a conflict. It was advocated in particular in the nuclear debates of the early 1980s, the period of the 'New Cold War'. Some argued that, if the NORTH ATLANTIC TREATY ORGANIZATION (NATO) was publicly to announce that it would never initiate such an attack, this might encourage ARMS CONTROL. Any such declaration, however, contradicted the official NATO policy of FLEXIBLE RESPONSE, which was deliberately ambivalent as to when any particular level of ESCA-LATION might be reached.

NOD Non-offensive defence.

No-fly zones This term has been since the 1990s by the UNITED NATIONS (UN) to refer to those zones in the former Yugoslavia and in Iraq in which it permits aircraft over-flights only by its own aircraft and those of another international organization in order to safeguard a protected population.

Non-aggression pact A term used for a special form of binding international TREATY by which two or more STATES promise not to engage in military action against one another. It creates confidence between the parties by reciprocally establishing peaceful intentions, and, unlike an ALLIANCE, which contains an obligation to act when a third party attacks one or more of the contracting parties a NON-AGGRESSION PACT obliges the parties to abstain from action. This form of agreement is especially identified with the years between 1918 and 1939 and the best-known example is the NAZI–SOVIET NON-AGGRESSION PACT (1939), which ended with the Nazi-German invasion of the USSR in June 1941.

Non-Aligned Movement (NAM) A group of nations organized during the COLD WAR and numbering more than a hundred member STATES that claimed to be neutral in the confrontation between the Western bloc lead by the USA and the Eastern bloc dominated by the USSR. It was inaugurated at the BANDUNG CONFER-ENCE (1955), where leaders of twenty-five Asian and African states proclaimed them-selves to be a third force in world affairs. The President of Yugoslavia Tito (1892–1980), the Indian Prime Minister Nehru (1884–1964), the President of Egypt Nasser (1918–70) and of Indonesia, Sukarno (1902–1970) emerged as the leading fig-ures in the movement. At the Belgrade Conference of the NAM in 1961 the partici-pants adopted a definition of non-alignment that stated that a non-aligned country must (1) pursue an independent policy based on PEACEFUL COEXISTENCE, (2) not par-ticipate in any multilateral military alliances with either of the SUPERPOWERS. In prac-tice, only those developing states allied with the West were prevented from joining it.

Non-Colonization Doctrine A major principle enunciated in the US MON-ROE DOCTRINE (1823). It stated that the USA would look with disfavour on any attempt to establish new colonies in the Western Hemisphere and that the hemisphere was 'closed' to further colonization. The originator was the US Secretary of State John Quincy Adams (1767–1848), who at the time was apprehensive about British and Russian ambitions to establish new colonies on the north-west coast of North America.

Non-discrimination rule A generally accepted principle in INTERNATIONAL LAW that holds that people residing within the territory of a foreign STATE are entitled to the same protection of person and property as allowed by the law of that state to its own citizens. In the early years of expropriation of foreign property by countries in the process of DECOLONIZATION, the offended parties often invoked the non-discrimination rule against their dispossessors.

Non-governmental organization (NGO) A private international organization that serves as a mechanism for cooperation among private national groups in international affairs, particularly in economic, social, cultural, humanitarian and technical fields. NGOs are also known as transnational associations. They have been active in international affairs for many years, some dating back over a century. Examples of NGOs include the INTERNATIONAL COMMITTEE OF THE RED CROSS (ICRC) and consumer and producer associations.

Non-intervention When used in international relations, this describes the situation where a STATE or group of states decides to avoid entanglement in a conflict. Non-intervention, for instance, was the declared policy of Britain and France among other powers during the SPANISH CIVIL WAR between 1936 and 1939.

Non-Intervention Committee (1936–9) This was formed in September 1936 at the suggestion of Italy, but with Britain taking the lead and running its headquarters in London. It was an attempt to prevent the SPANISH CIVIL WAR (1936–9) widening into a European conflict, and was also encouraged by fears that any French INTERVENTION might provoke a CIVIL WAR in France. The LEAGUE OF NATIONS delegated responsibility in this conflict to the Committee. The intention of blocking arms sales to both the Nationalists (the rebels) and the Republicans (government forces) failed miserably. In addition, Germany, Italy and the USSR intervened militarily. The British Prime Minister Stanley Baldwin (1867–1947) ruefully commented of it: 'A dam that leaks is better than no dam at all.' The last full meeting for dissolving the Committee was on 20 April 1939.

Non-Intervention Doctrine Included in the US MONROE DOCTRINE (1823), the Non-Intervention Doctrine advanced the objection of the USA to European INTERVENTION in the affairs of independent Western Hemisphere nations. This grew out of American suspicions of European plans to mount an expedition to recapture and recolonize Latin America for Spain. The subsequent ROOSEVELT COROLLARY (1904) prescribed US intervention in Latin America to ward off European intervention.

Non-Proliferation Treaty (1970) Signed in Washington, London and Moscow on 1 July 1968, this TREATY came into force on 5 March 1970. It was intended to prevent the spread of NUCLEAR WEAPONS and was subsequently endorsed by fifty-nine other states. It stipulated that the USA, Britain and the USSR would give no assistance to any other STATE in military nuclear programmes. Since then Israel, South Africa, India, Pakistan and possibly other states have developed nuclear capability. The treaty has been approved by the UNITED NATIONS GENERAL ASSEMBLY, which also included the pledge that nuclear powers should pursue DISARMAMENT.

Non-recognition The denial by another STATE or institution of the legitimate statehood of a country, or LEGITIMACY of a government. For instance, with the STIMSON DOCTRINE of 1932 the USA refused to recognize the Japanese PUPPET STATE of Manchukuo (previously Manchuria). Between 1917 and 1933 the USA refused to recognize the new Communist revolutionary order in Russia, claiming that it had seized power by FORCE and that the Bolsheviks were not representatives of the Russian people and could not be trusted to fulfil their international obligations. More commonly non-recognition is applied to a particular regime.

Non-self-governing territory A term that has been used by the UNITED NATIONS (UN) for a territory under the control of a colonial power. Article 73 of the UNITED NATIONS CHARTER charges all UN members responsible for administering non-self-governing territories to govern in such a manner as to promote the well-being of the inhabitants. This includes the political, economic, social and educational advancement of the territory in such a manner as to aid it to develop its own institutions. Since the end of the Second World War nearly all of these territories have become independent STATES, many interpreting Article 73 as a call for national independence.

Non-state actors In international relations ACTORS other than STATE governments. They include, for instance, multinational corporations, banks, agencies such as AMNESTY INTERNATIONAL (AI), and terrorist groups. Traditional views on international relations have been modified in recent years to give greater emphasis to such participants and their influence, with growing attention given to transnational links and linkages and to GLOBALIZATION.

Non-tariff barriers (NTBs) Restraints on international trade, such as quotas, domestic government purchasing policies and safety and technical standards that give advantage to domestic producers over foreign producers. The establishment of the SINGLE MARKET in the EUROPEAN UNION (EU) has involved the elimination of NTBs.

Nordic Council A Scandinavian inter-governmental and inter-parliamentary organization, established in 1952 by a common statute adopted by the national parliaments and composed of elected and appointed delegates. It was set up to advise the governments of Denmark, Finland, Iceland, Sweden and Norway on matters of common concern and to recommend coordinated policy actions. A high degree of collaboration has been achieved in some areas such as in the establishment of a common labour market and abolition of currency controls, but its brief has not extended to DEFENCE and foreign policy. One of its original objectives was to establish a Scandinavian COMMON MARKET, but this was suspended with the formation of the EUROPEAN FREE TRADE ASSOCIATION (EFTA) in 1959. Reforms in 1971 established a Council of Ministers with a supporting Secretariat. After this the Council of Ministers representing national governments became the focal point of cooperative proposals and activity. Its decisions had to be unanimous. Its structures were further organized in 1993, making it more like the EUROPEAN UNION (EU).

North This term came to be used during the 1970s in place of earlier expressions to cover the advanced economies. These had included 'the most developed countries', 'the West' or the ORGANIZATION FOR ECONOMIC COOPERATION AND DEVELOPMENT (OECD). 'North' includes the OECD countries of North America, Europe, Japan, Australia and New Zealand and the Russian Federation, though some STATES in the last, for instance, Tajikstan, may now, since the break-up of the USSR, be considered as belonging to the SOUTH.

North American Free Trade Agreement (NAFTA) This agreement was signed in December 1992 between the USA, Canada and Mexico with a view gradually to eliminate most of the barriers to the flow of goods and services among the three countries. It came into effect on 1 January 1994. All tariffs between them were to be removed within fifteen years. It was consistent with the goals of US trade policy, the achievement of a trading system with a minimum of official barriers and a maximum of global production. Canada was traditionally the USA's biggest trading partner and Mexico was its third largest export market. NAFTA led to considerable debate within the USA. Opponents cited in particular the likely depression of US wages by competition with Mexico and the increase of industrial pollution.

North Atlantic Cooperation Council (NACC) This was created after the end of the COLD WAR in Rome in November 1991 to arrange a framework for SECURITY and cooperation between the NORTH ATLANTIC TREATY ORGANIZATION (NATO) and the WARSAW PACT and other European STATES. The first meeting was held in the next month with 25 countries attending. It later came to include all the Soviet republics, but was soon overshadowed by the PARTNERSHIP FOR PEACE (PFP) programme instituted in 1994.

North Atlantic Council (NAC) The principal decision-making body of the NORTH ATLANTIC TREATY ORGANIZATION (NATO), based in Brussels, Belgium. It is chaired by the NATO Secretary-General and meets at various levels of government. Sometimes this is at the level of Heads of Government. Foreign ministers generally meet twice a year. When the Council meets at the level of permanent representatives, who act as ambassadors from the governments of the member states, it is known as the Council in Permanent Session.

North Atlantic Treaty (1949) This developed from the BRUSSELS TREATY of the previous year and was signed on 4 April 1949 by the five signatories of that pact together with the USA, Canada, Denmark, Iceland, Italy, Portugal and Norway. It provided for mutual support in the event of an attack in line with the right of COLLECTIVE SELF-DEFENCE recognized by ARTICLE 51 of the UNITED NATIONS CHARTER. The NORTH ATLANTIC TREATY ORGANIZATION (NATO) was established to implement the treaty provisions. Greece and Turkey joined in 1952 and West Germany in 1955. The principal Soviet response to the creation of NATO and the inclusion of West Germany was the WARSAW PACT (1955), which formally created the Warsaw Treaty Organization (WTO).

North Atlantic Treaty Organization (NATO) This was created by the NORTH ATLANTIC TREATY, which was signed in Washington on 4 April 1949, initially consisting of twelve states. This was at a time when the COLD WAR was markedly intensifying, particularly with the BERLIN BLOCKADE (1948–9) and the Communist assumption of power in Czechoslovakia. Fears of Soviet power and intentions (they had marked numerical superiority in conventional forces) increased yet more with their test explosion of an ATOMIC BOMB in August 1949 and the invasion of South by North Korea in 1950. The defensive TREATY subscribed to the principle that an attack on one of their powers was an attack on all. They were obliged to take such action as was deemed necessary to assist in resisting AGGRESSION. NATO was intended to defend but also to reassure, and its key political and military importance was that it coupled the USA with its conventional and nuclear forces to the defence of Western Europe, and with a force under a US Supreme Allied Commander. NATO's original purposes have been defined as keeping the Americans in, the Germans down and the Russians out. The original membership of twelve was later expanded; most notably, with the accession of West Germany (in 1955), at which point the WARSAW PACT, the Soviet Bloc's rival defence organization, also formally came into existence. NATO has been a highly durable alliance, though it has reflected transatlantic tensions, not least in the 1960s, when the French President Charles de Gaulle (1890–1970) removed France from the integrated military command structure, and in the 1980s with the 'New Cold War' and the EUROMISSILE controversy. Following the INTERMEDIATE-RANGE NUCLEAR FORCES (INF) TREATY of 1987 and the events of 1989, NATO leaders in 1990 declared the cold war at an end. The collapse of the Warsaw Pact forced reappraisal of the purpose of an ALLIANCE that had come into existence in the militarization of the cold war. Subsequently its troops were allowed to be at the disposal of the UNITED NATIONS (UN), and were deployed in Bosnia and against the Serbs in Kosovo. The PARTNERSHIP FOR PEACE (PFP) (1994) with the countries of EASTERN EUROPE was followed by the accession to NATO of the Czech Republic, Hungary and Poland. Reassessment of NATO's role has also been accompanied by geographical extension.

North–South axis A term for the political, cultural, economic and social relationship between the industrialized nations and the LESS-DEVELOPED COUNTRIES (LDCS) of the world. Awareness of the imbalance between them in terms of wealth and the problems arising from this for the world have been a conspicuously increasing concern in international relations since the 1960s.

North–South conflict The generalized term for the confrontation between the developing and the advanced industrialized countries. It became one of the central issues in international relations during the last third of the twentieth century, arising from the gulf between increasing wealth and higher standards of living and poverty.

Northern flank A term from the COLD WAR describing the northernmost reach of the NORTH ATLANTIC TREATY ORGANIZATION (NATO). It has normally referred only to Northern Norway, where NATO territory adjoined the USSR, close to the important Soviet military bases on the Kola Peninsula. It was given its own command, Allied Forces Northern Europe (AFNORTH).

Northern Territories The group of islands at the northern end of the Japanese archipelago that were occupied by the USSR at the end of the Second World War. The Soviet refusal to return these islands, Habomai, Shikoton, Kunashiri and Etorofu, which they claimed were part of the Kurile chain of islands, prevented the two countries from signing a formal PEACE TREATY.

Northern Tier The idea, advanced during the COLD WAR, that Turkey, Iraq, Iran and Pakistan formed a natural grouping of STATES for the DEFENCE of the Middle East. It evolved from a British wish to reaffirm relations with Iraq and from US and Turkish concerns to provide an effective regional defence system against the USSR. It became diplomatic reality with the signing of the BAGHDAD PACT (1955).

No-win policy This term was applied broadly in the period of the COLD WAR to the efforts of successive US administrations to achieve PEACEFUL COEXISTENCE and avoid nuclear war. It was first applied by critics of President Harry Truman (1884–1972) for his insistence on limited goals in the KOREAN WAR of 1950–3.

NPT See NON-PROLIFERATION (OF NUCLEAR WEAPONS) TREATY.

NSA See NATIONAL SECURITY AGENCY.

NSC See NATIONAL SECURITY COUNCIL.

NSC-68 This was one of the key documents in the development of the COLD WAR, presented by the US NATIONAL SECURITY COUNCIL in 1950 to President Harry Truman (1884–1972). It followed the explosion of the first ATOMIC BOMB by the USSR in August 1949 and addressed the question of the bipolar world conflict between the USSR and the USA and outlined Soviet efforts to achieve world influence and domination. It proposed that the USA resist the USSR through CONTAINMENT, by using military power to deter Soviet expansionism, and fighting limited wars if necessary. It advised against negotiations with Moscow and supported the development of the HYDROGEN BOMB and the build-up of conventional military forces. This required a willingness significantly to increase defence spending. It also advocated the mobilization of US society to the anti-Communist cause, the creation of a strong ALLIANCE system and propaganda to win over those under Communist rule. The outbreak of the KOREAN WAR (1950–3) in June 1950 seemed to confirm this analysis and strongly aided its implementation with greatly increased Western defence expenditure.

NTBs See NON-TARIFF BARRIERS.

Nuclear Club This phrase has normally been used to refer simply to those STATES that had developed NUCLEAR WEAPONS by the 1960s and openly admitted to their possession. These are the USA, the Russian Federation (previously the USSR), Britain, France and the People's Republic of China. In addition, India, Pakistan, South Africa and Israel are known to possess them.

Nuclear-free zone The idea of establishing weapon-free zones first appeared in the 1950s. It involved the exclusion of the production, storage, holding or use of NUCLEAR WEAPONS within specifically delimited geographical areas. The purpose was to contribute to international DÉTENTE. The best-known example is the RAPACKI PLAN (1957), which was under discussion until 1964 and proposed a nuclear-free zone, initially to include Poland, the Federal Republic of Germany and the German Democratic Republic, with the intention that it be later extended to other central European territories. Similar proposals have been put forward for other parts of the world. The ANTARCTIC TREATY (1959) included a ban on the stationing and use of nuclear weapons, but the only treaty to date establishing a nuclear-free zone for a highly populated region is the TLATELOLCO TREATY (1967), for the prohibition of nuclear weapons in Latin America.

Nuclear freeze A movement formed during the 'New Cold War' in the USA, which nevertheless lost momentum with the re-election of President Reagan (b. 1917) to the Presidency in November 1984. Already during the Presidency of Lyndon B. Johnson (1908–73) a proposal had been put forward for a mutual US–Soviet freeze on NUCLEAR WEAPONS and their delivery systems. The called-for freeze was voted down by a small majority in Congress in 1982, but the movement developed formal relationships with the PEACE MOVEMENT in Western Europe and some contacts with those in EASTERN EUROPE. At the same time it encouraged widespread public debate about ARMS CONTROL and helped to prepare the way for subsequent DISARMAMENT.

Nuclear Planning Group (NPG) Part of the NORTH ATLANTIC TREATY ORGANIZATION (NATO), this group was formed on 14 December 1966. It is responsible for planning and advising member governments of all nuclear DEFENCE-related matters. Membership is restricted to seven allied countries. These consist of the nuclear powers and a rotating membership among the other Alliance members. Meetings are held at the defence minister level.

Nuclear proliferation The spread of nuclear technology and NUCLEAR WEAPONS. During the ARMS RACE of the COLD WAR between the SUPERPOWERS, the USA and the USSR, VERTICAL PROLIFERATION was the major concern. Since the 1980s an agreement on limitation between these powers and the end of the cold war has meant that HORIZONTAL PROLIFERATION, the acquisition of nuclear potential by STATES that were not previously possessors of nuclear weapons has become more worrying. It is feared that these states, if involved in conventional war, might be tempted to resort to nuclear retaliation – for instance, in the Indian subcontinent, where both India and Pakistan possess these weapons.

Nuclear threshold The moment in an escalating crisis when NUCLEAR WEAPONS are used for the first time. During the COLD WAR strategists frequently referred to the need to 'raise the nuclear threshold' or expressed concern that deficiencies in Western conventional forces might 'lower the nuclear threshold'. The most common use of the concept was in relation to the FLEXIBLE RESPONSE STRATEGY for defending against an attack by the WARSAW PACT. It was assumed that the NORTH ATLANTIC TREATY ORGANIZATION (NATO) would be able to mount a conventional defence in Europe for only a strictly limited time before resorting to nuclear arms.

Nuclear umbrella A term from the COLD WAR to indicate that US NUCLEAR WEAPONS extended to the DEFENCE of Europe as well as the North American continent.

Nuclear weapons These now cover a range of devices from INTER-CONTINENTAL BALLISTIC MISSILES (ICBMS) to TACTICAL NUCLEAR WEAPONS. The first ATOMIC BOMBS, including the two dropped on Nagasaki and Hiroshima in 1945, derived their energy from fission, the splitting of atomic nuclei. Modern nuclear weapons, following the development of the HYDROGEN BOMB, are based on fusion, the joining-together of atomic nuclei at extremely high temperatures, the heat for which is created by an initial fission reaction. The subsequent chain reaction creates an enormous release of energy, causing massive destruction through the combined effects of heat, fire, shock and wind. High levels of radiation are the by-product of the uranium and plutonium used.

Nuclear winter A doomsday hypothesis first advanced in 1983 during the 'New Cold War' by a group of American scientists including the astronomer Carl Sagan (b. 1934), which provoked much debate. It argued that a nuclear conflict could lead to dust and soot in the atmosphere, which would block out sunlight and lead to a catastrophic global failure of agriculture, leading to the death of thousands of millions of people. Sagan commented that even a major FIRST STRIKE 'may be an act of national suicide, even if no retaliation occurs'.

Nuncio The official representative of the Pope at a court or capital of any country that maintains diplomatic relations with the HOLY SEE.

Nunn Amendment (1984) This was presented by US Senator Sam Nunn (b. 1938) of Georgia and reflected the belief in the USA that it was carrying a disproportionate burden of DEFENCE expenditure for Western Europe. It was proposed to withdraw up to one-third of American troops in Western Europe unless European members of the NORTH ATLANTIC TREATY ORGANIZATION (NATO) increased the support of conventional forces. It was defeated by 55 to 41 votes but revealed the tensions in transatlantic relations and led to a budget increase for defence by the European members. They responded favourably to the US Conventional Defence Initiative, which proposed the partial funding of some US defence procurement costs by Western Europe.

Nuremberg Trials (1945–7) The proceedings after the Second World War, which were conducted by judges from the USA, Britain, France and the USSR, before whom Austrians and Germans were accused of CRIMES AGAINST PEACE and CRIMES AGAINST HUMANITY and WAR CRIMES. The accused were alleged to have participated either in the planning, preparation and prosecution of the WAR, or in the actual murder, torture, enslavement and deportation of people during the war. Both the trials and subsequent execution of Nazi leaders have been criticized on a number of legal grounds, particularly because the judges and prosecutors were drawn from the victorious Allies. The trials were very important, though, not least because they helped to establish the legal basis for personal accountability during war. Simply claiming to have followed orders did not assure exculpation.

NWO See NEW WORLD ORDER.

O

OAPEC See ORGANIZATION OF ARAB PETROLEUM EXPORTING COUNTRIES.

OAS See ORGANIZATION OF AMERICAN STATES.

OAU See ORGANIZATION OF AFRICAN UNITY.

Occupied Territories During the Arab–Israel SIX DAY WAR (1967) Israel occupied various Arab and Arab-held territories, including the Sinai Peninsula, the GAZA STRIP, the GOLAN HEIGHTS, the WEST BANK and East Jerusalem. Though commonly referred to as the Occupied Territories, Israel has preferred to use the phrase 'Administered Areas'.

Oceania The island Pacific region, excluding Australia and New Zealand. It comprises Melanesia, Micronesia and Polynesia, consisting of about 10,000 islands. Following the UNITED NATIONS (UN) LAW OF THE SEA CONFERENCE, the Pacific island NATIONS in 1979 declared 200-nautical-mile EXCLUSIVE ECONOMIC ZONES (EEZS) around their archipelagos in order to protect their valuable marine and mineral resources. This greatly enlarged the territorial size of these MICRO-STATES.

October War See YOM KIPPUR WAR (1973).

ODA See OVERSEAS DEVELOPMENT ADMINISTRATION.

Oder–Neisse Line The boundary between Germany and Poland, with the line following the Western Neisse to the Czech border. Before 1938 the German territory to the east of this line had amounted to 24 per cent of Germany's territory and had supplied a large proportion of its food and coal. After the Second World War most of the land was incorporated into Poland to compensate the Poles for lands lost to the USSR in 1939. The German Federal Republic (West Germany) refused to recognize this demarcation until 1972 as part of *OSTPOLITIK* (East Germany had recognized it in 1950). Germany officially relinquished the area in 1990 after unification.

OECD See ORGANIZATION FOR ECONOMIC COOPERATION AND DEVELOPMENT.

OEEC Organization for European Economic Cooperation. See ORGANIZATION FOR ECONOMIC COOPERATION AND DEVELOPMENT (OECD).

Oil crises (1970s) An Arab embargo on oil shipments to the West following the YOM KIPPUR WAR of 1973 provoked a sharp price rise in oil. Before the embargo was lifted the ORGANIZATION OF PETROLEUM EXPORTING COUNTRIES (OPEC) had quadrupled prices, which were again doubled in 1979 with the Iranian Revolution. These rises stimulated worldwide inflation and provoked industrial recession. At the same time they caused a growing awareness of the need for energy conservation measures and ecological constraints, as well as for the development of alternative energy sources, including nuclear power and the rapid development of non-Arab reserves of Alaskan and North Sea Oil.

One Country–Two Systems Doctrine This was stated by the leader of the People's Republic of China Deng Xiaoping (1904–97) and referred to the different economic and social systems of Hong Kong and Taiwan, parts of 'one country', China.

According to the official Chinese statement, 'the idea of one country, two systems, is suitable, not only for Hong Kong, but for many other regions. It is definitely suitable for Taiwan.' The Chinese–Portuguese agreement on the transfer of Macao in 1999, signed in 1987, was also based on this doctrine. Macao has been granted the right to its own autonomy in matters other than foreign policy and DEFENCE until 2037.

One hundred per cent Americanism This phrase became common currency after the US President Woodrow Wilson (1856–1924) issued his war message to Congress in April 1917 leading to the US INTERVENTION in the First World War as an ASSOCIATED STATE. Nationalistic loyalty posed obvious problems for numbers of Americans of German origin, but also for anti-war socialists. This led to intolerance and persecution and subsequently, after the war, contributed to XENOPHOBIA, encouraging the passing of the National Origins Act of 1924, and to strong anti-radical currents, as seen in the so-called Red Scare of 1919–21 at a time when the USA was involved in the Russian Civil War against the new Communist government.

OPEC See ORGANIZATION OF PETROLEUM EXPORTING COUNTRIES.

Open diplomacy Reaction against the secret negotiations and undertakings that preceded the First World War led to a public demand for open diplomacy. This was conducted at international conferences open to the press and is sometimes described as conference diplomacy. It does not mean that all the negotiations are in public, but that the outcome, in terms of TREATIES and other arrangements, are. Because secret treaties impose commitments upon peoples of which they have no knowledge, are contrary to the principles of democracy and are a threat to international PEACE, both the LEAGUE OF NATIONS and the UNITED NATIONS (UN) have required that treaties or other international agreements entered into by members must be registered with the Secretariat and be published by it and that, until registered, a treaty is not binding.

Open Door Policy A US diplomatic principle that developed from the 'Open Door Notes' in 1899–1900 written by SECRETARY OF STATE John Hay (1838–1905) and his Assistant Secretary, and that reflected expanding commercial interests in the Far East. The notes requested that foreign powers operating in China give equal treatment to all commercial interests with their SPHERES OF INFLUENCE and that these powers respect Chinese territorial and administrative integrity.

Open Skies Agreement (1992) This was signed at the Helsinki session of the CONFERENCE ON SECURITY AND COOPERATION IN EUROPE (CSCE). The idea had originally been put forward by the USA in 1955 in the OPEN SKIES PROPOSAL and had been raised at Vienna in 1989 at a meeting of the CONVENTIONAL FORCES IN EUROPE (CFE) forum. A key stumbling block in reaching agreements over ARMS CONTROL had been the question of allowing VERIFICATION. This agreement established the right of low-flying surveillance to ensure there was compliance with arms control.

Open Skies Proposal (1955) A proposal made by the US President Dwight D. Eisenhower (1890–1969) to the USSR on 21 July 1955 at Geneva. It called for mutual aerial inspection, in which the USA and the USSR would provide each other with facilities for aerial photography and reconnaissance. It was rejected by the USSR.

Operation Overlord See D-DAY (1944).

Opt-out The phrase used to describe the dispensation within the EUROPEAN UNION (EU), according to which a member STATE need not accede to a specific provision of the EU treaties. This did not occur until the granting of opt-outs to the UK and Denmark during the negotiations leading to the TREATY ON EUROPEAN UNION (TEU) (1992), better known as the Maastricht Treaty, which was ratified in 1993. Specifically, the UK here declined to commit itself to the participation in a single currency and, although it has since accepted it, to the Social Chapter.

Optional clause One of the three principal means by which a STATE may consent to compulsory jurisdiction of the INTERNATIONAL COURT OF JUSTICE (ICJ), and contained within the statute of 1945. The statute of the previous PERMANENT COURT OF INTERNATIONAL JUSTICE (PCIJ) of 1920 proposed that the jurisdiction of the Court should be compulsory. This was not accepted and was replaced by Article 36, the Optional Clause. This enabled members of the LEAGUE OF NATIONS to declare that they recognized as compulsory *de facto* the jurisdiction of the Court in any or all of the classes of legal disputes concerning (1) the interpretation of a treaty, (2) any question of INTERNATIONAL LAW, (3) the existence of any fact that, if established, would constitute the breach of an international obligation. This obligation may be undertaken for a period of time or permanently, and other conditions may be attached.

Organization for Economic Cooperation and Development (OECD) This was preceded by the Organization for European Economic Cooperation (OEEC), which had been formed in April 1948 to coordinate the MARSHALL PLAN (the European Recovery Programme (ERP)) and reconstruction in Western Europe after the Second World War. This had involved most West European countries including Britain and the Western zones of Germany, with the USA and Canada as associate members. When the Marshall Plan ended in 1952, the OEEC was replaced by the OECD and the USA and Canada became full members. In addition to the commitment to encourage economic growth in Europe, the OECD also undertook to support expansion of the developing countries. It expanded over the years and by the 1970s had come to include nearly all the developed economies as a forum for cooperation and analysis of the issues of the world economy.

Organization for Security and Cooperation in Europe (OSCE) This came into existence in January 1995, succeeding the CONFERENCE ON SECURITY AND COOPERATION IN EUROPE (CSCE). CSCE had been a creation of the period of the COLD WAR with the brief of reconciling differences between the adversary BLOCS. This body faced a new SECURITY agenda, was described as 'in and for a new world', and has attended to broader areas of cooperation than its predecessor, including social and economic questions and, notably, issues relating to HUMAN RIGHTS. Members of OSCE include the USA and Canada, the countries of EASTERN EUROPE and Western Europe and the STATES that emerged from the USSR.

Organization of African Unity (OAU) Originally created in 1963 by thirty-two African states, in 2002 it has more than fifty members. It has focused on issues affecting the African continent, including DECOLONIZATION and the preservation of existing borders. It has attempted to reach a common African position in multilateral DIPLOMACY in the UNITED NATIONS (UN) and other organizations. More vaguely, it has promoted the idea of Pan-African continental unity. It has been divided on a number of issues, such as Nigeria and SELF-DETERMINATION in the Western Sahara, and has been less than forceful in its response to atrocities such as the GENOCIDE in Rwanda in 1994.

Organization of American States (OAS) By 1991 this body had achieved universal regional membership of the thirty-five sovereign American states. The idea of a regional organization for COLLECTIVE SECURITY was conceived at the Mexico City Conference of 1945 and came into existence at the Bogotá Conference of 1948. Its charter formalized the inter-American defence structure and integrated it into the UNITED NATIONS (UN) under the authority of ARTICLE 51. It has developed along the lines of multi-purpose cooperation, including such concerns as economic development, the environment and HUMAN RIGHTS. Using the mandate of the RIO TREATY of 1947 providing for hemispheric collective security, the OAS has managed to settle numerous minor disputes in Latin America.

Organization of Arab Petroleum Exporting Countries (OAPEC) This is a subgroup of the ORGANIZATION OF PETROLEUM EXPORTING COUNTRIES (OPEC), representing Arab producers. It includes Algeria, Bahrain, Egypt, Iraq, Kuwait, Libya, Qatar, Saudi Arabia, Syria, Tunisia and the United Arab Emirates.

Organization of Petroleum Exporting Countries (OPEC) This CARTEL was created in September 1960. Initially composed of Iran, Iraq, Kuwait, Saudi Arabia and Venezuela, it has subsequently added Qatar, Libya, Indonesia, the United Arab Emirates, Algeria, Nigeria, Ecuador and Gabon. It reflected the dissatisfaction of the oil-producing countries with their agreements with the oil companies. So, for instance, before 1960 the former had had no say in setting the price of oil. The pressure from this cartel became fully apparent in 1973–4 when, following the YOM KIPPUR WAR (1973), OPEC raised the cost of oil 400 per cent, and, temporarily, because of the latter's pro-Israel stance, banned the export of oil to the USA. It raised prices again in 1979 at the time of the Iranian Revolution, precipitating the recession of the early 1980s in the industrialized world. Subsequently, dissension among OPEC members over quota levels, and wars between them – the Iraq–Iran War and the GULF WAR (1991) – as well as the exploitation of non-OPEC oil and other energy reserves, have led to a relative weakening of the organization.

OSCE See ORGANIZATION FOR SECURITY AND COOPERATION IN EUROPE.

Oslo Accords (1993) These represented a key advance towards a PEACE settlement in the Middle East. In August 1993 two Israeli academics and an official from the PALESTINE LIBERATION ORGANIZATION (PLO) agreed in Oslo on a declaration of principles outlining an Israeli deployment from parts of the occupied WEST BANK and GAZA STRIP and the establishment of provisional Palestinian self-rule there. This concession would be reciprocated by PLO renunciation of TERRORISM. On 9 September a letter from the PLO leader Yasir Arafat (b. 1929) to the Israeli Prime Minister Yitzhak Rabin (1922–95) pledged PLO recognition of Israel, duly renounced terrorism and promised to remove from the Palestine National Charter the appeal for the destruction of Israel. Israel declared that it was willing to recognize the PLO as the legitimate representative of the Palestinian people. The accords were signed on 13 September by Israeli, Palestinian, US and Russian officials. On 24 September two years later a further agreement, called Oslo 'B', signed in Egypt, dealt with the specifics of Israeli troops withdrawals and Palestinian policing.

Oslo Final Document (1992) This agreement, which came into force on 5 July 1992, was to ensure that the successor STATES that emerged from the dissolution of the USSR assumed the obligations and rights inherent in all arms treaties that had been signed by the USSR. This meant that states such as Belarus and the Ukraine were able to become signatories of the CONVENTIONAL FORCES IN EUROPE (CFE) treaty. this, in turn, opened the way for the 1994 PARTNERSHIP FOR PEACE (PFP).

Ostpolitik The policy of the Federal Republic of Germand (FRG) (West Germany) associated in particular with Social Democrat Chancellor Willy Brandt (1913–92) of RAPPROCHEMENT between the FRG and EASTERN EUROPE and the USSR. It coincided with the initiatives in DÉTENTE between the SUPERPOWERS. The first major step was the German–Soviet Treaty of August and West Germany, which disavowed any territorial claims and confirmed its agreement that the borders of all European STATES were inviolable, including, crucially, the ODER–NEISSE LINE with Poland and that between East and West Germany. The *rapprochement* was underwritten in further agreements with Poland in 1970 establishing normal diplomatic relations and allowing the emigration of some ethnic Germans from Poland. 1971 saw the BERLIN QUADRIPARTITE AGREEMENT, which dealt with the question of access to and from West Berlin, which had been perilously fraught during the BERLIN BLOCKADE (1948–9) and the BERLIN CRISIS (1958–62). By signing the Basic Treaty in 1972 Brandt publicly accepted the German Democratic Republic (GDR) as a legitimate state. At the same time, the relations with East Germany were to be of a special nature, because the FRG insisted that there was one German nation (even if there were two German states) and that the GDR could not be treated just like any foreign country. In 1973 the FRG signed a treaty with Czechoslovakia in which the parties renounced the MUNICH AGREEMENT of 1938, which had ceded the SUDETENLAND to Nazi Germany, and established diplomatic relations. *Ostpolitik* also led to both Germanys being admitted to the UNITED NATIONS (UN) in 1975. *Ostpolitik* aroused considerable political controversy in West Germany, where from the start the Christian Democratic Union (CDU) alleged that it conceded LEGITIMACY to Communist and Soviet dominance in Eastern Europe without anything adequate in return, that it potentially endangered the DEFENCE of the West and that it could encourage diminished US commitment to Europe.

Ottawa Agreements (1932) The protectionist measures agreed at the British Imperial Economic Conference from 21 July to 20 August 1932 in the depths of the GREAT DEPRESSION. They involved a series of BILATERAL AGREEMENTS that established a system of IMPERIAL PREFERENCE between Britain and its colonies and dominions, excluding certain classes of goods from outside it.

Out-of-area capability The ability of a nation-state or ALLIANCE, for instance, the NORTH ATLANTIC TREATY ORGANIZATION (NATO), to take military action or involve itself in PEACEKEEPING actions outside its normal sphere of operations or responsibility.

Oval Office The official working office of the President of the USA, located in the WHITE HOUSE. It is also sometimes used as a term for the President and presidential policy.

Overkill This word is frequently used in a specific sense in debates over NUCLEAR WEAPONS. It refers to the fact that the destructive capability of the nuclear powers could eliminate the human race many times over. It was also used in an even more specific sense during the COLD WAR to emphasize the fact that the USA and the USSR could destroy each other.

Overseas Development Administration (ODA) The official British body that deals with development assistance to overseas countries. This assistance includes financing on concessionary terms and technical help. The ODA also assists developing countries in dealing with their national environmental problems and global environmental obligations.

Own path to socialism A phrase used during the COLD WAR to signify the freedom of each Communist party or country to choose the form of transition from CAPITALISM to COMMUNISM as appropriate to national, historical and other circumstances. In the traditional Marxist-Leninist interpretation, the transition was to be via violent revolution. The idea that the Soviet model under Stalin (1879–1953) was the only example to be followed was first questioned by the Yugoslav leader Tito (1892–1980), which led to his break with Stalin and expulsion from the COMINFORM. The new freedom was officially conceded by the Soviet leader Khrushchev (1894–1971) at the TWENTIETH PARTY CONGRESS (1956).

Own resources A term referring to the possession by the EUROPEAN UNION (EU) of resources that belong to it as of right. Contributed by the member STATES, they are collected from customs duties on imports, including agricultural ones, a proportion of the value-added tax levied by the states and contributions based on each member state's proportion of the overall production of the EU. This issue of the UK contribution to this budget was a particularly vexed one between 1979 and 1984, during the premiership of Margaret Thatcher (b. 1925).

Ozone layer The concentration of the gas ozone between about 12 and 30 miles above the earth's surface offers a vital protective shield against nearly all of the sun's ultraviolet radiation. A flight across Antarctica in 1987 appeared to indicate that there was a 'hole' in the ozone layer roughly equivalent to the size of the USA and in depth to the height of Mount Everest. The principal cause of depletion has been the production of chlorofluorocarbons (CFCs). This discovery has caused significant environmental concern. In 1989 the USA and the members of the EUROPEAN COMMUNITY (EC) committed themselves to abandoning all production of CFCs by the year 2000.

P

P5 This term is used by the UNITED NATIONS (UN) to refer to the five permanent members of the UNITED NATIONS SECURITY COUNCIL. These are the USA, Russia, the

People's Republic of China, Britain and France. Until 25 October 1971 the Republic of China (Taiwan) occupied the Chinese seat.

Paasikivi Line A line of DIPLOMACY named after Juho Paasikivi (1870–1956), President of Finland from 1946 to 1956. Finnish policy was much concerned with relations with its dominant neighbour, the USSR, with which it had been at WAR during the Second World War. This approach involved manifesting a clear understanding of the USSR's strategic concerns in the COLD WAR in order to escape greater Soviet pressure on Finland's independence. Fear in the West over such pressure on Western Europe was expressed in the term FINLANDIZATION.

Pacem in terris The Latin for 'peace on earth'. In international relations this refers, first to the Papal Encyclical *On Peace between all Nations, Based on Truth, Justice, Mercy and Freedom*, issued on 11 April 1963 by Pope John XXIII (1881–1963). It was the first time that the HOLY SEE had expressed official support for the UNITED NATIONS (UN) and joined Roman Catholics with people everywhere in an appeal for a world community of mutual understanding. Secondly, the phrase has been used as the name of international conventions on behalf of PEACE – for instance, during 1965 to honour the year designated as the Year of International Cooperation.

Pacific Rim The region bordering the Pacific Ocean in Asia and North and South America. This term has come into general currency with the dramatic growth of the Asian economies in the post-Second World War period, in particular Japan, China and the 'four little dragons', Singapore, Hong Kong, South Korea and Taiwan. In the 1960s the Asian economies were producing just 4 per cent of the world's economic output. By the 1990s this had risen to 25 per cent and US exports to Asia exceeded those to Europe.

Pacific settlement of disputes In international relations, the resolution of conflicts without recourse to FORCE. This can come about through a variety of techniques including ARBITRATION and MEDIATION. These techniques may be applied to disputes between STATES, between states and international organizations and between international organizations. As an example, the HAGUE PEACE CONFERENCES of 1899 and 1907 sought to codify procedures for establishing peaceful settlement. They proposed, for instance, that states postpone hostilities while MEDIATION was taking place. Subsequently, the LEAGUE OF NATIONS hoped to impose upon conflicting parties a delay of some months before hostilities occurred.

Pacification This has two meanings. First, it may refer to PEACE negotiations. Secondly, it may be used to mean the use of armed FORCE to suppress demonstrations or revolts, or to terrorize the population concerned.

Pacifism This term was coined in 1901, though it expresses an idea of opposition to WAR advanced throughout history. For the absolute pacifist this means opposition to all war, including CIVIL WAR and non-participation in conflict, except, sometimes, in a non-combatant role. Article 4 of the UNITED NATIONS CHARTER opens membership of the UNITED NATIONS (UN) to 'peace-loving states'. Governments are in theory committed to the ideal of PEACE over war. For those who have been absolute pacifists (a very small minority), many more have been, and are, what have been called 'pacifi-cists'. These regard war as evil but do not exclude the possibility of the JUST WAR, rec-ognizing that it may sometimes be necessary to go to war. As such, though, they have normally supported the idea of DISARMAMENT, ARBITRATION of disputes and effective imposition of INTERNATIONAL LAW. The recognition of the conscientious objector against military service started in many countries with the recognition of religious objection, which was particularly well represented in some of the Christian denom-inations and groups, such as the Society of Friends (Quakers). This has come to include recognition of those whose objection is based on secular ethical and humani-tarian grounds. The twentieth century – as a century of TOTAL WAR – also saw the growth of pacifism on an unprecedented scale and the attempt to set up structures for the preservation of international peace, notably the LEAGUE OF NATIONS and the UN. Socialist IDEOLOGY also, at least theoretically, encouraged peace and PEACE MOVE-MENTS. The pacifist debate has been given added urgency with the invention of NUCLEAR WEAPONS. The term 'nuclear pacifist' is sometimes used for those who, while completely repudiating any thought of recourse to nuclear war, nevertheless, in some circumstances, are willing to accept and to participate in conventional warfare.

Pact of Paris (1928) See KELLOGG–BRIAND PACT.

Pact of Steel The name given to the military alliance between Nazi Germany and Fascist Italy, signed on 22 May 1939, formalizing the Rome–Berlin AXIS and pledging mutual support if attacked.

Pacta sunt servanda The rule of general INTERNATIONAL LAW that TREATIES are binding and should be observed. It is the principle that establishes the legal basis whereby treaties constitute binding contracts between signatory STATES. The ration-ale for this is that, in the absence of an international enforcement agency, each mem-ber of the international community has the responsibility to keep its agreements.

Painting a country blue This phrase was coined by Douglas Hurd (b. 1930), British Foreign Secretary between 1989 and 1995. It means the work of international peacekeeping missions, which attempt to provide a range of services in territories where government has broken down. These may include AID, SECURITY, DISARMA-MENT and the creation of structures allowing political reconciliation. The United Nations Transitional Authority in Cambodia in the early 1990s, which included armed peacekeepers, election observers and civilian administrators, is an example of such a mission.

Palestine Liberation Organization (PLO) This organization was founded as an umbrella for a number of militant groups (dominated from 1967 by al- FATAH) in January 1964 and has become the officially recognized representative of the Palestinian people, representing the NATIONALISM of those displaced by the founda-tion of the State of Israel in 1948. Its original Charter rejected ZIONISM and the parti-tion of Palestine and called for the 'total liberation' of the latter. In 1974 it gained observer status with the UNITED NATIONS (UN), which accepted the principle of Palestinian SELF-DETERMINATION and national independence. Subsequently the PLO has become committed to a 'two-state' solution, as specified in UN Resolution 242, and to DIPLOMACY rather than guerrilla action. The Declaration of Principles (1993) laid down the formula of 'land for peace', of Israeli withdrawal from GAZA STRIP and the WEST BANK in return for Palestinian recognition of Israel, and therefore renunciation of its earlier insistence on Israel's destruction. Since 1969 the leader of the PLO has been Yasir Arafat (b. 1929). The PEACE process has been seriously impeded by the extremism of more radical Islamic organizations such as HAMAS, which instigated the INTIFADA, the popular Arab uprising, and by constraints within Israeli domestic politics, producing a recurrent cycle of violence, TERRORISM and repression.

Pan-Africanism The movement that originated after the First World War, partially under the influence of ideas for Pan-European INTEGRATION, as seen, for instance, in the Paneuropa Movement. It started among Arab and black students in universities in Britain, Belgium, France and Italy, initially without clearly defined political aims, and led to four congresses held between 1928 and 1939 in Britain. After the Second World War the Fifth Congress, held in Manchester in 1945, concentrated on racial equality and in subsequent years developed into an anti-colonialist movement. In 1958 the Pan-African Movement for Liberation of Central and East Africa was established. This was extended in 1962 to cover South Africa with the name of the Pan-African Freedom Movement of East, Central and Southern Africa.

Pan-American Union This organization to cover all the Americas was formally established at the Buenos Aires Conference, or the Fourth International Conference of American States (1910). It was intended to facilitate a great variety of inter-American activities, political, economic, humanitarian and cultural. Andrew Carnegie (1835–1919) donated the headquarters building located in Washington DC. The Pan-American Union had its roots in the purely commercial Bureau of American Republics, created in 1880, and now serves as the Secretariat of the ORGANIZATION OF AMERICAN STATES (OAS).

Pan-Germanism Originally this concept, which developed in the nineteenth century, was of a common identity of all Germanic peoples, similar to, and in reaction to, PANSLAVISM. By 1914 it was identified with extreme German NATIONALISM and a programme of territorial expansion, particularly in the Pan-German League, which had been founded in 1894. This idea, combined with extreme RACISM, was the dominant motivation in the Third Reich.

Panslavism The movement that, in its modern form, emphasizing ethnicity, called for the unification of all peoples speaking Slavic languages for common political, economic and cultural purposes. It developed in the early nineteenth century (the first Panslavic Congress met in Prague in 1848) and was used later to bolster Russian imperial ambitions. In the latter part of the century its basic premiss was that Russia was the possessor of a unique independent Slavic cultural heritage that was distinct from that of the Romano-Germanic world and incompatible with it. Panslavism was subsequently used by the USSR in propaganda during the Second World War and to support the idea of fraternal Soviet leadership in the early COLD WAR. It appeared significantly less credible with the rift between the USSR and Yugoslavia in 1948.

Paper blockade A blockade declared by a STATE but not maintained with a FORCE sufficient to prevent access to the coastline of the blockaded state.

Paper Tiger A term of contempt popularized during the COLD WAR by Mao-Zedong (1893–1976), the Chinese Communist leader. He used it first publicly in an interview with an American journalist in 1946, when she mentioned that the USA possessed the ATOMIC BOMB. The implication of his dismissiveness was that, though the Western Powers had military and technological superiority, their ideological conviction and fighting spirit were low. This view was continuously propagated by Communist China in the 1950s and 1960s and the criticism was extended to the USSR for, in its view, showing an accommodating attitude towards the West.

Para bellum A Latin term for the notion that, if you are seeking to preserve PEACE, you should prepare for WAR. This is an accompaniment to the assumption that the world is a perilous place requiring STATES to attend to constant DEFENCE preparedness. Much strategic theory, not least that about DETERRENCE in the nuclear era, has made this assumption.

Paramountcy A historical term for a special status or relationship in the British Empire. Between 1857 and 1947 (the date of Indian independence and partition) the princely rulers of India were allowed by the British Sovereign to retain their autocratic rule in return for pledges of loyalty. Paramountcy allowed the imperial authorities to intervene if the princes conspired with the enemies of Great Britain or were tyrannical. The term was also used in the conventions of 1881 and 1884 with regard to Britain and the South African Republic.

Pariah state See ROGUE STATE.

Paris, Club of See CLUB OF PARIS.

Paris Peace Accords (1973) A series of agreements signed in Paris in January 1973 by the People's Republic of China, France, North Vietnam, Britain, the USA and the USSR, together with representatives of the Vietnamese National Liberation Front. They concluded five years of negotiation over Vietnam. They were rejected by the South Vietnam leader President Thieu (1923–2001). After US withdrawal from the WAR, he fought on until the defeat of South Vietnam in 1975 and the unification of north and south under North Vietnam.

Paris Peace Conference (1919–20) This conference established the international settlement after the First World War and was dominated by representatives of the five victorious powers, Britain, France, Italy, Japan and the USA. The other powers, more than twenty of them, sanctioned the decisions of the BIG FIVE at plenary meetings. The following treaties were imposed on the defeated Central Powers: VERSAILLES (Germany), Saint Germain (Austria), Trianon (Hungary), Neuilly (Bulgaria) and Sèvres (the Ottoman Empire). The key figures were Georges Clemenceau (1841–1929), the French Premier; David Lloyd George (1863–1945), the British Prime Minister; and Woodrow Wilson (1856–1924), the US President. Frequently criticized for not having produced a durable settlement, it nevertheless faced very great problems, not least the consequences of the simultaneous collapse of four empires, post-war dislocation, conflicting nationalist claims with demands for SELF-DETERMINATION and significant divisions among the victorious powers. It also produced the LEAGUE OF NATIONS, which, from the start, was weakened by the non-participation of major powers, principally the USA.

Paris Peace Treaties (1946–7). The outcome of meetings in Paris between June 1946 and February 1947 to prepare peace terms for the allies of Germany during the Second World War – namely, Bulgaria, Finland, Hungary, Italy and Romania. Partly because all these STATES had broken with Germany before the end of the wa, the terms were reasonably moderate. The major terms involved territorial adjustments.

Paris Summit (1960) This was originally suggested at the CAMP DAVID SUMMIT, in September 1959, but it was fairly evident in advance of the Paris meeting that the Western powers were not going to make concessions over Germany to the Soviet leader Nikita Khrushchev (1894–1971). Neither the German Chancellor Adenauer (1876–1967) nor the French President de Gaulle (1890–1970) had favoured such a meeting. In the event it broke up only a couple of days after the leaders arrived in Paris because a fortnight earlier an American U-2 spy plane had been shot down over the USSR and its pilot captured. This incident and probable Soviet awareness of diplomatic stalemate doomed it from the start.

Partial Test Ban Treaty (1963) Signed in August 1963 between the USA, the USSR and Britain, this banned nuclear tests in the atmosphere, under water and in space. It followed growing public concern about the effects of radiation from the testing of NUCLEAR WEAPONS and was given urgency by the breakdown of a voluntary MORATORIUM that had operated since 1958, as well as the desire of the SUPERPOWERS to reduce risk taking after the CUBAN MISSILE CRISIS (1962).

Partnership for Peace (PfP) An association proposed by the Heads of State and Government participating in the meeting of the NORTH ATLANTIC COUNCIL (NAC) held at NATO headquarters in Brussels on 10–11 January 1994. It was a response to CENTRAL and EASTERN EUROPEAN STATES who wished to join NATO. Three of them, Poland, Hungary and the Czech Republic, were later to join. At this stage, NATO was particularly concerned not to alarm the Russian Federation with the prospect of an ENLARGEMENT which would look like a revival of CONTAINMENT. Instead it proposed cooperation and participation in military exercises and encouraged the Russian Federation to join the partnership together with the NEAR ABROAD STATES. The USA, Russia and the Ukraine also entered into an agreement on the reduction and disposal of NUCLEAR WEAPONS.

Pax Americana Latin for 'the American Peace' coined during the Second World War by the US publisher Henry R. Luce (1898–1968). Just as the Pax Romana had been the dominant force in the second century BC and the PAX BRITANNICA dominant in the nineteenth century, the Pax Americana, he argued, would prevail in the second half of the twentieth century.

Pax Britannica Latin term for 'the British Peace'. This was used from the nineteenth century to describe a world safeguarded by British naval power, of which a very large part was under the authority of the British Empire.

PCIJ See PERMANENT COURT OF INTERNATIONAL JUSTICE.

Peace In international relations, the absence of WAR. The word is also used more specifically to describe a TREATY terminating a conflict, e.g. Peace of Paris. In INTERNATIONAL LAW peace is considered to be the normal relationship between STATES and peacemaking has proceeded on this assumption. Frequently the breakdown of peace internationally has been related to internal conflicts – for instance, in the Middle East, in Korea (1950–3) or in the Balkans in the 1990s. One approach to the preservation of peace has been through COLLECTIVE SECURITY – for instance, through the LEAGUE OF NATIONS or the UNITED NATIONS (UN). Another has been through the BALANCE OF POWER and DETERRENCE. The recognition of an alternative to peace and war, non-war, underlines the fact that the absence of ARMED CONFLICT does not necessarily in itself mean peace, though it is a necessary condition for it. The English philosopher and political theorist Thomas Hobbes (1588–1679) in *Leviathan* (1651), commented as follows: 'the nature of war consisteth not in actual fighting, but in the known disposition thereto, during all the time there is no assurance to the contrary. All other time is peace.'

Peace Ballot (1934–5) The popular name for the National Declaration on the League of Nations and Armaments. This was a British nationwide referendum organized by the LEAGUE OF NATIONS Union in association with other groups following the breakdown of the WORLD DISARMAMENT CONFERENCE (1932–4). The questionnaire that was issued was intended to demonstrate the support of British public opinion for the League of Nations and the principle of COLLECTIVE SECURITY. More than eleven million cast a vote. The results showed massive support for the League, DISARMAMENT and the prohibition of private arms sales, strong support for the abolition of military and naval aircraft and 'economic and non-military measures' against an aggressor nation. It was not strictly pacifist, since 6.8 million voted for the use of FORCE against aggressors (with 2.4 million voting against). This helped to influence the tactics of the British government when it gave an insincere endorsement to the League at the time of the Abyssinian War (1935–6), which was exposed by the HOARE–LAVAL PLAN (1935).

Peace building This consists of actions taken after a conflict, primarily diplomatic initiatives that strengthen and rebuild civilian infrastructures and institutions in order to forestall a return to conflict. Military as well as civilian involvement is usually required. The most extensive peace-building efforts to date took place after the Second World War, in particular in Germany and Japan.

Peace Corps An idea that originated with US Democratic senators, was established by executive order under President Kennedy (1917–63) in May 1961 and was voted by Congress in September of the same year. The executive order called for the Peace Corps to 'be responsible for the training and service abroad of men and women of the United States in new programmes of assistance to nations and areas of the world'. Volunteers have been sent to developing countries to alleviate poverty, illiteracy and disease, and aid community and economic development. The original motivation was also to counter Communist aims in the THIRD WORLD, to project democratic values and to present the USA as a supportive power.

Peace dividend This phrase was much used at the time of the collapse of the Communist regimes of EASTERN EUROPE, the end of the COLD WAR and the disbanding of the WARSAW PACT. It suggested that the old adversaries would reduce DEFENCE spending and now have a larger budget to disburse on such areas as health and education.

Peace enforcement Military INTERVENTION to compel compliance with international SANCTIONS or resolutions designed to maintain or restore international PEACE and SECURITY. Armed personnel of this type of operation are allowed to go beyond the normal neutral stance of other peacekeepers and have permission to use FORCE to restore a ceasefire or bring to an end a breach of the peace.

Peace movement This term has been used to describe numerous movements committed generally to the preservation of PEACE, to the ending of WAR and to DISARMAMENT, or specifically in relation to particular conflicts such as the VIETNAM WAR (1960–75). With the mechanization and increasing destructiveness of war, such movements developed notably in the nineteenth century and as a consequence of the impact on public opinion of the carnage of the First World War. The inter-war years saw a significant increase and mass mobilization of opinion for movements embracing PACIFISM, disarmament, and campaigns for avoidance of military entanglement. In the period since 1945 the growth (or revival) of peace movements has coincided with periods of major international tension and acceleration of the ARMS RACE, notably at the height of the COLD WAR, such as during the BERLIN CRISIS (1958–62) and the CUBAN MISSILE CRISIS (1962), or during the early 1980s with the controversy over the deployment of EUROMISSILES. In Britain the dominant movement in these crises was the CAMPAIGN FOR NUCLEAR DISARMAMENT (CND) and at times the issue of NUCLEAR WEAPONS became a key one in party political debate. Though this and other movements did not prevent the deployment of these weapons, peace movements have stimulated wider discussion on the issues of DEFENCE and SECURITY, and continue to do so with conflicts that have succeeded the ending of the Cold War.

Peace operations A general term to cover peacekeeping, peace enforcement and other military operations conducted within a framework of diplomatic and political policies to establish and maintain PEACE.

Peaceful coexistence A term first used frequently in the mid-1950s in a period of comparative relaxation in East–West relations. It referred to the coexistence of Capitalist and Communist STATES, particularly the USA and the USSR, without WAR. The advent of NUCLEAR WEAPONS on both sides had forced a reappraisal of the earlier Communist dogma of the inevitability of war between CAPITALISM and COMMUNISM. At the same time, the Soviet leader Khrushchev (1894–1971), who advanced the principle at the TWENTIETH PARTY CONGRESS (1956), was becoming convinced that the USSR could succeed in peaceful competition with the West. Used as a slogan, it led to ideological controversies between the national Communist parties and those of the USSR and the People's Republic of China, and was treated sceptically by the Western Powers. Peaceful coexistence implied non-interference in each other's internal affairs, undertakings not to export revolution and counter-revolution, a slowdown in the ARMS RACE and competitive participation in international relations. It did not, nor was it intended to, imply that the USSR had renounced its belief in the ultimate triumph of the Communist system.

Peacekeeping This term may be applied to all efforts to prevent WAR. In recent decades it has also been used more specifically to describe the policy of the UNITED NATIONS (UN) of sending international forces, the BLUE BERETS, to police troubled areas such as Bosnia.

Pearl Harbor (1941) The US Pacific Fleet naval base in Hawaii, which was attacked on 7 December 1941. This was without declaration of WAR and brought the USA into the Second World War. Killing 2,043 servicemen and civilians, sinking shipping and destroying or damaging a large number of aeroplanes, it crucially missed the aircraft carriers, which were out of harbour on that day. It was a tactical victory, which led, though, to subsequent strategic defeat for Japan. It provoked six wartime inquiries and one post-war Congressional inquiry and has led to unsubstantiated allegations with the conspiracy theory that President Roosevelt (1882–1945) and the British Prime Minister Winston Churchill (1874–1963) knew about it beforehand and allowed it to happen to bring the USA into the war.

Peel Commission (1937) The British Royal Commission sent to investigate the situation in Palestine after the 1936 Arab Revolt. It proposed subdivision into two states, a Jewish and a Palestinian, with Transjordan being incorporated in the latter. The Arabs and Jews both rejected it and so, consequently, did the Palestine Partition Commission in 1938. The British White Paper in 1939, to pacify the Arabs, imposed an immigration quota on the Jews of 75,000 covering the period between 1939 and 1944.

Pentagon The name for the five-sided building of the US Defence Department constructed in Washington DC during the Second World War. Its official name until 1947 was the Department of War. From 1947 to 1949 it was called the National Military Establishment. Since 1950 it has been the Department of Defense. It contains the departments of the respective armed forces, the Committee of the Joint Chiefs of Staff, intelligence agencies and other command institutions of the US military.

Pentagon Papers The name given by the *New York Times* to a series of classified documents that were officially called 'History of US Decision-Making Process on Vietnam Policy'. They recorded how, progressively, the USA had become embroiled in the VIETNAM WAR (1960–75). Their initial importance was the revelation of the means by which the war had been extended through several separate administrations and the executive decision making that accompanied the long and ultimately unsuccessful attempt to prevent a Communist victory in Vietnam. Secondly, though, they raised a constitutional issue. The papers had been stolen in the spring of 1971, and their publication became a *cause célèbre*. The Nixon administration attempted to suppress publication on the grounds of national security, but this was overruled by the Supreme Court on the grounds of freedom of the press, and subsequent charges against the couple who had taken them were dropped when it was discovered that illegal means had been used to obtain evidence. The furore over the Pentagon Papers further undermined confidence in the war with US public opinion.

Percentages Deal An informal agreement between the British Prime Minister Winston Churchill (1874–1965) and the Soviet leader Stalin (1879–1953), reached in Moscow in October 1944 in the Second World War, as the Soviet Red Army was advancing in EASTERN EUROPE. Churchill was anxious to protect British influence in the Balkans, particularly Greece. It was agreed that Britain should have 90 per cent influence in Greece and that the USSR should have this percentage in Romania. It was to be 75:25 in favour of the USSR in Bulgaria and 50 per cent each in Hungary and Yugoslavia. Churchill had initiated the process that led up to the deal with the statement that 'Britain must be the leading Mediterranean Power and he hoped Marshal Stalin would let him have the first say about Greece in the same way as Marshal Stalin about Romania'. The exact significance of the agreement, and for how long it was intended to last, are still debated. The development of the COLD WAR made it inoperative.

Perestroika A Russian term meaning 'restructuring' that passed into common usage as a consequence of the call of Mikhail Gorbachev (b. 1931), the last General Secretary of the Communist Party of the Soviet Union (CPSU), for radical reform in the USSR. The motivations for it are debated – whether, for instance it was originally intended to strengthen the Communist system or genuinely move to democratization. The consequences, however, were dramatic, both within the USSR and, internationally, with the end of the IRON CURTAIN division of Europe.

Peripheral nationalism This term describes those autonomist or separatist movements in territories with different linguistic, religious and cultural traditions that are under the control of a STATE power that they hold to be unrepresentative of their interests. Campaigners for Scottish independence in Britain, Basque separatism in Spain or French separatism in Canada are examples.

Permanent Court of Arbitration A standing panel of jurists, established in 1900, based on the 1899 Hague Convention for the Pacific Settlement of International Disputes (1900) (subsequently revised in 1907). STATES can select arbitrators from this panel to resolve their disputes. The name is misleading, since in reality the Hague Convention did not create a court as such, but rather a machinery for facilitating the creation of arbitral tribunals as might be necessary.

Permanent Court of International Justice (PCIJ) This was the first permanent international global tribunal, and, as such, was of obvious significance as a precedent. It was brought into being by the LEAGUE OF NATIONS, according to Article XIV of its Covenant, to settle legal disputes between STATES and to give advisory opinions on any dispute or question referred to it by the League Council or Assembly. Its first session was held in 1922 and it was formally dissolved in 1946. In that year its functions were inherited by the INTERNATIONAL COURT OF JUSTICE (ICJ). The Permanent Court was not an integral part of the League, and only those states that ratified the Protocol were bound by the statute. By contrast, the ICJ is part of the UNITED NATIONS (UN). The principle of compulsory jurisdiction for the Permanent Court was rejected in favour of the so-called OPTIONAL CLAUSE. The Court dealt with a number of disputes in the inter-war years.

Permanent Representatives See COMMITTEE OF PERMANENT REPRESENTATIVES (COREPER).

Persona non grata A Latin term indicating that a diplomatic agent of a STATE is unacceptable to the receiving state. This can take place either before the agent is accredited, or after, in response to some real or alleged impropriety by the diplomatic agent. It is common for the other state to reciprocate in such circumstances, with mutual expulsion of diplomatic agents. Since it is an attribute of national SOVEREIGNTY for a state to be free to determine who is, or is not, acceptable to it, no reason needs to be offered for declaring someone *persona non grata*.

Petrodollars The common name for the dollar reserves of Arab countries deriving from the export of crude oil. The surplus of the BALANCE OF PAYMENTS of the petroleum-exporting countries was first put to use on Eurodollar markets, then on the markets of the USA, Britain and other countries of the ORGANIZATION FOR ECONOMIC COOPERATION AND DEVELOPMENT (OECD), as well as for international organizations and as funds for the aid of developing countries. A high proportion of petrodollars are returned to the markets of the highly developed industrialized economies.

PfP See PARTNERSHIP FOR PEACE.

Phoney War The period between September 1939 and April 1940. After the Nazi German invasion and occupation of Poland, there was a lull in the Second World War until the attack on Denmark and Norway in April, quickly followed by the invasion of France through the Low Countries.

Pillar This term is used to describe the organization of the EUROPEAN UNION (EU). Following the TREATY ON EUROPEAN UNITY (TEU) (1992), it consists of three 'pillars': the EUROPEAN COMMUNITY (EC) (Pillar One), the COMMON FOREIGN AND SECURITY POLICY (CFSP) (Pillar Two) and Justice and Home Affairs (JHA) (Pillar Three).

Ping-pong diplomacy This term was used by the world's press in 1971 to describe the way in which US relations were opened up with the People's Republic of China after a generation of hostility following the victory of Mao-Zedong (1893–1976). The RAPPROCHEMENT was signalled by the invitation to an American ping-pong team to take part in an international tournament in China. President Richard Nixon (1913–94) responded to this invitation by announcing the cancellation of a number of restrictions affecting trade, communications and visas with China. Since then this term has been used more widely to describe the initial steps towards establishing, or renewing, relations between hostile STATES.

Pivotal state A STATE that is considered to be of key importance for regional and/or international stability. The degree to which states are regarded as pivotal by individual powers is obviously a subjective one. During the nineteenth century, Turkey, 'the sick man of Europe', was regarded as crucially important, particularly in relations between Britain and Russia. During the COLD WAR, with the DOMINO THEORY, any state embroiled in the East–West confrontation tended to be considered pivotal. Examples of this include Germany, Greece, Egypt, Vietnam, Cuba and Afghanistan. In 1979 the USSR invaded Afghanistan and this became one of the major issues in the 'New Cold War', during which there were demands in the USA for a 'new pivotal strategy'. In 2002, though in a changed context, Afghanistan remains pivotal as a territory that has been harbouring international terrorists.

Plebiscite A public referendum or vote by a population of a territory to determine which STATE they wish to live under. It is often applied to the CESSION of territory from one country to another. From the nineteenth century onwards plebiscites gained in popularity as a device for putting into effect the principle of SELF-DETERMINATION and popular SOVEREIGNTY. The population in a ceded territory can lose their former citizenship as they come under new authority. Because of this, many TREATIES involving cession contain a proviso giving individuals the option of retaining their old citizenship or emigrating. Examples of plebiscites include those in Silesia and on the German–Danish borders after the First World War, that on the SAAR QUESTION in 1935 and that of India and Pakistan over Kashmir in 1949.

PLO See PALESTINE LIBERATION ORGANIZATION.

Pluralism As a concept in international relations theory, this term describes the view according to which NON-STATE ACTORS are important players in the international order and must be given full consideration in studying world affairs. It goes beyond the simplistic state-centric view of the international order. In addition, the STATE is not necessarily to be described as a unitary ACTOR or a 'rational' one. Policy making evolves through the interaction of different groups and bureaucracies, often in competition with one another. Furthermore, the agenda of world politics goes far beyond a simple concentration on SECURITY concerns. A range of other issues, including economic and environmental ones, are also of crucial significance.

Pogrom This term has come into general usage to describe any politically/racially inspired mass attack on a minority. Originally, it referred to the violent, spasmodic outbursts in pre-revolutionary Russia, before 1917, against the Jews and other groups that followed scapegoating after some unfortunate event.

Point Four Programme (International Development Act)
(1949) This marked the start of the post-Second World War US foreign aid programme to the developing world, involving capital investment and scientific and technical expertise. It was so called because President Truman (1884–1972) in his inaugural address on 20 January 1949 devoted his fourth point to support for the developing countries. It became law when the President signed the International Development Act on 24 June 1949. At first the programme was controlled by a special agency under the DEPARTMENT OF STATE, but in 1953 it was merged with other foreign aid programmes. It aimed to promote US influence in Africa, Asia and Latin America at a time when the confrontation of the COLD WAR was becoming the dominant international reality.

Polaris missiles Developed by the USA, these were the first SUBMARINE-LAUNCHED BALLISTIC MISSILES (SLBMS). Their first successful firing was in 1960. In December 1962 in the NASSAU AGREEMENT US President Kennedy (1917–63) acceded to the request by the British Prime Minister Harold Macmillan (1894–1986) to sell Polaris to Britain as a replacement for the cancelled Skybolt, and following the failure of the British BLUE STREAK project to provide the country with a credible deterrent and WEAPON OF LAST RESORT.

Polish October (1956) The liberal reaction against the Stalinist regime and economic austerity in Poland in October 1956, also known as the 'Polish Thaw'. The leadership of the Communist Party was taken over by Wladyslaw Gomulka (1905–82), who had been imprisoned. The ferment followed the denunciation of Stalin (1879–1953) at the TWENTIETH PARTY CONGRESS (1956) and the subsequent de-stalinization. It was also preceded by a significant revolt of workers in Poznan against oppression and low living conditions, which had been put down with loss of life. Some reforms were introduced and the worst abuses of the secret police reduced. However, after 1957 a slow return to authoritarianism set in.

POLITBURO The Russian acronym for the Political Bureau of the Central Committee of the Communist Party of the Soviet Union (CPSU), the highest policy-making and executive body of that party.

Polyarchy In international relations this means a world devoid of a dominant structure that adequately frames both conflict and cooperation. Polyarchy exists when nation states, subnational groups and transnational interests and communities compete for the loyalty of individuals. In a polyarchic system international politics is not confined to rivalry, conflict and cooperation between nation states. This is simply regarded as one SUBSYSTEM among others.

Polycentrism This term came into use in the COLD WAR in the world Communist movement to indicate that, rather than COMMUNISM being monolithic, there were a number of centres of power and decision making. The notion of polycentrism was developed by the Italian Communist leader Palmiro Togliatti (1893–1964) and advanced in 1956, a year of considerable upheaval in EASTERN EUROPE. He argued that national Communist parties should not be dominated by the Soviet party and that the world Communist movement should be a free union of autonomous national Communist parties that were agreed on general goals. There were no 'general laws for the construction of Socialism' but each party should be free to choose its own national strategies to achieve Socialism. In the 1970s this doctrine evolved into the even more liberal EUROCOMMUNISM.

Popular Front The idea of an alliance of Communists, Social Democrats and other left-wing groups to resist Fascism was proposed by the COMINTERN in 1935 following the Nazi consolidation of power and the suppression of other parties in Germany in 1934. It marked a revision of Soviet policy, which had earlier involved denunciation and belittling of parties other than Communist ones. Social Democrats, for instance, were ritually condemned by Stalin (1879–1953) as 'Social Fascists'. Popular Front governments were formed in France in 1936–7, Spain during the Spanish Civil War (1936–9) and Chile between 1938 and 1941. Soviet sponsorship of this idea ended with the Nazi-Soviet *RAPPROCHEMENT* of August 1939, the NAZI–SOVIET NON-AGGRESSION PACT.

Poseidon The US missile, also known as C3, which replaced the first SUBMARINE-LAUNCHED BALLISTIC MISSILE (SLBM) system, Polaris. It differed from its predecessor mainly in that it used MULTIPLE INDEPENDENTLY TARGETED RE-ENTRY VEHICLE (MIRV) technology. Britain did not adopt Poseidon. Instead, it modernized its Polaris system with CHEVALINE and subsequently purchased TRIDENT.

Post-cold war era The period considered generally to have begun in 1989 with the destruction of that key symbol of the COLD WAR, the BERLIN WALL on 9 November, leading to the reunification of Germany, accompanied by dramatic political and economic transformation in EASTERN EUROPE and Russia, with the ending of single-party Communist government.

Potsdam Conference (1945) Nicknamed 'Terminal', this was the last Allied conference of the Second World War, held outside Berlin from 17 July to 2 August 1945 after the Allied victory over Nazi Germany. The purpose of this meeting between the leaders was to discuss the operations to be conducted against Japan and to reach an agreement on a post-war international settlement. The POTSDAM DECLARATION demanded the UNCONDITIONAL SURRENDER of Japan and affirmed that the Allies would eliminate MILITARISM from that country. Germany was to be divided into four zones of occupation under the Allies. It was to be demilitarized and denazified, and democracy was to be introduced, while Nazi war criminals were to be punished. The conference approved the ODER–NEISSE LINE as the western boundary and the CURZON LINE as the eastern frontier of Poland, and the Allies recommended the resettlement of Germans from Poland, Czechoslovakia and Hungary.

Potsdam Declaration (1945) This was issued by the USA, Britain and China on 25 July 1945 at the POTSDAM CONFERENCE and later subscribed to by the USSR. It demanded the UNCONDITIONAL SURRENDER of Japan, its DEMILITARIZATION, demobilization and military occupation until a 'new order' was established. It also called for the punishment of war criminals, REPARATIONS, democratization and loss of territory as specified in the CAIRO CONFERENCE (1943). Japan accepted on 15 August 1945.

POW Prisoner of war.

Power According to the US realist international relations theorist Hans Morgenthau (1904–80), power 'may comprise anything that establishes and maintains control of man over man and it covers all social relationships which serve that end, from physical violence to the most subtle psychological ties by which one mind controls another'. Power has often been classified into five principal forms: FORCE, persuasion, authority, coercion and manipulation. It is a central feature of the international system, in which the exercise of power takes many forms, ranging from WAR, through economic pressure to cultural and ideological influence. This is particularly so because of the absence of effective international authority capable of imposing order on global affairs. It is, however, a problematic and 'essentially contested' concept. For instance, political scientists often distinguish power from influence, restricting the term 'power' to relations exercised through control. Power can be analysed in terms of quantity and of the distinction between power as capability to achieve objectives and as relationship. Some elements in power are very tangible, such a military or economic strength; others are vague, but influential, such as morale of population. In recent decades there has been growing interest in the varieties of power in international relations other than military power – for instance, oil power and the control over other precious resources such as water.

Prague Spring (1968) The period of reform in Communist Czechoslovakia associated with Alexander Dubcek (1921–92) between January and August 1968. The reforms, which included the abolition of censorship, were specified in the Action Programme of April that year. This liberalization significantly alarmed the leadership in the USSR and other neighbouring Communist states and was suppressed following invasion of Czechoslovakia on 21 August by the forces of the WARSAW PACT, whose presence was ratified by the Occupation Treaty two months later.

Pre-emptive war This is a WAR in which the country initiating hostilities does so because it considers itself to be about to be attacked. Those who defend such an action do so on the grounds that they are launching a legitimate defence ahead of the attack. It is mainly in order to remove the fears that could cause pre-emption that policies for ARMS CONTROL depend quite heavily on CONFIDENCE-BUILDING MEASURES (CBMS).

Preference agreement Mutual agreements between two or more countries, or groups of countries, on tariff reductions.

Prescription In international relations, the acquisition of a title to the possession of territory because of uncontested exercise of SOVEREIGNTY over an extended period of time. Derived from Roman civil law, this idea presupposes a prior power in occupation whose control over and title to it has lapsed through failure to occupy, abandonment, or neglect, wrongful claim or failure effectively to resist a new claimant. As an example of this principle, Britain's claim to the Falkland Islands has been advanced (as well as on the grounds of the wishes of the inhabitants) on the basis of continuous British occupation since 1833.

Preventive diplomacy This term was originally coined by the UNITED NATIONS SECRETARY-GENERAL Dag Hammarskjöld (1905–61) to describe such UNITED NATIONS (UN) peacekeeping efforts and MEDIATION as were directed to preventing regional conflicts erupting into head-on confrontations between the SUPERPOWERS, the USA and the USSR. At the time the Middle East and the Congo were particularly sensitive areas in this respect in the context of the rivalry of the COLD WAR. To begin with the term meant military as well as non-military INTERVENTIONS. In the 1990s the idea was advocated in a broader interpretation in *Agenda for Peace* (1992) by Boutros Boutros-Ghali (b. 1922), also UN Secretary-General. This reflected the fact that the reduction of East–West tension had not led to a pacific NEW WORLD ORDER. Preventive DIPLOMACY was now defined to mean not simply preventing existing conflicts spreading, but, through fact-finding missions, early warning and confidence-building measures, averting conflicts and DESTABILIZATION in the first place. Very much in mind in this reinterpretation were the events in the Gulf and in the former Yugoslavia, the latter in the 1990s in the process of disintegration. Obvious means would include DEMILITARISED ZONES (DMZS) and early deployment of peacekeepers, either through the UN or through other multilateral PEACEKEEPING organizations.

Preventive war A military STRATEGY that calls for an attack by a NATION, or a group of nations, that enjoys a temporary advantage in striking power. The theory of preventive war assumes that the other side in an ARMS RACE is determined to undertake future AGGRESSION, that time is on the opponent's side and that an immediate decisive action could destroy the pending threat. An example of this is the First World War. At this time there was conspicuous German fear of growing Russian power. Germans were to defend the war as one of legitimate defence ahead of attack and to claim that they were the victims of ENCIRCLEMENT.

Prisoner's Dilemma The theoretical game construct involving two prisoners in a separate cells who are invited independently to give evidence against each other. It that is sometimes used to explain and describe the development of ARMS RACES.

Programme aid This is AID that is designed to assist a country's ongoing development efforts, but without being tied to specific and itemized projects. Such aid will assist a faltering development process in a country by providing foreign exchange, so that the economy will be able further to develop and reach its potential. Controls over programme aid tend, consequently, to be more flexible than those over PROJECT AID.

Project aid Investment in a specific project producing visible results, usually in the form of some kind of construction – for example, a power station, dam or road system. Such projects have been favoured because they offer visible achievements and often also provide opportunities for related private-sector contracts. Most aid granted by the INTERNATIONAL BANK FOR RECONSTRUCTION AND DEVELOPMENT (IBRD) (World Bank) is tied to projects.

Proletarian internationalism A Communist catchphrase to emphasize the solidarity of the workers in different countries, transcending national boundaries. Communists argued that there could be no conflicts once the workers' common interests were clearly perceived and that they constituted a single class united by their struggle against the bourgeoisie and IMPERIALISM. The theoretical foundations of proletarian internationalism were laid in the Communist Manifesto of 1848, articulated in the slogan: 'Proletarians of all lands, unite!', and it became the guiding principle of the Communist internationals. After 1945 the more commonly used phrase was 'SOCIALIST INTERNATIONALISM'.

Proliferation In strategic analysis, negotiations and discussions over ARMS CONTROL, this term refers to the spread of NUCLEAR WEAPONS outside the so-called NUCLEAR CLUB – those countries that had developed nuclear weapons by the early 1960s and that admit, to greater or lesser extent, to basing their defence strategies on possession of these weapons. These are the P5 on the UNITED NATIONS SECURITY COUNCIL. A particular concern is that such arms, as well as other WEAPONS OF MASS DESTRUCTION, may come into the possession of, or be developed by, ROGUE STATES or even terrorist organizations.

Propaganda by the deed See ARMED PROPAGANDA.

Proportionality One of the criteria in the JUST WAR theory. It holds that the damage that any military action does can be justified only in terms of its proportionality to both the immediate military accomplishment it brings and the original justification for going to WAR. It is therefore a doctrine of moderation and restraint. It is a particularly moot and contentious issue with the great increase in the destructiveness of weapons, particularly, of course, the potential of NUCLEAR WEAPONS. For instance, it could be argued that a nuclear strike would be so appalling in its effects that, even if it were the only possible response to AGGRESSION, the rights of self-defence could never be seen as proportional to the damage inflicted.

Protectionism Creating barriers to the international flow of goods and services, protectionism is the theory and practice of using governmental regulation to control or limit the volume of types of imports entering a STATE. Tariffs, quotas, licensing arrangements, exchange control and other devices are used to reduce or eliminate imports, or to increase consumer cost of foreign articles that compete with domestic goods. Protectionism, leading to a dramatic fall in world trade, characterized the GREAT DEPRESSION. Even where nations openly embrace FREE TRADE, they often still employ a variety of covert practices and agreements to protect domestic industries.

Protectorate A legal status that has progressively become a historical one with the process of DECOLONIZATION since 1945. It indicates the situation in which a dependent STATE retains control over its internal affairs while leaving its external protection in the hands of another STATE. Brunei, the last protectorate state, became independent in 1984. Protectorates have been referred to under other titles, 'autonomous states', 'dependent states', 'semi-sovereign states' or 'vassal states'.

Protocol (1) An agreement that is less formal than a TREATY. It may be free-standing or supplementary to and/or clarifying another agreement, such as the secret clauses for the division of EASTERN EUROPE in the NAZI–SOVIET NON-AGGRESSION PACT of 1939. (2) Protocol is also used to mean diplomatic manners and courtesies.

Protocols of the Elders of Zion A forged publication, used among others by Nazi leaders in their campaign against the Jews. Most of it was copied from a French pamphlet of 1864. In Tsarist Russia the secret police, the Okhrana, adapted it to justify their POGROMS. The 'Protocols' purported to be an authentic report of the minutes of a secret Zionist congress aiming at the overthrow of Christian civilization. The document professed to contain the programme of one of the annual meetings held by an international Jewish government in Basel, Switzerland, simultaneously with the first Zionist Congress of 1897. The delegates were accused of conspiring to blow up major buildings in the capitals of Europe, destroy the Aryan race and set up a Jewish world state.

Psychological warfare Conducted mainly through propaganda or ideological campaigns based on carefully conceived strategies, this has become a major factor influencing foreign and military policy in the widest sense, including such fields as DIS- ARMAMENT and foreign AID. Already in the First World War very considerable use was made of psychological warfare – for instance, to weaken the resolve of the CENTRAL POWERS. This was developed significantly during the Second World War and the COLD WAR. In WAR it means all applications of propaganda pressure, including disinforma- tion, to effect the morale, discipline and efficiency of decision making of the enemy. It has also meant campaigns for winning over the HEARTS AND MINDS of populations facing GUERRILLA WARFARE INSURGENCY. Brainwashing refers to the use of such pressures and manipulative techniques with those who are captive subjects.

Pugwash Movement The official name is the 'Pugwash Conferences on Science and World Affairs', named after the village of that name in Nova Scotia where the first conference was held in July 1957. It is a gathering of scientists concerned to help prevent the harmful effects of scientific and technological invention, in particular the danger of nuclear war. In the early years it was the only forum at a subgovernmental level between informed and influential scientists from both East and West. Among other things, it has helped with international moves towards DISARMAMENT.

Puppet state An ostensibly independent STATE that in fact, in important matters, is under the control of another state. It was common, for instance, for the countries of EASTERN EUROPE during the COLD WAR to be referred to as puppet states of the USSR.

Q.

QMV See QUALIFIED MAJORITY VOTING.

Quai d'Orsay The street in central Paris where the French Ministry of Foreign Affairs is located. This is used as an international term for French foreign policy.

Qualified majority voting (QMV) This was introduced into the EUROPEAN COMMUNITY (EC) by the SINGLE EUROPEAN ACT (SEA) of 1987, without which it would have been very difficult to achieve the SINGLE MARKET. Since then, it has been applied more widely in the EUROPEAN UNION (EU). For legislative proposals to be adopted under those headings in which it applies there must be at least 62 votes in favour out of 87. The votes are based on size of population, with the major STATES having 10 votes and the smallest, Luxembourg, 2. It has been agreed that, if the votes for the largest states are increased with EU enlargement, they will give up their right to appoint a second Commissioner. QMV has circumvented in a number of policy areas the block imposed by the LUXEMBOURG COMPROMISE (1966).

Quarantine The compulsory segregation or isolation of people or animals, normally to guard against the spread of contagious disease. Until the First World War customary INTERNATIONAL LAW laid down the rule that the period of quarantine should be forty days on board a ship anchored in port, but away from other vessels. This was subsequently modified to facilitate isolation and segregation elsewhere. The term is also used in a metaphorical sense in international relations, for example, by the USA during the CUBAN MISSILE CRISIS (1962). The word was used then because BLOCKADE would have been technically an ACT OF WAR in an already highly tense situation. The imposition of SANCTIONS – for example, against South Africa during APARTHEID – was also described as quarantine.

Quid pro quo The Latin for 'something for something'. Negotiations are typically conducted on a 'quid pro quo' basis and depend on mutual compromises for success.

Any NATION or organization unable to demand a 'quid pro quo' in exchange for its own concessions is in an inferior bargaining position.

Quiet diplomacy A UNITED NATIONS (UN) term for private talks and negotiations aimed at settling or alleviating international disputes.

Quislings An international term after the Norwegian collaborator with Nazi Germany Vidkun Quisling (1887–1945), Prime Minister of Norway during the German occupation of his country, who occupied that post between 1942 and 1945. It is a synonym for collaboration. The UNITED NATIONS GENERAL ASSEMBLY resolution A/45 of 12 February 1946 recognized 'the necessity of clearly distinguishing between genuine refugees and displaced persons on the one hand, and the war criminals, quislings and traitors on the other'.

Quota A qualitative restriction established by a STATE to control the import of certain commodities. Quotas are used to limit foreign competition in the domestic market, to correct BALANCE OF PAYMENT deficits, to buttress PROTECTIONISM, to provide an instrument for the governmental direction of trade and to wage economic warfare. There are a number of variations in the imposition of quota systems, among them: allocated quotas, where the restrictions relate to specific countries, as against global quotas, where there is a general limitation; customs quotas, where the duties increase the greater the number of items that are imported, and quotas on import licensing, where individual quotas are imposed on specific companies.

R

Racism The belief that there are significant distinctions between races and that this provides grounds for differential treatment of human beings. This belief, expressed, for instance, in the system of APARTHEID in South Africa, has led to racial discrimination, racialism and, in some parts of the world, GENOCIDE. The Declaration on Race and Racial Prejudice (1978) by the UNITED NATIONS EDUCATIONAL, SCIENTIFIC AND CULTURAL ORGANIZATION (UNESCO) identifies the fundamental fallacy of racism in Article 1, which reads: 'All human beings belong to a single species and are descended from common stock. They are born in equal dignity and rights and all form an integral part of humanity.'

Radio Free Europe and Radio Liberty Also known as the 'radios', these were funded by the US CENTRAL INTELLIGENCE AGENCY (CIA) as part of a wider programme of anti-Communist operations in the COLD WAR. They started broadcasting, respectively, in 1949 and 1951. Their aim was both to act as the 'local free press' of EASTERN EUROPE and to project a positive image of the West. During the HUNGARIAN REVOLUTION (1956) Radio Free Europe was accused of encouraging Hungarians to risk their lives by promising Western assistance that never materialized. Subsequently broadcasts emphasized liberalization of COMMUNISM rather than revolution.

Raison d'état French for 'reason of state'. This term became current in the sixteenth century with the evolution of the modern STATE. It means a reason for state action, on the grounds of the interests of that state and its territory, and the SECURITY and well-being of its population, which override other considerations, particularly international ones. It has been acknowledged in INTERNATIONAL LAW since the Treaty of Westphalia (1648), which concluded the Thirty Years War.

Raison de guerre French for 'reason of war'. A doctrine that permits violations of the rules of JUST WAR, in cases where the objectives in the combat can be achieved in no other way. This originated at a time when warfare did not have a framework of regulation in INTERNATIONAL LAW. Such violations are justified by this doctrine only if the purpose is recognized as just. An example of such a justification would be the bombing of civilian targets if it is only by these means that combatants hiding among them could be forced to surrender.

Rapacki Plan (1957) A COMMUNIST BLOC initiative, first presented by the Polish Foreign Minister Adam Rapacki (1909–70) to the UNITED NATIONS GENERAL ASSEMBLY on 2 October 1957. It called for a central European NUCLEAR-FREE ZONE incorporating both German states, Poland and Czechosolovakia. It was to be supervised by the NORTH ATLANTIC TREATY ORGANIZATION (NATO) and the WARSAW PACT. The USA and Britain, which only two years earlier, after the French rejection of the EUROPEAN DEFENCE COMMUNITY (EDC) proposal, had engineered the rearmament of West Germany, rejected the Rapacki Plan. They argued that, because of the larger conventional forces, both in manpower and weapons, of the Warsaw Pact states, the plan would confer military advantage on the USSR and its allies.

Rapallo Treaties (1922) On 16 April 1922 Weimar Germany and the USSR established diplomatic relations, renounced financial claims against each other and pledged economic cooperation. In a secret exchange, the USSR granted German equality with the Allies of the First World War in any subsequent agreement on nationalized property. The Rapallo agreement, sometimes called 'the Treaty of the Outcasts', signalled the end of diplomatic isolation for each country and was a source of significant concern for the British and French, and even more so for Poland. By generating the vision of a powerful Russo-German combination in world affairs, it disrupted efforts at European cooperation and caused Germany difficulties in relation to discussions over REPARATIONS.

Rapid Deployment Force (Rapid Deployment Joint Task Force) (RDJTF) In the post-Second World War period Iran and its DEFENCE from Communist expansion were key considerations for the USA in its STRATEGY for the Middle East. In 1979 the Shah of Iran, Mohammed Pahlavi (1919–80), was overthrown (in February) and in December the USSR invaded Afghanistan. This led US President Carter (b. 1924) to reconsider US strategy in the Gulf region. It was decided to put into effect earlier plans to create a force of 100,000 troops drawn from the army and marine corps, which would be locally based, so that it could respond promptly to crises in the region. This force, representing a further manifestation of the US policy of CONTAINMENT, was in place by the spring of 1981. This defence programme was expanded by President Reagan (b. 1911) and through most of the 1980s planning typically assumed invasion of Iran by the USSR. Preparations for deployment proved very useful to the USA when, instead, Iraq invaded Kuwait in August 1990.

Rapprochement A term of French origin, in international relations it means a reconciliation of the interests of rival states after a period of estrangement or conflict and the re-establishment of normal relations. For instance, it is common to speak of the Franco-German *rapprochement* after 1945, which has made possible the emergence of the EUROPEAN UNION (EU).

Ratification In international relations this term refers to that act by which a TREATY becomes binding on a STATE. Though a treaty is said to be concluded when the parties to it sign it, it usually comes into force only when it is ratified. Each state has its own ratification process. For instance, in Britain Parliament ratifies; in the USA it is the Senate.

Reagan Doctrine Named after US President Ronald Reagan (b. 1911). It involved active, and well-funded, support for groups combating Soviet-backed regimes in Africa, Asia and the Western Hemisphere. A major example was the backing for Afghan ISLAMIC FUNDAMENTALIST rebels in the 1980s against the USSR after its invasion of Afghanistan, which had taken place in December 1979. Another was the backing for the Contras against the Sandinista government in Nicaragua. Whether overt or covert, these actions indicated a new global assertiveness by the USA, backed by a belief that there was a 'democratic revolution' at work in the world that deserved the support of the West.

Realism A major tradition in, and school of, international relations theory, sometimes called 'classical' realism. It makes the assumption that it is addressing the world as it is rather than as it might be, or ought to be, and is commonly contrasted with IDEALISM and the INTERNATIONALISM that was advocated particularly after the First World War. Realism has a pedigree that claims, among others, Machiavelli (1469–1527) and Hobbes (1588–1679). It emphasizes the realities of the pursuit of POWER and self-aggrandizement, conflict, the dominance of the STATE as the primary ACTOR in the international order, the importance of military strength and the maximization of SECURITY. Hans Morgenthau (1904–80), one of the leading realist thinkers, illustrated this perspective in defining statesmen as thinking and acting 'in terms of interest defined as power'. Realism attained particular prominence and apparent plausibility during the COLD WAR. Realists would argue against those who claim their position disregards ethical considerations that the national interest, in a world in which there is no genuinely effective authority higher than the state in world affairs, must be made secure enough before it can make action in support of other values a workable proposition.

Realpolitik This German term was coined in 1853 to describe the politics of REALISM and to encourage German Liberals, who had witnessed the failure of the 1848 nationalist revolutions, to pursue a 'policy of the possible', as was being advocated and was later effectively to be followed by Otto von Bismarck (1815–98), its future Chancellor, in the unification of Germany. It does not mean ruthless power politics and national egotism at all costs – Bismarck also knew when to limit and moderate demands – but it does involve a willingness to use FORCE where necessary. Because of the First and Second World wars, it is often used more negatively than its original sense implied, and is simply criticized as putting opportunism before principle.

Rebus sic stantibus Latin for 'in that state of affairs'. This is the controversial doctrine in INTERNATIONAL LAW that an essential change in the conditions under which a TREATY was concluded frees a STATE from its treaty obligations. It has been used to rationalize and justify unilateral renunciation of commitments. A grave example of this was the justification offered by Hitler (1889–1945) in 1936 for his occupation and REMILITARIZATION of the RHINELAND. He claimed that, because France and the USSR had just signed a treaty of mutual assistance threatening German interests, the previous agreement over the Rhineland in the LOCARNO TREATY (1925) was no longer binding. The Vienna Convention on the Law of Treaties (1969) rejects the doctrine as a justification for altering boundaries between states.

Reciprocity In INTERNATIONAL LAW this describes the relationship between STATES that give each other similar rights and privileges. The principle is implicit in the concept of sovereign legally independent states with governments that claim authority over their own territories and populations, free from external interference – the notion of national SOVEREIGNTY. In trade relations reciprocity is the basis for negotiating concessions, which are seldom lowered without reciprocation. At the same time, it can mean retaliation for higher foreign tariffs.

Recognition In DIPLOMACY, the practice of sovereign independent STATES or recognizing the authority and LEGITIMACY of each other's governments. The act of recognition (either *DE FACTO* or *DE JURE*), may take the form of a declaration to the effect, or may be implicit – for instance, in the addressing of a communication to another government. Recognition between states is usually accompanied by the exchange of AMBASSADORS and other envoys and the establishment of diplomatic offices in each other's capital cities.

Red Cross The worldwide humanitarian agency that also includes in its responsibilities the role of impartial and independent intermediary, assisting the military and civilian victims of WAR and CIVIL WAR. Founded in 1863. Its guidelines are laid down in the Geneva Convention of 1864, subsequently amplified in further conventions. The scope of its activities has increased enormously since its foundation. Its headquarters are based in Geneva, from which it coordinates many branches across the world. In Muslim countries the organization is called the 'Red Crescent'.

Red International This was a colloquial general term used for any of the seven Socialist Internationals from the First International of 1864–76 onwards. Sometimes the description has been applied specifically and only to the COMINTERN of 1919–43.

Red Peril A term first used in Europe in the inter-war years, it referred to the threat of COMMUNISM. This was held to come from two sources: (1), internally, from the local Communist parties instigating strikes and weakening governments; and (2), externally, from international Communism, for instance the COMINTERN. These fears were widely encouraged by right-wing extremists, especially fascists and Nazis, as a justification for strong nationalist and authoritarian governments.

Red Scare Specifically, a wave of anti-Communist agitation in several Western countries, including Germany and the USA, between 1918 and 1920. It was prompted by the Russian Bolshevik revolution of 1917, the ensuing civil war, the call for EXPORT OF REVOLUTION, industrial and agrarian unrest in Italy (the so-called two red years) and the establishment of Soviet republics in Bavaria, Slovakia and Hungary in 1919. The phrase has also been used more generally for other periods, such as during the early years of the COLD WAR with MCCARTHYISM and subsequent periods of high East–West tension.

Refugee The 1951 definition of a refugee by the UNITED NATIONS (UN), as amended in 1967, states that a refugee is a person who, 'owing to well-founded fear of being persecuted for reason of race, religion, nationality, membership of a social group, or political opinion, is outside the country of his nationality and is unable, or owing to such fear, is unwilling to avail himself to the protection of that country'. This definition has undergone some changes in some parts of the world – for example, to cover threats from external AGGRESSION or foreign occupation. In the USA, for instance, until 1980 foreign nations were accepted as refugees if they were fleeing from COMMUNISM. Since there are now many millions across the globe uprooted from their homes as refugees or 'internally displaced persons', of which a significant proportion are refugees for economic reasons, there has been a growing demand for redefinition of the term.

Refuseniks Those Jews in the USSR who were refused permission to emigrate to Israel from 1970 onwards. After the SIX DAY WAR (1967) the USSR had cut off diplomatic relations with Israel and mounted an anti-Zionist campaign. The issue became a key one in East–West relations and the debate over DÉTENTE. In the HELSINKI ACCORDS (1975) provisions were included for the rights of family reunification as well as the rights of minorities. With *GLASNOST* the situation was dramatically transformed. While only 900 were allowed to emigrate in 1986, by 1990 185,000 emigrated.

Regionalism In international relations, the concept that STATES situated in the same geographical area can cooperate with each other to resolve common problems or achieve objectives beyond the capacity of individual national attainment through a limited member organization. Such regional organizations include military ALLIANCE systems such as the NORTH ATLANTIC TREATY ORGANIZATION (NATO), economic arrangements such as the NORTH AMERICAN FREE TRADE AGREEMENT (NAFTA) and political organizations such as the ORGANIZATION OF AFRICAN UNITY (OAU). THE UNITED NATIONS CHARTER encourages regionalism as complementary to the world organization's aims, provided it is consistent with its principles. The period since the Second World War has seen a proliferation of regional organizations and significant moves towards regional INTEGRATION. The term is used also to denote the belief in, and practice of, regional government within states.

Regulation In the EUROPEAN UNION (UN) this term describes a legislative instrument setting down rules and guidelines applying in their entirety to all member STATES.

Reichswehr The armed forces of Germany between 1919 and 1935. Its structure was prescribed by the VERSAILLES TREATY (1919) and put into effect by DEFENCE regulations of 1921. The Army was not allowed to exceed 100,000, the Navy 15,000 and a German air force was prohibited. In practice, these restrictions were circumvented, not least by secret technical cooperation with the USSR. These restrictions were later openly rejected by the Third Reich.

Remilitarization The reintroduction of military forces into an area from which they have been removed, or removed themselves, under the terms of a PEACE agreement or other international accord by the NATION that has been required to end their occupation. One of the best-known cases is the remilitarization following reoccupation of the RHINELAND by Nazi Germany in March 1936. This contravened both the VERSAILLES TREATY (1919) and the LOCARNO TREATIES (1925) and it was of the greatest significance for the future, the first of several territorial moves by Hitler (1889–1945) that led to the Second World War.

Renversement des alliances A term meaning 'reversal of alliances' – leaving one ALLIANCE and entering into a new arrangement with a recent rival or enemy. Such changes may occur as a result of changing perceptions of what represents the NATIONAL INTEREST and/or a revolution within a country leading to diplomatic reorientation.

Reparations Payments made by defeated powers at the end of a WAR, commonly also called war indemnities. They serve two primary purposes: compensation for the damage and cost of war and the weakening of the economic and, therefore, also military capacity of the defeated power(s) in the future. The most famous and contentious case of reparations was over those imposed on Germany as a consequence of the VERSAILLES TREATY (1919) at the end of the First World War, which were not finalized until 1921, which were subsequently reduced in the Dawes Plan (1924) and the Young Plan (1929) and then, after the Nazi rise to power, repudiated. Following the fall of France in 1940, Germany extracted reparations and occupation costs. After the defeat of Germany in 1945, reparations were again imposed by the Western Allies and the USSR, though the former largely waived their demands in order to allow the German economy to revive, to avoid economic depression and accompanying anti-democratic political protest. The USSR's insistence on its reparations and failure to account for what it took from the Western zones of occupied Germany played a significant part in the early post-war deterioration of East–West relations, which soon led to the COLD WAR.

Repatriation The term is currently used to mean the policy of returning immigrants to their countries of origin, which has been specially espoused by political parties of the far Right. There has been particular controversy over the repatriation of prisoners of war by Britain at the end of the Second World War. These were Soviet citizens who had fought for the Germans and they were handed over to the Soviet and Yugoslav governments in 1945 to fulfil agreements made at the YALTA CONFERENCE (1945) – the so-called Victims of Yalta. Many were executed on their return.

Reservationists This term was used to describe those US Senators who, in the debate over the RATIFICATION of the VERSAILLES TREATY between 1919 and 1920, supported the addition of amendments or reservations to the Treaty. The majority of these related to the question of US participation in the LEAGUE OF NATIONS and its affiliated organizations. The qualifications included, for instance, the right of Congress to approve participation in COLLECTIVE SECURITY and in any matter involving the MONROE DOCTRINE (1823).

Reserve currency A currency held by countries as part of their foreign exchange reserves to meet foreign currency payments and manage their trade balances. It must be convertible and it will be the currency of a country that has an important share of world trade. Such currencies finance a major proportion of world trade. The US dollar is the most significant of the reserve currencies.

Retorsion A legal but deliberately unfriendly act by a STATE, short of the use of armed FORCE, against another state in retaliation for an unfriendly act with the intention of compelling it to change its behaviour. Means used are various, including severance of diplomatic relations, the restriction of freedom of movement of diplomats, and the curbing of fishing rights. An act of retorsion can become unlawful if it endangers international PEACE and SECURITY.

Revanchism From the French for 'revenge' (*revanche*). A revanchist policy is one based on vengeance. It was a term used particularly to describe the popular French wish after France's defeat in the Franco-Prussian War (1870–1) to take back ALSACE-LORRAINE.

Revisionism In international relations, a challenge to the existing order. Those powers have been described as revisionist that have attempted to change the distribution of POWER and territory to their own advantage. This was particularly illustrated and examined by the English historian of international relations and the USSR E. H. Carr (1892–1982) in *The Twenty Years' Crisis 1919–1939* (1939) with reference to the claims of the dissatisfied powers, Germany, Italy and Japan, which had in successive crises challenged COLLECTIVE SECURITY. The term has also been used specifically in the major historical debate over the origins of the COLD WAR, to describe those who have challenged the 'orthodox' pro-US /NORTH ATLANTIC TREATY ORGANIZATION (NATO) interpretation. Recently there has been further analysis and differentiation of the motivations behind revisionism, whether, for example, revolutionary or conservative militaristic. It has been also a term much used in denunciation within COMMUNISM, as, for instance, of the German Socialist Eduard Bernstein (1850–1932). Mao-Zedong (1893–1976), for example, stated that revisionism amounted to CAPITALISM.

Revisionspolitik German for 'policy of revision'. This aimed at the revision of the VERSAILLES TREATY of 1919, which had been imposed on Germany after the First World War. The primary targets were the territorial losses and REPARATIONS. The Treaty was generally resented in Germany, but the most vocal support for revision came from the right-wing political parties, demanding equality for their country and repossession of their territories, and to greatest subsequent effect by the Nazi Party.

Revolution in military affairs (RMA) This term means the impact of modern developments in weapons technology and information technology on modern warfare, STRATEGY and military CAPABILITY. Conventional strategy has now, for instance, to take account of NUCLEAR WEAPONS. It is now possible to strike over long distances, and very accurately, and achieve victory with minimum recourse to the use of ground troops. The key element in recent developments has been the collection and processing of INTELLIGENCE information and the achievement of dominance in the so-called information war, with the application of information to securing victory, with the use of SMART BOMBS. This has been very evident in such conflicts as that in the Gulf in 1991, over Kosovo in 1999 and in Afghanistan in 2001.

Reykjavik Summit (1986) The second summit conference between US President Ronald Reagan (b. 1911) and the Soviet leader Mikhail Gorbachev (b. 1931), held on 11–12 December 1986, which engaged in STRATEGIC ARMS REDUCTION TALKS (START). It was significant because of the mutual willingness of the leaders to see massive reduction in NUCLEAR WEAPONS. They agreed to reduce STRATEGIC nuclear weapons by 50 per cent within five years and President Reagan promised not to deploy the controversial STRATEGIC DEFENSE INITIATIVE (SDI) system for ten years, though he did not renounce the project.

Rhine River Commission The first modern international governmental organization (IGO). It was created by the VIENNA CONGRESS in 1814–15 and now promotes unrestricted navigation on the Rhine. Until 1918 this right extended only to those states through which the river flowed. The nations represented on its Commission are Belgium, France, Germany, the Netherlands, Switzerland and the United Kingdom.

Rhineland A Prussian ANNEXATION at the VIENNA CONGRESS (1814–15). After the First World War the VERSAILLES TREATY (1919) laid down that the Rhineland was to be occupied by Allied troops for fifteen years and that a 30-mile wide DEMILITARIZED ZONE (DMZ) was to be created on the right bank of the rhine. The LOCARNO TREATIES (1925) confirmed the DMZ but agreed the end of occupation by June 1930. Subsequently the Rhineland became the first object of Nazi territorial REVISIONISM when, on 7 March 1936, Hitler (1889–1945) ordered German troops into the DMZ, refortifying the area, and encountered only verbal protest from Britain, France and the LEAGUE OF NATIONS. Later, the reoccupation of the Rhineland came to be regarded as the most favourable moment when Nazi aggrandizement might have been halted.

Riga Axioms The analysis of Soviet behaviour worked out by US foreign service officers in Riga, Latvia, during the inter-war years. This interpreted the USSR as motivated by Marxist IDEOLOGY and seeking world conquest for its revolutionary ideas. They concluded from their assumptions and observations that, as it was a revolutionary rather than a traditional STATE, negotiations with the USSR would be pointless and even dangerous.

Right of legation See LEGATION.

Rio Conference (1992) See UNITED NATIONS CONFERENCE ON ENVIRONMENT AND DEVELOPMENT.

Rio Treaty See INTER-AMERICAN TREATY OF RECIPROCAL ASSISTANCE (1947).

RMA See REVOLUTION IN MILITARY AFFAIRS.

ROE See RULES OF ENGAGEMENT.

Rogue state A term that originated in the USA, meaning those STATES that pose a threat to international PEACE and that should be considered outside the circle of civilized nations. It has been used especially to point the finger of accusation at those countries that are hostile to Western interests and have been sponsors of international TERRORISM, such as Iraq and Libya, and/or may be developing WEAPONS OF MASS DESTRUCTION, such as North Korea, which presents a potential nuclear threat.

Rollback A strong anti-Communist critique of the US policy of CONTAINMENT in the COLD WAR. In the late 1940s and early 1950s this was particularly intense among those who argued that, with the domination of EASTERN EUROPE, the 'loss of China' and the KOREAN WAR (1950–3), containment was not working and that the USA should support 'liberation' of peoples from COMMUNISM rather than simply limiting its advance. It reinforced the misperception that Communism was monolithic with Moscow as the puppet master. The actual response of the USA to upheavals in Eastern Europe, such as the HUNGARIAN REVOLUTION (1956), was rhetorical rather than interventionist. The idea of rollback revived though during the 'New Cold War' in the 1980s with the REAGAN DOCTRINE.

Rome, Club of See CLUB OF ROME.

Rome Treaties (1957) (1) The founding TREATY of the EUROPEAN ECONOMIC COMMUNITY (EEC), which was signed by France, Germany, Italy, Belgium, Holland and Luxembourg on 25 March 1957. It established a COMMON MARKET to be phased in originally over a twelve-year period. At the end of this it would have a common external tariff (CET) and free circulation within the market of capital, labour, goods and services. It would also extend to agricultural goods with the COMMON AGRICULTURAL POLICY (CAP). Its provisions take precedence over national law. The original membership has expanded to fifteen, with other states due to accede to the Treaty, which has been amended by subsequent enactments, notably the SINGLE EUROPEAN ACT (1987) and the TREATY OF EUROPEAN UNION (TEU) (1992). (2) A second Treaty of Rome signed at the same time in 1957 established the EUROPEAN ATOMIC ENERGY COMMUNITY (EURATOM).

Roosevelt Corollary (1904) This was announced to Congress by the US President Theodore Roosevelt (1858–1919) on 6 December 1904 in his Annual Message. It was an extension of the MONROE DOCTRINE of 1823, in asserting the right of the USA to intervene in the affairs of Latin American STATES in order to prevent INTERVENTION by a European state. At the time several Caribbean and Central American states were deeply in debt to various European powers. These were threatening forcible collection of what was owing to them. The Roosevelt Corollary clearly indicated that it would regard any such intervention, particularly in the area of the proposed Panama Canal, as a threat to its SECURITY.

Ruhr occupation (1923) The Franco-Belgian occupation of the major German heavy industrial area in January 1923, which followed German failures to meet the schedule of REPARATIONS demanded after the First World War. This led to passive resistance, accompanied by hyper-inflation and intensification of German hostility to the VERSAILLES TREATY (1919), fuelling radical NATIONALISM. The Ruhr occupation was also criticized by Britain and the USA.

Rules of engagement (ROE) These are directives issued by commanders that control the use of military FORCE, sometimes severely restricting it. The term is of recent origin, and detailed standards and criteria were developed during the COLD WAR. This was partly in response to the changing technology of warfare and the enhanced destructiveness of new types of weapon.

Russification The policy that, over the centuries, has attempted to assimilate non-Russians into Russian culture. As the Tsarist empire expanded into Siberia, Central Asia, and Europe during the seventeenth, eighteenth and nineteenth centuries, russification became the official policy of the Crown. Occupants of any position of importance had to speak Russian. Those who practised a religion other than Russian Orthodox Christianity, notably the Jews, were persecuted under the formula of 'autocracy, orthodoxy and nationality'. Though the Bolsheviks came to power in 1917 with the promise of equality to all nations, Stalin (1879–1953) repeatedly purged non-Russian elements for 'bourgeois nationalism' and propagated Russian as the language of COMMUNISM in the USSR. During the COLD WAR Russian was also compulsorily taught throughout EASTERN EUROPE as the second language.

Russophobia Anti-Russian sentiment, which has been a recurrent theme in public opinion, not simply in countries such as Poland and Hungary adjacent to Russia/the USSR. By the mid-nineteenth century, for instance, there was a strong current of Russophobia in British public opinion, which included those fearful of Russian expansion at the expense of the British Empire and those who regarded the Tsarist order as the bastion of oppression. Towards the end of the century this was aggravated by the POGROMS against the Jewish population. Whether encouraged by fears of territorial advance or of ideological abhorrence, this sentiment was yet further developed by the effects of the Russian Revolution of 1917 and the COLD WAR.

S

Saar Question The issue of whether the Saar would be returned to Germany after the Second World War or be given international status under France. A highly industrialized area, rich in coal deposits, the Saar is culturally German. After the First World War it was placed under the jurisdiction of the LEAGUE OF NATIONS, which allowed France to administer it from 1919 to 1935. In a 1935 PLEBISCITE Saarlanders voted overwhelmingly to be returned to Germany. After the Second World War France again attempted to annex the Saar or to keep control of its economy. When this met with opposition, it tried to prevent Germany from controlling the land by promoting the plan for an independent free territory. In October 1955 the Saarlanders were asked to vote on a charter that would have given the territory status within the WESTERN EUROPEAN UNION (WEU). They rejected this by a 68 per cent vote and in the following year France and Germany agreed that the territory should be politically united with the Federal Republic of Germany (FRG). On 1 January 1957 the Saar became the tenth *Land* in the FRG and its economy was fully integrated with that of West Germany three years later.

SAC See STRATEGIC AIR COMMAND.

SACEUR Supreme Allied Commander Europe, responsible for training, equipping and assigning all the NORTH ATLANTIC TREATY ORGANIZATION (NATO) forces, including US troops committed to the DEFENCE of Europe.

SACLANT Supreme Allied Commander Atlantic, the officer responsible for all NORTH ATLANTIC TREATY ORGANIZATION (NATO) naval commands in the Atlantic Ocean, responsible for training and, in the event of conflict, guarding its sea lanes and islands. The British Isles and the English Channel come under the separate command of CINCHAN, Allied Commander-in-Chief Channel.

Safe areas Six 'safe areas' were established by the UNITED NATIONS (UN) in Bosnia-Herzegovina in 1992 in an attempt to protect Muslims from Bosnian Serbs. The peacekeepers moved into six Muslim-dominated towns, including Sarajevo and Srebrenica. This did not prevent a number of massacres, and shelling of Muslims continued until the NORTH ATLANTIC TREATY ORGANIZATION (NATO) intervened militarily.

Safe havens The term for the areas established in northern Iraq by the UNITED NATIONS (UN) for the protection of the Kurds from the forces of Saddam Hussein (b. 1937), following the GULF WAR of 1991, and to provide them with humanitarian assistance. They extended from Iraq's northern border to the 36th parallel. The term 'haven' replaced 'enclave' in order not to prejudice Iraqi territorial integrity.

Sahel The Arabic for 'border', this refers to those West African countries located at the edge of the Sahara Desert, characterized by little or no rainfall. The Sahel includes Burkina Faso, Cape Verde, Chad, the Gambia, Guinea-Bissau, Mali and Mauretania.

SALT I and II See STRATEGIC ARMS LIMITATION TALKS AND AGREEMENTS.

San Francisco Conference (1945) Properly known as the United Nations Conference on International Organizations (UNCIO), this was held from 25 April to 26 June 1945, resulting in the approval of the UNITED NATIONS CHARTER and the Statute of the INTERNATIONAL COURT OF JUSTICE (ICJ). The proposals before the fifty STATES that participated had been formulated at the DUMBARTON OAKS CONFERENCE (1944) by the USA, Britain, the USSR and Nationalist China. The first session of the UNITED NATIONS GENERAL ASSEMBLY, which ratified the decisions of the San Francisco Conference, was held in London on 24 October in the same year. Two key disputed issues were, first, the power of VETO on the UNITED NATIONS SECURITY COUNCIL. Here the ruling that emerged was that there could be a veto on action, but not on topics of discussion, the so-called YALTA FORMULA. Secondly, there was the question of the relationship between the Security Council and any regional SECURITY organizations, such as the subsequent NORTH ATLANTIC TREATY ORGANIZATION (NATO), created in 1949. This was covered by ARTICLE 51 of the UN Charter, which authorized 'individual and collective self-defence against armed attack until the Security Council has taken the (necessary) measures'.

San Remo Agreement (1920) This agreement in April 1920 embodied decisions taken by the Council of the LEAGUE OF NATIONS. It specified that Britain and France would decide the nature of the MANDATES for the Middle East and submit their proposals to the League. Britain was awarded Palestine and Mesopotamia (later Iraq). France was awarded the mandates for Syria and Lebanon. The British Mandate for Palestine incorporated the BALFOUR DECLARATION (1917).

Sanctions Coercive measures adopted or threatened against a STATE violating INTERNATIONAL LAW and disregarding its obligations. In the absence of an international executive, the imposition of sanctions depends on the degree of consensus in the international community and on the willingness of each member to see them enforced, as was all too evident, for instance, in the failure of a COLLECTIVE SECURITY during the Abyssinian War of 1935–6. To be effective sanctions should create more hardship for the offending state than the sanctioning state. Sanctions are also harder to apply effectively against non-democratic states, where all too often the population carry the brunt but are not in a position to do anything about it. Similarly, sanctions often enforce isolation without achieving compliance, and are sometimes easily circumvented. Enforcement measures are provided for in Chapter VII of the UNITED NATIONS CHARTER and military sanctions were authorized by the UNITED NATIONS SECURITY COUNCIL against Korea in 1950 and Iraq in 1990. Examples of economic sanctions include those against Southern Rhodesia and South Africa.

Sanctuarisation élargie The DEFENCE policy associated with French President Valéry Giscard D'Estaing (b. 1926), which called for French DEFENCE of a wider area than the French homeland. It involved expansion of military capabilities for overseas operations and greater cooperation with the NORTH ATLANTIC TREATY ORGANIZATION (NATO), and led to an increase in naval forces in the Indian Ocean and military intervention in a number of French-speaking African states. His successor, President Mitterrand (1916–96), continued many of these policies, as, for example, French involvement in CIVIL WAR in Chad in 1983.

Satellite state A STATE that is tied by political, economic and ideological links to a more powerful state, which constrains its freedom while nominally allowing it independence. This term, for instance, fairly described the members of the WARSAW PACT within the Soviet SPHERE OF INFLUENCE during the COLD WAR.

Schengen Agreement (1990) An agreement for free movement of persons with the abolition of border controls throughout the EUROPEAN COMMUNITY (EC) originally negotiated in February 1985. The original negotiations were conducted by Belgium, France, the Federal Republic of Germany (FRG), Luxembourg and the Netherlands. It was essentially incorporated in the AMSTERDAM TREATY (1997), though Britain and Eire were granted OPT-OUTS. The result of protracted negotiations and long delays, dealing with such complexities as arranging a common policy for ASYLUM, it commits the continental member STATES of the EUROPEAN UNION (EU) to open their internal borders by 2004. The area of agreement covered is called 'Schengenland'.

Schlesinger Doctrine Named after James Schlesinger (b. 1929), who became US Secretary of Defense in May 1973. His doctrine revolved around the need to have a range of nuclear options, and strategic flexibility, with which to respond to any nuclear attack on the USA, rather than simply relying on ASSURED DESTRUCTION.

These ideas were subsequently incorporated in Presidential Directive (PD) 39 issued by President Jimmy Carter (b. 1924).

Scramble for Africa The term used for the competitive partition of Africa in the age of the so-called New Imperialism by the European powers between 1880 and 1911. This was for a variety of motives, financial, commercial, strategic, national prestige, and missionary. The main beneficiary, simply in terms of territory, was France, with nominal SOVEREIGNTY over more than a third of Africa's surface.

SDI See STRATEGIC DEFENSE INITIATIVE.

Sea Lion The code word for the German invasion of England for which Hitler (1889–1945) ordered preparation in his directive number 16 on 16 July 1940, after the fall of France. In spite of this, Hitler still hoped to persuade Britain to conclude PEACE. Operation Sea Lion envisaged a speedy invasion of southern England, but on 14 September it had to be postponed until the intended destruction of the Royal Air Force was complete. The invasion never took place, because of the RAF victory in the BATTLE OF BRITAIN (1940). In addition, Germany would have had to ward off the Royal Navy. Without command of the air and the Channel it would have been a highly perilous operation for Nazi Germany.

SEA See SINGLE EUROPEAN ACT.

Seabed Treaty (1971) Signed by sixty-three nations on 11 February in Washington, London and Moscow, this prohibited the installation of NUCLEAR WEAPONS on the ocean floor. This was part of the wider DISARMAMENT initiative, the STRATEGIC ARMS LIMITATION (SALT I) process. It barred from the seabed, outside the 12-nautical-mile coastal zone of TERRITORIAL WATERS, 'any nuclear weapons and launching installations, or any other facilities specifically designed for storing, testing or using such weapons'.

SEATO See SOUTH EAST ASIA TREATY ORGANIZATION.

Secession The political expression of willed separation of a region from an existing political structure. This is commonly accompanied by violence and communal conflicts. Modern examples include the secession of Eastern Nigeria as Biafra between 1967 and 1970, leading to CIVIL WAR and of East Pakistan as Bangladesh in the 1970s, or the wish of the French Canadians of Quebec to secede from Canada.

Second centre of decision making One of the justifications that British governments have advanced from the early 1960s for the UK's nuclear deterrent. The knowledge that the UK (and France) had NUCLEAR WEAPONS as well as the USA, it was argued, would act as an additional deterrent to any risk taking by the USSR, because it would increase Soviet uncertainty. If, for instance, the USSR had convinced itself that the USA would not risk nuclear retaliation for Europe, the existence of the European deterrents would continue to give it significant pause for reconsideration and caution. It was an argument of DETERRENCE by uncertainty.

Second Front The term used during the Second World War, after the invasion of the USSR by Nazi Germany in June 1941, for a cross-Channel invasion of the Continent, which materialized with D-DAY (Operation Overlord) on 6 June 1944. The Soviet leader Stalin (1879–1953) and the US High Command initially called for such an invasion as early as 1942, but the British Chiefs of Staff argued for delay until preparations were fully advanced and Germany was weakened enough for success to be assured. They stressed the logistical difficulties of mounting a premature amphibious operation against a fortified coastline. This argument was sustained by the Dieppe Raid of 1942, in which half a force of 6,000 were lost. The USSR was highly critical of the delay, during which the Western Allies mounted the invasion of North Africa and Italy, claiming that they, the Russians, were deliberately being forced to bear the brunt of the Nazi war effort. In the event, British caution proved wholly justified and realistic.

Second generation peacekeeping This term has been applied to operations mounted after 1989 by the UNITED NATIONS (UN). In addition, simply by keeping belligerents apart ('traditional peacekeeping'), this also involves humanitarian assistance and rebuilding the civil order after conflict, with such work as monitoring elections.

Second strike capability A STATE's ability to survive an initial nuclear attack on it and counter-attack with its own NUCLEAR WEAPONS. It was at the heart of the concept of the BALANCE OF TERROR in the COLD WAR. This capability has been maintained in a variety of ways, by increasing the number of missiles, locating them in hardened silos underground, placing them in submarines or mounting an effective ANTI-BALLISTIC MISSILE (ABM) SYSTEM.

Second Tier A phrase used to describe countries lacking a stable democracy, a market economy and significant industrial development.

Second World A phrase used to describe the USSR and its East European satellites during the COLD WAR.

Secret Speech The attack on Stalin (1879–1945) by the Soviet leader Nikita Khrushchev (1894–1971) at the TWENTIETH PARTY CONGRESS in 1956. The speech was entitled 'On Personality Cult and its Consequences' and lasted six hours. It was delivered to a select group of 140 delegates and was not published in the USSR at the time, but it soon found its way via the CENTRAL INTELLIGENCE AGENCY (CIA) to the West. Denouncing Stalin's disregard for legality, his TERRORISM, self-glorification and abuse of POWER, its disclosures caused a sensation throughout the world and produced considerable ferment within the COMMUNIST BLOC.

Secret treaties Historically, very many treaties or protocols have been secret. This term came to be used critically, though, in the context of the demand for OPEN DIPLOMACY and a new international order, which was advocated most prominently by US President Woodrow Wilson (1856–1924) during and after the First World War. In the FOURTEEN POINTS of 1918 he called for 'open covenants openly arrived at' and, therefore, for an end to such arrangements as the London Treaty (1915), which had made promises to Italy that created major problems after the WAR.

Secretary of State The chief adviser to the US President on foreign affairs and Head of Department of State. This office was created together with the Department of State in 1789. The Secretary ranks first among Cabinet officers and first among the non-elected officials in the line of presidential succession. Though the President is ultimately responsible, some secretaries of state have been allowed virtually a free hand in managing US external relations.

Secretary-General (United Nations) See UNITED NATIONS SECRETARY-GENERAL.

Sectoral integration A gradualist approach to INTEGRATION in contrast to an immediate federal approach. It found expression in the EUROPEAN COAL AND STEEL COMMUNITY (ECSC) (1951), inspired by Jean Monnet (1888–1979). By integrating economic sectors the national economies of the member STATES would become so interlocked that a common political structure and decision-making authority would be both desirable and inevitable. The assumption was that economic integration would eventually lead to political unification.

Security The absence of threat – an ultimate goal and top priority of STATE behaviour and government policy. Traditionally, the emphasis has been on the military aspects, against perceived threats of external attack and invasion or subversion with, or without, internal upheaval and CIVIL WAR, and on the importance of DEFENCE spending. If world politics is an INTERNATIONAL ANARCHY, then both military elements and the economic base essential to sustain them are required. So, for instance, in the pre-Second World War years the British government very much emphasized the need for the 'fourth arm' of economic strength, stability and durability (in addition to the armed services) in the face of any international conflict. Concepts of what makes for effective security are highly subjective. Necessary defensive capability for one state is often perceived by others as excessive and potentially offensive. At the same time, security is rarely discussed as an absolute but in terms of greater or lesser security. Since the end of the COLD WAR the security agenda has tended to embrace a wider agenda of risk in addition to threat. A particularly salient element now is concern over the global environment and the need for environmental protection. Others are the impact of economic disparities and DESTABILIZATION in the world and the growth of international TERRORISM. Since the GULF WAR (1991) there has also been revived interest in the idea of COLLECTIVE SECURITY under the UNITED NATIONS (UN).

Security community This is a concept associated with the work of the US political scientist Karl Deutsch (b. 1912), prominent in the theory of INTEGRATION. His argument, which derived from his analysis of the NATION STATE, was that convergence, brought about through communications and growing interaction, for instance, through regional trade, would reduce inter-state hostility. In a security community, which Deutsch has envisaged as either 'amalgamated' or 'pluralistic', the 'no-war' principle would establish itself. This idea has been particularly applied to post-war Europe.

Security Council See UNITED NATIONS SECURITY COUNCIL.

Security dilemma A term coined by the US international relations theorist John Herz (b. 1908). It describes the situation in which a STATE may increase its

DEFENCE CAPABILITY simply to defend itself and yet other power(s) interpret this as aggressive intention and themselves rearm, generating less SECURITY and encouraging an ARMS RACE. Sometimes 'security dilemma' is used more generally simply to denote the lack of central authority in the international order.

Security studies
This is a subfield in the study of international relations, which is concerned with the question of SECURITY and its impact on national and global affairs. Traditionally, security studies has tended to concentrate on military issues – for instance, the threats posed by nuclear war and the PROLIFERATION of weapons. Since the end of the COLD WAR there has been greater attention paid to the interrelationship between security and such issues as the environment, population movements and economic instability and disparities. 'Security' has tended to embrace a significantly wider definition.

Selective coexistence
A term sometimes used during the COLD WAR to qualify the notion of PEACEFUL COEXISTENCE, which limited the scope for DÉTENTE. In the COMMUNIST BLOC it was stressed that peaceful coexistence meant avoidance of nuclear war and trade, technological, financial and cultural relations, but that it did not mean ideological concessions or retracting support from WARS OF NATIONAL LIBERATION. In the West, selective coexistence tended to mean flexibility of approach to COMMUNISM. In particular, it meant modification of the view of communism as a monolithic BLOC. The West should treat different communist countries according to their current foreign policies and specific cultural and historical circumstances, and in the light of the best interests of Western countries and the Western Alliance. Two obvious examples of this were policy towards Tito's Yugoslavia and, at least initially, Ceaucescu's Romania. This differentiation was developed further in the DÉTENTE policy of the USA in the early 1970s.

Selective strike
A military attack with a precise and carefully delimited target. Selective strikes are intended to maximize military value and to send a very clear message to an adversary, be it a STATE or terrorist organization. At the same time they are intended to minimize ESCALATION.

Self-determination
The right of a people to choose their own legal and political institutions, and to independence. It was articulated notably in the FOURTEEN POINTS in 1918 and in the UNITED NATIONS DECLARATION ON THE GRANTING OF INDEPENDENCE TO COLONIAL COUNTRIES AND PEOPLES (1960). Self-determination is advanced as a political concept, a theoretical principle and a legal right and has also become a very disputed concept. At the same time, the UNITED NATIONS (UN) guarantees the right to territorial integrity of member STATES. Conflicts have frequently arisen between the right of a state to maintain its integrity and the demand for self-determination of minority national groups within it, as, for example, in the Balkans, or with the Kurds. Given the vague concept of 'the people', the existence of dissatisfied ethnic minorities and the fact that the end of COLONIALISM or, for that matter, the Hapsburg Empire, for example, usually did not mean well-defined territories coterminous with logical demarcation of ethnic groupings, self-determination has frequently proved highly problematic.

SEM
Single European Market. See SINGLE MARKET.

Servitudes In international relations, restrictions on the exercise of SOVEREIGNTY over territory; a binding obligation on a STATE to permit a specific use to be made of all or part of its territory by another state.

SHAPE See SUPREME HEADQUARTERS ALLIED POWERS EUROPE.

Shuttle diplomacy A phrase used originally to describe the MEDIATION by the US Secretary of State Henry Kissinger (b. 1923) in the Arab–Israel conflict at the time of the YOM KIPPUR WAR (1973). It was so-called because of his frequent flights between Israel and Egypt. The phrase has been used of subsequent diplomatic interventions, as, for example, the missions of US Secretary of State Alexander Haig (b. 1924) between London, Washington and Buenos Aires during the FALKLANDS WAR (1982).

Si vis pacem, para bellum Latin phrase meaning: 'If you want peace, prepare for war.'

SIGINT Signals intelligence.

Sinatra Doctrine Named after the famous US singer, it refers to the policy of NON-INTERVENTION by the WARSAW PACT in 1989. The members of the Warsaw Pact in November 1989 agreed that member STATES had the right to determine the direction of their own social and political doctrines. They could, in the words of the popular song, 'do it their way'. This amounted to a negation of the interventionist BREZHNEV DOCTRINE, justifying mutual assistance against threats to the Communist system.

Single European Act (SEA) (1987) This Act revised the ROME TREATY (1957) in a variety of ways. It facilitated the introduction of the internal market, reformed the structure of the EUROPEAN COMMUNITY (EC), extended its competence into new areas and strengthened EUROPEAN POLITICAL COOPERATION (EPC). Institutional changes restricted the VETO power of national governments by reducing the range of decisions requiring unanimous consent as well as increasing the role of the EUROPEAN PARLIAMENT (EP). It obliged the member STATES to work for further harmonization, and, with the reform of the veto, was an essential accompaniment to the introduction of the SINGLE MARKET.

Single European Market (SEM) See SINGLE MARKET.

Single Market The creation of a COMMON MARKET in the EUROPEAN COMMUNITY (EC), which officially came into existence in January 1993. While the ROME TREATY (1957) had enacted the removal of tariffs and quotas on member STATES, there were still numerous NON-TARIFF BARRIERS (NTBS) limiting the potential for intra-Community trade. The elimination of these followed the SINGLE EUROPEAN ACT (SEA) (1987) and the White Paper produced by the Commissioner Lord Cockfield (b. 1916) listing some 300 measures to be taken.

Sino-Soviet Split The conflict of IDEOLOGY and NATIONAL INTEREST between the USSR and the People's Republic of China, which in the late 1960s even led to military skirmishes along the Ussuri River. The growing dispute was visible to the outside world from at least 1956 when the Chinese leaders repudiated the proposal of the notion of PEACEFUL COEXISTENCE and the denunciation of Stalin (1879–1953) by the Soviet leader Khrushchev (1894–1971) in his SECRET SPEECH at the TWENTIETH PARTY CONGRESS. In June 1959 the USSR refused to supply nuclear materials and technology to China (thereby breaking the SINO-SOVIET TREATY of 1950), and in August 1960 all Soviet technical experts were recalled from China. This conflict was formally announced in the Moscow Statement of November 1960, which acknowledged the existence of unresolved problems between the two parties. In 1962 the USSR and Communist China began to denounce each other vigorously in the international arena and each intensified its efforts to canvas the support of the other Communist parties in the world. This split opened up opportunities for the US policy of DÉTENTE in the early 1970s.

Sino-Soviet Treaty of Friendship, Alliance and Mutual Assistance (1950)

This was signed on 14 February 1950 and marked a high point in relations between the two Communist STATES. It was subsequently interpreted to suggest a greater harmony of view than in fact existed between the POWERS. The CHINA LOBBY in the USA used it to argue that world COMMUNISM was monolithic and under the control of the USSR and that, accordingly, Communist China should be denied diplomatic RECOGNITION and a seat in the UNITED NATIONS (UN). Its terms were as follows: (1) It was to last for thirty years. (2) If either China or the USSR were attacked by Japan or 'another state that directly or indirectly would unite with Japan in acts of aggression', the other country would 'immediately render military or other aid with all means at its disposal'. (3) China and the USSR pledged to respect each other's 'sovereign and territorial integrity', practise 'non-intervention in the internal affairs of the other country' and render each other 'every possible economic aid'. Originally, the USSR promised China NUCLEAR WEAPONS in exchange for Soviet determination of Chinese foreign and DEFENCE policy. This promise never materialized and, following the SINO-SOVIET SPLIT the TREATY was renounced.

SIPRI See STOCKHOLM INTERNATIONAL PEACE RESEARCH INSTITUTE.

Six Also called the 'Europe of the Six', this refers to the original founder members of the EUROPEAN COMMUNITY (EC) from the Schuman Plan of 1950 and the ROME TREATY (1957) through to the first enlargement of the Community in 1973 when Britain, Denmark and Eire also joined. The Six were Belgium, France, Italy, West Germany, Luxembourg and the Netherlands.

Six Day War (1967) This was fought between Israel and its three Arab neighbours Egypt, Syria and Jordan. It started on 5 June 1967; at the end of six days Egypt had lost the Sinai Peninsula, Jordan the WEST BANK and East Jerusalem, and Syria the GOLAN HEIGHTS, which Israel regarded as particularly important for its SECURITY. It was the third war between Israel and its neighbours. It led to an increased number of Palestinian REFUGEES, further inflaming Arab NATIONALISM, and uniting Arabs against Israel. It also brought the closing of the Suez Canal, a temporary oil embargo against the USA, the breaking-off of diplomatic relations between the USA and Egypt and Syria, and some advance of Soviet influence in the Middle East.

SLBM See SUBMARINE-LAUNCHED BALLISTIC MISSILE.

Smart bombs Smart bombs, or any other 'smart' weapons, are those that have some capacity to guide themselves on to their targets. These may be through laser direction or infra-red heat-seeking detectors, used, for instance, as anti-tank weapons.

Smithsonian Agreement The currency agreement between Western countries in December 1971 at the Smithsonian Institute, Washington DC, which attempted to provide some of the stability of fixed EXCHANGE RATES that had been provided by the agreement reached at the BRETTON WOODS CONFERENCE (1944). Currency fluctuation was to be fixed at 2.25 per cent on either side of a new par value against the US dollar. It failed to cope with chronic international financial instability, not least that generated by the oil price rises following the YOM KIPPUR WAR (1973), and was abandoned in 1974.

Social Fascism This term was propagated by the Soviet leader Joseph Stalin (1879–1953) in the early 1930s in his denunciation of social-democratic political parties in Europe and in his STRATEGY of persuading Communist parties not to form coalitions, or collaborate with them. This term appeared in the propaganda issued by the COMINTERN, but originated in the KPD (the German Communist Party). By 1936, with the growth of the power of Nazi Germany and the outbreak of the SPANISH CIVIL WAR (1936–9), Stalin reversed this policy and pressed for the formation of the POPULAR FRONT against FASCISM.

Social imperialism This propagandist term was used by the People's Republic of China after 1960 in the SINO-SOVIET SPLIT. China accused the USSR of only paying lip service to COMMUNISM, of in fact running a system of state monopoly CAPITALISM, of being guilty of 'imperialism in deed'. It claimed that the USSR was in the hands of a 'Soviet revisionist clique' in the process of making it an imperialist power. This critique, aimed at influencing opinion in the THIRD WORLD, cited bases in Asia and Africa, naval expansionism, large weapons sales and collusion with the USA in dividing the world into SPHERES OF INFLUENCE.

Socialist Bloc See COMMUNIST BLOC.

Socialist internationalism Before 1945 the more commonly used phrase for this was PROLETARIAN INTERNATIONALISM. It was used in particular to emphasize the international cooperation between Communist STATES and the Communist parties that controlled them in the period of the COLD WAR, in the context, for instance, of the WARSAW PACT or the COUNCIL FOR MUTUAL ECONOMIC ASSISTANCE (CMEA/COMECON). This term has also been used to describe international cooperation between the non-Communist social-democratic parties of the world.

SOFA See STATUS OF FORCES AGREEMENT.

Soft power A term coined by the US international relations scholar Joseph S. Nye (b. 1937) to describe the intangible elements, non-military, non-economic, of STATE POWER, such as cultural influence and ideological appeal.

Solidarity (Polish: *Solidarnosc*) This free trade union movement, the only one in the COMMUNIST BLOC that was independent of the Communist Party, was formally established on 22 September 1980. It developed in particular out of the factory strike coordination committee led by Lech Walesa (b. 1943) in Gdansk. This had protested against shortages, rising prices, the authoritarianism and privileges of the Party elite, oppressive living and working conditions and disregard for HUMAN RIGHTS. Its claim for liberalization within COMMUNISM aroused concern elsewhere in EASTERN EUROPE and especially in the USSR, not least because of the demand for the right to strike for democracy and the abolition of censorship and the advocacy of similar groups elsewhere in EASTERN EUROPE. Solidarity was suppressed by MARTIAL LAW under General Jaruzelski (b. 1923) on 12 December 1981 and made illegal in October 1982. Legality was restored to the movement in April 1989 and subsequently the union formed a Civic Committee as a political party.

South The term 'South', as an alternative to THIRD WORLD, came into general use during the 1970s when the concept of North–South dialogue attracted attention. In 1987 a South Commission was established under the chairmanship of the Tanzanian President Julius Nyrere (b. 1927). Used interchangeably with Third World, both terms cover the developing countries of Africa, Asia, Latin America, the Caribbean and OCEANIA, many of which emerged as newly independent STATES after the Second World War, having belonged previously to one or other of the European empires.

South East Asia Treaty Organization (SEATO) An ALLIANCE between the USA, Britain, France, Australia, New Zealand, Pakistan, the Philippines and Thailand that was part of the US STRATEGY of CONTAINMENT, to prevent the further spread of COMMUNISM. It was created in September 1954 after the humiliation of France in Indochina. Its members pledged mutual defence as well as extending defence to other designated countries, South Vietnam, Cambodia and Laos against AGGRESSION and subversion. The US hope that it would be as effective as the NORTH ATLANTIC TREATY ORGANIZATION (NATO) was to be disappointed. For instance, only three member STATES sent troops to assist the USA in the VIETNAM WAR (1960–75), and in 1977 SEATO was officially dissolved.

Southern Cone That part of South America that includes Argentina, Chile, Brazil, Bolivia, Paraguay and Uruguay. It is a region characterized both by rivalries, as for instance, between Argentina and Chile, and moves towards economic INTEGRATION, for example, MERCOSUR.

Southern flank A NORTH ATLANTIC TREATY ORGANIZATION (NATO) term for the Mediterranean area, including Greece, Italy and Turkey. The cohesion of the alliance in this area has been damaged by Graeco-Turkish hostility and rivalry over Cyprus and the Aegean and by considerable public hostility towards NATO and the USA, in particular in Greece.

Sovereignty Domestically, the idea of independent, final and supreme authority, the attribute of a STATE that refers to its right to exercise complete jurisdiction over its own territory. According to the German theorist Max Weber (1864–1930), the sovereign should enjoy the monopoly over the legitimate use of FORCE. In relation to the outside world (the external aspect of sovereignty), the state should be the arbiter of its own fate. In international relations, the state as a sovereign unit has a right of autonomy from other states. Again, while they may differ in size and power, states as sovereign entities are legally equal. Therefore the concept is integral to INTERNATIONAL LAW, DIPLOMACY and the RECOGNITION of states. This idea becomes a central concern from the sixteenth century onwards, being given a particularly clear exposition by the English thinker Thomas Hobbes (1588–1679), as the modern state system asserts itself against the background of competing jurisdictions of the Middle Ages, particularly the ecclesiastical. With GLOBALIZATION and regional INTEGRATION, with reference to such ideas as 'pooled sovereignty', and a common European currency, the notion is currently much debated.

Sovietization The policy and tactics of making the Communist parties outside the USSR accept the Soviet patterns of party and STATE organization and practices as opposed to other versions of COMMUNISM. Originally known as Bolshevization, it became prominent with the condemnation of TROTSKYISM by Stalin (1879–1953) in the inter-war years. It appeared to most effect in EASTERN EUROPE after 1945, when leaders loyal to Moscow were installed in power. All opposition parties were eliminated and purges and show trials removed Communists accused of disloyalty to Stalin's line. Approximately a quarter of party members were purged. This process was both encouraged by and contributed to the rift between the USSR and Yugoslavia in 1948–9.

Spaceship earth This phrase, coined in the 1960s, reflects the growing ecological awareness of human dependency on the environment, of the threat of resource depletion and the need to avoid the reckless exploitation of nature in the interests of consumption.

Spanish Civil War (1936–9) The armed struggle that came about as a consequence of the revolt of commanders in Spanish Morocco led by Francisco Franco (1892–1975) against the anti-clerical Popular Front Government, claiming that the latter was provoking the 'disintegration of the fatherland' and Communist revolution. Though its origins were very much internal, the WAR became an ideological battleground for Europe in the years leading to the Second World War. Germany and Italy intervened on the Nationalist side, while the USSR supported the Spanish Republic. Britain and France followed a policy of NON-INTERVENTION under the NON-INTERVENTION COMMITTEE, to prevent the conflict widening, but this, in the circumstances, aided the Nationalists. About 60,000 volunteers went to support the Republic in the International Brigades, seeing this as a crusade against FASCISM. Franco declared victory on 1 April 1939. It has been described as the first modern CIVIL WAR, with the use of air power. (The Luftwaffe bombardment of Guernica was one of the most notorious episodes.) Over half a million were killed during the conflict and large numbers were executed in reprisals afterwards.

Special drawing rights See DRAWING RIGHTS.

Special Relations Agreements These were signed by the EUROPEAN COMMUNITY (EC) and West European countries in the early 1970s, which at that stage did not wish to join the EC. With the creation of the SINGLE MARKET all the STATES that had signed the agreements had either applied or indicated their willingness to do so.

Special relationship A term that has been used with particular reference in international relations to Anglo-US relations since the Second World War, though it has been used more widely, for instance, to describe US relations with Israel, or implied in the description by US President George Bush Sr (b. 1924) of 'partnership in leadership' between the USA and Germany. It has usually been more stressed and referred to by Britain than the USA since Sir Winston Churchill (1874–1965) gave it popular currency. Prime Minister Mrs Thatcher (b. 1925) was to describe it as the 'extraordinary relationship'. The phrase refers to shared language, culture, political outlook and, particularly, strategic and military ALLIANCE and close sharing of INTELLIGENCE (not least D-DAY (1944), adoption of the POLARIS and TRIDENT nuclear system and liaison with GOVERNMENT COMMUNICATIONS HEADQUARTERS (GCHQ)), a pattern established from the time of the US entry into the Second World War and sustained in the GULF WAR of 1991 and in opposition to TERRORISM. It has not been without its troubles, for instance, the SUEZ CRISIS of 1956, and it has become increasingly difficult to disentangle it from European–American relations in general since Britain's entry into the EUROPEAN COMMUNITY (EC) in 1973. Given Britain's relative economic decline and the emergence of the USA as a SUPERPOWER, it has never, since 1945, been remotely an equal relationship in terms of POWER.

Sphere of influence An area dominated by a foreign power without being formally brought under its sovereign jurisdiction. Peoples in the area are often required to grant the dominant power special military, political and commercial rights and are, in various ways, restricted. During the COLD WAR EASTERN EUROPE was in the Soviet sphere of influence. The ROOSEVELT COROLLARY (1904) effectively claimed Latin America as a US sphere of influence. Sometimes the division into spheres of influence can be informally done, as with the PERCENTAGES DEAL (1944), or it can be formal, as when, in the Anglo-Russian Convention of 1907, Britain and Russia partitioned Persia. Dominant powers will usually regard their spheres of influence as areas of vital interest and allow themselves the right of INTERVENTION there without fear of external interference.

Spillover A term used in discussions of INTEGRATION, in particular with reference to European integration in the early years, before the ROME TREATY (1957), which established the EUROPEAN ECONOMIC COMMUNITY (EEC). The argument was that SECTORAL INTEGRATION, such as with coal and steel in the EUROPEAN COAL AND STEEL COMMUNITY (ECSC), would lead to more and more sectors coming together. Secondly, once institutions had been established to oversee this process, other organizations would more and more look to them rather than national governments to achieve their objectives. Spillover therefore had both an economic and a political dimension.

Sputnik I The first artificial satellite to orbit the earth, launched by the USSR on 4 October 1957. It created particular alarm in the USA, both because the USA was not to put its own satellite into space until the end of January in the following year and because the USSR had already managed to launch an INTER-CONTINENTAL BALLISTIC MISSILE (ICBM). Americans formed the impression that they were lagging in the ARMS RACE, leading to later misapprehensions over a MISSILE GAP, intensifying international tension and delaying negotiations for a nuclear test ban treaty.

Stab-in-the-back myth The false legend disseminated at the end of the First World War and afterwards that Germany had not faced military collapse, but had been brought down by domestic subversion. According to the legend, Germany's capitulation was brought about by defeatism and left-wing pacifists and revolutionaries within Germany. During the period of the Weimar Republic (1919–33), it was used as an argument of the parties of the Right, most effectively by the Nazi Party, against the exponent of the accommodation of Germany with the post-war settlement, the so-called FULFILMENT POLICY.

Stalin Line This was a series of deep defensive fortifications (which could also be used for offensive purposes) set up along the Soviet border with Poland in the 1930s to protect the western borderlands of the USSR, organized in thirteen regions. In purpose it was similar to the French MAGINOT LINE, though greatly more extensive, stretching from the Baltic to the Black Sea. With widely spaced fortresses it was easily vulnerable to the Nazi German onslaught of Operation BARBAROSSA in June 1941. But by then it had largely been dismantled, since in September 1939 the USSR occupied eastern Poland.

Stalin Notes (1952) In these the Soviet leader, faced with the prospect of West German rearmament, revived the prospect of discussions to resolve the problem of a divided Germany. He proposed reunification, the withdrawal of all foreign troops, free elections and a neutral STATE. It is usually thought that this was a tactical move to wrong foot the West, who were committed to German rearmament, which came about within the NORTH ATLANTIC TREATY ORGANIZATION (NATO) three years later, and who were afraid that a neutral Germany could well gravitate towards the Soviet sphere.

Stalingrad (1942–3) The battle in Russia, known also as the Battle of the Volga, between Russian troops and, on the other side German, Romanian and Hungarian forces. After the failure of BARBAROSSA to obtain a speedy victory over the USSR in the Second World War, Nazi Germany attempted to obtain control of the economic resources of southern Russia. On 5 September General Von Paulus (1890–1957) commanding the German Sixth Army with the Fourth Panzer Army advanced on Stalingrad and the Lower Volga. The Russians then mounted a defensive operation until 18 November when General Zhukov (1896–1977) launched a counter-offensive with six armies, cutting off the German lines of communication, which led to German surrender at the end of January 1943. This was the turning point of the WAR on the EASTERN FRONT, as a result of which the Red Army gained the initiative and pressed its advantage until the final collapse of Germany in May 1945.

Star Wars See STRATEGIC DEFENSE INITIATIVE.

START I AND II See STRATEGIC ARMS REDUCTION TALKS.

State Also commonly referred to as nation state, a politically organized community under a sovereign government. The concept of the state is central to the development of modern political thought and analysis of the state and its role is a major concern of international relations, and absolutely central to realist interpretations of it. As an international ACTOR with its RECOGNITION under INTERNATIONAL LAW the SOVEREIGNTY of the state implies its autonomy and its ability to ensure both its frontiers and that its nationals are respected by other states. A state becomes a state under

INTERNATIONAL LAW only when it is recognized as such by other states, and by the UNITED NATIONS (UN). According to the classic definition of the Montevideo Convention on Rights and Duties of States (1933) a state should possess (1) a permanent population; (2) a defined territory; (3) government capable of maintaining effective control over its territory and (4) of conducting international relations with other states. There are in 2002 about 200 states in the international system. The role of the state internationally is particularly discussed in relation to the challenges posed by GLOBALIZATION, economic interdependence and the role of NON-STATE ACTORS such as multinational corporations; and to the development of SUPRANATIONALISM as, for instance, with the EUROPEAN UNION (EU). These, at the very least, compel redefinitions of concepts that first evolved clearly in the early modern period, the state and, associated with that, sovereignty.

State-centrism An approach to the analysis of international relations that gives precedence to the STATE as the dominant element or ACTOR. This is associated with REALISM, which envisages an international order in which inter-state rivalry, competition and conflict are of the essence, and in which there is no effective global authority over and above the states. This approach traditionally has given particular attention to issues of DEFENCE, SECURITY and military competition.

State terrorism The sponsorship by a STATE of terrorist groups to carry out attacks against enemies outside its boundaries, or, alternatively, the use of its own agencies to this end. It violates both HUMAN RIGHTS and the SOVEREIGNTY of other nations. With the destruction of the New York World Trade Centre on 11 September 2001, the issue of international TERRORISM and the extent to which it may be sponsored by states, something that has grown dramatically in recent decades, became a dominant one in international relations. Where a government directs terror and oppression against its own inhabitants, such as in Stalinist Russia, or with the DEATH SQUADS in some states in Latin America, this has normally been regarded as a human rights problem. However, this has also attracted international censure and, in some cases, as with APARTHEID in South Africa, led to international SANCTIONS.

Status of Forces Agreement (SOFA) This defines and regulates the arrangement by which military forces from a foreign power are installed on a permanent, or long-term basis in peacetime on the territory of a HOST STATE – for example, US Air Force personnel in Britain, from the 1940s onwards. Such agreements usually provide for exclusive jurisdiction by the contracting STATE over its own military where military law has been violated, for instance, by insubordination or desertion, and normally for the exclusive jurisdiction of the host state for violations of its own laws. In those cases where offences violate the laws of both states, there may be concurrent jurisdiction.

Status quo In international relations any POWER that pursues a status quo policy wishes to maintain the existing territorial, ideological or power distribution. It will be likely to seek stability and resist change and maintain a basically defensive posture, faced with new challenges. Britain in the inter-war years offers a good example. Its increasing difficulties came from a combination of relative economic decline, imperial overextension, where it was becoming more and more difficult to defend its possessions, and the challenges of REVISIONIST powers, principally Germany, Italy, Japan and the USSR to the international order established at the end of the First World War.

Statute of Westminster (1931) This codified the transformation of the self-governing parts of the British Empire into the COMMONWEALTH OF NATIONS. Canada, Australia, New Zealand, South Africa and the Irish Free State were freed from most aspects of surviving imperial subordination. It embodied the formula put forward in the BALFOUR DEFINITION (1926). Since 1931 many aspects of the Statute have been modified to adapt to the constitutional evolution of the various countries of the Commonwealth.

Sterling Area Those countries, mostly members of the Commonwealth defined in the British Exchange Control Act of 1947, that pegged their currencies to, and held their foreign exchange balances in, sterling. It originated from earlier British dominance in the world economy, but declined from the 1950s as the British share of world trade decreased and countries diversified their reserves into other currencies.

Stimson Doctrine (1932) A statement of the doctrine of NON-RECOGNITION expressed by the US SECRETARY OF STATE Henry L. Stimson (1867–1950) in January 1932 by means of a diplomatic note to China and Japan. It was provoked by the Japanese invasion and conquest of Manchuria from 1931 and stated that the USA could not recognize any TREATY or *de facto* government that impaired treaty rights with China or any situation brought about in violation of the KELLOGG–BRIAND PACT (1928). Subsequently most members of the LEAGUE OF NATIONS, which endorsed it, refused to recognize the Japanese PUPPET STATE of Manchukuo. It did nothing to restrain subsequent international AGGRESSION in the 1930s.

Stockholm Accord (1986) Signed on 21 September 1986, this was a result of the Conference on Security and Confidence-Building Measures and Disarmament in Europe. It stated that the NORTH ATLANTIC TREATY ORGANIZATION (NATO) and the WARSAW PACT would give each other advance notification of military exercises and troop movements. In this way there would be less risk of any conflict breaking out in Europe between the alliances through misapprehension, and therefore of ACCIDENTAL WAR.

Stockholm Convention (1959) Signed in November 1959, this took effect in May 1960, establishing the EUROPEAN FREE TRADE ASSOCIATION (EFTA), the organization set up in response to the EUROPEAN ECONOMIC COMMUNITY (EEC). The original signatories were Austria, Britain, Denmark, Norway, Portugal, Sweden and Switzerland. The Seven, as they were called, were subsequently joined by Finland, Iceland and Lichtenstein.

Stockholm International Peace Research Institute (SIPRI) The world's leading independent centre for peace research, it is funded primarily by the Swedish government. It publishes data on stockpiles of nuclear and conventional armaments and an annual survey of agreements on ARMS CONTROL and their implementation. It also monitors arms sales on a worldwide basis.

Stockpiling The accumulation of reserve supplies of raw materials and finished products for use in the event of WAR when supplies might be cut off. This may enable a country to survive a BLOCKADE, enemy control of the seas, or other disruption of supplies. During the inter-war years Germany stockpiled large quantities of material to avoid a repetition of the First World War experience when the Allied blockade helped to bring about German defeat. During the COLD WAR the USA amassed the world's largest stockpile of over seventy-five STRATEGIC MATERIALS.

Stop at the water's edge A phrase used particularly in the USA to indicate that domestic party political rivalry should be suspended when national interests are under external threat, and that there should be BIPARTISANSHIP.

Strategic The primary meaning of this term is as the adjective from STRATEGY. However, it is also used in modern DEFENCE and military phraseology to refer, in a more specific sense, to long-range and powerful weapons, in particular nuclear ones. It is in this sense, for example, that it is used when one refers to the STRATEGIC ARMS LIMITATION TALKS (SALT). A strategic missile is one with inter-continental range and very high destructive capability, such as that provided by TRIDENT.

Strategic Air Command (SAC) The US Air Force branch with the responsibility for long-range offensive operations, established in 1946. During the COLD WAR it was charged with the responsibility of a nuclear attack against the USSR in the event of a general war. SAC controlled both the bomber force as well as the INTER-CONTINENTAL BALLISTIC MISSILES (ICBMS) and became the largest of the commands, not least because of the belief within the Air Force that air power was likely to be the most decisive weapon in any future war. With the reorganization of the Air Force in 1992 it disappeared as a separate command.

Strategic Arms Limitation Talks and Agreements (SALT I and II)
These were negotiations between the USSR and the USA, originating in the policy of DÉTENTE, which resulted in agreements in 1972 and 1979 to limit STRATEGIC WEAPONS. SALT I resulted in the ANTI-BALLISTIC MISSILE (ABM) TREATY (1972) restricting the deployment of anti-ballistic missile defences. This was with a view to stabilizing DETERRENCE. In the same year the Offensive Arms Agreement limited the number of INTER-CONTINENTAL BALLISTIC MISSILES (ICBMS) and SUBMARINE-LAUNCHED BALLISTIC MISSILES (SLBMS). The SALT II agreement, which was never ratified, but generally observed, became a casualty of the 'New Cold War'. This set limits to the numbers of each missile and (with the MULTIPLE INDEPENDENTLY TARGETED RE-ENTRY VEHICLES (MIRVS)) the number of warheads each delivery vehicle could carry. This process was continued further by the STRATEGIC ARMS REDUCTION TREATY (1991), after the end of the COLD WAR.

Strategic Arms Reduction Talks (START) These bilateral negotiations between the USA and the USSR were begun in 1982, abandoned in 1983 and then revived in 1985 when Mikhail Gorbachev (b. 1931) had come to POWER as Soviet leader. The word 'reduction' was chosen to indicate significant advance on the earlier STRATEGIC ARMS LIMITATION (SALT) negotiations, which referred simply to 'limitation' of arms. The first START TREATY was signed in July 1991 and reduced each country's long-range missile launchers to 1,600, and warheads to 6,000. In December 1992 the US and Russian leaders signed a second agreement halving the number of warheads on each side.

Strategic bombing offensive See AREA BOMBING.

Strategic coupling A military and/or political link between two regions or countries that ensures that one comes to the assistance of the other. A key issue in international relations after the Second World War has been the link between the USA and Canada and Europe in the NORTH ATLANTIC TREATY ORGANIZATION (NATO) and the extent to which Europe could expect support in a major CRISIS. There was particularly intense debate over this between the 1960s and 1989. The breaking of such links is called DECOUPLING.

Strategic Defense Initiative (SDI) This programme, which was popularly known as 'Star Wars', was announced by US President Ronald Regan (b. 1911) in March 1983. Its purpose was to create a space-based DEFENCE against a BALLISTIC MISSILE attack using laser interception or anti-missile missiles. The President said that he hoped it would make NUCLEAR WEAPONS 'impotent and obsolete' and replace reliance on MUTUAL ASSURED DESTRUCTION (MAD) with 'assured survival'. It aroused considerable controversy. Critics argued that it breached the ANTI-BALLISTIC MISSILE (ABM) TREATY of 1972, that it would encourage an isolationist 'Fortress America' attitude, that it would undermine any prospect of credible ARMS CONTROL with the USSR; that it was technologically unfeasible and would not be able to guarantee complete protection. Congress also recoiled from its cost implications. Under subsequent administrations and with the end of the COLD WAR the research programme for SDI was given less and less priority. In 1991 President George Bush Sr (b. 1924) announced a reorientation of the SDI programme away from developing strategic defences to a system: Global Protection against Limited Strikes. The notion of missile defence has, however, been given a higher place on the agenda of his son's administration.

Strategic materials Raw materials and semi-finished and finished products essential for fighting a modern WAR, which are a significant component in the determination of national POWER, or the power of a coalition. The number of materials considered strategic has increased dramatically with the modernization of warfare in the twentieth century. In order to secure its position a country may resort to STOCKPILING, development of synthetic substances, pre-emptive buying or ANNEXATION of territories with such materials.

Strategic studies The scholarly enquiry into military affairs, broadly defined.

Strategic weapons INTER-CONTINENTAL BALLISTIC MISSILES (whether land-based ICBMs or submarine-launched missiles) armed with nuclear warheads.

Strategy From the Greek term 'generalship'. The use of political, economic, military force and propaganda, as necessary during PEACE or WAR, to support policies, secure victory and diminish the chances of defeat. Defining the means policy-makers use to achieve desired ends, it is to be distinguished from TACTICS. It is most often used in military affairs, in which the makers of strategy will attempt to secure the objectives of national, or alliance policy by the application of force, or threat of force. In military policy there are three main categories – offensive, defence or deterrent strategy. The term 'grand strategy' describes overall strategy, as, for instance in the Second World War.

Structural determinist In the study of international relations, one who believes that the structure of the international system largely determines the behaviour of individual STATES and consequently circumscribes the choices before their governments. This applies also to other ACTORS in international relations. The form that discussion takes on this issue is of apportioning greater or lesser influence to the structure.

Sublime Porte The term commonly used in Europe for the Ottoman or Turkish government until the Ottoman Empire was dissolved at the end of the First World War.

Submarine-launched ballistic missile (SLBM) A missile carried in nuclear-powered submarines capable of delivering nuclear warheads. Examples include POLARIS and TRIDENT. The following states possess SLBMs: Britain, the People's Republic of China, France, the Russian Federation and the USA.

Subsidiarity A principle that seeks to establish the appropriate location of authority between various levels of government. It has been much discussed in recent years in the EUROPEAN UNION (EU) following the TREATY ON EUROPEAN UNION (TEU) (1992), though it originated in Roman Catholicism to express, within a highly centralized institution, the need to enhance the role of the localized churches and orders. The principle basically recommends that authority for decision making should be at the level of those most affected by them and it has been particularly pressed by Germany, as a leading proponent of FEDERALISM in the EU, anxious to safeguard the constitutional position of its individual STATES (*Länder*). Within the EU it has not become an absolutely clear guide, because views tend to differ as to whether an issue over, for instance, the environment is a local one or a much wider one. Some states, for instance, Britain, have tended to interpret it as enhancing national, as against EU-wide decision making.

Subsystem A subordinate system within the global in international relations. It usually means a particular area of the world and the phrase used is frequently 'regional subsystem', for instance, with regard to the Middle East or Far East. In the modern WORLD ORDER issues within a subsystem frequently become something of far wider significance and impact. For instance, the KOREAN WAR (1950–3) or the YOM KIPPUR WAR (1973), both of which were conflicts of global concern, involved the UNITED NATIONS (UN) and had a significant effect on the world economy.

Succession States The states established in the aftermath of the defeat of the CENTRAL POWERS in the First World War. These were on territory belonging, wholly or in part, to the Austro-Hungarian Hapsburg monarchy, otherwise known as the Dual Monarchy after the constitutional compromise of 1867, the *Ausgleich*. These states were Austria, Czechoslovakia, Hungary, Poland, Romania and Yugoslavia. Although Italy acquired former Hapsburg lands in the Alto Adige (a previous demand of Italian nationalist IRREDENTISM), Italy is not generally classified as a succession state.

Sudetenland This had been part of Austria-Hungary, which was assigned to the new SUCCESSION STATE of Czechoslovakia after the First World War. It contained more than three million ethnic Germans, who became the focus of strong Nazi agitation for their inclusion within the Third Reich. This was orchestrated within

Czechoslovakia by the Sudeten German Party led by Konrad Henlein (1898–1945), who was instructed by Hitler (1889–1945) to press for more than the Czechs could reasonably concede. Under threat of an international war, the Sudetenland was incorporated into Nazi Germany by the MUNICH AGREEMENT of September 1938. In 1945 the area reverted to Czech control and the ethnic German inhabitants were expelled.

Suez Crisis (1956) This followed the nationalization of the Suez Canal on 26 July 1956 by the Egyptian leader Colonel Nasser (1918–70) as a consequence of the withdrawal of the promise of US and British funding for the Aswan High Dam project. Protracted negotiations got nowhere and Britain, France and Israel agreed secretly for Israel to attack Egypt, after which Britain and France would occupy the Canal zone on the pretext of separating the combatants, in order to keep the Canal open. Israel duly attacked on 29 October. The subsequent Anglo-French invasion aroused widespread protest across the world, including, decisively, the US government. The USA was on the eve of a presidential election. Faced with a massive run on sterling and US pressure, as well as Soviet threats, Britain, followed by France, halted the invasion on 6 November. They accepted unconditional withdrawal and the introduction of a UNITED NATIONS (UN) PEACEKEEPING force. The CRISIS and outcome of the conflict demonstrated, both internationally and to their domestic populations, the relative decline of Britain and France. It also illustrated that, in spite of the COLD WAR and of the SPECIAL RELATIONSHIP, the USA would not be unquestioningly supportive.

Summit diplomacy This involves personal meetings of heads of state or government, as contrasted with DIPLOMACY at the ambassadorial or ministerial level. It developed during the age of absolute monarchy, was given considerable public profile by the PARIS PEACE CONFERENCE (1919–20) after the First World War and has become a key part of contemporary international relations, whether in discussions of military conflicts, DISARMAMENT or the world economy. Some summits have been spectacularly unproductive or abortive – for instance, the PARIS SUMMIT of 1960. This form of diplomacy is usually most successful when decisions and agreements have been worked out at lower levels in advance of the meeting.

SUNFED Special fund of the UNITED NATIONS (UN) for economic development.

Superpower During the post-Second World War period this term, first widely publicized in William Fox's *The Super-Powers* published in 1944, has been used to describe the USA and USSR. They have been distinguished by the absolute and relative size of their military predominance, particularly their nuclear arsenals, and their capacity for global influence. At the same time, this period has also seen the development of what have been described as 'civilian superpowers' – major economic powers without the military CAPABILITY of the superpowers, notably the EUROPEAN UNION (EU) and Japan. Because of Russia's economic weakness, some have argued since the 1990s that there is now essentially one superpower in the full sense of the term, the USA.

Supranationalism Institutions and laws are supranational when not confined in their powers or application to any one STATE. It exists where governmental functions are exercised at a level over and above the states over which they are exercised. As a term, supranationalism gained currency in the 1950s, particularly with the development of

West European INTEGRATION. The EUROPEAN COMMISSION of the EUROPEAN UNION (EU), for instance, is an example of a supranational institution that initiates policies, functions as an executive body and makes decisions within prescribed areas that are binding upon member states, organizations and individuals. The question of supranationalism has attracted particular attention and occasioned widespread debate in relation to the issue of the loss, or diminution, of national SOVEREIGNTY, as, for example, over ECONOMIC AND MONETARY UNION (EMU) or the issue as to whether majority voting should be introduced for decision making in European foreign policy.

Supreme Headquarters Allied Powers Europe (SHAPE) The headquarters of the NORTH ATLANTIC TREATY ORGANIZATION'S (NATO) European Military Command. Until France withdrew from the integrated military structure of NATO under President de Gaulle (1890–1970) in 1966, SHAPE was based at Versailles near Paris. Since then it has been located near Mons in Belgium.

Sustainable development The concept of reconciling economic development with environmental conservation in a world where very many live in great poverty while there is the excessive consumption by an affluent minority. This idea was promoted by the UNITED NATIONS CONFERENCE ON ENVIRONMENT AND DEVELOPMENT (UNCED) (1992) (the Earth Summit) held in Rio de Janeiro. This conference discussed the 'carrying capacity' of the earth and the threats to the environment, global warming through pollution and the exhaustion of the earth's resources. It produced an overall plan called AGENDA 21 in which the THIRD WORLD agreed to limit its industrialization and the advanced nations agreed to give it technological assistance. Finally, it set up the Sustainable Development Commission to monitor progress, though this has lacked an enforcement mechanism.

Suzerainty The quasi-sovereign status of certain territories where the local sovereign is a subject of another sovereign and yet exercises most of the powers of government over that territory.

Swaddling theory of soviet international behaviour Among various Western attempts to analyse the motivation of the USSR in the COLD WAR, this was one of the most bizarre, but illustrative of the justifications of CONTAINMENT, and seemingly giving it anthropological endorsement. It derived from a co-authored book published by Geoffrey Gorer (1905–85), an English anthropologist, *The People of Great Russia: A Psychological Study* (1949). It argued that the infant experience of being swaddled explained the XENOPHOBIA of the Russians, their insecurity and fear of CAPITALIST ENCIRCLEMENT. It concluded that 'if Russia is faced with permanent strength, firmness and consistency there would appear to be no reason why a tolerable and durable "modus vivendi" should not be maintained indefinitely.'

T

Tactical nuclear weapons NUCLEAR WEAPONS for use in the context of a battle. They have low YIELD and short range, such as nuclear shells, almost all of them being under DUAL-KEY SYSTEMS.

Tactics As a military term, the employment of units in combat; or the ordered arrangement and manœuvring of units in relation to each other and/or to the enemy in order to use their full potentialities. Tactics are specified and defined in relation to an overall plan or STRATEGY.

Tehran Conference (1943) Held between 28 November and 1 December, this marked the first meeting of the BIG THREE. The USSR, previously critical of Britain and the USA for their failure to open a SECOND FRONT against Germany, were promised an Anglo-American landing in France in 1944. Stalin (1879–1953) committed the USSR to joining the war against Japan once the war in Europe was over and pressed the Western Allies over a Soviet SPHERE OF INFLUENCE in EASTERN EUROPE. The conference also discussed post-war control of Germany and the setting-up of the UNITED NATIONS (UN).

Ten Year Rule A ruling first adopted by the British government after the First World War, in 1919. It stipulated that British DEFENCE policy should plan on the assumption that there would not be a major WAR during the following ten years. On this basis substantial defence cuts were imposed and Britain accepted the restrictions following the WASHINGTON CONFERENCE ON THE LIMITATION OF ARMAMENTS (1921–2). It was restated in 1926 and 1927 and thereafter on a yearly basis until it was abandoned in 1932, a casualty of growing international conflict and tension. This included the Japanese invasion of Manchuria in 1931 and Nazi advances in Germany.

Terminal See POTSDAM CONFERENCE (1945).

Territorial particularism National/ethnic identity focused on a distinct territory that one regards exclusively as one's own.

Territorial waters Otherwise known as 'territorial sea', that part of the sea over which the authority of a STATE is considered to extend. It forms a belt between the coast and the HIGH SEAS and is sometimes called the 'maritime belt' or 'marginal sea'. The generally accepted view is that states have rights amounting to SOVEREIGNTY over the territorial sea, though some international lawyers treat them as qualified sovereignty rights only.

Terrorism Terrorism is coercive intimidation, the use of murder, injury and destruction, or the threat of these things, to produce a climate of terror. It is a form of protracted warfare carried out now particularly, though not exclusively, for political aims, often with the sponsorship of foreign governments or groups. It is also a form of ARMED PROPAGANDA, which compels public attention by its random violence. Though it has a long pedigree as a means of challenging governments within countries – for instance, with the terrorist outrages in nineteenth-century Russia – in the 1970s the term 'terrorism' came increasingly to be used to describe acts of political violence committed by groups outside the territory in which they were primarily active. This has become one of the major challenges facing the international community, as was dramatically illustrated in the terrorist destruction of the World Trade Centre in New York on 11 September 2001. Terrorism commonly opposes violence and oppression with violence in the name of freedom. This means that the leaders of terroristic groups in one generation have not infrequently become national leaders in the next. The commonest form of terrorism is that within communities, such as in Northern Ireland, or Lebanon or with the ETA Basque movement in Spain. It compels governments to mobilize considerable resources. It also centrally poses the problem as to whether terrorists should be treated by means of repression or engaged in political discussions, or a mixture of both. 'STATE TERRORISM' is used as a term to describe the intimidation of populations by government repression, the waging of organized terror on the part of the STATE, as with the 'reign of terror' during the French Revolution in the early 1790s, or the Stalinist terror in the USSR.

Test Ban Treaty (1963) See PARTIAL TEST BAN TREATY.

TEU See TREATY ON EUROPEAN UNION (1992).

Thalweg The channel taken by vessels navigating a river or other stretch of water. As a term of INTERNATIONAL LAW, the Thalweg rule is used to mark territorial jurisdiction over rivers, bays and estuaries that are boundaries. The boundary is understood to be the middle of the main navigable channel (or its principal channel, if the river has more than one). The emphasis is on navigable. The idea is that adjoining STATES should have equal use of the waterway for commerce and travel. The rule permits adjustment, since the main channel may shift through accretion. If the river or other stretch of water were simply divided down the middle, this might deny one of the parties the right of navigation.

Thaw Historically, a term that refers to the relaxation in East–West relations after the death of the Soviet leader Stalin (1879–1953) and the ending of the KOREAN WAR (1950–3) in 1953. It was also used to describe the relative liberalization that occurred in EASTERN EUROPE at this time, also known as de-stalinization, associated with his successor Nikita Khrushchev (1894–1971). The term is now sometimes used more generally describing an easing of hostilities in, or opening-up of, diplomatic relations.

Theatre nuclear weapons Any NUCLEAR WEAPON with a range of less than 3,500 nautical miles. These are subdivided into TACTICAL NUCLEAR WEAPONS with a range of less than 120 nautical miles and designed for battlefield use and intermediate-range weapons.

Theatre of operations The geographical area within which a war is fought.

Thermonuclear bomb See HYDROGEN BOMB.

Third party Person or body that is recognized as being independent of the parties involved as concerns the issue in question.

Third state A STATE that is not party to a TREATY.

Third World This term was first used in the 1950s when the newly independent nations of Asia, led by India's Pandit Nehru (1889–1964), wanted to stress their NEUTRALITY in the COLD WAR between the FIRST WORLD of the industrialized West and the SECOND WORLD of the COMMUNIST BLOC. It later became more and more a general term for the LESS DEVELOPED COUNTRIES (LDCS). Also known as the SOUTH, the Third World is now seen to include those countries of Africa, Asia, Latin America and Oceania that are designated by the INTERNATIONAL BANK FOR RECONSTRUCTION AND DEVELOPMENT (IBRD) (World Bank) as lower-income, lower-middle-income or upper-middle-income economies.

Thirty-eighth parallel Latitude 38 degrees North, the symbol of the division of Korea since 1945, which cuts across the country at roughly its middle point. In fact the Military Demarcation Line between communist North Korea and South Korea runs, for most of its length, somewhat to the north of this line. The parallel was chosen in some haste in August 1945 when the USSR declared war on Japan and moved troops into Korea and became of crucial international significance during the KOREAN WAR of 1950–3.

Three Worlds Theory This was proposed by the Chinese Communist leader Mao-Zedong (1893–1976) in 1974. He argued that the world was divided into (1) the SUPERPOWERS, (2) the economically developed world, Europe, Canada, Japan, Australia, New Zealand and South Africa, and (3) the THIRD WORLD, consisting of the rest of Africa, Asia (excluding Japan) and all Latin America. He presented the SECOND WORLD as exploited by the Third, but both as exploited by the FIRST WORLD. Accordingly, he called for the Second and Third worlds to unite against the super-powers, which he described as the common enemies of the world.

Tiananmen Square Protest (1989) The demonstration between 15 April and 4 June 1989 in Beijing in support of political liberalization and the Democracy Movement and calling for an end to corruption. Starting as a student protest, it soon involved people from all walks of life and spread to other cities in the People's Republic of China. In June the Chinese government brought in heavily armed troops to suppress the demonstration, killing more than a thousand protestors and bystanders. This aroused public opinion internationally, but led to only minor Western SANC-TIONS. In the USA, for instance, there were calls in Congress for the termination of MOST-FAVOURED-NATION STATUS for China in support of HUMAN RIGHTS. This demand was sidestepped by the Bush administration.

Tied aid In very many cases overseas development aid is tied to specific projects for an agreed development or it is tied to the recipient purchasing goods from the donor country. Aid is often defended politically in donor countries with the argument that it will increase exports from those countries. The BRANDT REPORT (1980) called for a relaxation of tied aid along these lines on the grounds that it often meant poor countries would not be able to buy in the cheapest markets.

Titoism The theory and practice of the national road to COMMUNISM as advanced by the Yugoslav communist leader Joseph Broz Tito (1892–1980). Titoism emerged as a new doctrine in 1948 when Tito rejected the monolithic approach to world COMMUNISM advanced by the Soviet leader Joseph Stalin (1879–1953) under which national Communist parties were expected to accept the direction and control of the Communist Party of the Soviet Union (CPSU). For Tito NATIONALISM and

Communism were complementary doctrines that should be fused into a new movement that permitted each Communist STATE to retain full political independence and
choose its own 'road to socialism'. After the rift with Stalin, Yugoslavia followed a policy associating itself with the NON-ALIGNED MOVEMENT (NAM) in international affairs.
Titoism encouraged POLYCENTRISM.

Tlatelolco Treaty See Treaty for the Prohibition of Nuclear Weapons in Latin
America (1967).

Tobar Doctrine (1907) Proposed by the Ecuadorian politician Carlos Tobar
(1854–1920), this argued that there should be collective NON-RECOGNITION of governments that had come to power through non-democratic means. He stated that it was
in the interest of all existing governments to establish constitutionalism and democratic processes as the means of effecting political change, and that, as far as the international community was concerned, a new STATE or government could be formed
only with the assent of the other members of the state system. This was challenged by
the ESTRADA DOCTRINE (1930), which claimed that a government should be automatically recognized when it is shown to be in control of the territory and population
concerned.

Tokyo Round The seventh series of negotiations held under the auspices of the
GENERAL AGREEMENT ON TARIFFS AND TRADE (GATT) on further tariff reductions in
international trade. The Round began in 1973 and was concluded in 1979. The agreement stipulated reductions in customs duties of around one-third. These reductions
came into force in 1980.

Tonkin Gulf Resolution (1964) An Act of Congress, passed in August 1964,
authorizing the President of the USA to take 'all necessary steps, including the use
of armed forces', to prevent further Communist AGGRESSION in South East Asia. It
was specifically directed against the North Vietnamese attack on American vessels in
the Gulf of Tonkin, regarded as international waters. On the basis of this resolution,
President Johnson (1908–73) ordered the bombing of military bases in North
Vietnam, which began in 1965, and stepped up aid to South Vietnam. The resolution
was repealed by President Nixon (1913–94) in 1971.

Total war The First World War was the first total war in history. The Second
World War was the most destructive war in history, and since 1945 NUCLEAR
WEAPONS have created the possibility of previously unimagined destructiveness. Total
war involves confrontation across the globe with the involvement of whole populations in the war effort, greatly increased destructiveness of weapons, mass mobilization of peoples, unprecedented use of propaganda and the terrorization of civilians.
It has also meant demand for UNCONDITIONAL SURRENDER and for the reconstruction
of defeated STATES according to the dictates of the victor.

Tous azimuts A French military term used to indicate that its NUCLEAR WEAPONS
were pointed 'in all directions'. This was first stated in 1967 when the *FORCE DE FRAPPE*
was being deployed and President de Gaulle (1890–1970) was in the process of
pulling France out of the integrated command structure of the NORTH ATLANTIC

TREATY ORGANIZATION (NATO). It was essentially an expression of French autonomy, and of the classic French doctrine that the possession of nuclear weapons can only credibly be intended for self-protection, and must not in any way be restricted by alliance obligations.

Transnationalism This is both the medium and the consequence of an international environment and WORLD ORDER in which, with increasing mobility and the growth of communications, populations are exposed to influences, cultures, ideas, economic pressures and so on, originating outside their own STATE or territory. Isolation from such currents has become increasingly unrealistic. Transnationalism is particularly evident in financial and economic GLOBALIZATION, in political INTERDEPENDENCE, and in significant movements of populations. It has also meant the vulnerability of national borders and frontiers to international TERRORISM and organized crime.

Transparency In international relations transparency indicates openness in diplomatic settlements and the CREDIBILITY of STATES' agreement to them. It applies to relations not only between previous adversaries, as, for instance, in the negotiations between the West and the USSR at the end of the COLD WAR, but also between allies and organizations on the same side. Transparency is one of the essentials of confidence building in international relations.

Treaty This word is often used generally to describe any international instrument of a contractual nature. It is a written agreement between two or more STATES that becomes INTERNATIONAL LAW. It may also, if applicable, as with the treaties of the EUROPEAN UNION (EU), become part of the national law of the nations assenting to it. Many treaties are bilateral, binding on two parties and creating 'particular' INTERNATIONAL LAW Multilateral treaties, involving a number of parties, are called 'general' International Law. The fundamental principle of the law of treaties is *PACTA SUNT SERVANDA*, which means that pacts in good faith should be preserved. At the beginning of the new millennium 45,000 treaties are registered with the UNITED NATIONS SECRETARIAT.

Treaty for the Prohibition of Nuclear Weapons in Latin America (1967)

Also known as the TLALETOLCO TREATY, this was signed on 14 February 1967 by all nations in Latin America with the exception of Cuba and Guyana. It banned NUCLEAR WEAPONS from Central and South America and the Caribbean, their manufacture, testing, acquisition, storing or deployment. It did not rule out the use of atomic energy for peaceful purposes.

Treaty of Accession The document signed by the EUROPEAN UNION (UN) and a STATE applying for membership once the terms of its entry have been negotiated and agreed. There must be unanimous acceptance among the existing members for a new state to join. Each TREATY must also be ratified by the national legislatures of all the existing member states and, since 1986, by the EUROPEAN PARLIAMENT (EP).

Treaty of Friendship (1963) Signed on 22 January between France and the Federal Republic of Germany (FRG). It provided for Franco-German institutional cooperation in DEFENCE, foreign policy, education and culture. It was the consequence of the deliberate policy of *RAPPROCHEMENT* of the French President Charles de Gaulle (1890–1970) and the German Chancellor Konrad Adenauer (1876–1967) and came only a few days after the French rejection of the first attempt by the UK to join the EUROPEAN ECONOMIC COMMUNITY (EEC). The subsequent pattern of strong cooperation between France and Germany, sometimes called 'the Franco-German axis', has been a dynamic feature in the development of European integration. De Gaulle's hope, though, that Germany would look more to France than to the USA for defence was to be disappointed.

Treaty on European Union (TEU) 1992 Better known as the Maastricht Treaty, this was a significant revision of the ROME TREATY (1957), which had created the COMMON MARKET. It was intended further to advance the economic and political INTEGRATION of the EUROPEAN COMMUNITY (EC). Maastricht formally established the EUROPEAN UNION (EU), consisting of three PILLARS, the EC, the COMMON FOREIGN AND SECURITY POLICY (CFSP) and Justice and Home Affairs (JHA). It introduced the notion of a common EU citizenship, laid special emphasis on the opening of international borders and established a firm commitment to EUROPEAN MONETARY UNION (EMU) by 1999. It also agreed to further integration in social affairs in the form of the Social Chapter. The treaty met with significant opposition in several countries. In Denmark, for instance, it was initially rejected by referendum, while in Britain it had a difficult passage through Parliament and provoked sharp controversy, particularly over monetary union.

Treaty ports The ports in China that foreign powers forced the Manchu Qing Dynasty to open to foreign residents and trade in the mid-nineteenth century. This followed the Nanking Treaty of 1842 and subsequent UNEQUAL TREATIES. These became the base for substantial economic activity in China and many developed large European quarters. By the end of the Dynasty in 1911 there were forty-eight treaty ports.

Treaty rights These concern the legal status of TREATIES. Some constitutions, such as that of the French Republic, fully incorporate treaties so that they are supreme over domestic legislation. Other countries, such as the UK, argue that a treaty is an agreement between sovereigns and that it cannot have effect within Britain unless Parliament expressly legislates for it to do so. Hence the legislation for UK membership of the then EUROPEAN COMMUNITY (EC), which led to accession in 1973, empowered British courts to take notice. The issue of the domestic applicability of treaties is particularly significant, internationally, in the field of HUMAN RIGHTS.

TREVI An acronym for Terrorisme, Radicalisme, Extrémisme, Violence Internationale, a body set up by the EUROPEAN COMMUNITY (EC) in 1975. It is a forum for inter-governmental cooperation over organized crime, TERRORISM, internal security, asylum and immigration policy. It forms the basis of the Justice and Home Affairs PILLAR as laid down in the TREATY ON EUROPEAN UNION (TEU) (1992), which entered into force in 1993.

Triad The triad, or nuclear triad, is the three-part structure of nuclear strategic forces, consisting of air force bomber squadrons, the land-based INTER-CONTINENTAL BALLISTIC MISSILE (ICBM) force and the SUBMARINE-LAUNCHED BALLISTIC MISSILE

(SLBM) fleet. Three of the five members of the NUCLEAR CLUB (France, the Russian Federation and the USA) deploy their forces in this triad.

Triangular diplomacy This term was coined by US SECRETARY OF STATE Henry Kissinger (b. 1923) to describe the DIPLOMACY of DÉTENTE with the USSR and the People's Republic of China in the early 1970s with the USA engaging with both of these powers at the time of the SINO-SOVIET SPLIT.

Trident The SUBMARINE-LAUNCHED BALLISTIC MISSILE (SLBM) SYSTEM developed in the USA as the successor to POLARIS MISSILES and POSEIDON MISSILES. The D-5 missiles have a range of 6,000 miles and the system is designed to be less vulnerable to anti-submarine warfare than its predecessors. In 1982 the British government signed an agreement for the acquisition of this system, continuing British dependence on US nuclear technology.

Trigger Thesis This was one of the arguments advanced by Britain and France during the COLD WAR to justify the CREDIBILITY of their own nuclear deterrents. The argument was that, though their overall nuclear capacity was small compared to that of the SUPERPOWERS, they could trigger a supportive US attack against the USSR if they made a strike in their own defence. This was advanced to answer the argument that the USA might not wish to use its NUCLEAR WEAPONS in defence of an ally.

Trilateralism An analysis of world affairs that dated from the early 1970s and influenced the thinking of US President Jimmy Carter (b. 1924) and other US policy-makers. It emphasized the existence of three major industrial poles in the non-Communist world, the USA, the EUROPEAN COMMUNITY (EC) and Japan, and their interdependence. It also stressed the role of such non-state ACTORS as multinational companies.

Tripartism Also called 'Tridominium', the proposal made to the US and British governments by the French President Charles de Gaulle (1890–1970) in 1958 by a 'directorate' of France, Britain and the USA. The alleged purpose was to maintain French military superiority over Western Germany, to give France a say in nuclear policy and to gain security assurances for French overseas interests. It was rejected by the other two parties and by the Secretary-General of the NORTH ATLANTIC TREATY ORGANIZATION (NATO), an organization that would have been subordinated in the plan. Subsequently, in 1966, de Gaulle was to withdraw France from the integrated military command structure of NATO.

Tripwire thesis A COLD WAR term describing the role of conventional forces on the CENTRAL FRONT during the 1950s and early 1960s. At this time, the doctrine of MASSIVE RETALIATION called for nuclear attack if the USSR mounted a major invasion of Western Europe. The tripwire argument was that initial conventional armed resistance would convince the USSR of the West's resolve. At the same time it carried the warning to the USSR that the US government would do everything to protect its own troops in Europe.

Trotskyism The theories of Leon Trotsky (1879–1940), the leading Russian Communist revolutionary who challenged Joseph Stalin (1879–1953) for the leadership of the USSR after the death of Lenin (1870–1924). After the Bolshevik Revolution of 1917 and the Civil War Trotsky argued for using the Communist base in Russia for the achievement of world revolution. As against this, Stalin stressed the importance at the time of strengthening COMMUNISM in one country, to make it impregnable to capitalist counter-revolution. Trotskyism became a synonym for REVISIONISM and deviation from the Stalinist line, and Trotsky was assassinated on the Soviet leader's orders in 1940.

Truce The ending of armed conflict or hostilities pending negotiations for an ARMISTICE. According to the ruling of the HAGUE PEACE CONFERENCE (1907), during a truce 'no aggressive action by the armed forces . . . of either party shall be undertaken, planned or threatened against the people or the armed forces of the other'.

Trucial States Seven Arab emirates on the Persian Gulf were called the Trucial States from the 1820s until 1971, when they became known as the United Arab Emirates. The name came from the annual TRUCE that the British enforced by which they disavowed maritime warfare. Further controls were imposed on arms and slave trading and in the Exclusion Agreement of 1892 Britain assumed control of the external affairs of these territories.

Truman Doctrine (1947) This was announced to a congressional joint session on 12 March 1947 by US President Harry Truman (1884–1972). It committed the USA to a global policy aimed at preventing the spread of COMMUNISM, pledging to support 'free peoples who are resisting attempted subjugation by armed minorities or by outside pressures'. The background to this was a warning by Britain on 21 February that it could no longer fund support for conservative forces in Greece who were combating Communism and for Turkey, which was being pressurized to make treaty concessions by the USSR. Truman both asked Congress for an initial $400 million for Greece and Turkey and framed a more open-ended commitment, which anticipated the DOMINO THEORY.

Trust territory A former LEAGUE OF NATIONS MANDATE or NON-SELF-GOVERNING TERRITORY, placed after the Second World War under the UNITED NATIONS (UN) trusteeship system. All League mandates that had not achieved independence became trust territories, with the exception of the South African mandate of South-West Africa. Only one additional territory, Italian Somaliland, was placed under trust as a consequence of the war. Each trust territory was brought into the arrangement by a special agreement drawn up by the administering STATE and approved by the UNITED NATIONS GENERAL ASSEMBLY. By the mid-1980s all trust territories with the exception of the Trust Territory of the Pacific Islands, administered by the USA, had been granted independence. In 1990 the League-sanctioned mandate of Namibia became an independent state.

Trusteeship An arrangement created under Chapters XII and XIII of the UNITED NATIONS CHARTER by which a TRUST TERRITORY would be administered by another STATE or by the UNITED NATIONS (UN) itself under the supervision of the TRUSTEESHIP COUNCIL of the UN. It replaced the MANDATES set up after the First World War by the LEAGUE OF NATIONS. Its purpose was to supervise the political, economic and social betterment of the populations in the territories concerned until such time as self-government and then independence would be granted. An interesting feature of the trusteeship system was that territories could be placed under the Trusteeship Council. Under the mandate system such an option did not exist. Administration was simply by another state.

Trusteeship Council This organ of the UNITED NATIONS (UN) was vested in 1945 with the responsibility of supervising the administration of the TRUST TERRITORIES, the colonies taken from the defeated powers with a view to their subsequent SELF-DETERMINATION 'exercised without any condition or reservation'. With the independence of all countries concerned, bar one, the Council has been directed towards new tasks of helping to manage the GLOBAL COMMONS, those areas outside national jurisdiction, which belong to all peoples, and dealing with global environmental issues.

Twentieth Party Congress (1956) The meeting of the Communist Party of the Soviet Union (CPSU), which was also attended by delegates from other national Communist parties. It is best known for the SECRET SPEECH (which was nevertheless leaked to the West) made by the Soviet leader Nikita Khrushchev (1894–1971), which attacked Joseph Stalin (1879–1953) for his dictatorial tyranny, brutality and cult of personality. More importantly for international relations, Khrushchev stressed the need for PEACEFUL COEXISTENCE between East and West and conceded that there could be 'different roads to Socialism'. In EASTERN EUROPE these statements encouraged a belief that the USSR was willing to relax its controls. Subsequently minor reforms were carried out and the worst aspects of Stalinism removed. However, the limits of relaxation were clearly emphasized in the Soviet military suppression of the HUNGARIAN REVOLUTION in 1956.

Twin-Track Policy See DUAL-TRACK POLICY.

Two-and-a-Half Wars Doctrine/One-and-a-Half Wars Doctrine
The description of US military thinking in the 1960s, which called for military preparedness and resources for the USA to be able to wage two-and-a-half wars simultaneously on separate continents. To begin with the VIETNAM WAR (1960–75) was calculated as one-half of a WAR. The reverses faced by South Vietnam and the USA led the US administration to VIETNAMIZATION and to judge its country capable of engaging in one-and-a-half wars at the same time. This meant looking for greater support from allies.

Two-Enemies Doctrine A Polish foreign policy and strategic doctrine arising from Poland's vulnerable position between two dominant neighbours, Germany and Russia. Rather than NON-AGGRESSION PACTS or one-sided alliance with Germany or Russia, this advanced the view that Poland could survive if it cooperated closely with other SUCCESSION STATES in CENTRAL EUROPE and EASTERN EUROPE and allied with the major Western powers. This alliance with the Western powers was triggered by the invasion of Poland in September 1939, but did not rescue it from incorporation in the COMMUNIST BLOC after 1945.

Two-Plus-Four Talks The discussions between the Federal Republic of Germany (FRG), the German Democratic Republic (GDR) and the Second World War Allies, the occupying powers, Britain, France, the USA and the USSR, leading to German reunification. These took place in 1990 and the Final Settlement with respect to Germany was signed by the six foreign ministers in Moscow on 12 September in that year. Two key issues were the NORTH ATLANTIC TREATY ORGANIZATION (NATO) and Germany and the border between Poland and Germany. The West insisted that the reunited Germany be part of NATO. This was agreed by the USSR in return for the Western undertaking that no NATO forces would be stationed on the territory that had previously been the GDR. After the end of the Second World War the West had refused to accept the ODER–NEISSE LINE. Now, as a consequence of these negotiations, Germany renounced claims to lands east of the Line. The question of Berlin was settled on 1 October 1990 in New York when the Allies signed an agreement terminating their rights and responsibilities in Germany.

Two-Power Principle The rule that the British Navy should be equal to the other two strongest navies in the world in combination. It was announced in 1893, though Britain had operated it before and since the Battle of Trafalgar in 1805 had been the dominant naval power. With the development of German naval power from the end of the nineteenth century and the emergence of the US and Japanese navies, the principle was quietly abandoned. In the WASHINGTON CONFERENCE ON THE LIMITATION OF ARMAMENTS (1921–2) Britain agreed parity with the USA.

Two-Speed Europe See VARIABLE GEOMETRY.

U

U-2 Incident (1960) A US spy plane engaged in reconnaissance of nuclear sites in the USSR was shot down on 1 May 1960 and its pilot captured. US President Eisenhower (1890–1969) was forced to admit to and accept responsibility for spy flights. Shortly after, this incident contributed to the collapse of the PARIS SUMMIT (1960).

UDC See UNION OF DEMOCRATIC CONTROL.

UDHR See UNIVERSAL DECLARATION OF HUMAN RIGHTS.

UDI Unilateral Declaration of Independence.

UKUSA See UNITED KINGDOM–UNITED STATES AGREEMENT.

Ultimatum A communication containing final and categorical terms with respect of a dispute. Rejection may lead to the breaking-off of diplomatic relations or conflict.

ULTRA The codeword the Allies used to identify INTELLIGENCE produced by decrypting enemy communications during the Second World War. The British Admiralty first used the word in May 1940 to enable commanders to evaluate the source of the intelligence sent them. By 1945 it was in official use by American, Australian, Canadian as well as British intelligence agencies and Allied forces worldwide. ULTRA had a major beneficial effect on the Allied campaigns, shortening the war in both the Atlantic and Pacific theatres.

UN See UNITED NATIONS.

Unanimity Principle The voting procedure in international organizations that provides that no STATE may be bound by a decision without giving its consent. The usual rule is that a single member, by voting against a decision, can defeat it. Some organizations, though, have the rule that dissent means the dissenter should leave the organization. The unanimity principle derives in this context from the idea that a sovereign state can be bound only by those decisions to which it consents.

UNCED See UNITED NATIONS CONFERENCE ON ENVIRONMENT AND DEVELOPMENT (1992).

UNCLOS See LAW OF THE SEA CONFERENCES.

Unconditional Surrender The surrender of a defeated power without negotiated conditions, particularly associated with the idea of TOTAL WAR. The victors may impose whatever conditions they wish. At the Casablanca Conference (1943) US President Franklin D. Roosevelt (1882–1945) and the British Prime Minister Winston Churchill (1874–1965) called for 'unconditional surrender by Germany, Italy and Japan . . . That . . . does not mean the destruction of the population of Germany, Italy and Japan, but it does mean the destruction of the philosophies of those countries which are based on conquest and the subjugation of other people.' Motives for this declaration included the desire of Britain and the USA to convince the USSR that they were not intending to reach a separate peace with Germany, and further to rally opinion in the USA behind the war effort. Another important consideration was to avoid any attempt by Germany to repeat the STAB-IN-THE-BACK MYTH and to argue, as it had after 1918, that it had been tricked into an ARMISTICE in the expectation that the peace settlement would be on other terms (the FOURTEEN POINTS) than those that were subsequently imposed on it at the VERSAILLES TREATY (1919). The demand for unconditional surrender has aroused historical controversy. In May Germany did surrender unconditionally, but some have argued that the knowledge that there would be no negotiations prolonged the Nazi war effort, undermined support for the Resistance within Germany and, of course, saddled the Allies with the responsibility of governing the conquered territory. It has also been argued that it influenced the decision to use NUCLEAR WEAPONS against Japan. During the KOREAN WAR(1950–3) the USA briefly contemplated imposing unconditional surrender on North Korea in order to force the unification of North and South Korea. In the event, the INTERVENTION of the People's Republic of China forced the USA to realize that the costs of such an objective were too high and the WAR, though very costly, was a limited one.

UNCTAD See UNITED NATIONS CONFERENCE ON TRADE AND DEVELOPMENT.

Unequal Treaties A term used by the Chinese to describe the TREATIES that were imposed by European powers on China in the nineteenth century, staring with the Nanking Treaty of 1842. Under these arrangements the Chinese had to cede lands and rights to the Europeans. The treaties were not finally abolished until 1943.

Unequal Treaties Doctrine The controversial doctrine, invoked particularly since the Second World War, that claims that treaties that have not been concluded on the basis of sovereign equality of the parties are invalid. Where, for instance, Western nations have used economic and political pressure, supporters of this doctrine have argued that the use of such pressure amounts to FORCE. The 1969 Vienna Convention on the Law of Treaties leaves the matter open by not defining 'force', while referring to the prohibition of the use of force in the UNITED NATIONS CHARTER.

Unfriendly act This term in the language of DIPLOMACY is used for an action likely to result in WAR.

UNICEF See UNITED NATIONS CHILDREN FUND.

UNIDO United Nations Industrial Development Organization.

Unilateralism Support for a policy of surrendering use and deployment of NUCLEAR WEAPONS, which, among others, was supported by members of the British CAMPAIGN FOR NUCLEAR DISARMAMENT (CND). Instead of relying on unilateral DISARMAMENT to lead other governments to give up their weapons, multilateralists have argued that mutual nuclear disarmament is the only way to PEACE and SECURITY. This issue in the early 1960s and in the 1980s was a highly divisive one in the British Labour Party. As a general term, it means a policy of self-reliance in international affairs. This can mean ISOLATIONISM, NEUTRALISM or unilateral INTERVENTION without reference to allies.

Uninterrupted revolution Also known as 'continuous revolution', this was a key concept in Chinese Communist ideology under Mao-Zedong (1893–1976), which was strongly promoted during the Chinese Cultural Revolution of 1966–76. He argued for a constant state of political struggle to ensure the 'ultimate liberation of the working class and people as a whole', and that revolutionary fervour should be maintained, in contrast with the USSR. From 1978 the Cultural Revolution has been officially condemned and the idea of uninterrupted revolution dropped both in theory and in practice.

Union of Democratic Control (UDC) This was a British PEACE organization formed in 1914 under the leadership of E. D. Morel (1873–1924). It campaigned to replace 'secret diplomacy' by a foreign policy under the control of Parliament, and during the First World War advocated a negotiated settlement without annexations or indemnities. Its ideas exercised some influence on thinking about international relations in the inter-war years, in particular in the Labour Party.

Unipolarity An international order in which one ACTOR is dominant. If one power could establish global HEGEMONY or if there were to be a WORLD GOVERNMENT, then one could credibly talk about unipolarity. With the dissolution of the USSR there has been some speculation and comment to the effect that this might offer a 'unipolar moment', or opportunity for the USA as the one surviving SUPERPOWER. This view has not attracted much support, however.

Unitary state A STATE with a single sovereign body, the central government, as contrasted with FEDERALISM.

United Kingdom-United States Agreement (UKUSA) (1947) This

agreement established a close post-war partnership among the electronic INTELLIGENCE organizations of Britain, the USA, Canada, Australia and New Zealand. It originated in the earlier British–United States Agreement (BRUSA) of 1943, which followed British success in cracking the Nazi ENIGMA code. UKUSA provided for exchange of intelligence, personnel and equipment and divided the world into areas of responsibility for surveillance.

United Nations (UN) This was established as successor to the LEAGUE OF

NATIONS by Charter in San Francisco on 26 June 1945 as a voluntary association of sovereign STATES and formally came into existence on 24 October of that year. The preamble to the Charter states that its principal objective is 'to save succeeding generations from the scourge of war'. Under ARTICLE 51 it accepts that states have a right of individual and COLLECTIVE SELF-DEFENCE if attacked and in Chapter 8 recognizes the LEGITIMACY of regional security organizations such as the NORTH ATLANTIC TREATY ORGANIZATION (NATO) (which came into existence in 1949). Otherwise, it states all forms of WAR to be illegal and asserts the UN's own right to preserve PEACE. With its headquarters in New York, its three central institutions are the UNITED NATIONS SECURITY COUNCIL(the executive body with five permanent members, and six others elected for two years at a time), the UNITED NATIONS GENERAL ASSEMBLY(representative of all member states) and the UNITED NATIONS SECRETARIAT. Its executive powers are stronger than those of the League, but it has often been paralysed by the VETO power in the Security Council, notably throughout the COLD WAR. The UN is also dissimilar to the League in the range of its specialized agencies, such as the ECONOMIC AND SOCIAL COUNCIL (ECOSOC) and the TRUSTEESHIP COUNCIL and in the fact that member states are called on to contribute armed forces to serve as peacekeepers. Attitudes to the UN PEACEKEEPING rule have been ambivalent. While there is general welcome for the idea of an effective international body, it has not been welcome when it has attempted to obstruct major national interests. Since the end of the cold war, in which the adversaries would routinely block each other, there has been a resurgence of interest in the UN as a body capable of legimating and supporting COLLECTIVE SECURITY and peacekeeping in the world as a credible authority. So, for example, the UN provided a mandate for the Allied opposition to Iraq in the Gulf in 1990–1.

United Nations Charter The document establishing the UNITED NATIONS

(UN). It was signed by the representatives of fifty STATES at the SAN FRANCISCO CONFERENCE on 26 June 1945, coming into effect on 24 October of that year. As a multilateral TREATY it specifies the obligations of member states and the purposes, organizational structure, powers and procedures of the UN. The Charter, consisting of 111 articles in eighteen chapters, is three times the length of the LEAGUE OF NATIONS COVENANT, containing, among other things, lengthy provisions for the TRUSTEESHIP system and detail on economic, social and humanitarian agencies and programmes.

United Nations Children Fund (UNICEF) In 2002 this organization

extends throughout the world and is particularly involved in LESS DEVELOPED COUNTRIES (LDCS). It was originally set up by the UNITED NATIONS GENERAL ASSEMBLY to provide for those children who were destitute, homeless and hungry as a consequence of the Second World War. Its original name was the United Nations International

Children's Emergency Fund (UNICEF) and it was made permanent in 1953 and its name changed (though the original acronym remained). To its traditional contribution to education, health and housing, it has, since the 1980s, added campaigning for the Convention on the Rights of the Child (CRC) (1989), and against landmines.

United Nations Conference on Environment and Development (UNCED) (1992) Also known as the Earth Summit, this conference was held in June 1992 in Rio de Janeiro, being attended by more than 100 heads of STATE or government. Following two years of intensive preparatory work for the conference produced principally: (1) AGENDA 21, a detailed plan for global action, (2) the Rio Declaration, consisting of twenty-seven principles for SUSTAINABLE DEVELOPMENT, (3) a set of principles for the management of the world's forests, (4) a convention on climate change, and (5) a convention on biological diversity. To monitor progress, the UNITED NATIONS (UN) created a Commission on Sustainable Development.

United Nations Conference on Trade and Development (UNCTAD) This agency was established by the UNITED NATIONS GENERAL ASSEMBLY to develop trade policies encouraging economic development. It began in 1964 as an *ad hoc* conference at the suggestion of countries from the THIRD WORLD, became a permanent body and is convened every three to four years. Its Secretariat is in Geneva and it has a Trade and Development Board, which formulates and proposes policy. One of its major successes has been the adoption of a GENERALIZED SYSTEM OF PREFERENCES (GSP), by which developed industrial countries have facilitated exports from Third World countries by tariff reductions.

United Nations Declaration (1942) This was the joint declaration of the nations allied against the AXIS during the Second World War and was issued on 1 January 1942 in Washington DC. In the first instance it was signed by the USA, Britain, the USSR and China. The signatories pledged to support the ATLANTIC CHARTER (1941), to secure the defeat of the enemy and not to conclude a separate peace. Twenty-two countries soon endorsed it, eventually followed by nineteen others. These countries formed the nucleus of the UNITED NATIONS (UN) created in 1945.

United Nations Declaration on the Granting of Independence to Colonial Countries and Peoples This key declaration was passed by the UNITED NATIONS GENERAL ASSEMBLY in 1960 immediately after the admission to the UN of seventeen former colonial states. It was described as putting into effect the UNITED NATIONS CHARTER in announcing the rights of all peoples to political independence and self-rule. What a 'people' was left undefined. The next year the UN General Assembly created a committee to oversee DECOLONIZATION.

United Nations Educational, Scientific and Cultural Organization (UNESCO) This organization was formed by the UNITED NATIONS (UN) in November 1946. Its task is to contribute to PEACE and SECURITY and respect for HUMAN RIGHTS by encouraging collaboration between peoples and nations through education, science, culture and communication. For instance, it runs teacher-training centres to make provision for the LEAST DEVELOPED COUNTRIES

(LDCS). In the mid-1980s the USA, Britain and Singapore temporarily suspended their contribution to its funds, alleging anti-Western political bias.

United Nations General Assembly One of the six major organs of the UNITED NATIONS (UN). It is essentially its central organ, since its agenda encompasses the whole range of UN issues and all of the other organs report to it. Unlike the UNITED NATIONS SECURITY COUNCIL, it lacks the authority to pass resolutions legally binding on its members. All UN members have one vote. Certain matters require a simple majority of those present and voting. Its major functions and powers include: (1) discussing any issue that is within the scope of the United Nations Charter, (2) considering general principles of cooperation for the maintenance of international PEACE and SECURITY and making recommendations based on these principles, and (3) calling to the attention of the UN Security Council any situation that is likely to endanger international peace and security. It admits STATES to membership, and may expel them. It is also responsible for the UN's finances.

United Nations Partition Plan (Palestine) (1947) This was the majority recommendation of the United Nations Special Committee on Palestine (UNSCOP), adopted by the UNITED NATIONS GENERAL ASSEMBLY on 29 November 1947, which called for the division of Palestine into a Jewish and a Palestinian STATE with Jerusalem placed under the supervision of the UN. The plan offered the Jews 56 per cent of the land of Palestine at a time when they owned only 7 per cent and represented a third of the population. The plan was rejected by the Palestinians and the Arab world, who refused to truncate Arab Palestine or to recognize a separate Jewish state. As the British prepared to pull out, the Zionists sought to gain control of as much territory as possible. The subsequent war of 1948–9 led to Israel's control of more than three-quarters of Palestine, including the coastal areas.

United Nations Protection Force (UNPROFOR) This was the collective name for the international military forces mandated by the UNITED NATIONS (UN) in 1992 as PEACEKEEPING forces in the former Yugoslavia. It had three separate components, one deployed in the Serb-populated areas of Croatia, one in Bosnia-Herzegovina and a third in Macedonia.

United Nations Relief and Rehabilitation Administration (UNRRA) (1945–7) The special post-Second World War relief agency, agreed on by representatives of forty-four nations in 1943, which took over responsibilities for the needs of displaced persons in July 1945. Over the next two years in Europe, Africa and the Far East it supplied more than a billion dollars worth of humanitarian assistance and promoted resettlement. Disbanded in June 1947, its REFUGEE protection function was assumed by the International Refugee Organization.

United Nations Secretariat One of the six main organs of the UNITED NATIONS (UN). Its main role is to carry out the responsibilities as specified under the UNITED NATIONS CHARTER. The UNITED NATIONS SECRETARY-GENERAL, as the chief administrative officer of the UN, is charged with presenting an annual report to the UNITED NATIONS GENERAL ASSEMBLY and has the responsibility for drawing to the attention of the UNITED NATIONS SECURITY COUNCIL issues that threaten international PEACE and SECURITY.

United Nations Secretary-General

The chief administrative officer of the UNITED NATIONS (UN), head of the UNITED NATIONS SECRETARIAT, who supervises the organization on a day-to-day basis. The holder of this office is chosen by the UNITED NATIONS GENERAL ASSEMBLY on the recommendation of the UNITED NATIONS SECURITY COUNCIL.

United Nations Security Council

One of the six principal organs of the UNITED NATIONS (UN). It is assigned primary responsibility by the UNITED NATIONS CHARTER for maintaining PEACE and SECURITY in the world. Its role of preserver of peace provided for it, under the Charter, to attempt PACIFIC SETTLEMENT OF DISPUTES or it may call on members to undertake collective action against a NATION that is agreed guilty of an act of AGGRESSION, or threatening the peace. It has five permanent members (the P5), the People's Republic of China, France, Britain, the Russian Federation and the USA, and ten, originally six, elected members, serving two-year terms. Half of the elected members are chosen by the UNITED NATIONS GENERAL ASSEMBLY each year, under a GENTLEMAN'S AGREEMENT that apportions them to major geographical regions. All decisions require an affirmative vote of nine members, but (and this has, historically, been the major restraint on its effectiveness), on substantive rather than procedural decisions, decisions may be vetoed by a permanent member. Nations that are not represented on the Security Council may be invited to participate if a dispute concerning them is under consideration.

Uniting for Peace Resolution

This was adopted by the UNITED NATIONS GENERAL ASSEMBLY in November 1950 at the time of the KOREAN WAR (1950–3). It called for the General Assembly to be convened within twenty-four hours if the UNITED NATIONS SECURITY COUNCIL should be unable to agree on a course of action in situations involving a threat to PEACE and SECURITY. The UN had agreed support for South Korea against the Communist North, but this had only happened because the USSR was boycotting it, rather than exercising its VETO, and this boycott ended in August 1950. The resolution also requested members to designate military units for UN service, and to establish a Peace Observation Commission and a Collective Measures Committee.

Universal Declaration of Human Rights (UDHR) (1948)

The proclamation by the UNITED NATIONS (UN) intended to establish 'a common standard of achievement for all peoples and all nations' in the observance of civil, economic, political, social and cultural rights. Prepared by the ECONOMIC AND SOCIAL COUNCIL (ECOSOC), it was adopted on 16 December 1948 by the UNITED NATIONS GENERAL ASSEMBLY. In 1954 the UN began working on two covenants to make the rights legally binding, which became known as the INTERNATIONAL BILL OF HUMAN RIGHTS. Now this Bill is a collective term applying to four major international instruments in the field of HUMAN RIGHTS, the Declaration, the International Covenant on Economic, Social and Cultural Rights, the International Covenant on Civil and Political Rights, its optional Protocols and the International Convention on the Elimination of all Forms of Racial Discrimination.

Universalist rule A rule that recognizes no intrinsic limits to the extension of its authority.

UNO United Nations Organization.

UNPROFOR See UNITED NATIONS PROTECTION FORCE.

UNRRA See UNITED NATIONS RELIEF AND REHABILITATION ADMINISTRATION.

Uruguay Round The eighth series of negotiations on world trade under the GENERAL AGREEMENT ON TARIFFS AND TRADE (GATT), which began in Punta del Este in 1986. Previous rounds had concentrated on manufactured goods. This extended to other areas, including agriculture and services. There were sharp differences between the USA and the EUROPEAN UNION (EU), particularly over agriculture, and the round was only concluded four years later than anticipated at the end of 1994. This was the last round before GATT was transformed into the WORLD TRADE ORGANIZATION (WTO).

Ussuri Incident (1969) Clashes between Russian and Chinese border troops in March 1969 on the island known to the Chinese as Zhinbao and to the Russians as Damansky, on the Ussuri River, which marks China's north-eastern border with Russia. It was the most serious incident in the SINO-SOVIET SPLIT.

Uti possidetis The rule that leaves in the hands of the victor what has been captured in WAR.

Vandenberg Resolution (1947) A US Senate resolution sponsored by Republican Arthur Vandenberg (1884–1951) and adopted on 11 June 1948. It favoured US participation in regional security agreements within the framework of the UNITED NATIONS (UN). This was significant in preparing the way for the NORTH ATLANTIC TREATY (1949) and US acceptance of commitment to the NORTH ATLANTIC TREATY ORGANIZATION (NATO). In the inter-war years Vandenberg had been an isolationist. His conversion to BIPARTISANSHIP and CONTAINMENT was particularly reassuring to those in Europe who feared that the USA might revert to ISOLATIONISM.

Variable geometry A phrase coined by the President of the European Commission Jacques Delors (b. 1925) to explain the possibility of common policies being developed and put into effect at different rates by individual member states of the EUROPEAN COMMUNITY (EC). Variable geometry envisaged the possibility of a two- or even three-speed Europe in the process of integration. The OPT-OUTS by the UK, for instance, over the single currency and the Social Chapter in the TREATY ON EUROPEAN UNION (TEU) (1992) indicate this variation.

Vatican See HOLY SEE.

Velvet Divorce A term used to describe the peaceful break-up of the Czechoslovakian federation, after the collapse of COMMUNISM in EASTERN EUROPE, into two independent STATES, the Czech Republic and Slovakia, on 1 January 1993.

Venice Declaration (1980) This was issued by the then nine-member EURO-PEAN COMMUNITY (EC) following a European summit on 12–13 June and it reflected cool relations between the EC and Israel. Consisting of eleven points, it reaffirmed previous declarations opposing changes in the status of Jerusalem and stressing the inadmissibility of acquiring territory by FORCE, broke new ground by calling for Palestinian SELF-DETERMINATION and the need to associate the PALESTINE LIBERATION ORGANIZATION (PLO) with PEACE negotiations. The Nine stated that they were willing to participate 'within the framework of a comprehensive settlement in a system of concrete and binding international guarantees'. The Declaration also called on Israel to stop building settlements, to end the military occupation of the WEST BANK and GAZA STRIP and to cease claiming exclusive control over Jerusalem. It was in the longer term significant in encouraging a more flexible approach to a very intractable problem. This initiative irritated the USA, however, and was denounced by Israel as a 'Munich-like capitulation to totalitarian blackmail' and as an attempt to subvert the CAMP DAVID ACCORDS of 1978.

Verification The process and means by which parties to an agreement are able to determine with confidence that other parties are abiding by the terms of that agreement. Its principal application has been with regard to agreements over ARMS CONTROL, as, for example, those between the USA and the USSR during the COLD WAR, and for enforcing multilateral agreements to prevent the spread of WEAPONS OF MASS DESTRUCTION.

Versailles Treaty (1919) This TREATY, which also incorporated the LEAGUE OF NATIONS COVENANT, concluded the First World War and came into effect on 10 January 1920. It was signed by thirty-two nations, but rejected by the US Senate. It punished defeated Germany and was imposed on it as a *Diktat*, both Germany and Russia being excluded from the negotiations. It consisted of 440 articles and the Germans objected in particular to ARTICLE 231 (the 'War Guilt Clause'), which blamed Germany and its allies exclusively for starting the First World War. It imposed REPARATIONS on Germany and an Allied occupation of the Rhineland and Saar for fifteen years. Germany was disarmed, and its Army was reduced to 100,000 soldiers, with CONSCRIPTION being abolished. ALSACE-LORRAINE, which had been lost in 1871, was returned to France, and Belgium gained three small ENCLAVES. Most controversial among the territorial clauses were the loss of all its colonies, which became MANDATES, of territory to Poland, which included the so-called Polish Corridor and DANZIG (now Gdansk), declared a FREE CITY under the LEAGUE OF NATIONS, and the ban on union between Austria and Germany. The US rejection of the Treaty and of the League was to prove crucial. Not least, the arrangement for an Anglo-US guarantee of French security lapsed. Germany was excluded from the League until 1926, and German public opinion overwhelmingly regarded it as unjust and was united in opposition to it. This disquiet was echoed abroad in the famous polemic by the British Treasury official and economist John Maynard Keynes (1883–1946) in the *Economic Consequences of the Peace* (1919). In practice, while the terms of the Treaty gave

Germany a great sense of grievance, they did not impede its revival. The Nazi Party was the ultimate beneficiary of the unpopularity of Versailles and its REPARATIONS clauses, and DISARMAMENT restrictions were soon repudiated after Hitler's accession to power in 1933.

Vertical fusion The feature of international organizations where, because delegates are appointed by their national governments, they follow instructions from their governments rather than developing an independent voice of their own.

Vertical proliferation An increase in the number and destructive force of NUCLEAR WEAPONS in those STATES that already possess them.

Veto A vote that forbids or blocks the making of a decision, such as that, for instance, that may be exercised by any of the P5 (permanent five members) on the UNITED NATIONS SECURITY COUNCIL.

Vichy A resort in the Auvergne in France. After the defeat of France by Germany in 1940, it became the provisional capital of France under the government of Marshal Pétain (1856–1951). This government remained in Vichy until the Allied liberation of 1944. The name became a symbol of betrayal, collaboration and capitulation.

Vienna Congress (1814–15) The peace conference following the Napoleonic Wars, which set out to establish a durable international settlement and to prevent renewed French domination of Europe. It agreed to periodic consultations among the powers, which became known as the CONGRESS SYSTEM, and was intended to create a more developed international system and to institutionalize cooperation for the preservation of PEACE and against revolution. Its main preoccupations were with the DEMARCATION of boundaries, the establishment of regimes in Europe, and, outside, arrangements for colonies. More specifically, it created the German Confederation (*Bund*), guaranteed the NEUTRALITY of Switzerland and gave northern Italy to the Austrian Empire. In the Final Act it also gave the first explicit recognition and guarantee of the rights of national minorities, adopted a declaration for the abolition of the slave trade and codified the procedures of DIPLOMACY.

Vienna Summit (1961) The only summit meeting between US President John F. Kennedy (1917–63) and the Soviet leader Nikita Khrushchev (1894–1971). Kennedy, who had recently been humiliated by the fiasco of the BAY OF PIGS INVASION (1961), was faced with an intransigent adversary who demanded RECOGNITION of the German Democratic Republic (GDR) and reiterated his support for WARS OF NATIONAL LIBERATION. The only positive outcome was that the leaders agreed there should be 'a neutral and independent Laos'. That it did not improve US–Soviet relations is evidenced in the resumption of nuclear testing by the USSR and in the CUBAN MISSILE CRISIS (1962).

Vietnam Syndrome This term refers in general to the pervasive and long-lasting impact of the Vietnam conflict on the national consciousness of the USA. This has been seen subsequently in government caution and public reluctance to commit, in particular, US ground forces in military actions abroad. While the War Powers

Resolution (1973) imposed Congressional restraints on the President, the likely impact of US casualties on domestic public opinion was also significantly constraining. Though President George Bush (b. 1924) and others argued that the military victory in the Gulf in 1991, with minimal US casualties, had laid the 'ghost of Vietnam' to rest, US hesitancy was conspicuously apparent in the protracted crisis in Bosnia-Herzegovina during the first half of the 1990s.

Vietnam War (1960–75) The conflict in South East Asia involving South Vietnamese government forces, backed by the USA, and Communist guerrilla forces supported by the North Vietnamese, the Vietminh. The potential loss of South East Asia was defined in the USA as threatening its SECURITY and that of the FREE WORLD nations. Washington was much traumatized by the accusation of the 'loss of China' in 1949. This WAR followed the INDOCHINA WAR (1946–54), which had resulted in the division of Vietnam into two separate STATES. North Vietnam had proclaimed itself a Communist state, and had established close relations with the USSR and the People's Republic of China, and its government was regarded as an agent of global COMMUNISM. In 1957 Communist forces, the Vietcong, began a guerrilla campaign in South Vietnam with the aim of overthrowing the government and uniting Vietnam. Seeing this as vindication of the DOMINO THEORY, President Dwight D. Eisenhower (1890–1969) and then John F. Kennedy (1917–63) stepped up support for South Vietnam, believing that, if they abandoned South Vietnam, the USA would lose credibility across the globe. Kennedy's successor, Lyndon B. Johnson (1908–73), expanded the conflict with the authority granted him by Congress in the TONKIN GULF RESOLUTION (1964), initiated bombing raids on North Vietnam and despatched large forces, eventually reaching over half a million. The Resolution promised to support 'all necessary measures' to defend US forces and to prevent further AGGRESSION in the region. The war was limited, however, to the extent that Soviet and Chinese support for North Vietnam stopped short of direct INTERVENTION and the USA ruled out an invasion of North Vietnam. With the Tet offensive of 1968 already faltering, support by public opinion in the USA developed into significant outright opposition. The government was criticized, on the one hand, for intervening and intensifying the military effort and, on the other, for failure to win the war. Under Johnson's successor, President Richard Nixon (1913–94), the USA offered a mixture of negotiation, ESCALATION of the bombing and VIETNAMIZATION of the war. This led to agreement in 1973, which allowed US military withdrawal. This did not resolve the internal conflict and Saigon fell to North Vietnam in April 1975, as a consequence of which Vietnam was united under the Communists. The war was a local struggle for HEGEMONY complicated by foreign intervention. The USA failed to fit military STRATEGY effectively to achieve its goals. The so-called VIETNAM SYNDROME was subsequently invoked to explain US hesitancy in involving itself militarily in later crises.

Vietnamization The US policy initiated by President Richard Nixon (1913–94) in 1969 of phasing out US forces and turning the war responsibilities over to the South Vietnamese. While continuing material support to the South Vietnamese army and strengthening it, strategists hoped that South Vietnamese forces would become progressively able to oppose the Viet Cong without US support. This policy reflected the growing political and public opinion pressure within the USA for the government to extricate the country from the conflict.

Visegrad Group A grouping of STATES formed in February 1991 by Czechoslovakia, Hungary and Poland, named after the town where the inaugural meeting took place. The main purpose of the group was defined as cooperation over economic matters, specially with a view to their common ambition to be admitted to the EUROPEAN COMMUNITY (EC), and over SECURITY issues.

Voice of America (VOA) This agency was originally established by the USA in 1942 to project US aims by radio and oppose the propaganda of the AXIS. It came to broadcast in more than fifty languages. In 1948, with the development of the COLD WAR, President Truman (1884–1972) signed legislation making it permanent under the aegis of the DEPARTMENT OF STATE. In 1953 it became part of the US Information Agency and in 1995 it was subsumed under the International Broadcasting Bureau.

Voidance of treaties The loss of binding force for a TREATY for reasons other than it has expired or been renounced.

W

War ARMED CONFLICT between independent political units; hostilities between STATE, or within a state or territory (CIVIL WAR) undertaken by means of armed FORCE, involving violence. When two or more states declare officially that a condition of hostilities exists between them, war is recognized according to INTERNATIONAL LAW, which incorporates legal rules originating in traditional views of what does and does not constitute JUST WAR. War may range from TOTAL WAR, to limited war or to INSURGENCY, and the objectives may range from total destruction of the adversary to modest territorial adjustments. It should be said that limited wars may be limited for a major power but devastating for a minor one. It is possible to have declarations of war without combat and vice versa. Since the twentieth century, with the intensification of war and the greatly increased destructive capacity of weapons, there has been a significant interest in, and analysis of, the multifarious causes of war and of individual and/or interrelated wars (for instance, very great, and continuing, debates over the First World War or the COLD WAR, and in the role of IDEOLOGY in international conflict). At the same time, the scale and trauma of modern war, in particular the involvement of civilians in it, have encouraged the development of ideas for war prevention, for the outlawing of war, such as COLLECTIVE SECURITY and ARMS CONTROL, and organizations such as the LEAGUE OF NATIONS and the UNITED NATIONS (UN). This interest in PEACE preservation contrasts with a traditional view of war, which has historically seen it as legitimate means for the pursuit of state interests. This has become particularly so since the invention of NUCLEAR WEAPONS.

War crimes One of three categories of criminality concerning WAR. The others are CRIMES AGAINST PEACE and CRIMES AGAINST HUMANITY. War crimes include, but are not limited to, killing and wounding combatants who have surrendered or asked to surrender; killing, wounding or subjecting to ill-treatment prisoners of war; pillage or plunder; deportation of populations for forced labour or any other purpose; abusing the dead and wanton destruction. Since 1945 those responsible can be held accountable nationally or internationally, and cannot claim extenuation on the basis of 'superior orders'.

War fighting This phrase was used to describe the argument advanced in the 1970s and 1980s that NUCLEAR WEAPONS were more credible and therefore more deterrent if one had the weapons and doctrines that could sustain the idea of a possibly prolonged nuclear war. This departed from the common view that there would be no winners in a nuclear war. Critics pointed out that preparation to fight a nuclear war would enhance, not diminish, its probability and that the cost of such an arsenal would be prohibitive.

War games Simulations of military operations using data, rules and procedures, which are designed to depict an actual situation and predict responses. A few months before the Falklands War of 1982, for instance, the Argentinian forces practised war games, which led them to the mistaken conclusion that Britain would not react militarily to occupation of the islands by FORCE.

War Guilt Clause See ARTICLE 231.

War indemnities See REPARATIONS.

War Powers Resolution (1973) A US joint congressional resolution passed on 7 November 1973 over the veto of US President Richard Nixon (1913–94), which represented the determination of Congress to reassert control over foreign policy following the experience of the VIETNAM WAR (1960–75). It has been a contentious issue with successive presidents, who have objected to its constraint on them as chief executive, and have resorted to various ploys to circumvent it. The resolution requires the President to notify Congress of any use of armed force in a hostile situation and to withdraw any forces within sixty days unless Congress authorizes otherwise. Another part of the resolution grants Congress the power to withdraw forces at any time by passage of a concurrent resolution.

Wars of National Liberation Insurgencies of an anti-Western and anti-capitalist nature against the established colonial authorities in the developing world as a STRATEGY for achieving world COMMUNISM. This doctrine was first openly championed by the Soviet leader Nikita Khrushchev (1894–1971). Mao-Zedong (1893–1976) similarly called for an uprising of peasants in all class-dominated societies. It was argued by Communists that, as long as the West 'exports counter-revolution', aid must be given to support indigenous revolutions, hence support for insurgency in Vietnam and Ethiopia among other places. The REAGAN DOCTRINE gave this a contrary twist by supporting insurgencies against the USSR and Communist influence in Afghanistan, Angola and Mozambique.

Warsaw Pact (1955) Officially known as the Warsaw Treaty Organization (WTO), this military and political organization originally consisted of Albania, Bulgaria, Czechoslovakia, East Germany, Hungary, Poland, Romania and the USSR. It was instituted on 14 May 1955, just after the RATIFICATION of West Germany's entry into the NORTH ATLANTIC TREATY ORGANIZATION (NATO). Up to this point the other countries had been bound to the USSR with bilateral ties. After the HUNGARIAN REVOLUTION (1956), Moscow centralized decision making in the Pact. Its purpose was to form a counterpoise to NATO and to enable the USSR the better to control EASTERN

EUROPE. It was always under the control of a Soviet general. The decision to invade Czechoslovakia in 1968 was put into effect by the WTO. In that year Albania left. With the collapse of COMMUNISM in Eastern Europe the Warsaw Pact, as both a military structure and a political organization, was dissolved in 1991.

Warsaw Treaty Organization (WTO) See WARSAW PACT.

Washington Conference on the Limitation of Armaments (1921–2) (Washington Naval Conference) An international confer-
ence for the limitation of naval armaments and the adjustment of Far Eastern questions. It resulted in three major agreements. The Five-Power Treaty, which served as the basis for the so-called ten-year 'naval holiday' (subsequently extended to fifteen years), reduced naval tonnage in capital ships to a ratio of 5:5:3:1.75:1.75 for the USA, Britain, Japan, France and Italy respectively. A Nine-Power Treaty committed the signatories to the principle of the OPEN DOOR POLICY and the territorial integrity of China. The Four-Power Treaty (signed by Britain, France, the USA and Japan) pledged the signatories to consultation in the event of AGGRESSION in the Far East.

Watergate The US scandal between 1972 and 1974 that ended with the resigna-
tion of US President Richard Nixon (1913–94) on 9 August 1974 and that otherwise would have resulted in impeachment. This followed exposure of the fact that he had been complicit in concealing the break-in at the headquarters of the Democratic National Committee, located in Washington DC, on the night of 17–18 June 1972. This issue reflected deeper tensions between the executive and Congress arising, not least, from the conduct of the VIETNAM WAR (1960–75). The scandal came at a tense time in international relations, in particular with the YOM KIPPUR WAR (1973) and cast a shadow over Nixon's policy of DÉTENTE. The WAR POWERS RESOLUTION (1973), which reflected the weakened position of the President, meant that subsequently South Vietnam did not receive the military support it had expected after the signing of the PARIS PEACE ACCORDS (1973), and contributed to its defeat in 1975.

Weapon of last resort A term used with reference to NUCLEAR WEAPONS, par-
ticularly in relation to the British nuclear force. This is how the Ministry of Defence (MOD) commonly describes this CAPABILITY. The 'last resort', in this case, would be for retaliation against a nuclear attack against Britain.

Weapons of mass destruction This term is used collectively to describe
NUCLEAR WEAPONS and CHEMICAL AND BIOLOGICAL WEAPONS (CBW). It came into wide public usage at the time of the GULF WAR (1991) and during subsequent attempts to enforce DISARMAMENT on Iraq. The Western governments have expressed particular concern about such weapons in the hands of ROGUE STATES.

Weapons states A term used to describe small or medium-size STATES that are
armed with WEAPONS OF MASS DESTRUCTION and possess the means to deliver them.

Wehrmacht The name for the German armed forces between 1935 and 1945,
the collapse of the Third Reich. It was based on rearmament and CONSCRIPTION, both

a rejection of the terms of the VERSAILLES TREATY (1919), and willingly collaborated with the Nazis in the preparation for, and conduct of, the Second World War.

Weighted voting Voting that is not on the basis of one-person, or one-country, one-vote, but according to criteria such as population or scale of financial contribution. An example of this is the QUALIFIED MAJORITY VOTING (QMV) established under the SINGLE EUROPEAN ACT in the EUROPEAN UNION (EU), where the number of votes a member STATE has depends on its population. The USA has, as another example of this principle, attempted to press for weighted voting on the budget in the UNITED NATIONS (UN), with the nations who make more of a financial contribution to the organization having a greater vote.

Weinberger Doctrine Named after the US Secretary of Defence Caspar Weinberger (b. 1917), who on 28 November 1984 announced six principles that should govern the use of military FORCE by the USA. They were the following: (1) that forces would be used only in support of a 'vital national interest'; (2) that they would be committed only with 'the clear intention of winning'; (3) that they should support only clearly defined military and political objectives; (4) that the relationship between objectives and use of military forces should be 'continually reassessed and readjusted if necessary'; (5) that military commitment must have the support of Congress and the people of the USA; (6) that the use of troops should be only a last resort. This statement followed the withdrawal of US marines from the Middle East (241 marines had been killed by a suicide bomber in Beirut the previous year) and reflected the VIETNAM SYNDROME.

Weltpolitik A term for German imperial policy, involving persistent INTERVENTION in world affairs. The claim by Germany for world power status and 'a place in the sun' was strongly advanced in the reign of the Emperor William II (1859–1941). It involved Germany in the construction of a large naval fleet and a forward colonial policy, an addition to its older demand for dominance in MITTELEUROPA. It was regarded by other powers as reckless and provocative. In particular, Britain regarded the German *Weltpolitik* as a threat to its own imperial interests.

West Bank Part of the area that was allotted by the UNITED NATIONS (UN) in its partition plan of 1947 for the Palestinian Arabs. The term for this area of 3,700 square miles, bordered on the west by the 1949 GREEN LINE and on the east by the river Jordan, was annexed by Jordan in 1950.

Western European Union (WEU) This DEFENCE agreement, signed in 1955, extended the BRUSSELS TREATY (1948) to include the Federal Republic of Germany (FRG) and Italy. This was part of the arrangement, following the collapse of the idea for a EUROPEAN DEFENCE COMMUNITY (EDC), which allowed the rearmament of Germany and reassured its European neighbours, together with the commitment of British troops in the BRITISH ARMY OF THE RHINE (BAOR). After this it was an essentially inactive body until the mid-1980s. In 1984, with a particular push from France and Germany, there was an attempt to reinvigorate it as the means for creating a more distinctive West European defence and SECURITY identity. This aroused some apprehensions, particularly with the British government, that this would open up divergences between Europe and the USA. After the end of the COLD WAR, the TREATY ON EUROPEAN UNION (TEU) **(1992)** incorporated the WEU within the EUROPEAN UNION (EU) in the second PILLAR, the COMMON FOREIGN AND SECURITY POLICY (CFSP).

Westminster Statute   See STATUTE OF WESTMINSTER (1931).

Westphalian System   The European order established with the Treaty of Westphalia (1648), which ended the Thirty Years War. It marked the triumph of the concept of the STATE, sovereign, in control of its own domestic affairs and independent of external control, which had developed since the end of the fifteenth century.

WEU   See WESTERN EUROPEAN UNION.

White House   Since November 1800 the official executive office and personal residence of the President of the USA, located in Washington DC. It is commonly used too as shorthand for presidential policy.

WHO   See WORLD HEALTH ORGANIZATION.

Wilhelmstrasse   The street in central Berlin that included the German Foreign Ministry (Auswärtiges Amt) between 1871 and the collapse of Nazi Germany in 1945. It is commonly used to refer to German foreign policy and DIPLOMACY over this period.

Wilson Doctrine (1913)   This was advanced by US President Woodrow Wilson (1856–1924) to justify US intervention in Central and Latin America and amounted to a further elaboration of the ROOSEVELT COROLLARY of 1904, which had invoked the international policing role of the USA. It followed difficulties with Mexico that led to the US occupation of Veracruz. Wilson stated: 'We do not sympathize with those who establish their government authority in order to satisfy their personal interests and ambitions . . . We must teach the Latin Americans to select the right man.'

Wilsonianism   After US President Woodrow Wilson (1856–1924), this term is normally used to indicate an idealistic approach to international relations based on moral principles and values and on a rejection of simple power politics. Wilson was particularly identified after the First World War with support for SELF-DETERMINATION and the LEAGUE OF NATIONS and the universalist preservation of PEACE. During the COLD WAR his legacy was denigrated by advocates of REALISM, who argued that Wilsonianism neglected NATIONAL INTEREST, SECURITY, POWER and the value of military strength. With the end of the COLD WAR, there is, perhaps, an opportunity to reappraise his ideas more sympathetically.

Window of vulnerability   This apprehensive phrase was used by some US strategists, rather like the term MISSILE GAP was in the late 1950s. Because of the build-up of Soviet INTER-CONTINENTAL BALLISTIC MISSILES (ICBMS) with MULTIPLE INDEPENDENTLY TARGETED RE-ENTRY VEHICLES (MIRVS), they predicted that the USSR might in the early 1980s possess a FIRST-STRIKE CAPABILITY and be able to destroy a very high proportion of the US land-based missiles before they could be launched.

World Bank See INTERNATIONAL BANK FOR RECONSTRUCTION AND DEVELOPMENT (IBRD).

World Commission on Environment and Development (Brundtland Commission) This was created by the UNITED NATIONS GENERAL ASSEMBLY in 1983 for the purpose of examining potential conflicts between economic growth and the protection of the environment. It was chaired by Gro Harlem Brundtland (b. 1939), Norwegian Prime Minister. Its report was produced in 1987, addressing the question of SUSTAINABLE DEVELOPMENT, discussing the impact of the GREENHOUSE EFFECT and the requirement for greater energy efficiency.

World Council of Churches (WCC) This organization, based in Geneva, was formally established in 1948 in Amsterdam to promote cooperation between the Christian churches. It originated from the joining of two earlier movements 'Life and Work' and 'Faith and Order'. With the exception of the Roman Catholic Church and the Unitarians, the Council includes churches from all the main Christian confessions and denominations, including nearly all the Eastern Orthodox churches. Apart from its spiritual ecumenical priorities, it has also involved itself in issues such as the campaign against racial discrimination and APARTHEID and on behalf of REFUGEES.

World Court See INTERNATIONAL COURT OF JUSTICE (ICJ).

World Development Report This is an annual publication issued by the INTERNATIONAL BANK FOR RECONSTRUCTION AND DEVELOPMENT (IBRD) (World Bank), which has appeared since the mid-1970s. It represents one of the most comprehensive regular examinations of questions relating to economic development and AID. It provides a general overview and also, sometimes, deals with a particular topic.

World Disarmament Conference See Conference for the Reduction and Limitation of Armaments (1932–4).

World Food Programme This was initiated in 1963 as a joint enterprise between the UNITED NATIONS (UN) and the Food and Agriculture Organization (FAO). It began with a $100 million fund pledged by governments. One of its most notable features is the food-for-work concept that is intended to improve nutrition among the rural poor. It is involved in both development and emergency projects and much of its work has been in sub-Saharan Africa.

World government The idea of a global institution that would create a supreme authority to oversee affairs of the world community, and that would result in the obsolescence of the STATE. Movements for world government have often been combined with PACIFISM and the wish to move beyond the INTERNATIONAL ANARCHY of nation states in rivalry with one another. It would also involve the surrender, or severe limitation, of national SOVEREIGNTY. In practice the world confronts us with both growing economic INTERDEPENDENCE and political fragmentation and divisions.

World Health Organization (WHO) This was founded on 7 April 1948 and is one of the most important specialized agencies of the UNITED NATIONS (UN). Its declared aim is the attainment, globally, of the highest level of health care. It has concentrated particularly on the provision of primary health care – for instance, mounting programmes for the control of malaria, of ACQUIRED IMMUNE DEFICIENCY SYNDROME (AIDS) and the provision of infant immunization. It has also set up research programmes and trained medical personnel.

World order The structure of international society, its institutions and its procedures. Analysis of the concept of world order has involved two fundamental assumptions, first, that there is a single human community and, secondly, that WAR need not, inescapably, be the fate of the human condition. In his *Anarchical Society: A Study* of *Order in World Politics* (1977) Hedley Bull (1932–85) defined world order as 'those dispositions of human activity that sustain the elementary or primary goals of social life among mankind as a whole'.

World system A concept developed by the US sociologist and historian of economic development Immanuel Wallerstein (b. 1930) in the 1970s – for instance, in his book *The Modern System* (1976). His view has been that the world economy must be studied as a whole; and he specifies three categories of nation in the world system: (1) the 'core' countries (or 'centre'), the industrialized countries, (2) the 'peripheral', the countries of the THIRD WORLD and (3) the intermediate 'semi-peripheral' countries. Reviewing the global economic evolution over the last half-millennium, his argument accounts for the unequal distribution of power and wealth across the world and the continued dependency of the poorer countries on the 'core'. This approach led to a whole number of debates and hypotheses by other scholars on such issues as the interdependence of 'core' and 'periphery', on the role of market forces and class differentiation, and even as to whether there is not one but several 'world systems'.

World Trade Organization (WTO) The WTO was set up in Geneva in 1995 as the successor to the GENERAL AGREEMENT ON TARIFFS AND TRADE (GATT), following the conclusion of the URUGUAY ROUND of trade negotiations. It is intended to boost the growth of world trade by the reduction of barriers in a non-discriminatory and transparent way and is the principal organization responsible for the rules of global trade. It provides the resources and forum for the resolution of trade disputes through independent panels. A member is bound to accept the ruling of the WTO Appeals Tribunal. Recently it has become a prominent target of protestors against GLOBALIZATION, as was seen in the demonstrations in Seattle in 1999.

World Zionist Organization (WZO) This was founded on the initiative of Theodore Herzl (1860–1904) at the First Zionist Congress at Basel in August 1897; the WZO campaigned for and materially assisted the foundation of the State of Israel. Its ruling body is the Zionist Congress, with delegates elected from all countries except Israel, where the Zionist parties receive their representation on the basis of elections to the KNESSET (Israeli Parliament).

WTO See WORLD TRADE ORGANIZATION.

WTO See WARSAW TREATY ORGANIZATION.

WWMCCS World-wide military command and control structure.

WZO See WORLD ZIONIST ORGANIZATION.

X-article A famous article that was published in the US journal *Foreign Affairs* under the authorship of 'Mr "X"' with the title 'The Sources of Soviet Conduct'. The author was George F. Kennan (b. 1904), diplomat and between 1947 and 1949 Director of the Policy Planning Staff of the DEPARTMENT OF STATE. It restated an analysis of Soviet foreign policy contained in his no less celebrated 'Long Telegram' and is significant for its advocacy of the policy of CONTAINMENT of the USSR and COMMUNISM. Many years later, during the 'New Cold War', he expressed his regret that this analysis had led to a highly militarized policy of containment, which, he argued, had not been his intention.

Xenophobia Fear or distrust of foreigners and of the policies and objectives of other states. Playing on nationalistic emotions and ethnic desires for exclusivity, it is commonly manipulated by governments and STATES to their own ends. A historical example of this is China, which, traditionally, refused to deal with foreigners on a basis of equality. At the same time, xenophobic sentiments have commonly expressed themselves against Chinese minority populations in other Asian states.

Yalta Formula This term refers to the agreement reached over the use of VETO in the future UNITED NATIONS SECURITY COUNCIL. It was reached at the YALTA CONFERENCE by the BIG THREE in February 1945.

Yalta Conference (1945) The meeting of the three Allied leaders during the Second World War, US President Franklin D. Roosevelt (1882–1945), the British Prime Minister Winston Churchill (1874–1965) and the Soviet leader Joseph Stalin (1879–1953), held between 4 and 11 February 1945 at Yalta on the Crimean Peninsula. The leaders addressed the issues presented by the pending defeat of Germany, agreeing the partition of its territory into four military zones and the principle of REPARATIONS. As far as Poland was concerned, the most complicated and controversial question before the leaders, the conference agreed that the CURZON LINE would be the eastern border, which meant ceding to the USSR a large sector of eastern Poland. Poland was reciprocally given German territory in the west. The Allies were unable to agree the final DEMARCATION of the ODER–NEISSE LINE. A Polish Provisional Government of National Unity was to be created. It was evident that it would be dominated by Communists, but was to include 'democratic' leaders, and the government was supposed to organize free elections to the Polish parliament as soon as possible. The Yalta decisions were strongly protested against by the Polish Government-in-Exile (the 'London Poles') and critics of Roosevelt accused him of a sell-out to COMMUNISM at Yalta. From a symbol of Allied cooperation, Yalta soon became used as a synonym for APPEASEMENT. The agreement soon provoked dissension, in particular over Poland and Germany, which led quickly to the alienation of the COLD WAR. The Conference also endorsed the creation of a new international security organization, the UNITED NATIONS (UN). A separate agreement between Roosevelt and Stalin specified that the USSR would join the WAR against Japan three months after the defeat of Germany.

Yaoundé Conventions Signed in 1963 and 1970, these were treaties between the EUROPEAN ECONOMIC COMMUNITY (EEC) and the APC states, former French, Belgian and Italian colonies. They arranged for duty-free access to the EEC for most of their products on a non-reciprocal basis, and to European loans and grants.

Year of Europe (1973) The declaration of a 'Year of Europe' with its appeal for a 'New Atlantic Charter' by Henry Kissinger (b. 1923), National Security Adviser and then SECRETARY OF STATE to US President Richard Nixon (1913–94). It was an abortive attempt, at a time when the US government had been very preoccupied with DÉTENTE with China and the USSR, to improve transatlantic relations. Calling for coordination over trade, foreign and DEFENCE policies, this statement gave offence by saying that, while Europe had regional responsibilities, the USA had global ones. Tensions, which had developed particularly as a consequence of the political and economic consequences of the VIETNAM WAR (1960–75), were further aggravated by the Arab-Israeli YOM KIPPUR WAR (1973) later in the year.

Yellow peril This term has been used to denote the Western fear that Asians, especially the Japanese, might overrun areas populated by, or seen as important for, the settlement of whites. It first came into use after the defeat of Russia by Japan in 1905. It contributed to the refusal of the LEAGUE OF NATIONS to adopt a position favouring racial equality, as Australia, Britain and the USA strongly objected. It was an integral part of propaganda against Japan during the Second World War and led to widespread discrimination against Asians in the USA. Since the Second World War, it has been used sometimes to refer to the economic power of the Far East, particularly that of Japan.

Yen power A phrase indicating Japan's status as an economic SUPERPOWER in the period since the Second World War, and a major rival in the global marketplace. Sometimes Japan's role as one of the three major industrial poles with the USA States and the EUROPEAN UNION (EU) is referred to as the 'Pax Nipponica'.

Yield The power of a nuclear explosion is measured as yield, which covers the entire range of energy released and its impact. It is expressed in megatons, where one megaton is equivalent to one million tons of TNT or kilotons, with one kiloton equalling a thousand tons of TNT.

Yishuv The Jewish minority community in Palestine in the period of the British MANDATE after the First World War. The term means 'settlement' and it was often defined as 'a state in the making' or 'a state within a state'. During this period, though, there were almost no continuous areas of Jewish settlement without Arab population. Statehood was not established until the foundation of the State of Israel in 1948.

Yom Kippur Statement (1946) The statement by US President Harry Truman (1884–1972) on the Jewish Day of Atonement, 4 October 1946, which called for the British to admit 100,000 Jewish REFUGEES and displaced persons into Palestine immediately. He also announced that a plan to partition the British MANDATE between Jews and Arabs 'would command the support of public opinion in the United States'. This proved highly controversial because of the level of tension between Jews and Arabs and the resistance of the British to further significant Jewish immigration.

Yom Kippur War (1973) So-called because the Egyptians and Syrians attacked Israel during the Jewish Yom Kippur religious holiday, it is also known as the October War. After a fortnight both Israelis and Arabs accepted a UNITED NATIONS SECURITY COUNCIL ceasefire on 22 October. The aftermath of the WAR saw very active SHUTTLE DIPLOMACY by the US SECRETARY OF STATE Henry Kissinger (b. 1923). During the war the USA had intervened with military equipment and aid and did so decisively. However, it disproved the assumptions that Israel could count on a quick victory in any conflict with the Arabs and that the USSR would keep well clear. The outcome and shuttle diplomacy did not produce a PEACE TREATY, but led to the restoration of the US–Egyptian diplomatic relations, pledges between Egypt and Israel to engage in peace negotiations, and the granting of increased US financial support to both Israel and the Arab states. They also led, though, to the oil embargo by the ORGANIZATION OF PETROLEUM EXPORTING COUNTRIES (OPEC) in November 1973 and the dramatic increase in oil prices that precipitated major economic and financial upheavals and strained relations between the USA and Western Europe.

Yoshida Doctrine This was the single-minded Japanese drive for economic stabilization and revival after the Second World War, laying the basis for the dramatic success of Japan in world markets. It was named after Shigeru Yoshida (1878–1967), who was Prime Minister in the period between 1946 and 1954, during much of the US occupation.

Z

Zeitgeist German for 'the spirit of the age', a term suggesting a particular mood for a particular time; for instance, 'the *Zeitgeist* on the eve of the First World War'.

Zero option A proposal made by US President Ronald Reagan (b. 1911) to the USSR in 1981 during the 'New Cold War' concerning INTERMEDIATE-RANGE BALLISTIC MISSILES (IRBMS). In return for the dismantling of its own SS-20, SS-4 and SS-5 missiles, the USA offered to cancel the proposed intermediate-range CRUISE AND PERSHING MISSILE deployment to Europe. This issue was proving very controversial at the time and there was a strong revival of the PEACE MOVEMENT. The USSR responded with the following offer: it would freeze the number and quality of the NUCLEAR WEAPONS already installed in European Russia and have a MORATORIUM regarding the replacement of the SS-4 and SS-5s by SS-20s, providing the USA did not deploy its missiles. Both proposals were rejected.

Zero-sum game A term in GAME THEORY. A competitive situation in which the success of one person or, in international relations, STATE must come at the expense of another or others. A gain for one is automatically a loss for the other. Perception by the parties that a conflict is zero-sum makes it evidently more difficult to resolve.

Zimmermann Telegram (1917) This was purportedly written by the German Under-Secretary of State to the German Minister in Mexico on 16 January 1917. It proposed that, if the USA joined in the First World War against the CENTRAL POWERS, a German–Mexican ALLIANCE should be created. Mexico should receive financial support and the restoration of the Mexican Cession in return for supporting Germany against the USA. Intercepted by British INTELLIGENCE, it was passed on to the administration of US President Woodrow Wilson (1856–1924). When published on 25 February, it aroused a storm of hostility against Germany in the USA and accelerated American entry into the war.

Zionism This cultural and political movement, which began in the nineteenth century, is particularly associated with the work of Theodore Herzl (1860–1904) for the establishment of a homeland for the Jewish people. The term is derived from Mount Zion in Jerusalem, which has been used as a symbol for the Jewish homeland in Palestine since the time of the Babylonian Captivity in the sixth century BC. Alternative areas, including Argentina and Uganda, were considered for a possible homeland. However, the movement, with the aid of the British BALFOUR DECLARATION (1917), which promised support for a 'national home' in Palestine, and Zionist-sponsored emigration to Palestine, led to the establishment of the State of Israel in 1948. Since 1948 the Israeli government and the WORLD ZIONIST ORGANIZATION (WZO) have continued to encourage this emigration.

Zone of peace An international term for denuclearized and demilitarized areas of the world, either land or sea. For instance, the RAPACKI PLAN (1957), proposed to the UNITED NATIONS (UN) in October 1957, envisaged a NUCLEAR-FREE ZONE of PEACE in CENTRAL EUROPE and EASTERN EUROPE. In the POST-COLD WAR ERA, the phrase has also come to mean more broadly those parts of the world where democratic governments, prosperity and stability are considered to be the norm.

Zone of separation See BUFFER ZONE.

Zones of turmoil Those parts of the globe in which poverty, instability, insecurity and conflict seem to be endemic, as, for instance, in sub-Saharan Africa.

Bibliography

The following is a short selection from an enormous range of materials available to the reader. It is divided into three sections: historical background, introductory text and theory, and web sites. Unless otherwise specified, place of publication is London.

HISTORICAL BACKGROUND

Bell, P. M. H., *The World since 1945* (2001).
Bull, H. and Watson, A. (eds.), *The Expansion of International Society* (Oxford, 1984).
Calvocoressi, Peter, *World Politics 1945–2000* (8th edn, 2000).
Carr, E. H., *The Twenty Years' Crisis* (1995). (Reissue of a classic text in international relations covering the inter-war years.)
Cassels, A., *Ideology and International Relations in the Modern World* (1996).
Clark, I., *Globalization and Fragmentation: International Relations in the Twentieth Century* (Oxford, 1977).
Crockatt, R., *The Fifty Years' War: The United States and the Soviet Union in World Politics 1941–1991* (1996).
Dinan, D., *Ever Closer Union: An Introduction to European Integration* (Boulder, CO, 1999).
Dunbabin, J. P. D., *International Relations since 1945*, i. *The Great Powers and their Allies*; ii. *The Post-Imperial Age: The Great Powers and the Wider World* (1994).
Gaddis, John Lewis, *We Now Know: Rethinking Cold War History* (Oxford, 1997).
Hobsbawm, E. J., *Nations and Nationalism since 1870* (2nd edn, Cambridge, 1992).
Holsti, K., *Peace and War: Armed Conflict and International Order, 1648–1989* (Cambridge, 1991).
Iriye, Akira, *Japan and the Wider World: From the Mid-Nineteenth Century to the Present* (1997).
Kennedy, Paul, *The Rise and Fall of the Great Powers* (1988).
Keylor, W. R., *The Twentieth Century World: An International History* (4th edn, Oxford, 2000).
Kissinger, Henry, *Diplomacy* (1994).
Mazower, M., *Dark Continent, Europe's Twentieth Century* (1998).
Ovendale, Ritchie, *The Origins of the Arab-Israeli Wars* (2nd edn, 1992).
Reynolds, David, *One World Divisible: A Global History since 1945* (1999).
Shlaim, A., *The Iron Wall: Israel and the Arab World* (2000).
Urwin, D.W., *Western Europe since 1945* (5th edn, 1997).
Waites, B., *Europe and the Third World: From Colonization to Decolonization c.1500–1998* (New York, 2000).
Wallerstein, I., *The Capitalist World Economy* (Cambridge, 1979).

Watson, A., *The Evolution of International Society* (Oxford, 1992).

Woods, Ngaire (ed.), *Explaining International Relations since 1945* (Oxford, 1996).

Yapp, M. E., *The Near East since the First World War* (1991).

Young, J. W., *Cold War Europe: A Political History 1945–1991* (1996).

Young, J. W., *The Longman Companion to America, Russia and the Cold War 1941–1998* (1999).

INTRODUCTORY TEXTS AND THEORY

Archer, C., *International Organizations* (3rd edn, 2001).

Baylis, J. and Smith, S., *Globalization of World Politics* (Oxford, 1997).

Booth, K. and Smith, S., *International Relations Theory Today* (Oxford, 1995).

Brown, Chris, *International Relations Theory: New Normative Approaches* (Hemel Hempstead, 1993).

Brown, Chris, *Understanding International Relations* (1997).

Bull, Hedley, *The Anarchical Society: A Study of Order in World Politics* (2nd edn, Oxford, 1995).

Burchill, S. and Linklater, A. (eds), *Theories of International Relations* (1996).

Cimbala, S., *The Past and Future of Nuclear Deterrence* (Westport, CO, 1998).

Creveld, M., *The Rise and Fall of the State* (Cambridge, 1999).

Elliot, Lorraine, *The Global Politics of the Environment* (1997).

Evans, G. and Newham, J., *Dictionary of International Relations* (1998).

Freedman, L., *The Evolution of Nuclear Strategy* (1989).

Gellner, E., *Nations and Nationalism* (Oxford, 1983).

Gilpin, R., *The Political Economy of International Relations* (Princeton, NJ, 1987).

Groom, A. J. R. and Light, M., *Contemporary International Relations: A Guide to Theory* (1994).

Handel, Michael I., *Masters of War: Classical Strategic Thought* (1996).

Haslam, J., *No Virtue like Necessity: Realist Thought in International Relations since Machiavelli* (2002).

Higgins, R., *Problems and Process: International Law and How We Use It* (Oxford, 1995).

Hocking, Brian and Smith, Michael, *World Politics: An Introduction to International Relations* (2nd edn, 1995).

Hollis, Martin and Smith, Steve, *Explaining and Understanding International Relations* (Oxford, 1990).

Hurrell, Andrew and Kingsbury, Benedict, *The International Politics of the Environment* (Oxford, 1992).

Jackson, Robert and Sorenson, Georg, *Introduction to International Relations* (Oxford, 1999).

Keens-Soper, M., *Europe in the World: The Persistence of Power Politics* (2000).

Kegley, Charles W., *Controversies in International Relations Theory* (New York, 1995).

Kegley, Charles W. and Wittkopf, E. R., *World Politics: Trend and Transformation* (6th edn, 1997).

Luard, Evan, *Basic Texts in International Relations: The Evolution of Ideas about International Society* (Oxford, 1992).

Mayall, J., *Nationalism and International Society* (Cambridge, 1990).

Morgenthau, Hans, *Politics among Nations: The Struggle for Power and Peace* (New York, 1985).

Nicholson, M., *International Relations: A Concise Introduction* (1998).

Nye, Joseph S. Jr, *Understanding International Conflicts* (2nd edn, New York, 1997).

Olson, W. and Groom, A. J. R., *International Relations Then and Now: Origins and Trends in Interpretations* (1991).

Paret, P. (ed.), *Makers of Modern Strategy: From Machiavelli to the Nuclear Age* (Princeton, NJ, 1986).

Rengger, N., *International Relations, Political Theory and the Problem of Order* (2000).

Reynolds, Philip, *An Introduction to International Relations* (3rd edn, 1994).

Roberts, A. and Kingsbury, B., *United Nations, Divided World: The UN's role in International Relations* (Oxford, 1993).

Stern, G., *The Structure of International Society: An Introduction to the Study of International Relations* (1995).

Strange, Susan, *States and Markets* (2nd edn, 1994).

Taylor, P., *International Organization in the Modern World* (1993).

Vaquez, John, *The War Puzzle* (Cambridge, 1993).

Waltz, Kenneth, *Theory of International Politics* (New York, 1979).

Walzer, M., *Just and Unjust Wars* (3rd edn, New York, 2000).

Wight, Martin, *International Theory: The Three Traditions* (Leicester, 1991).

Williams, M., *International Relations Theory and European Integration: Power, Security and Community* (2000).

WEB SITES

Academic Council on the United Nations System, http://www.yule.edu/acuns

Academic Info: Human Rights, http://www.academicinfo.net/human.html

Academic Info: Nuclear Studies and Resources, http://www.academicinfo.net/histnuke.html

Amnesty International, http://www.amnesty.org

Arab League, http://www.arab.de/arabinfo/league.htm

Armed Forces of the World, http://www.cfcsc.dnd.ca/links/milorg/index.html

Asia Pacific Economic Cooperation (APEC), http://www.apec.org/

Association of South East Asian Nations (ASEAN), http://wwwasean.or.id/

Carnegie Commission for Preventing Deadly Conflict, http://www.ccpdc.org/

Central Intelligence Agency, http://www.cia.gov/

Centre for Defence and International Security Studies, http://www.cdiss.org/hometemp.htm

Centre for Defence Information, http://www.cdi.org/

Centre for Strategic and International Studies, http://www.csis.org/

Centre for the Study of Intelligence, http://www.odci.gov/csi/index.html

CNN's Cold War Site, http://www.cnn.com/SPECIALS/cold.war/

Cold War International History Project (CWIHP), http://www.cwihp.si.edu/default.htm

Conflict and Conflict Resolution Resources, http://www.cfcsc.dnd.ca/links/intrel/confli.html

Constitutions, Treaties and Declarations, http://www.psr.keele,ac.uk/const.htm

Contemporary Conflicts, http://www.cfcsc.dnd.ca/links/wars/index.html
Council of Europe, http://www.coe.fr/index.asp
Council on Hemispheric Affairs, http://www.coha.org/
Economic Policy Institute, http://www.epinet.org/
Economist, http://www/economist.com
European Union (EU), http://europa,eu.int/
Financial Times, http://www.news.ft.com/
Greenpeace, http:///www.greenpeace.org/
Harvard Project on Cold War Studies, http://www.fas.Harvard.edu/hpcws/
Institute for Global Cooperation and Conflict, http://www-igcc.ucsd.edu/
Institute of Development Studies, http://www.ids.ac.uk
International Affairs Network – Virtual Library, http://www.etown.edu/vl/
International Court of Justice (ICJ), http://www.icj-cij.org/
International Development Studies Network (IDSNet), http://www.idsnet.org
International Institute for Strategic Studies, http://ww.isn.ethz.ch/iiss/
International Institute for Sustainable Development, http://www.iisd1.iisd.ca/
International Law, http://www.cfesc.dnd.ca/links/intrel/intlaw.html
International Relations Data Page, http://home.regent.edu/kevipow/dta.html
International Relations Resources on the Web, http://mitpress.mit.edu/journals/
    INOR/deibert-guide/TOC.html
Jane's, http://www.janes.com/
Major International Instruments on Disarmament and Related Issues, http://
    www.unog.ch/frames/disarm/distreat/warfare/.htm
National Security Archive, http://www.gwu.edu/nsarchiv/
North America Free Trade Association (NAFTA), http://www.mac.doc.gov/nafta/
    nafta2.htm
North Atlantic Treaty Organization (NATO), http://www.nato.int/
North–South Institute, http://www.nsi-ins.ca/
Organization for Economic Cooperation and Development (OECD), http://
    www.oecd.org/
Organization for Security and Cooperation in Europe (OSCE), http://www.osce.org/
Organization of African Unity (OAU), http://www.oau-oua.org/
Public International Law, http://www.law.ecel.uwa.edu.au/intlaw/
Stockholm International Peace Research Institute, http://www.sipri.se
Terrorism Research Centre, http://www.terrorism.com/
United Nations (UN), http://www.un.org/
United Nations and Disarmament, http://www.un.org/Depts/dda/index.html
United Nations High Commission for Human Rights (UNHCHR), http://www.
    unhchr.ch/
United Nations Peacekeeping Operations: Past and Present, http://www.clw.org/pub/
    clw/un/unoperat.html
World Bank, http://worldbank.org
World Governments, http://www.polisci.com/almanac/world.htm
World Resources Institute, http://www.wri.org/wri/
World Trade Organization (WTO), http://www.wto.org

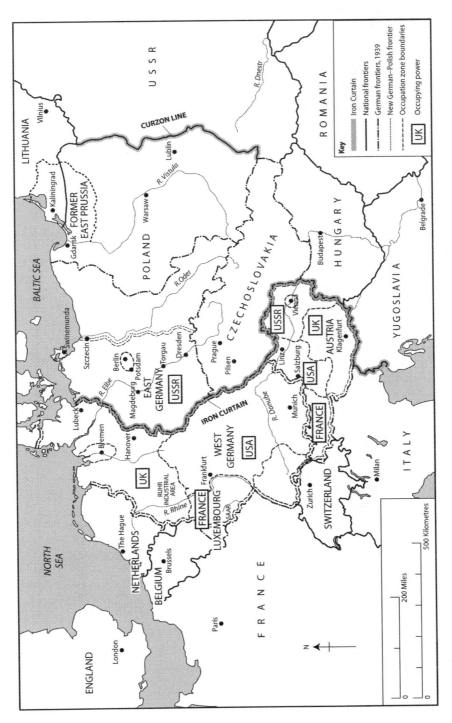

Map 1 Central Europe and the Iron Curtain

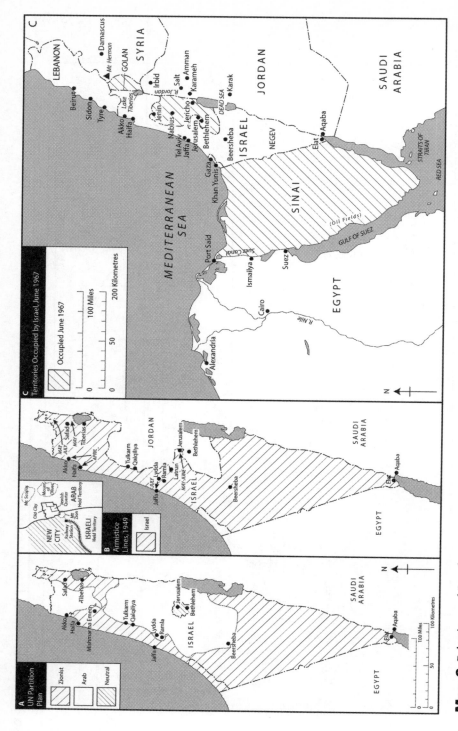

Map 2 Palestine and Israel

Map 3 China and its neighbours

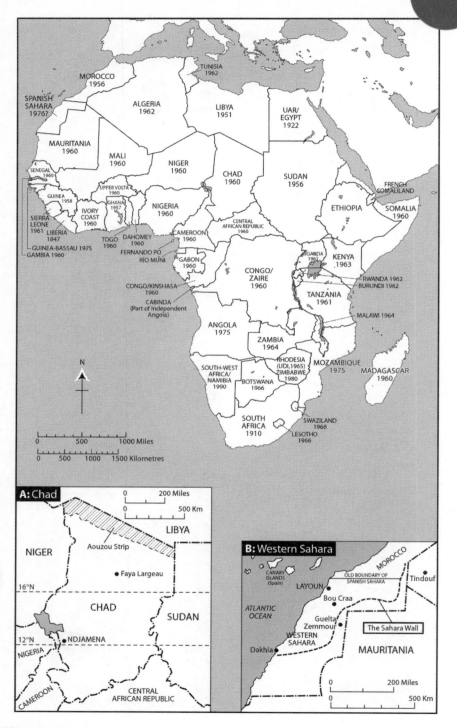

Map 4 Africa, showing dates of independence